The Salt Companion to Charles Bernstein

WILLIAM ALLEGREZZA teaches literature and creative writing at Indiana University Northwest. He has published ten books, such as *The City Visible: Chicago Poetry for the New Century, La alteración del silencio: Poesía norteamericana reciente, Fragile Replacements, Collective Instant,* and *In the Weaver's Valley,* and he has published nine poetry chapbooks. His articles, translations, reviews, and chapbooks have been published in many countries, and he has books forthcoming with The University of New Orleans Press, Otoliths, and Furniture Press. He also edits *Moria,* an e-zine for poetry and poetics.

The Salt Companion to
Charles Bernstein

Edited by

WILLIAM ALLEGREZZA

CROMER

PUBLISHED BY SALT PUBLISHING
12 Norwich Road, Cromer, Norfolk NR27 0AX

The selection and introduction © William Allegrezza, 2012
individual contributions © the contributors, 2012

The right of William Allegrezza to be identified as the
editor of this work has been asserted by him in accordance
with Section 77 of the Copyright, Designs and Patents Act 1988.

Salt Publishing 2012
Reprinted with corrections 2012

Printed and bound in the United Kingdom by Lightning Source, UK

Typeset in Swift 10/12

ISBN 978 1 84471 485 8 paperback

3 5 7 9 8 6 4 2

Contents

1

WILLIAM ALLEGREZZA

Introduction

Charles Bernstein has been and continues to be a central figure in U.S. poetry debates. Often associated with the Language poets, he writes poetry, theory, librettos, and reviews. Early in his career, he was considered an outsider, an anti-poet of sorts, but his work has gained acceptance, as evidenced by the recent publication of his selected poems, *All the Whiskey in Heaven*, by Farrar, Straus and Giroux. The debate that centered on his work and that of other Language poets has largely dissipated, yet critics, including a few in this book, are trying to figure out still how a poet who takes a stance against the "Official Verse Culture" fits into the American poetry scene.

In Bernstein's poetic works, he examines meaning through language. He reworks syntax, challenges the notion of an authorial voice, deconstructs the reading experience, and in general upsets preconceived notions about how language signifies. Bernstein uses a variety of techniques to achieve this disorientation or deconstruction, such as using indeterminacy, abstraction, parataxis, and fragmentation, being non-representational and poly-referential, and avoiding closure. His poetry does not allow one to sit back and accept a standard narrative. In addition to his poetry, Bernstein has written many theory articles, and he has helped foster a poetic community by publishing others' works, by teaching, and by presenting. His practice has aided in creating a space for poetry outside of any use value, of which it has little under capitalism, and has helped offer poetry as a space where the individual, not the collective, is important. His outreach projects influenced many poets, and many of his students have followed his example and created presses and reading venues themselves; thus, his works influenced many poets.

Throughout the decades, Bernstein's poetry has changed significantly. For example, *Girly Man*, a somewhat recent work, largely relies
on humor and accessibility. His early books are not known for accessibility. Nonetheless, his themes of making a space for the individual
in a consumer based society, of the importance of poetry for intellectual life, of the need to challenge mainstream thought and power are
still apparent. Moreover, the process of writing poetry is more significant for Bernstein than the actual outcome, for the process itself
makes one question preconceived notions, preconceived language,
and/or deceptive language. The process of reading and writing poetry
helps make one an individual, and the process of reading Bernstein's
work also pushes one to rethink language itself.

Bernstein grew up in New York. He attended Harvard and studied philosophy and avant-garde literature. Years after graduating,
he and Bruce Andrews started the *L=A=N=G=U=A=G=E* magazine,
which was a starting point for the Language poetry movement, a
loose group with similar poetic penchants that includes such writers as Ron Silliman, Lyn Hejinian, Barret Watten, Ron Silliman,
Michael Palmer, and Susan Howe. Bernstein became a professor at
the State University of New York–Buffalo, where he co-founded the
Electronic Poetry Center, a web portal for innovative poetry. He has
since become a professor at the University of Pennsylvania, where
he co-founded PennSound, an extensive online library for poetry and
poetry related sound files.

Many scholars have written articles about Bernstein's works,
and his poetry and poetics have been the subject of several disserta-
tions; still, this collection is the first to bring together a variety of articles on his work in book form. Part of the motivation for this book
is to foster a wide discussion of Bernstein's poetry and poetics. Up to
now, his theoretical articles have received more published attention
than his poetry, but the writers in this collection examine his poetry,
theory, pedagogy, sound projects, and influences. The book includes
poetic reactions to his work from friends, students, and writers not
personally connected to his work.

The collection starts with a nice introduction to Bernstein's
work by Caroline Bergvall that is useful both to the first time reader
of Bernstein's work and to scholars. Having an introduction from a
British poet also signals Bernstein's international interests, interests
that have become more pronounced in recent years due to his work
with poets from many countries. In fact, he currently directs *Sibila*, a
journal based in Brazil, with Régis Bonvicino. In the past four years,

he presented lectures in Korea, Denmark, France, Portugal, Canada, Britain, Sweden, China, and Finland.

The other articles in the book cover his major influences like Wittgenstein, Marx, Brecht, Stein and compare his ideas to those of many writers, such as Baudrillard. The articles examine his outsider status and explore his use of poetic techniques like poly-referentiality, anti-absorption, and defamiliarization. The authors examine his use of sound, explore changes in his work, look at his composition theory, and examine his poetics in relation to reader-response theory. For example, Kimberly Lamm discusses the influence of Gertrude Stein on Bernstein's work, claiming that Stein's work pushed him to explore the way identity is retained in language and to critique ideas of masculinity. Lamm argues that Stein's works do not allow one to use contemporary notions of identity, and her works provided a starting point for Bernstein since much of his work explores identity as a social construct, one which he tries to deconstruct in his early work by writing against authorial voice.

Discussing similar ideas, Thomas Fink argues that Bernstein uses the list poem to complicate single perspectives by providing a large number of competing perspectives or objective perspectives that do not seem so objective. Fink explores a variety of list poems in which the lists deal with war, poetic fashions, and cultural correctness. Fink suggests that Bernstein complicates the way the reader sees the identity of the poet, but he also claims that Bernstein is pointing with the list poem to the myriad poetic selves that a poet uses, has to use, because of the nature of language. In other words, numerous discourses occur in any given poem, acknowledged or not, and Bernstein points that out in his work.

This idea of multiple voices is explored further in Steve Salmoni's article, for he explores the shadow of *Shadowtime* partially by examining the legacy of Benjamin in *Shadowtime* and in Bernstein's work as a whole. In this exploration, he shows the way the shadow can be other texts (literary, social, and/or political) behind one's text and the way in which those things intrude or condition the text. Ultimately, Salmoni see the shadows as a connective device constructed in a non-productive way to show us language as constructed.

Michael Angelo Tata picks up this theme by looking at Bernstein's pointing to the myriad voices embedded in language, but he examines Bernstein's use of language as open allowing for direction/ misdirection and multi-referentiality and how this aspect of his work grounds it and makes it more politically useful. Like Salomi and Fink, he focuses on Bernstein's ideas of language, but he examines how

Wittgenstein's work provides a theoretical background to Bernstein's ideas.

Tim Peterson's article also discusses the political nature of Bernstein's poetry, but Peterson tackles the question of change in Bernstein's work from the early poems to the more recent ones. He compares Bernstein's defamiliarization, fragmentation, and general anti-absorptive techniques to those of Berthold Brecht. He then goes on to ask how one reconciles the commodified self of the early work with the clear self of *Girly Man*. He argues that Bernstein complicates the self of *Girly Man* by giving us a divided self who embraces similar liberation strategies as the GLBTQ community. Bernstein has essentially taken Schwarzenegger's girlie-man slur of the Democrats as a rallying cry after 9-11 for responding to co-opted language.

In a related article, Carlos Gallego explores the function of anti-absorption in Bernstein's work, how it both pushes the reader back from normative thought patterns and pulls the reader into the alternative patterns of poetry. Gallego argues that with his focus on materiality Bernstein forces us away from abstraction and back to the real world and that this refocusing makes us realize our individual importance. In his discussion, Gallego ties Bernstein's thought to both Marx and Wittgenstein.

Paul Stephens turns away from these two influences to explore the idea of the sophist in Bernstein's work. He suggests the sophist makes us question sincerity and irony and how Bernstein's use of the sophist helps explain his idea community/uncommunity for Language poets. Stephens pays close attention to Bernstein's use of irony and contrasts it with writers like Richard Rorty and Hegel and argues that Bernstein's irony is rhetorical and that it shows his writing as being embedded in larger language networks.

Like Peterson, Megan Jewell starts out with a discussion of Bernstein's place as an insider and outsider in academia, but then she takes a different direction than the other writers by looking at Bernstein's compositional theories related to Composition Studies as taught in the U.S. She argues that Bernstein stresses situational reading strategies and that his stress is similar to that of recent composition theorists like Gerald Graff. She also argues that his push against a normative I, as in *The Sophist*, is similar to contextual reading in the academy and that his innovative pedagogy is connected to his poetry practice, suggesting that Bernstein sees the process of questioning literary practices in all aspects of his life as important.

Also quite different than the other writers, Michael Hennessey explores Bernstein's interest in sound and recording by discussing Bernstein's early work *Class*. Hennessey provides close readings of each track, focusing on the techniques of recording/composition. He argues that Bernstein's early work in sound experimentation sets the foundation for his poetics later and for his recording projects, such as the reading series and PennSound.

The other articles in the book cover equally fascinating topics, such as the relation of Bernstein's poetry to conceptual art in Allen Fisher's article, the argument in Peter Monacell's article that Bernstein's work is firmly anti-suburban in nature, or the close examination of visual poetic strategies that occurs in James Shiver's article. Overall, the twenty-five writers in this book explore the most often debated aspects of Bernstein's work, and I hope the publication of the book will help deepen the discussion around his work, especially his poetry.

Lastly, beyond the joy of seeing so many articles on Bernstein's work published, I consider this book a tribute to one of my primary influences. I found Charles Bernstein's work while scanning the book stacks during my graduate school years. At that point, I knew the Modernists and some of the first Post-Modernists, but I did not know many names in the innovative American tradition. Their books were not being sold in bookstores in the South, and one could only get them from a small press or a library that paid attention to the small press world. His early poetry volumes led me to his theory, and from there, I became engaged with the innovative tradition in the United States.

2

CAROLINE BERGVALL

Charles Bernstein or an Insistence to Communicate [1]

I have read, used, and admired Charles Bernstein's work ever since I came across it in the early 90s when I first arrived in the UK. They were selling his poetry and criticism, alongside a rack of other poets and all sorts of radical literary, philosophical and political works, in a great bookshop now long gone called Compendium, which sold a great number of European and American imports. It was a time when counter-culture still visibly had bookshops in the high street. The As and Bs under poetry could only be reached by standing at the top of a high ladder, which was so much fun that my introduction to contemporary English-speaking poetry for a long while never got beyond Brathwaite. For years, I carried Bernstein's collection of early essays, *Content's Dream*, in my bag. And when *Dark City* came out, that took its place. There was so much stuff in this deep, two-leveled bookshop that magazines such as the essential *Re/Search* compilations were being sold in a box on the floor. Their shelving was strange and wonderful, in itself a lesson in social science. In a section reserved for "male cult writers," they had shelved Kathy Acker, and that's how I came across her work. Compendium had to fold in the year 2000 when the whole of Camden Lock was sold to real estate developers and the area was drastically turned into a highly lucrative commercial avatar of its former anarchist and punk years, now selling chains and torn T-shirts made in China. But for the first decade of my life in

---

1 Slightly edited from the Opening Address, Oslo Poetry Festival, 23 Oct 2009

London, it introduced me to many of the English-speaking writers that have come to have such a strong influence on my own work.

It's impossible to summarize Bernstein's impact and reputation in just a few words, so I approach the aspects of his work that have been the most important for me. At its very heart, Charles Bernstein's poetry signals the idea of performance, in the sense of its construct-edness, explicit artefactuality, and distantiation. One recognizes this from LANGUAGE Poetry, and he was one of the main voices of this intellectual, anti-movement in the 70s. And although his poetry has changed radically since that time, it continues to be poetry as a sample of a thinking process. It is a thinking process that plays, but refuses to be played by the romances of poetic production. Its inner life is the bolts and screws of language. He doesn't want his reader to necessarily agree or emote with the text. Rather, he makes the reader become aware of some of the ambient politics of language in use, and poetic knowledge in use.

There are lot of voices, and a lot of fighting and conflict in Bernstein's poetry. Nothing heroic—it's more like a rumour, a small ulcer, a meal with friends, an urban ambience. Usage of the English language is presented as a chaotic, compounded mode of behavior, full of interjections, half knowledge, gossip, verbal games, juxtaposi-tions, junk mail and recyclings from mass culture. This allows for a whole range of verbal personas, ventriloquised from official and unofficial sources. These personas are often at odds with one another; they seem unhappily housed alongside one another; they want more room; they fight for our attention. This makes for a crowded, noisy space of unresolved disagreement that's very irritating to read, and also very funny. It's like being in a crowded bar, or on a bus stuck in a traffic jam, when you can't get out. Such a poetry bases its hope and its foundation on what Bernstein calls language as a "commonness of being, through which we see & make sense of & value."[2] It wants to show you how language and social performance think you, think for you, not with you, as soon you don't pay attention.

Bernstein is always aware of the complicated, interrupted, re-inter-preted history of the language that he uses, working explicitly as he does with a poetry written in American English. He writes some-where that American poetry is a poetry that historically was writ-ten by writers for whom English is a second language. For a poetry such as his and that of many others (he mentions especially Stein),

---

2   Charles, Bernstein, *Content's Dream* (Los Angeles: Sun & Moon, 1986), 32.

it is also the history of such an actual foreignness and the processing of language acquisition, which carries over into the make-up
of poetry. It makes it a poetry concerned primarily with language,
and secondly, with literature. In fact, one could nearly say that it is
secondly concerned with music, and then with literature. I say this
because of the way Bernstein uses music to reflect on recent poetic
history, notably that of the Objectivists, but also of the revolutionary influence of African American music and linguistic history on
American modes of poetics. He sees how American resistant poetics
are not only inspired by "non standard language practices" largely
inherited from a Eurocentered modernism, but also by the inclusion
of strands of previously ignored, rejected, localized and homegrown,
yet also always diasporic language practices.

   Then there is the level of re-sounding, resounding and presenting. Bernstein's highly favourable approach to live readings is well
known. He is himself a lively, acerbic reader, a great performer of
his own work, a poet not adverse to entertaining. For him the live
reading is a complementary, not a secondary, mode of poetic involvement. His interest in the audiophonic impact of poetry is also very
clear from his dedication to PennSound, a now truly vast archival site
that he founded, providing online storage and free access to readings,
performances and talks by poets. No doubt, the early 21st century's
digitalisation is revolutionizing access to the written text away from
publishing. It is also rapidly changing the way and value some poets
put into audio recordings for our writing practices. Bernstein's own
interest has largely stayed close to the spoken text and its demands
on the live reading, but of course audiographic texts are applicable
beyond this to audioworks, sounded installations and even vaster
ongoing fields of aural manifestations that use language structure as
their basis.

   His best poetic work for me so far is his recent full-length libretto
Shadowtime around Walter Benjamin's life, death, and thought. He
calls it a "thought opera." It starts at the excruciating moment of
Benjamin's final night and thereafter is a reflection on the philosopher's work through various characters, such as the Angel of History,
Einstein, Hitler, Hölderlin, as well as Bernstein's own Marx broth-
ers, Karl and Groucho, and Madame Moiselle. This arc dynamises
Bernstein's language games and critical voices, his connection
with Continental Philosophy and its Jewish legacy into a powerful
dramatic structure. It is as though such a demanding motif and the
collaborative work with a composer had placed an added, external
pressure on to the composition of the textual matter itself.

To conclude, let me just mention one more recent piece where the connection between written and spoken performance is so tenuous as to be nearly reversed. Or rather, where the performance of speaking assists the writing and where the politics of engagement take place at the point of the delivery. His recent piece *Recantorium* is a piece based on models of historic and frequently religious acts of public recanting. Such acts of recantation, frequent in the early Catholic church, notably to contain intellectual dissent, were written mainly to be spoken. This was part of the act in its humiliation. By being spoken, the words would be signed. There is coercion and the disciplining of belief in such an act, whose function it is to force the individual to renege on their convictions prior to allowing them re-entry into the collective group. It is a performative act in the strictest sense. It stamps and gives the individual back to the collective — Only If. It conventionalizes the rule of the strong into a rule of law. This is of course the whole point behind the very idea of "heresy." Bernstein uses the heretical analogy here to declare his new found allegiance to the rule of the one poetic aesthetic, mainstream culture, what he calls "official verse culture," and he gives himself over to this dominant culture. Here are the opening lines. "I was wrong, I apologize, I recant. I altogether abandon the false opinion that National Poetry Month is not good for poetry and for poets." Implicating the listener in a satirical piece that blends cultural coercion against a backdrop of religious and political trials is a masterly, timely, well-shaped comedy. The Aristophanes of the *Wasps* would have been proud of this. The Jarry of *Caesar Antichrist* would have endorsed it with relish. The repetition, the sloganeering, the simplistic formulations of allegiance are also timely reminders of the bloated bombast of the conservative culture we find ourselves in. At another level, it also recognizes the poetic act as one that must at times disengage from the perniciously consensual demands of poetry's besieged micro-collective to provoke instead strident gestures within one's own group as much as towards a larger cultural group. What the British thinker Paul Gilroy has called "the necessity to practice a form of local disloyalty for social change."

The piece is subtitled "Recantorium (A bachelor machine after Duchamp after Kafka)." This of course references a history of literary modernity that has long since gone full circle. As a duchampian principle, it is tied up in the visual arts and does also remember that it is a model for a self-perpetuating, non-functioning machine-sculpture of the future. Now a useless piece of libidinal machinery with a suitcase full of notes to go with it. The suitcase is a sign that all is not well, that departure is imminent. It then projects itself back to the nihilistic and fantastical world of that alienated European, Frank Kafka, the perpetual prisoner—now that's you and me, without many keys and none that seem to fit in a tightening, walled-in world of freedom.

Bernstein's *Recantorium* and its vast field of polemics does beg the question: when the radical terms and tactics of one's artform seem either archaic or thoroughly commodified, how does it find the ideological terms and methodological tools that will enable new modes of disloyalty and heresy? On what terms and to what end shall we continue practicing poetry, and perform its poetics? As he writes: "The question may well be art versus culture not art as culture."

3

TIM PETERSON

Either You're With Us and Against Us: Charles Bernstein's *Girly Man*, 9/11, and the Brechtian Figure of the Reader

The twentieth book of poems by Charles Bernstein, *Girly Man*, signifies a departure and a renewal in this poet's oeuvre. These changes seem to have been prompted by the political climate following the 9/11 attacks on the World Trade Center. Whereas Bernstein's earlier range of multi-voiced styles created an analogy between the goals of Language poetry and Brecht's alienation effect, *Girly Man* adopts new methods of critique, responding to the new political situation that stifles public dialogue and dissent.

1. The Brechtian Figure of the Reader

Bernstein's sharp-edged, often sarcastic earlier poetry frequently employed a multi-voiced social critique and was known for being humorous and critical rather than empathetic. A range of critics have previously noted key characteristics of this classic Bernstein style. Tenney Nathanson, in an article on Bernstein's 1980 book *Controlling Interests*, argues that this poetry's critique of the commodified cold war self was achieved by collaging together multiple reified versions of this self. According to Nathanson's reading, this earlier style in Bernstein's poetry saw the self and narrative as linked symptoms of underlying cultural malaise, and adopted a strategy of interrupting this narrative by destabilizing the traditional notion of the speaker's monologic voice in poetry. This strategy in Bernstein's early work offered what Nathanson calls a "rather chilling demonstration of that fading of person into discursive position" as a kind of post-Fordist allegory in which "there is less of a sense of people using language to say what they mean than of discourse recruiting them to mean what it says." [1] A related approach is offered by Hank Lazer in his review of Bernstein's 1992 book *Dark City*; Lazer discusses how Bernstein's work foregrounds cultural modes of "manipulation and targeting," achieving a "subversion and defamiliarization of the 'transparent' communication used in the world of commodification and consumption." [2] This process occurs in Bernstein's poems through a dysraphism or "mis-seaming" of multiple utterances from different contexts.[3] Both critics' interpretations point to an over-arching strategy for a certain portion of Bernstein's early poetry: the achievement of social and aesthetic critique through anti-absorptive techniques, meaning gestures through which the reader is alternately drawn into and bounced out of the text being read.

This anti-absorptive strategy is not unlike that of playwright Bertolt Brecht, who proposed a concept of "Epic Theater" in contrast to Stanislavski's naturalistic emotive Method. Others have noted these similarities before: in "After Language Poetry," Jena Osman draws an explicit analogy between the Aristotelian model in theater and the epiphanic model in poetry, placing Bernstein's work in the context of the anti-Aristotelian or Brechtian theater.[4] The cornerstone of Brecht's Epic Theater became the "Alienation Effect" or *Verfremdungseffekt*, an approach to acting in which the viewer of the play was to be at all times reminded that he or she was watching a play. Brecht wanted to prevent the audience from lapsing into complacent absorption in the entertainments, and instead argued for the importance of keeping the viewer's mental faculties active at all times. The key work for establishing a connection between the

---

1 Tenney Nathanson, "Collage and Pulverization in Contemporary Poetry: Charles Bernstein's Controlling Interests," *Contemporary Literature* 33, no.2 (Summer 1992): 307.

2 Hank Lazer, "Charles Bernstein's Dark City: Polis, Policy, and the Policing of Poetry," in *Opposing Poetries* (Evanston, IL: Northwestern University Press, 1996), 139.

3 Lazer, 136.

4 Osman, Jena. "After Language Poetry," *OEI* 7, no. 8, 2002. (reprinted in English on-line at www.ubu.com/papers/oei/osman.html)

alienation effect and Bernstein's anti-absorptive techniques would be *The Threepenny Opera*, Brecht's musical which presents a multi-voiced, shifting collage of emotional and ideological perspectives while adopting a gleefully critical attitude towards all of them. The theme of Brechtian critique first coalesced as an overtly stated poetic strategy for Bernstein's readers with the publication of his essay "The Artifice of Absorption," which drew explicit connections between the anti-absorptive and Brechtian devices in the writing:

> Brecht figures prominently in my verse essay 'Artifice of Absorption' because I am interested in the dynamic of both being absorbed in the textual 'action' and at the same time remaining aware of the structures producing the effect. Like the Russian futurist's idea of ostranenie (making strange), Brecht's *Verfremdungseffekt* is a crucial model for breaking the empathic connection between reader and poem, where one reads through the words to get to the idea of content 'on the other side.' [5]

This influential critique by Bernstein of voice, speech, and the self-forged a space of resistance in poetry outside of "Official Verse Culture" throughout the eighties and nineties. As Nathanson notes, claims for the value of the argument went hand-in-hand with a liberatory rhetoric regarding the freedom of the reader to make meaning. Such claims ranged from Steve McCaffery's emphasis on "producing one's own reading among the polysemous routes that the text offers" to Bruce Andrews' insistence that "The constitutive rules of meaning are not taking the words away from us. We can create those rules as we go along." [6] These are all compelling claims. Yet is Bernstein's writing so open to interpretation that it can be easily misread or read against its own values by an unsympathetic reader? On the contrary, I think there are an abundance of clues, hints, directional vectors, and especially metaphorical framing devices which in retrospect make the politics of Bernstein's critique abundantly clear.

So we might ask, how does the aesthetic form of the poetry in some ways guide us toward this politics, and how does the reader figure in? Walter Benjamin in his essay "What Is Epic Theater?" made

---

5 Charles Bernstein, "An Interview with Hanna Möckel-Rieke," in *My Way: Speeches and Poems* (Chicago: University of Chicago Press, 1999), 68.

6 Nathanson, 310.

an observation about Brecht's work which I think illuminates the political use of alienation throughout Bernstein's earlier writing. Benjamin in this essay describes the goal of the Alienation effect as being "to discover the conditions of life" in a way that diverges from the assumed version of naturalism, and his figure for this phenomenon is the eyes of a stranger:

> This discovery (alienation) of conditions takes place through the interruption of happenings. The most primitive example would be a family scene. Suddenly a stranger enters. The mother was just about to seize a bronze bust and hurl it at her daughter; the father was in the act of opening the window in order to call a policeman. At that moment the stranger appears in the doorway. This means that the stranger is confronted with the situation as with a startling picture: troubled faces, an open window, the furniture in disarray. But there are eyes to which even more ordinary scenes of middle-class life look almost equally startling. [7]

Benjamin's description of this stranger coming in from outside and seeing the bourgeois family from a startling new viewpoint is like the perspective often adopted by Bernstein's earlier poetry, in which the detritus of commodified capitalist selves are collaged together and held up for critical examination as if "exhibit A," "exhibit B," and so on. For example, this passage from "Emotions of Normal People" in *Dark City*:

At which point

You can connect a bi-directional

Buffer or dumb terminal to the

Module's digital inputs & relay

Outputs with crystal-controlled

---

7   Walter Benjamin, "What is Epic Theater?" in *Illuminations* (New York: Schocken Books, 1968), 150.

External trigger for jitter-free

Duplex data compression & protocol

Source codes.

    Dear Fran & Don,

    Thanks so much for
    dinner last night. You two
    are terrific—we knew that about
    you, Fran, but, Don—we don't
    meet rocket engineers such as
    yourself very often and so
    meeting you was a special treat!
    Next time—our little
    Italian restaurant!

        Warm Regards,

        Scott & Linda

Suddenly, in spite of
worrisome statistics that had unnerved
the Street,we
developed conviction and acted on it. Aside
from the arbs
and the rumor mill, the major trend remains up regardless of
street noise.
The liquidity is there, so any catalyst
should hasten the major direction. The market's internal technical condition is far from overbought, which leaves
room to rally back to October's
2500.

I think our big problem is inhibiting post-normalization.[8]

This poem collages together a number of recognizable personas
through abrupt transitions. The cloying "Fran & Don" correspond-

---

8   Charles Bernstein, *Dark City* (Los Angeles: Sun and Moon, 1994), 87-88.

ence (probably the closest thing here to "the bourgeois family scene"
discussed above) is revealed from an outside perspective as just one
of a number of different technological and jargonized languages. The
"personal" message is exposed here for Bernstein as a language which
traffics in something very different—emotion, comfort, and perhaps
sycophancy as a means for creating a false sense of intimacy. The eyes
of Benjamin's stranger which cause middle class life to look startling
and strange are like the perspective of the implied or ideal reader for
Bernstein's poetry. This readerly perspective is here provided by cues
created partially through the actual tone of utterance and partially
through an overlay of sarcasm implied by the collage juxtapositions.
As a consequence, all speech acts in the language have a perva-
sively doubled quality for any reader, creating explosive moments of
humor when the transition from one scene to the next incongruous
one occurs. None of these speakers seem trustworthy or authoritative in any sense. As in Nathanson's readings of Bernstein, the poem
therefore has a kind of built-in dramatic irony which destabilizes
all the discourses that inhabit it. The critique of our situation under
capitalism, the polemic, is not directly spoken but rather negatively
implied through tone and through juxtaposition of evidence, much
like in a documentary which coyly encourages the reader to form his
or her own conclusions. But the fact remains that the writing itself
takes a political position through its formal technique, and in doing
so allows us direct access to the view of Benjamin's stranger walking
in on the bourgeois family from outside.

So who might inhabit this perspective and these eyes, and how
does that relate to the politics in Bernstein's earlier poetry? In
Brecht's writings about theater, there is this note about the playwright's early developing interest in Marxism:

> When I read Marx's *Capital* I understood my plays.
> Naturally I want to see this book widely circulated. It
> wasn't of course that I found I had unconsciously written
> a whole pile of Marxist plays; but this man Marx was the
> only spectator for my plays I'd ever come across. For a man
> with interests like his must of necessity be interested in
> my plays, not because they are so intelligent but because
> he is—they are something for him to think about. [9]

---

9 Bertolt Brecht, *Brecht on Theatre* (trans. John Willett) (New York: Hill and Wang,
1957), 23-24.

In Bernstein's work, as in Brecht's, it might be argued that the stranger coming in from the outside and seeing the bourgeois family from a strange new perspective is implied to be Marx himself. This stranger is an absent figure for the utopian reader of Language Poetry, a possible reader who would adopt a critical eye towards the facile naturalism and emotions of art under a capitalist society.

2. Either You're With Us or You're With the Terrorists

By the time we reach Bernstein's book *Girly Man*, everything has changed. Rather than sarcastic Brechtian collages, this work demonstrates an entirely different tonal range. Early on in this new book, one encounters passages such as the following:

> At about 6, Felix, Susan and I walked down to the Hudson. I wanted to see New Jersey, to see the George Washington Bridge. The sun gleamed on the water. The bridge was calm. Folks were bicycling and rollerblading. The scene was almost serene; just five miles from the Trade Center.[10]

Sincere and urgent statements here such as "I wanted to see New Jersey, to see the George Washington Bridge" make it initially hard to believe that we are dealing with the same poet who wrote the earlier caustic multi-voiced scenarios. Perhaps the most vociferous critic of the self, the memory poem, and the voice in previous years, Bernstein is noticeably breaking several of his own earlier rules about poetics in "Some of These Daze" and is writing for the first time in an overtly biographical and narrative style. Where are the sardonic ironies, the collage assemblage, and the multiple voices used as polemical props? Where is the implied perspective of critique? Instead we are presented with short prose paragraphs, a way of evoking bits of narrative in a process that flits between relating a clear story and figuring the process of writing ("By mistake I first wrote "Word Trade Center."). The tone seems bleaker and perhaps foggier, as if the speaker is working through the process of enduring a shock:

> *They thought they were going to heaven.*

---

10 Charles Bernstein, *Girly Man* (Chicago: University of Chicago Press, 2006), 19.

I find myself walking around making up arguments in my
head, but when I try to write them down they dissolve in a
flood of questions and misgivings. I value these questions,
these misgivings, more than my analysis of the situation.

A new sport is checking not what stores have put up flags
but which ones don't. Still, there is one Afghani joint in
midtown that has no flag in sight. Stu and I head over to
try out the lamb kebab. [11]

In this poem 'Report from Liberty Street,' an outside voice ("They
thought they were going to heaven") is introduced, but the earlier
poetry's atmosphere of pervasive irony regarding outside voices is
now absent. Instead the statement "They thought they were going
to heaven" becomes quite literal, a symbolic or thematic rhyme
which chimes in between the note-taking gestures of this piece. The
emphasis on the value of doubt here (valuing one's own questions
and misgivings, eating at the only Afghani restaurant without an
American flag) causes "They thought they were going to heaven" to
stand in contrast to the stunned speaker's distrust of a confident argument that might be brandished as a weapon. Narrative and the self
are no longer seen as symptoms of monologic discourse as they were
in Bernstein's earlier writing. The Self that is reintroduced in these
new poems is not a monologic construction but is rather internally
divided in a continuous process of reflection, as in 'Broken English:':

What are you fighting for?

What are you fighting for?[12]

The speaker-as-poet has been reintroduced as only one of many possible witnesses for getting at the real subject: the attack on the world
Trade Center and its aftermath in the culture.

Why does this poetry feel so different from Bernstein's earlier
writing, yet so timely? What is it about the old form of multi-voiced
Brechtian critique that seems no longer tenable after 9/11 for this
poet? Perhaps there's something about the new political context
which appears to be itself at times pre-emptively Brechtian, as in the

---

11 Bernstein, 28-29.

12 Bernstein, 48.

case of Dick Cheney shooting someone and then making jokes about
it at a press conference. How does one parody or even critique that,
for instance? As Bernstein notes in a recent article on Bob Dylan's
legacy, "We are all Brechtians now."[13] Given this political climate,
that already-appropriated poetic strategy is potentially headed for a
place that's too bleak or cynical, a dilemma which becomes clear in
Bernstein's hilarious poem "Self Help," originally published on the
Buffalo Poetics List shortly after the reelection of George Bush in
2004:

> Hurricane crushes house.—You never seemed so resilient.

> Brother-in-law completes second year in coma.—He seems
> so much more relaxed than he used to.

> $75 ticket for Sunday meter violation on an empty street
> in residential neighborhood.—The city needs the money
> to make us safe and educate our kids.

> Missed last episode of favorite murder mystery because
> you misprogrammed VCR.—Write your own ending!

> Blue cashmere pullover has three big moth holes.—What
> a great looking shirt!

> Son joins skinhead brigade of Jews for Jesus. —At least
> he's following his bliss.[14]

The attempt here to consistently find the upside to a bad situation
creates inadequate aphoristic solutions that try to project booster-
ism but continuously fail. These ridiculous responses demonstrate an
Orwellian way of naming the current political situation (like a "Clear
Skies" initiative that in reality poisons the environment) and also a
way of rushing to the wrong solution to a dilemma too quickly. Yet
the poem also evokes a larger political difficulty for liberals under the
Bush administration after 9/11, the fear that language itself has truly
become an inadequate means for changing reality—it is almost as if

---

13 Charles Bernstein, "Knockin' on Heaven's Door: Bob Dylan and the Adolescent
    Sublime." *The Brooklyn Rail* (September 2006) http://www.brooklynrail.org/2006/09/
    books/knockin-on-heavens-door
14 Charles Bernstein, *Girly Man* (Chicago: University of Chicago Press, 2006), 172-173.

language itself has been co-opted in advance and rendered unable to refer directly to reality or to solutions that might solve a real problem. From such a perspective, "anti-absorptive" comes to have a much less triumphant meaning. In "Self-Help," reality happens (and is correspondingly silenced) during that repeated em-dash which acts as a bridge between phrases. The poem reveals and performs the limits of satire through its exasperated tone, demonstrating in the process how this approach is ultimately a rhetorical (and perhaps a political) dead end because the poem is ultimately trapped in its own closed circuit. Fortunately, the angle of critique is torqued at the end of the poem where there is an attempt by the author to impose a frame: "Self help—other drowns." We might recognize the old critique of the self here from Bernstein's earlier work, yet it's barely recognizable as the carnivalesque collage of the earlier writing. Instead it feels bleaker and more frustrated, much less sure of its own moral superiority.

While we all may be pre-emptively Brechtian in a post-9/11 context, pre-emptively "performing," only some of those performances are considered worthy of being recognized or legitimized by the news media. In the months and years following the 9/11 attacks, a certain critical function of journalists toward our government was suspended, and for a significant period of time there was less toleration of public dissent. A "with-us-or-against-us" mentality developed in which disagreeing with President Bush's ideas was translated as "Bush-bashing." Judith Butler recounts this period in her book *Precarious Life*, published in 2004 the year Bush was re-elected and the Iraq War was already in full swing:

> The voicing of critical perspectives against the war has become difficult to do, not only because mainstream media enterprises will not publish them (most of them appear in the progressive or alternative print media or on the internet), but because to voice them is to risk hystericization and censorship. In a strong sense, the binarism that Bush proposes in which only two positions are possible—'Either you're with us or you're with the terrorists'—makes it untenable to hold a position in which one opposes both and queries the terms in which the opposition is framed . . . .At the beginning of this conflict, to oppose the war meant to some that one somehow felt

sympathy with terrorism, or that one saw the terror as justified. [15]

After 9/11, hawkish politicians and media personalities alike obviously made it clear that they thought they were going to heaven. A famous example of this phenomenon was a speech by Arnold Schwarzenegger, the newly-elected Governor of California, in which he denounced the democratic legislature resistant to his outrageous budget proposal as "girlie-men" for supporting "special interests" such as the Unions.[16] Bernstein's title, a parody on this quotation, evokes the state of emergency in which dissent was silenced, in the process gesturing toward a possible realization of that negative capability in which "one opposes both and queries the terms in which the opposition is framed."

The dilemma Butler articulates, where to participate in public dialogue was to risk hystericization, has been accounted for in a slightly different way by linguist George Lakoff as a dilemma in which liberals lacked the proper cognitive and metaphorical frames to get their ideas across. In his book *Moral Politics* and the post 9/11 popular version *Don't Think of an Elephant*, Lakoff described two underlying cognitive and metaphorical frames for all public discourse between conservatives and liberals, the conservative one being the "strict father" frame, and the liberal one being the "nurturing parent" frame. Whereas in the conservative worldview, "the strict father is the moral authority who has to support and defend the family, tell his wife what to do, and teach his kids right from wrong," the liberal alternative of the nurturing family is focused on "empathy (feeling and caring how others feel) and responsibility (for taking care of oneself and others for whom we are responsible)."[17]

Given these options, what is a liberal to do in an argument? Nurture the heck out of his or her opponent until they cry "uncle"? Is it possible to develop a rhetorically strong activist poetics out of those twin themes of empathy and responsibility, and what would such a poetics look like? For Bernstein, there is still a certain distrust

---

15 Judith Butler. *Precarious Life: The Powers of Mourning and Violence* (London: Verso, 2004), 2.

16 Peter Nicholas, "Schwarzenegger deems opponents 'girlie-men' — twice: Governor's rhetoric incites mall crowd, infuriates others," *Los Angeles Times*, Sunday, July 18, 2004.

17 George Lakoff, *Don't Think of an Elephant!* (Vermont: Chelsea Green Publishing, 2004), 40.

of the empathy inherent in getting absorbed in the performance too readily:

> That still, small voice may not be the root of all evil but it's no innocent bystander either. [18]

> War is an excuse for lots of bad antiwar poetry.[19]

As these lines from 'Sign Under Test' and 'War Stories' indicate, The poems in *Girly Man* consistently explore a range of alternate paths to the with-us-or-against-us rhetoric of the popular media as well as the binary posed by Lakoff which suggests that liberals quite literally cannot fight. Bernstein accomplishes this by shifting the target of critique. Rather than the earlier poetry in which a mono-logic consumer Self appeared as chief symptom of cultural malaise, Bernstein's more recent writing is a battle cry against the mono-logic implications of Unilateralism. At a reading for the anthology "Enough!" in 2003, Bernstein noted:

> At these trying times we keep being hectored toward moral discourse, toward turning our work into digest-ible messages. This too is a casualty of the war machine, the undermining of the value of the projects of art, of the aesthetic . . . 'Unilateralism' is not just the course the Executive branch is pursuing, with disastrous conse-quence, in foreign policy, but also the policy it pursues domestically, in its assault on our liberties, on the poor, and indeed on our aspirations for a democratic society. [20]

This is one of the challenges taken up by Bernstein's book: how is it possible to take a political position in one's writing without being prematurely "hectored toward moral discourse" and reducing one's work to "digestible messages" that are always already co-opted?

One answer is to celebrate one's own dividedness, emphasizing the parallels between provisionality, doubt, and dissent. Bernstein's book makes these connections through the figure of the Girly Man who acts as a synecdoche for many of the work's central concerns.

---

18   Charles Bernstein, *Girly Man* (Chicago: University of Chicago Press, 2006) 158.

19   Bernstein, 151.

20   Charles Bernstein, "Enough" in *Enough: An Anthology of Poetry and Writings Against the War*, Ed. Rick London and Leslie Scalapino (Oakland: O Books, 2003).

The position of the author, too, is multiple and complex; rather than adopting a signature style, more than ever before Bernstein seems to be many different poets within a single volume. *Girly Man* is divided into seven sections, each of which pursues a different style (and some of which were originally published as discrete chapbooks): "Let's Just Say", the aforementioned "Some of These Daze," "World on Fire," "Warrant," "In Parts," "Likeness," and "Girly Man." In addition to the personal narrative of 9/11 recounted in "Some of These Daze," some other styles the book employs include wide-ranging philosophical fragments:

> Now I am getting weary of ideology and would like to give it up entirely but it seems the more I give it up the more it has me by the throat. I write so I can breathe.
>
> Or let's say trying to re-imagine the possibilities of sentience through the material sentience of language.
>
> Don't ask me to be frank. I don't even know if I can be myself. [21]

In this poem, 'Sign Under Test,' the leaps between sections represent a kind of note-taking rather than a collage in the sense of the earlier work. The troubled, haunted utterances come from one speaker who appears at times to be addressing himself, at times talking to someone else. There is no over-arching rhetorical perspective or implied reader supplying a Brechtian critique in the earlier sense of *The Threepenny Opera*. If there is a Brechtian aspect here, it would be more redolent of something like the Brecht who wrote *Galileo*, the (rewritten) last scene of which portrays the protagonist at once angered at being silenced by the papacy and troubled by his own discoveries and the role they have in creating a notion of "progress:"

> Threats and bribes fill the air. Can the scientist hold out on the numbers? For what reason do you labor? I take it that the intent of science is to ease human existence. If you give way to coercion, science can be crippled, and your new machines may simply suggest new drudgeries.[22]

---

21 Charles Bernstein, *Girly Man* (Chicago: University of Chicago Press, 2006), 162.
22 Bertold Brecht, *Galileo* (New York: Grove Press, 1966), 123-124.

The diminished role for sarcasm in Bernstein's work evokes a similar kind of troubled sadness. In the spirit of Butler's comments about hystericization, it is harder "to be frank" when one is compelled to respond to ridiculous ultimatums such as "Either you're with us or you're with the terrorists." While Bernstein's older work saw the ironic anti-absorptive as a way to evade commodification, it is no longer necessarily possible to accomplish this when everyone is Brechtian. Rather, in this new book there is a certain attempt at sincere communication of a multitude of ideas. The strategy has become a mobile, localized questioning of what values are in operation from moment to moment.

This theme of the divided self in the book extends to the micro level of how certain utterances are constructed and then reversed. More than anything else, the aphoristic seems to be the emphasis here rather than the ironic or the sarcastic. At times a barrage of skewed aphorisms, the book proceeds from one cockamamie truism to another through a clustering of flatfooted cliché expressions given new life through minor surgery. In "A Flame in Your Heart," such rhetorical turns act as an underlying framework for the play of sounds:

> As slow as Methuselah and as old as
>
> molasses, time passes but nobody ever
> does anything about it—the soda water
>
> at the club on Tuesday so much more fishy
>
> than it used to be and the giant marmoset
> in the bedroom wants more cookies and milk
>
> before fading into memory's skipped disk.[23]

The wan, lingering irony in this passage may be seen as influenced by John Ashbery's deadpan befuddled gestures recalling a vague colloquial American idiom. Yet in Bernstein's version, the wan statements derive their humor from allusions to pre-existing aphoristic structures such as folk sayings. One example of this occurs in the poem 'Let's Just Say':

---

23 Charles Bernstein, *Girly Man* (Chicago: University of Chicago Press, 2006), 52.

Every lake has a house . . .
& every house has a lake ²⁴

And as these lines from 'There's Beauty in the Sound of the Rushing Brook as It Forks & Bends in the Moonlight' indicate, Bernstein's version is also spun in a decidedly bleaker, more Althusserian mode than Ashbery would ever attempt:

When I die I'm
sure America
will have
taken hold.²⁵

3. *The Girly Man*

The final and most memorable piece in the book, the title poem "Ballad of the Girly Man," reveals this dividedness of the author to be a volatile, politically transgressive principle by embodying that dividedness in a speaker who is an allegory for (and a solution to) many of the book's larger concerns. Also a stylistic departure from earlier Bernstein modes, this poem stages a direct polemic articulated in song form:

The truth is hidden in a veil of tears
The scabs of the mourners grow thick with fear

A democracy once proposed
Is slimmed and grimed again
By men with brute design
Who prefer hate to rime²⁶

The first few lines feel at once simple, innocent, awkward, and somewhat archaic, in the manner of a nursery rhyme or doggerel verse. The vatic, incantatory language stands in stark contrast to the irony in many of Bernstein's other poems; any Althusserian smugness has disappeared and been replaced by a sense of bemoaning, a mythic performance mapping the political dilemma:

---

24 Bernstein, 13.
25 Bernstein, 156.
26 Bernstein, 179.

Thugs from hell have taken freedom's store
The rich get richer, the poor die quicker
& the only god that sanctions that
Is no god at all but rhetorical crap[27]

The Bernsteinian tendency toward aphorism here emerges in the warped truism "The rich get richer, the poor die quicker," as a strategic, provisional prompt to turn away from the Orwellian "rhetorical crap" that makes that aphorism possible. Dedicated in the epigraph to Felix, Bernstein's son, the poem is recited by a single speaker who gives the sense of explaining something extremely complicated to a child in a simplified way. This speaker's Cassandra-like cry demonstrates a divided voice that is vulnerable yet defiant, fretting in protest, finally mapping the poem's addressee onto the reader in an exhortation to action:

So be a Girly Man
& take a gurly stand
Sing a gurly song
& dance with a girly sarong.[28]

In an unprecedented gesture, Bernstein intertwines Schwarzenegger's epithet "girlie-man" with a Stonewall-like gesture of defiance, deliberately misreading the epithet and turning it on its head as a celebratory label, in the process shifting the entire metaphorical frame of the political discourse. Dissent, figured here as a kind of sophist doubt, is something to be celebrated rather than shamed by:

We girly men are not afraid
Of uncertainty or reason or interdependence
We think before we fight, then think some more
Proclaim our faith in listening, in art, in compromise.[29]

While the earlier Bernstein would have been terrified of the pathos in such gestures, here he appears to be quite serious, and pathos against power is very much the point. The key turn in the poem, the

---

27 Ibid.
28 Ibid.
29 Ibid.

place where the frames shift, happens in the second of the fugue-like choruses when the speaker says:

> Sissies and proud
> That we would never lie our way to war[30]

The first line here calls upon the legacy of the gay rights movement, and the second line calls upon the collective voice of the left's protest against the war. This is an aphoristic gesture like so many of Bernstein's skewed truisms, but upon closer inspection, it makes an inspired kind of sense. This pairing and intersection in a post-9/11 context is neither accidental nor forced, as Judith Butler reminds us in a discussion of feminist and LGBT responses to 9/11:

> We tend to narrate the history of the feminist and lesbian/ gay movement, for instance, in such a way that ecstasy figured prominently in the sixties and seventies and midway through the eighties. But maybe ecstasy is more persistent than that; maybe it is with us all along. To be ec-static means, literally, to be outside oneself, and thus can have several meanings: to be transported beyond oneself by a passion, but also to be beside oneself with rage or grief. I think that if I can still address a 'we,' or include myself within its terms, I am speaking to those of us who are living in certain ways beside ourselves, whether in sexual passion, or emotional grief, or political rage.[31]

Finding the ecstasy of the sixties revived in the current sense of being "beside oneself" post-9-11, we can start to see how Bernstein is forming this sense of a "we" and why it feels convincing. By queering language and queering the left, Bernstein's speaker momentarily becomes a representative figure both for the poet speaking and for the state of being "beside oneself" in mourning for the victims of 9-11, angry at the aftermath and the U.S. government's abuse of its own people. This defiant position snowballs as the poem continues, picking up additional identities, additional cohorts in a Hardt and Negri-like assemblage:

---

30 Ibid.

31 Butler, Judith. *Precarious Life: The Powers of Mourning and Violence* (London: Verso, 2004), 24.

The girly men killed Christ
So the platinum DVD says
The Jews and blacks & gays
Are still standing in the way[32]

The Girly Man becomes a kind of accumulative figure for the left
in their protest against the neocon agenda and the dismantling of
democracy. But we're not out of the woods yet, the poem reiterates
in its final lines, the same lines with which it began:

The truth is hidden in a veil of tears
The scabs of the mourners grow thick with fear[33]

This is the menacing world of words we're left with at the end of
the poem. Does this move indicate, as in "Self Help," the acknowledgement of language's inability to directly change reality? Is it the
poignant result of "turning our work into digestible messages" after
entering discourse? Or is it a caution against being self-congratula-
tory, a reminder that much more needs to be done and changed "out
there"? The interpretation of the ending is ultimately left up to the
reader, inviting a different kind of participation and a different way
of making meaning.

The way in which the Girly Man figure turns an epithet inside out and
draws strength from that position can be seen as a direct response to
the dilemma that Lakoff describes for the left when he places the
family in the center of his metaphorical schema:

> Conservatives know that politics is not just about policy
> and interest groups and issue-by-issue debate. They have
> learned that politics is about family and morality, about
> myth and metaphor and emotional identification. They
> have, over twenty-five years, managed to forge conceptual
> links in the voters' minds between morality and public
> policy. They have done this by carefully working out
> their values, comprehending their myths, and designing
> a language to fit those values and myths so that they can

---

32   Charles Bernstein, *Girly Man* (Chicago: University of Chicago Press, 2006) 179.
33   Ibid.

evoke them with powerful slogans, repeated over and over
again, that reinforce those family-morality-policy links,
until the connections have come to seem natural to many
Americans, including many in the media. As long as liberals ignore the moral, mythic, and emotional dimension of
politics, as long as they stick to policy and interest groups
and issue-by-issue debate, they will have no hope of understanding the nature of the political transformation that
has overtaken this country and they will have no hope of
changing it.[34]

Lakoff's emphasis on the development of alternate myths here
suggests that the family (the "Fran & Don" of Bernstein's earlier
poem) is not dismissable as merely bourgeois or merely a curiosity—on the contrary, it turns out to matter very much how we go
about reconceptualizing this notion in liberal political discourse.
Bernstein would perhaps agree with this assessment of the problem,
but ambivalently, and that restlessness of perspective allows him to
discover certain options that may not have been available to Lakoff.
That very "we" in "Sissies and proud / that we would never lie our way
to war," bypasses Lakoff's entire binary by evoking a different kind
of family or community, one composed entirely of "sissies." Here the
return of the Brechtian occurs. In the poem's doggerel moments and
occasional flatfootedness as well as its overt political statement of
dissent against the war, it achieves a moment more truly Brechtian
than any amount of distancing attempted in other contexts. It accomplishes this by using pathos as a broad form of identification. It is
joyfully and blatantly celebratory and blatantly manipulative—for a
more overtly stated cause this time. The mobilization of queer rhetoric, iconoclastic values, and an implied notion of the family here in
the figure of the Girly Man evokes once again the Brechtian figure
of the reader, the ghostly presence of Marx himself. But in this situation Benjamin's stranger is no longer the potential reader of the
text. For the first time, this stranger appears in the position of the
speaker who utters the poem and who exhorts others to be other. In
a single and ingenious stroke, Bernstein at once reveals a way out for
the left and proves that the opposite of liberalism is neither family
nor morality, but empire.

34　George Lakoff. *Moral Politics: What Conservatives Know That Liberals Don't* (Chicago:
University of Chicago Press, 1996), 19.

4

mIEKAL aND

The Cave Children of New York Are Never Free

THE CAVE CHILDREN OF NEW YORK ARE NEVER FREE

A dime is no longer than the air of misery the day of yearning forgot. Who twisted when mounting all ages of wobbling. Hurry border. Hurray fits sat. Avenue child anagram. Who alerted taxi is the criminal of media of fight of knife a document. Sense tense, cent tense.

THE CAVE CHILDREN OF NEW YORK ARE NEVER FREE

I had six of that many. Under the newspaper delivery the door slipped like an ominous doorbell. Stake lock of who should come. E not satisfying by why show that matters. A done the first new year in platters a shelf of fingertips destroy destroy. Outer wear, terrain came, a plausible, dint he bite trigger, narrow lames of beautify them. As if it shall comment. Dont? Tariff protrudes almost twice the cracking. Book of Of. Every shelf in every dream bat. Only too long the vamber's locked grooves undulate triumph after footloose furry fury. I bang enough impressions thought total like traps. No deloraloriolius. A cute as fire four fickle fingers blunt & mute.

THE CAVE CHILDREN OF NEW YORK ARE NEVER FREE

Ask a dispute the derivation conjugal. Nax of powerful tankas, ok brethren, navally. Deed or something like other than availability. A hundred & an estimate equals an astral length a-ma-bob, if you comp? Laid a fair enough away worth is esteem. Notch of agreement as if tandem in quadruple. Stationary Amsterdam swile the many jersied gamut as if the geomorph studied late for once. Checking up on occupations damned the noble. The church isn't. But stood in line to exchange bread for chromatics. She rang "lay-lay" arenas after I'd already arrived extant. The last book suffered. Stood in lamb for watery game. Like the mouth likes. Ain't avenue from the right the first on the left? Looking at the windows –

THE CAVE CHILDREN OF NEW YORK ARE NEVER FREE

Plentus knew O was to rendevous with U. Mr Went included a marginal reminder. The damnedest to fathom, or went there think-ing alike. Brags the haphazard unbecoming the literal. Tangent royalty waiting for shoe or grave machine. Qua ethnic sultry day in day out, rosy crucifix under a therapeutic garter. Honesty teller over library trouble waged ear after ear of fitness longings. Whom not, I'm one, core of bloodless A & a botched painting out of sight rocks the metropolis. "It's what you do best" a doppelganger if ever the crust broke. Blind junk tumbles or feathers where flowers stumble. Stood up to & rusted shut a stipple afore the rackmount slavery.

THE CAVE CHILDREN OF NEW YORK ARE NEVER FREE

Gone over like a shower. Rocks plug the guiles, the willies, the afraid gone under without daytime. Somewhere England stands. Trying twisted from taking out of. One too many disjuncts proven fatality slivers proper dress a day as a tease. God bears withals & a hefty axe clefts Alexandria. All years occupation nailed it together. The signs in their eyes yelped data spewed. Maxims numbered alternately against a fraction of the instinct the cavern held. Many shelves-high I looked up. Natal reading habits pretend out thanks. Evidence to the contrary, even a light switch, held sway the conse-quent thinkers. The spindle, its latest, headed the chronology. Under no contions, be at remove, that is, codify dehibilitations.

THE CAVE CHILDREN OF NEW YORK ARE NEVER FREE

Bit much, the dread & her bakery lunatic kept quiet all these years. Lasting a pungent, curiosity mechanique an omnibus certitude. No good'll be weary, street beneath warpage, thread whilst combat whistler imagines. Ho chilles men. Much read, must of been only keen trackest for the last gymnastic. In circles radios treble, a hermetic message-roper animates rorschach scenery. Reductive linguistics inordinate topical digression. Innkeeper's wider screen (said beacon deconstructs . . .) private reference is what guarantee.

THE CAVE CHILDREN OF NEW YORK ARE NEVER FREE

A freedom feels. Like everyone tells. The kiss years from now. Deepened & opened out onto. Used to be how anxious. Decent tries attract buyers. Them that. Lessen fears unto the door. He isn't, is he? But while the bravery smears...wakable laxation guillotine. Letters=attach=novelisme=guiltless=u tile=anti=gradule=envelope. Word aims diagrams arrive. At standing postal discretion avowed her another thankless. We as them operate. Youse badger the wiggins but doon power the mudder-be's.

Draconian measures is stanza understatement. Hopping swoggle blays toothe fin. My antics buy time. New York creams its afterlife, the single heroic villager. Man O man popping. Destiny player's forgery. I cambert justice nor tackle Ho Chi Minh.

Believer yesterday more than concession. Who would make, anyway?

THE CAVE CHILDREN OF NEW YORK ARE NEVER FREE

Vector discussions are limited in climax but physical nomenclature has extensive masternation by giving, granted a disastrous diplomacy on my venue's wavering, or it isn't slightly baroque lecturnalia, ya know, stood by hence the legend reminder, but giving given prior stupor my client isn't a thinker whose standard alientates a trimmed & plushest kind of bodice; that till now wore frankly tender but no more, please you to plare meece, a vint is no spoof worth drabbing around, I'll titilate avuncular & speed head-wise lithe photography rank, bottle after the day a fester rose.

THE CAVE CHILDREN OF NEW YORK ARE NEVER FREE

Bouncing bondage nostalgia fled cabbies mixed tax-drop h'ors
douerves at price net, bet a card the meant was enough rope. Lettrist
fixates taper an irregular-only mark. Mark black & white dense city
on a bank rot map, if teeth fit the cabinet trend, remember her
when his whims killed the fair, slanted hermaneutics for centuries
inspired. Day little consequence capsized flurries as if antiquity
time line printed clearly ever. 2 tomes E held lantern only lit dark
stoops, pal distance carried distent concentrate. Twining vault-garret
progress had the effect, <u>nom</u> <u>plus</u> career attache/down under went
no fast spell & draft a worried terror dice.

THE CAVE CHILDREN OF NEW YORK ARE NEVER FREE

Kept budging but A fought. The diary changed the externals of
chemistry, her crying made. Q jet continent met tomorrow on a
hybrid. They played for days without making a decision. November
started the weather landlubbers wanted. Keep it clean he jerks me
more. Us ignore their hiding plenty, arms & everything, maybe if
we spread everywhere, the test could work. Hoopala nightly, & a red
lantern jury hung around well past the western lady. Lag of form
or culture tongue bravado. May last. May last. Mr Went had dithers,
corruption features & a masque of a spanish hero. No one had any
time it seemed or the adventure index.

THE CAVE CHILDREN OF NEW YORK ARE NEVER FREE

Some shifting fortunes abbreviate distractions. A multiple riser
lept uncontrolled, my many, her labor, them is altogether picked.
& uncanny, yes under the popular we met there unhinged, quartz
bride & bunches of tickets & fist-gamble in fits. Lo inept candies,
overtry no. ll alento debaff, first heard in fragment (read fragments)
& filled? Well, patter some since nobody wanted mentors or suitors
or tremors. I kinda. A conversation dichotomy abrupts thence, cher-
okee hath swept but buried lip. Favor in the Letter. Splatter black
without erasure, between red brown the splice is material. History
women compress phallus ably. Of in ordinary plan or that edge term
led benter the gammon. Now tool unlay anxious bridge-worn spiel,
learn tapping at once. By stress a breath & not hot fence. Her beal
chapped tidal. Of course heir child silent squeal.

THE CAVE CHILDREN OF NEW YORK ARE NEVER FREE

I should sit in the shrift of tiding there would amount to be that many. You are a tire defeated vocabulary. O tells the design to the planet there are many of . . . adle the milk laid for hours the fear of trying would not protect the other scheme. Do not say do not say only body lately. After taste dour work. Lip glaze the smack smashed. Do aunt try the O. About anything there is nothing of content inept. Intent. Or another blue see-thru mending. I blood the the then or up till gaffer stroke out of the way he jake the buck light. Nobody lays under rocks for long or even their head beside any boulder stopped short of.

THE CAVE CHILDREN OF NEW YORK ARE NEVER FREE

Honus Cobb met the ways his trap kelpt dustive turnder. No else could think talk that way. Why ways followed where O wanted, how tabulating counted for exit chase doomster. I ist nomeromerorder ismist. There a tunx, placent chabbers belded avouled ert trobuley-ant. Come out of it as mobile pragmite, taken venom molder anti-unti cursive, played out button ammo. Knock turn hammer change-up tool blend. Only looking yo U but not A vowelese. This modern whore furnace muscled down he'lls, else we'd all go where'd a noun clout could make it big, a bit like a legendary ball-hop back some game ago. A sport aches overly fluent rousting felt Roman, dirty ile & all that.

THE CAVE CHILDREN OF NEW YORK ARE NEVER FREE

Bank shrift mocks. Celt block some time ago. Distance story starred. Travel phallanx shifted motive or granite being stood chub & broad where happiness trog courted an alcove, a cove, an oven. Marry druther & shakespeare fetish blanced car dom vu—lape away twails, nasty gares, tell vernly blaws. Aerhoo blared coxhill wike my tuned-a-tune-o-total-o-tidal-u-teetography. Further tribs banked rare court & ravener trump. Her days Alice could keep undercover final literature & a taste mundane alphist dogmatizing, a spin round the hedge back of thirty, no gads the bibles left undone, undo. Thbook.

5

MICHAEL ENG

The Metaphysical Mouth and the Asylum of the Everyday: Charles Bernstein and Contemporary Continental Philosophy of Language

Charles Bernstein's notion of "the metaphysical mouth" offers us an opportunity to demonstrate the alignment of this thought with the reflection on language found in the post-Heideggerian continental tradition. For reasons that I aim briefly to address, the reflection on language in continental thought has not been considered as belonging to the field of philosophy of language as it is conventionally conceived. Thus, part of my aim in bringing Bernstein's work into conversation with reflections on language following Heidegger is to show how he enables at once the possibility of thinking a contemporary continental philosophy of language, a view of what this philosophy of language might look like and perhaps most importantly, a consideration of what is at stake in the type of relation to language this thought advances. Both Bernstein and contemporary continental thought share a concern with language that places language itself at stake as part of the movement of that concern, a concern that I will argue is ultimately a reflection on the relationship of language to human finitude. However, the juxtaposition of Bernstein and contemporary continental thought makes visible the fact that this concern with language and human finitude is connected directly with to the possibility of a thinking life within institutions—in particular, that institution that passes for the institution of thought, viz., the university—and actually calls for us to engage this possibility as part of a relation to language.

In order to unfold the formulations I just offered, my discussion will proceed first with a reading of Bernstein's Introduction to his edited volume *Close Listening: Poetry and the Performed Word* (1998), in which the concept of the metaphysical mouth appears most prominently. After rehearsing the role the concept of the metaphysical mouth plays in Bernstein's argument in the volume's introduction, I will survey the connections to continental reflections on language his concept of the metaphysical mouth inspires, focusing specifically on what I described above as their shared concern with the question of language and the possibility of thinking within the university. I would like to conclude my analysis with a reading of Bernstein's "Asylum" (1975) and consider the poem as both an intervention into the relation among language, finitude, and critical life in the institution, as well as an invitation to 'sound the words' of this intervention along with him. I identify "Asylum" as an exemplary instance of the relationships I seek to describe in this essay; in my assessment, the poem conveys Bernstein's attempt and invitation to think at the same time, through a method of sounding, the limits of institutional language and language itself as an institution.[1]

I. *Close Listening*: Sounding Language

The volume *Close Listening* is devoted to bringing "critical attention to modern poetry and performance," which Bernstein claims in his introduction "has been negligible" up until the present moment, especially concerning "the sound of poetry" in its performance.[2]

---

1   This essay is very much an attempt to take up the invitation Bernstein issues in describing the organization informing his writing. Based on the following description in his essay "The Revenge of the Poet-Critic," which is echoed in different ways in much of his critical essays, I will be reading Bernstein's criticism (which I prefer to think of as theory) as poetic and his poetic work as forms of theory. Regarding the arrangement of paragraphs in his critical writing, Bernstein writes, "The idea is that the order of the paragraphs could be shifted, and, more importantly, that space is left for new paragraphs to be inserted, something like leaving room for (more) thought" ["Revenge of the Poet-Critic, or The Parts are Greater Than the Sum of the Whole," in Charles Bernstein, *My Way: Speeches and Poems* (Chicago: University of Chicago Press, 1999), 7]. Taking-up his invitation to insert new paragraphs, this essay views Bernstein's practice of writing as an invitation to write and think the contours of language along with him.

2   Charles Bernstein, ed., *Close Listening: Poetry and the Performed Word* (New York: Oxford UP, 2008), 3.

That attention to the question of poetry's sound should remain ignored at the same time that its performance has become one of the primary vehicles for the dissemination of poetic works in North America since the 1950s is a contradiction that Bernstein attempts to explain through distinctions between listening and hearing on the one hand, and between "orality" and "aurality" on the other hand.[3] Listening for meaning within the poetic performance obscures the ability to hear the language of the poem. Similarly, privileging the voice of the poet, which is what Bernstein calls "orality," prevents the aural dimension of language from being sounded and heard. These distinctions are intended by Bernstein to make it clear that his aim is not to argue for a return to, or primacy of, the voice of the poet. Instead, Bernstein's concern is with a fidelity to the poem as an event of language; in performance, language is sounded, and the poem appears in its material presence; it "matters," as Bernstein is dedicated to saying.[4] Performance is thus a pragmatics of language for Bernstein, one which "calls" the language of the poem "into use by saying, or hearing, the words aloud."[5]

"Aurality" emphasizes the hearing of the poem's writing over the poet's "breath, voice, and speech," or "orality," which Bernstein designates with the phrase "the metaphysical mouth" because it implies the poet's sovereignty over the poem as an object of his or her expressive creation.[6] To be sure, and as we have already noted, Bernstein is also not denying the necessity of the material presence of either the poet or reader who would perform the poem. Nor does he deny the necessity of the material presence of the audience, of those who would be addressed by the poem. Both poet/reader and audience/listener are required by language in order for it to appear through the poem. Bernstein explicitly brackets listening from his theorization, for listening already implies a listening for meaning, while what he is concerned with is the sounding of language as a condition of meaning. Language in this way becomes the matter of poetic performance through a separation of sound and meaning. It is only "[w]hen sound ceases to follow sense, when, that is, it *makes* sense of sound, [that] we touch on the matter of language."[7] "This,"

---

3 Ibid., 5; 13.
4 Ibid., 21.
5 Ibid., 7.
6 Ibid., 13.
7 Ibid., 21.

says Bernstein, "is the burden of poetry; this is why poetry matters."[8] A few lines further down in the same passage, Bernstein asserts, "Sound brings writing back from its metaphysical and symbolic functions to where it is at home, in performance."[9]

Rather than appeal to or reinforce any metaphysical unity of either the work or the poet, Bernstein theorizes performance as demonstrating a poem's "fundamentally plural existence" in each performative event.[10] Were there no performance of poetry, Bernstein implies, the experience of poetry would be literally muted, and the poem would be identified solely with its form on the printed page. By attuning us to the sounding of language and the plural existence of the work, the performance of poetry is at once an experience of the language of the work and a gathering of "different, dissonant voices: a multivocality."[11] This multivocality, writes Bernstein, "foregrounds the dialogic dimension of poetry"; it makes audible the fact that the work calls for and invokes an audience that would be in dialogue with it as the condition of its appearance.[12]

Bernstein's claim concerning the power sounding language in performance has to free language from its metaphysical reduction to an expression of a creative self, or from its role as a vehicle of communication (also a metaphysical conception of language), resonates at first glance with Ludwig Wittgenstein's *Philosophical Investigations* (1951), which Bernstein appeals to periodically throughout his writings. In particular, Wittgenstein's idea from §115 of the *Investigations* of being held captive to a certain image of language is a recurrent theme in Bernstein's thinking. Bernstein powerfully combines Wittgenstein's image of being held captive to specific modes of language to his own notion of "frame lock" elaborated out of Erving Goffman's work on conceptual frames of reference. Sound, Bernstein contends in the present context, having been traditionally kept 'out of the frame' of poetic criticism, has the ability to disrupt established frames in which we approach and use language once we allow it to appear in performance.[13]

---

8   Ibid.

9   Ibid.

10   Ibid., 9.

11   Ibid., 15.

12   Ibid.

13   Ibid., 5. Cf. "Writing and Method," in Charles Bernstein, *Content's Dream: Essays 1975-1984* (Evanston: Northwestern UP, 1986) and "Frame Lock," in *My Way: Speeches and Poems*.

Nonetheless, Bernstein's conception of sound's ability to liberate writing from a metaphysics of presence appears to echo most directly §116 of the *Investigations* in which Wittgenstein famously claims, "What *we* do is to bring words back from their metaphysical to their everyday use."[14] Of course, the question which immediately arises is 'who' answers to the 'we' Wittgenstein invokes. Closer inspection of this section of the *Investigations* makes it is difficult to say whether Bernstein actually belongs to this 'we,' since Wittgenstein explicitly criticizes philosophy for allowing language to 'go on holiday' or 'run idle' and privileges everyday uses of language over the reified language-game of philosophy.[15] Whoever this 'we' is, they are not philosophers in the conventional sense, according to Wittgenstein.[16]

In any case, it is quite clear in Bernstein's writings that he does not share Wittgenstein's privileging of the everyday. On the contrary, he routinely calls out the quotidian forms of popular media, such as *Time* magazine and *The New York Times'* Op Ed pages, for the role they play in perpetuating what is in fact a metaphysics of the everyday. [17] The concept of the everyday is metaphysical to the extent that it is structured to appear as commonsensical (i.e., as *not* a concept at all) and to mark as silly any kind of critical thought brought to bear upon it.[18] The media through which the metaphysics of the everyday accomplishes itself gives us a relationship to language that, to paraphrase Heidegger, prevents us from experiencing language *as language*. We may use language in the everyday, but that does not mean we have a relationship to it. Or rather, our everyday relationship to language is only a simulacrum of one, buttressed with a host of metaphysical presuppositions of the nature of language. We therefore don't have to look very far for the metaphysical mouth; it is speaking to us constantly from the likes of The Grey Lady and its derivatives.

---

14 Ludwig Wittgenstein, *Philosophical Investigations*, trans. G.E.M. Anscombe (Oxford, UK: Blackwell, 1958).

15 Ibid., §38 and §132.

16 Wittgenstein's intentions here won't prevent those working in his wake, however, from using the distinction between philosophy and the everyday to promote opposing approaches in philosophy of language, one directed at constructing an ideal meta-language to analyze how meaning is constructed and another directed at understanding meaning in language's everyday, or "ordinary," employments.

17 Cf. "Writing and Method" and "The Revenge of the Poet-Critic."

18 Cf. "What's Art Got to Do with It? The Status of the Subject of the Humanities in an Age of Cultural Studies," in *My Way: Speeches and Poems.*

However, Bernstein's reluctance to pursue a lockstep retracing of the Wittgensteinian project is significant, because it opens a space to think an alignment of his work with Heidegger, who articulated similar paths for recovering a fundamental relation to language. Moreover, while Wittgenstein shared with Heidegger a conviction that the question of human existence was tied up with the question of language, the same could not be said of the tradition of language philosophy inaugurated by Wittgenstein's thought. Post-Heideggerian continental philosophy, in contrast, has taken it upon itself to elaborate the problem of language and human finitude in a manner that aligns with Bernstein's reflections on language. Bernstein's claim, for example, in *Close Listening* that "[i]n sounding language we ground ourselves as sentient, material beings, obtruding into the world with the same obdurate thingness as rocks or soil or flesh" brings him closer in sensibility to Heidegger, post-Heideggerian thought, and most importantly the *stakes* of this thinking than philosophy of language conventionally conceived.[19]

In my next section, I should like to sketch the basic contours of Heidegger's reflections on language, focusing specifically on what I would call his theorization of an "antagonism of language" and his reversal of the relationship of language and use through a provocation of language's sounding. I do not wish to enter into a long exegesis of Heidegger's texts, but since what I am arguing for in this essay is a consideration of Bernstein's work as a thinking along with post-Heideggerian reflections on language, I feel I need to offer as a foundation for this argument more than a simplistic parallel between them.

II. Heidegger and the Metaphysics of Language

Heidegger's engagement with language is typically considered not to have taken place until later in his thought and is also often reduced to his proclamation in his 1947 essay, the "Letter on Humanism," that "Language is the house of Being."[20] However, Heidegger's preparation for issuing such a claim, as well as for undertaking the reflec-

---

19 *Close Listening*, 21.

20 "Letter on Humanism," in Martin Heidegger, *Basic Writings*, ed. David Farrell Krell, revised & expanded ed. (New York: HarperCollins, 1993), 217.

tions on language in the essays from the 1950s collected under the title *Unterwegs zur Sprache* (1959) (*On the Way to Language*),[21] can be traced within his originating project of recovering the question of Being, which he named "fundamental ontology." To use one of Wittgenstein's phrases, the "struggle with language," as Heidegger notes in the "Letter on Humanism," was always present within the project of fundamental ontology, but this project was not fully able to overcome what Heidegger characterized as the language of metaphysics.[22]

At the center of the project of fundamental ontology is "Dasein," which in traditional philosophical usage means "existence," but which Heidegger employs to redefine human existence as fundamentally "being-there." Heidegger's casting of human existence as Dasein was an attempt free "the human" from traditional definitions of subjectivity and belonged therefore to the general task Heidegger identifies in *Being and Time* of "destructuring" the history of metaphysics.

Traditional theories of subjectivity—specifically, the language of subjectivity—through which human existence was thought, had the result, so Heidegger claimed, of blocking access to human finitude. "Dasein," therefore, is not simply a replacement for the names for the subject which philosophy furnished throughout its history, such as the Greek essence or "hypokeimenon," the Latin substance or "subiectum," or the Cartesian *ego cogito*. As da-sein, being-there, Dasein points to the fact that human existence is directed toward the future, always ahead of itself, not sub-jected, thrown under, but pro-jected, thrown ahead. "Dasein" un-grounds metaphysical subjectivity, but unlike the Cartesian subject who grounds itself in its self-representations, Dasein is also fundamentally un-grounded in existence.

The project of recovering the question of Being through a theorization of human finitude as thrown existence required for Heidegger what one might refer to in basic terms as a defamiliarization of the language of metaphysics. This is one side of the antagonism of language that I argue unfolds in fundamental ontology, and if we were interested in maintaining some kind of alignment between

---

21   In English translation, these essays are divided among two works: *On the Way to Language*, trans. Peter D. Hertz (New York: Harper and Row, 1971) and *Poetry, Language, Thought*, trans. Albert Hofstadter (New York: Harper and Row, 1975).

22   "Letter on Humanism," 231.

Heidegger and Wittgenstein, then this is one moment in which such an alignment might be read. Establishing such an agreement between the two would only contribute to a simple scholarly accounting, though, rather than attend to what is at stake in the question of language for both these thinkers.

Seeing where Heidegger and Wittgenstein depart is more instructive than their convergence, for their departure also allows us to see how Bernstein's critique of language aligns with the antagonism of language Heidegger articulates. While Heidegger engages one slope of this antagonism along the terrain of the language of metaphysics, he identifies the antagonism's other slope within the language of the everyday, which Wittgenstein does not sufficiently interrogate in his later thought and instead privileges as a point of access to how language really is and should be used. For Wittgenstein, philosophy mystifies language by abstracting it from use, thus rendering it "idle" or letting it go "on holiday"; for some reason he never specifies, Wittgenstein does not consider philosophy a legitimate use of language.

Heidegger, however, not only questions the metaphysical constructions of language; he views the language of the everyday (even the idea of the "everyday" itself) as an extension of the metaphysics of language. Everyday language, for Heidegger, belongs to the public realm (*die Öffentlichkeit*), which he characterizes as anonymous, impersonal and filled with modes of experience that distract the human Dasein from engaging in a thinking-questioning of one's existence. Many will recognize the phrase "das Man" or the "they" Heidegger uses to name this realm. Within it, 'our' concerns are always conditioned, so Heidegger contends, by the fact that we have to accomplish certain tasks of everyday living. We have to get things done, and what we are presented with as goals to accomplish in our everyday experience has been given to us always in advance from an abstract "they": we think and act as "they" tell us to.[23]

We would not be thrown ahead of ourselves as beings 'in-the-world' if our existence were not conditioned fundamentally by our finitude—our understanding of Being that makes possible the fact of existence is a matter of our concern. However, the concern with our existence quickly threatens to be diluted the more we are absorbed by everyday existence. The demands belonging to our quotidian life

---

23 See Sections 25-27 of *Being and Time*, trans. John Macquarrie and Edward Robinson (Oxford: Blackwell, 1962), 149-68.

easily eclipse attempts to reflect on the fact of our existence; we end up taking all things that exist—and therefore Being itself—for granted, lost in the "they," as Heidegger says.

While lost in the "they," we take language for granted, as with our everyday relationship to any other existing thing. In our ordinary engagements, we tend not to ask the question, 'What is language?' If we do, the typical answer, the answer shared by both linguists and 'the man on the street,' conceives language as an instrument of communication that expresses the thoughts of the subject who employs it. Though this conception of language seems self-evident, it is metaphysical through and through; it presupposes the stability of both language and a subject who represents the world to him- or herself. For Heidegger, if we find ourselves in a struggle with language, it is not because, as Wittgenstein personified it, language bewitched us into believing it had powers it does not have; rather, our struggle is one of recovering a relationship to language that allows us to experience the question of Being *as a question*.

In *Being and Time*, Heidegger claims the form language takes in the realm of the "they" is *die Gerede*—"idle talk" or "chatter."[24] In the everyday, language may be useful and may aid us in realizing goals pertinent to day-to-day activities, but it has ceased to be meaningful in attending to the fact of existence. In "Letter on Humanism," Heidegger writes, "Language thereby falls into the service of expediting communication along routes where objectification—the uniform accessibility of everything to everyone—branches out and disregards all limits. In this way language comes under the dictatorship of the public realm, which decides in advance what is intelligible and what must be rejected as unintelligible."[25] Within the public realm, language is taken for granted, and so is the idea that everything can be communicated. Language in the public realm belongs to the structure of viewing everything that exists as accessible, available, and differing only in degree. There is no thought of difference as such from language in the public realm. Furthermore, in directing all language to reproduce itself in recognizable ways, the public realm is not unlike what Bernstein calls "official verse culture": it decides in advance what can be said (and by default, what falls outside of the sayable).[26]

---

24 See Section 35.

25 "Letter on Humanism," 221.

26 Heidegger's description of the public realm's role in determining the sayable and

With the essays of *Unterwegs zur Sprache* (*On the Way to Language*), Heidegger willingly acknowledges both the usefulness as well as correctness of the everyday conception of language. However, he quickly notes that both the ideas of utility and correctness belong to the logic of technocratic rationality which Heidegger joins many in diagnosing as the chief organizing force of modernity. Language is thus a subject of this modernity as much as its human inhabitants: it is allowed to appear solely within a utilitarian role as either a tool of communication, or, in the form of what is communicated as information, and it is theorized according to the very logic that determines the bounds of its appearance. In his essay "The Nature of Language," Heidegger finds little help in attending to language as *language* from philosophy of language as it is has been formed by analytic thought. Concerning analytic philosophy's self-characterization as "metalinguistics," Heidegger writes, "That sounds like metaphysics—not only sounds like it, it *is* metaphysics. Metalinguistics is the metaphysics of the thoroughgoing technicalization of all languages into the sole operative instrument of interplanetary information." With an appropriate flourish, he adds, "Metalanguage and sputnik [sic], metalinguistics and rocketry are the Same."[27]

That the logic that created Sputnik and sent it into space to orbit the globe is the same logic that organizes both daily life and the life of the disciplines (philosophy especially in this case) should not be surprising, at least to those who feel the force of this connection as it persists in our postmodernity. Bernstein is certainly to be counted among those who have registered such a feeling, and like Bernstein after him, Heidegger identifies poetry as a site in which the antagonism of language may be articulated and made visible. In a reading of Georg Trakl's "A Winter Evening" whose echoes might be heard in Bernstein's theorization of aurality, Heidegger describes the work of the poem as clearing a space for the speaking and sounding of language.[28] In poetic practice language is not a vehicle of communication, expression or representation; rather, through poetry, Heidegger contends, "*die Sprache spricht*"—"language speaks." What is at stake in the poetic act's overturning of language? The possibility of experi-

---

unsayable here anticipates Michel Foucault's concept of the archive. Cf. Foucault's, *The Archaeology of Knowledge*, trans. A.M. Sheridan Smith (New York: Pantheon, 1972).

27 Heidegger, *On the Way to Language*, 58.

28 Heidegger, "Language," in *Poetry, Language, Thought*.

encing language as an event of Being and as a site of human finitude. Both movements belong to one another: Being appears in concrete, material instances, moments in which we are engaged with Being as a matter of existential concern (and there is no concern that is not existential). But the call of language in poetry also designates an event in which language "uses" human beings in the scenic presentation of Being. Poetry 'works' as a scene because it allows us to witness the event of Being's appearance as a question for us (and as an event that places us into question).

The movement I have just summarized rather rapidly is what Heidegger thinks as the "appropriating event" (*Ereignis*) of Being. As Christopher Fynsk has painstakingly demonstrated, another way Heidegger thinks the event of Being's appropriation is in terms of usage (*der Brauch*). *Der Brauch* has the dual meaning of need or use. Thus, Being needs and uses human beings in order to appear. As Fynsk has also discovered, Heidegger remarkably theorizes the appropriating event of Being in language bodily. "We" don't use language. Language uses the bodily presence of human beings for its sounding.[29]

In his description of poetry reading as "*a public tuning*,"[30] Bernstein reminds us that our being-called by language is a collective experience. This reminder corresponds nicely with the work of Jean-Luc Nancy, whose contribution to the reception of Heidegger's text is to show how our understanding of Being, and therefore our being-in-the-world, is a socially shared one and one that is never finished.[31] As Bernstein speaks both of sounded poetry's potential to "[spin] out into the world [. . .] a new series of acoustic modalities" and constitute new audiences around these events of poetry,[32] he shares Nancy's intuition about the ever-open possibility of a social experience of language as a collective experience of existence.

---

29 As Fynsk recounts, Heidegger writes rather obliquely in a marginal note in *Unterwegs zur Sprache* the following formulation: *Lauten und Leiben — Leib und Schrift* ("Sounding and Bodying — Body and Writing") [*Unterwegs zur Sprache*, vol. 12 of the *Gesamtausgabe* (Frankfurt am Main: Klostermann, 1985), 249, quoted in Christopher Fynsk, *Language and Relation . . . that there is language* (Stanford: Stanford UP, 1996), 98].

30 *Close Listening*, 6, italics Bernstein's.

31 See Jean-Luc Nancy, "Sharing Voices," in Gayle L. Ormiston and Alan D. Schrift, eds. *Transforming the Hermeneutic Context: From Nietzsche to Nancy* (Albany: SUNY Press, 1990), as well as Jean-Luc Nancy, *The Inoperative Community*, ed. Peter Connor, trans. Peter Connor et al (Minneapolis: University of Minnesota Press, 1991).

32 *Close Listening*, 6; 22.

Bernstein also helps to remind us that the experience of existence is mediated more and more comprehensively through institutions. Heidegger's theorization of the public realm recognized this, as did his call for a reorganization of the university according to the project of fundamental ontology, but we all know how that turned out. Heidegger's joining of his project with that of National Socialism's proves there are no guarantees. But that does not mean his diagnosis of the technocratic logic governing everyday life was any less sound.

Bernstein has yet to offer a focused reflection on poetry's potential contribution to critical interrogations of what Bill Readings called the "posthistorical university," many of which, as I will shortly point out, take their departure from the Heideggerian schema sketched above.[33] But it is worth noting that Bernstein casts a fair share of suspicion on poetry's role in perpetuating the metaphysics of language as a discipline, field and industry ("official verse culture," as noted above). In my final section, I would like to conduct a reading of Bernstein's poem "Asylum" (1975) to underscore the seamless critique of the language of the institution and the institution of language (language as an institution). I will preface this reading first by pointing out briefly moments in post-Heideggerian continental reflections on language that intersect with Bernstein's efforts here, but my intention is to read "Asylum" as a kind of call to 'deconstruct' the institution of language and the language of the institution in the way Nancy conceives the project of deconstruction following Heidegger: "It is to present, to expose[,] the construction to itself."[34] At stake for those thinking within this movement of deconstruction is the possibility of new forms of existence in and through language.

III. The Language of the Institution /
The Institution of Language

My rehearsal of Heidegger's project above and my remarks just offered concerning deconstruction feel, if I am to be honest, quite anachronistic. I 'came of age,' so to speak, in my graduate studies in the late 1990s, when deconstruction and its adjuncts—Theory, in

---

33   See Bill Readings, *The University in Ruins* (Cambridge, MA: Harvard UP, 1996). A work that reflects on the attempts to re-imagine the university from Heidegger's engagement, and is also itself an engagement with the university following Heidegger's gestures, is Christopher Fynsk's *The Claim of Language: A Case for the Humanities* (Minneapolis: University of Minnesota Press, 2004).

34   Jean-Luc Nancy, "Our History." *Diacritics* 20.3: 104.

general—was falling out of fashion (though I didn't realize it then, and no one felt the need to clue me in on this fact). Now, however, though Derrida really is dead as I compose this essay, and though I am quite aware of the fact that Bernstein has been critical of deconstruction,[35] the stakes of deconstruction feel no less exigent today than they were in deconstruction's heyday, which some "deconstructionists," admittedly, as Bernstein states, may have invented out of a *nostalgia for there to be stakes* in reading. (Talk about meta![36])

I would like to submit that the anachronistic feeling I am describing *points* to something. If I repeatedly appeal to this pointing as something felt, it is because I am convinced there is an affective dimension to the question of language, both in the moments it appears and especially in the moments it fails to appear (or appears as a kind of failure). To be more precise: the anachronistic feeling I have when teaching students even such basic skills as critical reading of texts as a form of a relation to language belongs to the knowledge they and I both share that we are part of a world that cares nothing for criticality, save the requisite lip service and window dressing that accompany the marketing of college educations to students and the accreditation of curricula. It is the *same* anachronistic affect that surrounds recent appeals to the administration of Middlesex University to reverse the decision it rendered just recently to close its Philosophy program.[37]

---

35 Cf. "The Academy in Peril: William Carlos Williams Meets the MLA," in *Content's Dream*, 244-51.

36 Ibid. Bernstein's use of the moniker "deconstructionists" is telling about who he might have identified as perpetuating such a theater of stakes at the time of his provocation at the MLA. Whether he would concede this fact or not, I should hope it unnecessary to add that those who identified themselves as "deconstructionists" at the time, or as "deconstructionists" now, whether in the fields of literature, philosophy, architecture, etc., very likely constituted this identity from a willful inattention to the guiding textual interventions marking deconstruction as a practice of language. In this way, "deconstructionists" and those who oppose deconstruction have much in common.

37 See http://savemdxphil.com/about/. The decision was apparently communicated to the Philosophy Department's faculty in April 2010. It seems to me, however, that efforts either to point out the contradictory nature of the Middlesex administration's claims that the Philosophy Department does not contribute anything "measurable" to the university despite its acknowledgment of the high research ratings the department received in the United Kingdom or to demonstrate some measurable—i.e., useful—value of the study of philosophy play into the very logic informing the decision to close the department in the first place. The administration, I would imagine, either does not understand such appeals (i.e., they

If the university is no longer a place where a call to engage the question of language as a question of existence can be heard, perhaps it never was. As distressing as this possibility is, there is something paradoxically affirming in the anachronistic affect I just described, for it reminds me that the engagement with language in many of the key, guiding works of post-Heideggerian thought were conceived precisely as antagonisms both to the kind of writing possible in the academy at the time of their publications and to the very casting of the question of language in the university in the form of "the linguistic turn." I of course cannot perform here the sustained readings this claim I am offering requires, but I will draw attention to the fact that Michel Foucault's *The Order of Things* (1966) and *The Archaeology of Knowledge* (1969) and Derrida's *Of Grammatology* (1967) all set out with the observation that the very modes by which language is named as an object of analysis in the human sciences actually serve to cut off access to the existential stakes of engaging language *as a question*.[38] While Jean-François Lyotard's *The Postmodern Condition* (1979) and *The Differend* (1983) perform as straight-faced submissions of Official Academic Speech, to paraphrase Bernstein's "official verse culture," thereby enacting the very differend Lyotard diagnoses in the latter text, all these texts by Foucault, Derrida and Lyotard can be seen to be attempting a realization of "research" defined by Maurice Blanchot in *The Infinite Conversation* (1969): a relation to language in which language itself is at stake.[39]

While it typically takes substantial preparation in philosophy and literature for students to be able to read the texts named above, they often have no problem knowing that we are touching on something that engages their lives when we encounter an instance of a relation to language that requires us *not to question* the experience of language, such as the interpellation of the individual by the language

---

fall outside the language the administration speaks) or simply laughs them off as quaint. As much as I am in agreement with its premises, Martha Nussbaum's recent argument in her *Not For Profit: Why Democracy Needs the Humanities* (Princeton: Princeton UP, 2010) strikes me as equally quaint, as if anyone today actually cares about the fate of democracy in its real sense—i.e., in a sense separate from the advance of global capital.

38   Not insignificantly, Derrida employs the term "inflation" to describe the reification of language by the discipline of linguistics [*Of Grammatology*, trans. Gayatri Chakravorty Spivak (Baltimore: Johns Hopkins UP, 1976), 6].

39   *The Infinite Conversation*, trans. Susan Hanson (Minneapolis: University of Minnesota Press, 1993), 6.

of ideology, as Louis Althusser details in his famous essay. Perhaps this is why articulating the question of language as a question of existence (and vice-versa) in the classroom often feels like an inter-ruption and caesura, like a tangent but also like we've accidentally stumbled upon something essential, like "reality" is at stake at that very moment in which we are struggling with the text.[40] My experi-ence of such a moment is one of feeling that if we turn to look at the object of our concern directly—that is to say, existence—then it will disappear from view, not unlike the story of Orpheus and Eurydice, which Blanchot retold in his work. If we make existence the issue of the class, then everything we discuss simply becomes schoolwork. However, if we attend to the fact of schoolwork and the feeling everyone (not just the students, by the way) has that schoolwork and school in general foreclose asking about not only one's own existence but our shared existence together, then the question of what we are doing in relation to the speech we are learning is able to be felt.

Though one of Bernstein's earliest published works, "Asylum" strikes me as 'more deconstructive,' if such a phrase makes sense, than his quite witty and cutting performances that give the lie to the literal investment institutions, as well as other disciplines within the university, 'make' in poetry and poetic practice.[41] Of course, such performances do indeed expose the construction to itself in ways

---

40 The "reality" I have in mind is the one Fynsk draws out in his reading of Celan's Bremen and Darmstadt addresses as statements of poetry's engagement with the reality of language 'after Heidegger' (*Language and Relation*, 135-160).

41 In ways that are quite consonant with Derrida's remark concerning the infla-tion of language through linguistics, Bernstein has at times employed the tactic of restoring the capitalist logic of cultural and academic production by speak-ing of poetry as a financial vehicle. I am thinking, for example, of the state-ment Bernstein issued at an event at the New School marking the release of *Best American Poetry 2008*, in which he employs the language of finance capital to call for a bailout of American poetry (Charles Bernstein, "Poetry Bailout Will Restore Confidence of Readers," *Harper's Magazine*, September 26, 2008, http://harpers.org/archive/2008/09/hbc-90003617). Another moment that stands out takes place in an interview conducted by Allison M. Cummings and Rocco Marinaccio. In response to a question concerning the authority of poetic criticism, Bernstein suddenly breaks into a kind of non-sequitur of financial jargon, proclaiming, "Still, poetry's assets would have been overdrawn long ago if it did not have, as a genre, the authoriza-tion to coin new money. This new currency has underwritten both the greatest and the most reprehensible poetic projects of the past years. Of course, science is the only really blue-chip truth stock, but poetry is a good investment because it remains significantly undervalued. I would certainly recommend including it in any diversified epistemologic portfolio" ["An Interview with Charles Bernstein," *Contemporary Literature*, Vol. 41, No. 1 (Spring, 2000): 6].

faithful to Nancy's definition of deconstruction, and they also expose the language of the institution to itself in the vicious, unmerciful way that justly matches the cynical appropriation of the stakes of poetry and the humanities in general by institutions when it suits them. However, what these particular 'in-your-face,' 'cut-through-the-crap' performances by Bernstein lack is the affective experience of language containing at once the accidental and essential in the manner I described above and which I would hold has been so far an under-theorized component in the reception of deconstruction in North America.

"Asylum," in contrast, enacts an affective experience of language, I contend, through its assemblage of architectural, disciplinary and diagnostic phrases culled from Erving Goffman's *Asylums: Essays on the Social Situation of Mental Patients and Other Inmates* (1961). The poem, following a leitmotif Bernstein establishes throughout his work, is about "closed systems," he tells us.[42] It is not surprising that he has chosen to reprint it a number of times following its initial offering as the opening poem of *Asylums* (1975).[43] The poem's use of the page's space creates a rhythm in which Goffman's phrases are condensed closely together and then opened-up, directing the reader/listener, as Bernstein will later say, through opaque enclosures punctuated with occasional openings for light—or flight.[44] The poem opens as if stepping into the recitation of a bureaucratic report:

rooms, suites of rooms, buildings, plants

in line. Their encompassing or total character

intercourse with the outside and to departure

such as locked doors, high walls, barbed

---

42 Thom Donovan, "Interview with Charles Bernstein (Part I)," *Harriet: a blog from the poetry foundation*, http://www.poetryfoundation.org/harriet/2010/04/interview-with-charles-bernstein-part-i/.

43 In addition to opening *All the Whiskey in Heaven*, Bernstein published "Asylum" also in *Islets/Irritations* (1983).

44 "The Book as Architecture," in *My Way*, 57.

wire, cliffs, water, forests, moors

conflicts, discreditings, failures

of assimilation. If cultural change

the outside. Thus, if the inmates stay

victory. They create and sustain

a particular kind of tension

dangers to it, with the welfare

jails, penitentiaries, P.O.W.
camps, concentration camps[45]

Bernstein describes "Asylum" as a dark poem,[46] which seems a bit
understated to me. If I cannot speak for the general reader/listener,
I at least can admit to feeling quite distressed reading the text, and
especially typing it into this essay as I quote from it. Following the
falling into line of bureaucratic containers ("rooms, suites of rooms,"
as in an office park, and "buildings" instead of "architecture," the

---

45 "Asylum," in Charles Bernstein, *All the Whiskey in Heaven: Selected Poems* (New York:
    Farrar Straus Giroux, 2010), 3. The combined effect of density and flow is most
    pronounced in the original publication of the poem in *Asylums* (1975), which was
    manually typed. The typing of the original retains the trace of the machine, along
    with the unevenness of the indentation of each typewriter stroke. In addition,
    Bernstein disregarded the margins of the page in the original publication, begin-
    ning lines quite close to the edge of the page, or concluding them near the edge.
    For facsimile images of the original publication, see the "Eclipse" archive of the
    text at http://english.utah.edu/eclipse/projects/ASYLUMS/asylums.html.

46 "Interview with Charles Bernstein (Part I)."

ambiguity of "plants"—industrial plants or plants of the organic variety?), we are immediately confronted with the institution's interest in "Their encompassing or total character" and thereby the institution's totalizing drive.

The degree of distress increases (again, at least for me), as "failures / of assimilation" implies assimilation as an active goal of the institution rather than some effort at acclimating mental patients and the "other inmates" of Goffman's title to their environment. (Neither possibility is particularly uplifting.) However, luckily—gladly?—there is "victory" for the institution "if the inmates stay," for "They create and sustain / a particular tension."

Already with the opening movements of the poem the accidental and essential come together. Years ago, a teaching assistant I had for Psych 101 once declared that reading a psychology textbook is always accompanied by stages of self-realization: first, you think that everything the book is describing applies to you and that you are the one who is 'sick.' Then you realize that it's not you who has all the disorders the book describes—it's everyone else. In the case of "Asylum," it seems more like the experience of reading the DSM IV, except one never gets past the first stage and the realization that the language the poem is describing is the language we all—*all*—live and breathe, the language of the everyday. The asylum the poem is describing is not only a closed physical space, and not only the closed space of institutional language, which are both material, but also language as such (including the poem, "Asylum," itself), language as a kind of asylum, the asylum of the everyday. It now seems like we know who the "other inmates" are to which Goffman's book refers.

A particularly striking passage appears about a third of the way into the poem:

cycle, the time

advancement, in

"civil death"

world. The process

well. We

life history, photographing, weighing, fingerprinting, assigning numbers, searching, listing, personal possessions for storage, undressing, bathing, disinfecting, haircutting[47]

Had we not known that the list linking together archival/surveillance activities with hygiene practices was taken from Goffman's analysis, we would most likely have assumed it was from Foucault's *Discipline and Punish* (1975). Neither Goffman nor Foucault frame the list with the disturbing clause, "the time / advancement, in / 'civil death.'" What does the poem restore to this list with that phrase? What does the institution understand about "'civil death,'" which it places in scare quotes as if to convey it were not real, as if it were the hallucination of one of the mental patients or "other inmates"? Or is "civil death" a category among other categories that the institution tracks and measures? There is a "time advancement in 'civil death,'" an increase in its occurrence. In that case, the institution's measurement and tracking of "civil death's" frequency implies the institution exists in some way in order to measure and track it and therefore *requires* "civil death" to take place to rationalize the institution's existence. Still the worst possibility? That "civil death" is what the institution seeks to advance. Again, the poem's language articulates a knowledge that I believe a great many have always felt.

"Civil death." The quotation marks indicate that someone is speaking. Is it the language of the institution? Is this what institutional language cannot *not* say, even as it submits the concept of "civil death" to questioning and interrogation? Though "Asylum" is very much a deconstructive reading because it is not 'original' but reorganizes the constitutive language of the institution and thereby exposes the construction of the institution to itself, my aim is not to say simply that Bernstein is a "deconstructionist" (again, whatever that is). By providing a space for the language of the institution to say what it cannot *not* say — "civil death" — Bernstein touches on, and helps us recognize, stakes shared by the reflections on language following Heidegger. At stake in poetry for Heidegger was always the

---

47 *All the Whiskey in Heaven*, 8.

possibility of having an experience of everyday existence that did not let us take our existence for granted. Once we allow ourselves to take existence for granted, we also allow for its everyday administration by the technocratic logic of the institution and its languages. Bernstein, I would argue, helps point the way to understanding a set of textual practices reflecting on language following Heidegger as asking about—and drawing out a sensibility to—how "we" move (so easily) from a collective, social experience of finitude to a collective, social, "civil" death.

6

MADELINE GINS

Voluming Dimensionalizing Gazoop What Gazoop Gazoop In A Restless World Like This Gazoop

in 2012 for Charles Bernstein who holds to the fire the feet
of the restless WORLD like this is

The voluming dimensionalizing of PERSON and WORLD gazoop
quite a feat.
And it does not end there.
Voluming Dimensionalizing gazoop (the) considering that
fills the air as atmospheric initiative.
And you cannot do what you cannot do, except
when you go against the grain severally,
for which you p-p-poet remarkably have the knowhow.
And any tightening up on voluming dimensionalizing
gazoop treacherous, in that it impedes too harshly and cuttingly
(the) considering that fills the air as atmospheric initiative.

Architectural embodying gets lost dissipated
when there gazoop no prompts in place for
honing perspicaciousness.

Mitosis and its faint, soft cleaving analogues
beg for and demand to be taken into consideration
when voluming dimensionalzing
gazoop gazooping considered initiatively.

We gazoop considering along out into the architectural surround.

Or I could imitate that person
by tensing voluming▨dimensionalizing.
Or I could imitate one of my jagged selves, irritation in tow,
by tensing, some say armoring, voluming▨dimensionalizing.
Or I could imitate imitating, duh.

Give the voluming▨dimensionalizing a chance,
the whole of its chance in many parts.
If the voluming▨dimensionalzing gazoop not there,
initiative goes limp—not much traction.
O organicness. O dear puzzle friend.
Voluming▨Dimensionalizing save us from
knotted dissipation—all un-initiative.
Voluming▨Dimensionalizing gazoop what gazoop gazoop.

▨ ≈ gazoop

[In 2011, when working on the Reversible Destiny Foundation's
website (reversibledestiny.org), S. Cesarini saw the need for a new
symbol for connecting items within a terminolgical junction,
a group of synonymous, nearly synonymous and closely related
terms, convinced M. Gins of the pressing need for such a symbol,
and, within a matter of months, together they had convened on the
ASCII symbol▨which stands for and encompasses not only the
copula but conjunction and disjunction alike.]

7

KIMBERLY LAMM

Girly Men Ballads: (Il)legible Identities in Charles Bernstein and Gertrude Stein

I.

This essay traces Charles Bernstein's engagement with the work Gertrude Stein in order to bring his take on identity in contemporary American poetry into sharper relief. Increasingly, cultural and literary critics from across the political spectrum stress that identity is an obsolete critical category.[1] Many contend that since becoming unhinged from the social movements of the 1960s and 1970s, identity politics have been appropriated by dominant culture as a tool of assimilation rather than the assertion of difference. Bernstein has contributed to conversations that put pressure on the reification of identity in the study and practice of contemporary poetics, and analyses of and allusions to Stein's literary innovations in language often help him underscore the inadequacies of identity as a category for interpreting and registering literature's unique contributions and potential. For Bernstein, Stein's work is an important counterpoint to the appearance of identity in what Bernstein describes as "offi-

---

1 For an overview of the ways in which "identity" and "identity politics" have transformed over the last two decades, particularly in literary and cultural studies, see the essays collected in "Is There Life After Identity Politics?" *New Literary History* 31.4 (Autumn 2000). The ideas about identity I put forward in this essay have been influenced by James Clifford's "Taking Identity Politics Seriously: 'The Contradictory, Stony Ground . . .'" in *Without Guarantees: In Honour of Stuart Hall*, eds. Paul Gilroy, Lawrence Grossberg, and Angela McRobbie (London: Verso, 2000), 94–112.

cial verse culture," in which "figures of difference are often selected because they narrate in a way that can be readily assimilated . . . into the conventional forms of the dominant culture."[2] In "Stein's Identity" (1999), for example, Bernstein establishes Stein as an anti-identitarian writer, more interested in literature as a theatrical arena for productively playing with, reflecting upon, and enacting the relationship between language and mind than she is interested in establishing the ready-made appearances of identity: "Stein questions identity constructions, she does not affirm identity. Her syntactic and grammatic investigations show how language forms consciousness, how our words make as well as reflect experience."[3]

Borrowing from Bernstein's recent poem "The Ballad of the Girly Man" (2006), the first part of my title is meant to highlight the fact that Stein's work is also one of Bernstein's crucial models for rendering the imbrications among identity, gender, and literary genres. This rendering, in turn, contributes to his productive destabilization of dominant masculinity. For Bernstein, Stein's work shows how gender, as a set of recognizable forms for identifying, categorizing, and containing sexual difference, and genealogy, as a discernible line of both familial and literary inheritance, inform the connection between identity and literary genre: "In literature, genre, with its etymological roots suggesting both genealogy and gender, is a fundamental site of identity politics. Throughout her career, Stein plays with, in the sense of reforming and reformatting, genre, genealogies, and genders."[4] Of course "reforming and reformatting" identities and literary genres is quite different than wholly rejecting them, and Bernstein's alliterative phrase points to a more complicated and diffuse argument moving through his work: namely, that dismantling or escaping legible generic and gender identities cannot simply come about through stubborn will or good intentions, nor is it as politically desirable as one might readily assume. Stein is also a model for this aspect of Bernstein's argument, for he claims that her work "is not an escape from determinants of self nor the self-consciousness of personality. The play is dialectical."[5]

2 Charles Bernstein, "State of the Art," *A Poetics* (Cambridge: Harvard UP, 1992) 6.

3 Charles Bernstein, "Stein's Identity," *My Way: Speeches and Poems* (Chicago: U Chicago Press, 1999) 141.

4 Ibid.

5 Ibid., 143. To my knowledge, Bernstein does not explain his definition of the term "dialectical," but I think he uses it to account for the ways in which Stein's representation of identity highlights its contradictory dimensions. I employ the term

Bernstein describes his own work as "dialectical play," and taking this phrase as a point of departure, I want to follow the dialectical movement between legible and illegible gender identities in the writing of both Stein and Bernstein. For Bernstein, the dialectical play between legibility and illegibility makes itself present in Bernstein's undermining and scrambling of masculinity, which announces itself unequivocally in many of his essays and in poems such as "The Ballad of the Girly Man." In "The State of the Art" (1992), Bernstein makes a strong plea for men to renounce the masculinized voice as a tool of power and authority:

> I sometimes even wonder whether men can understand the voice of the women we live next to and from whose bodies we have come, since I hear every day the male version of the universal voice of rationality trying to control, as if by ventriloquism, female bodies. Though as men we have to make it clear that these men do not speak for us, do not represent us, but mock what men could be but too rarely are.[6]

The feminist imperative to renounce the power and domination necessary for upholding masculinity is unequivocally articulated here, but this line of thinking in Bernstein's poetry has yet to be fully discussed. Therefore, while tracing Bernstein's engagement with Stein and analyzing the dialectical play with identity in both bodies of work, this essay also devotes itself to revealing the critique of masculinity in Bernstein's poetry, which he extends to the patterns of patriarchal literary inheritance through which normative masculinity becomes established as a habit, both within institutions and language itself.

Bernstein's critique does not indulge in the fantasy of completely undoing gender identity or difference. An important aspect of Bernstein's work suggests that making gender identities and genres legible is not necessarily a capitulation to conservative essentialisms, but highlights instead the collective dimensions of language and the political and psychological necessities of recognition. Bernstein's work engages with what Judith Butler, following Gayatri Spivak,

---

dialectic and its association with two contradictory ideas held together in tension to show that the impulse to dissolve identity and make it illegible relies upon and even requires identity's legibility.

6 Charles Bernstein, "State of the Art," 5.

names as "the necessary error of identity," a formulation that attests to the strategic importance of laying claim to identity categories so as to refute their narrow and punitive deployments in political and daily life.[7] Throughout his work, Bernstein subtly argues for the strategic necessity of legible gender identities and literary genres, particularly in moments of political crises. Revealing the impact of Stein's work on Bernstein's play with the dialectics of legibility and illegibility in identity not only requires charting Bernstein's lifelong engagement with Stein but also tracing the multifaceted representation of recognition in Stein's autobiographical writing.

II. Patriarchal Poetry: Bernstein's Stein

Stein had a generative impact on Bernstein's work from the beginning. He was first introduced to Stein by Susan Bee, who was enrolled in one of Catharine Stimpson's Women's Studies courses at Barnard College. Discussing his introduction to Stein and the effect it had upon him, Bernstein exclaims: "I was completely knocked out: this is what I had been looking for, what I knew must exist, and I was giddy with excitement."[8] At Harvard, Bernstein wrote his undergraduate thesis on Stein and Ludwig Wittgenstein. Commenting upon the fortuitous connection he happened to make bringing these two linguistic innovators together, Bernstein states, "I can't explain how when I was 21 I fell upon a matrix of thinking and writing that would continue to occupy me until this day. For the writing and thinking I was starting to do then is very much of a piece with my work now. Let's say it was intuition that bore out."[9] The relationship Bernstein establishes between Stein and Wittgenstein in his early thinking not only appears in his poetry, but bears interestingly on his denaturalizing of normative masculinity.

One can get a sense of the argument Bernstein makes in his undergraduate thesis in an essay titled "Inventing Wordness: Gertrude Stein's Philosophical Investigations," an excerpt that was published in a collection of critical essays on Gertrude Stein entitled *Gertrude*

---

7 Judith Butler, *Bodies That Matter: On the Discursive Limits of 'Sex'* (New York: Routledge, 1993) 229. For an extended discussion of the arguments informing "the necessary error of identity," see Gayatri Chakravorty Spivak, "In a Word. Interview," *Outside in the Teaching Machine* (New York: Routledge, 1993), 1-24.

8 Bernstein, "An Autobiographical Interview," *My Way*, 243.

9 Ibid., 242.

Stein Advanced (1990). This essay is focused primarily on *The Making Of Americans: Being A History Of A Family's Progress* (1903–1911), Stein's modernist version of the immigrant story that centers upon a German-Jewish family and their increasingly Americanized descendants. "Inventing Wordness" shows that Bernstein was interested in the transition *The Making Of Americans* enacts between the nineteenth and twentieth centuries, and the distinct genres, characters, discourses, and perceptions associated with them. Bernstein begins by discussing *The Making Of Americans'* relationship to the nineteenth-century novel, which was intensely preoccupied with "the struggle between the public and the private," the family as the microcosm of the church and the state, and the anomalous central protagonist who rebelled against the family and the multiple forms of authority the family coalesces.[10] Together these preoccupations culminated in what Bernstein describes as the nineteenth-century novel's "dialectic struggle between our inner lives and the external world."[11]

According to Bernstein, *The Making Of Americans* fits well into this nineteenth-century picture of the world because rather than despite the fact that Stein struggles against it: "And so Stein moved into the twentieth century grounded in the nineteenth. The recurring motif of that century had been to represent (even allegorize) the family as setting limits that were acknowledged or transgressed."[12] Stein had a name for the anomalous protagonist who rebels against the family and the society it allegorizes — the "singular individual" — and David Hersland is the character in *The Making Of Americans* who represents this rebellious singularity. However, in her attempt to represent David Hersland's innovative rebellion, Stein came up against the limits of, as Bernstein puts it, "traditional prose and its established genres. Indeed the very publicness and intelligibility of the established forms seemed to deny [David Hersland's] privacy and distance from others."[13] Against the recognizability of established genres, Stein develops what Bernstein calls "wordness," which is an attention to language "so dense that meaning is no longer to be found in what

---

10 Charles Bernstein, "Inventing Wordness: Gertrude Stein's Philosophical Investigations" in *Gertrude Stein Advanced: An Anthology of Criticism,* ed. Richard Kostelanetz (Jefferson, N.C.: McFarland, 1990), 58.

11 Ibid., 58.

12 Ibid.

13 Ibid.

the words represent, or stand for, but in their texture: the repetition, juxtaposition and structure of phrases, sentences, and paragraphs."[14]

Bernstein turns to Wittgenstein's *Philosophical Investigations* (1951) to show how the density Stein achieves in *The Making Of Americans* represents more than a struggle against literary genres but a struggle within and against language itself. Before citing Wittgenstein's famous statement "*[t]he limits of my language* mean the limits of my world," Bernstein writes, "We are limited to language: for language provides the bounds of our intelligibility—of what can be meant. We see everything *through* our language."[15] In Bernstein's last sentence, language has its own internal lenses and becomes a "frame" through which one sees. Recall that in *Philosophical Investigations* (1951), Wittgenstein draws attention to the set of visual perceptions embedded within language: "A *picture* held us captive. And we could not get outside it, for it lay in our language and language seemed to repeat it to us inexorably."[16] Wittgenstein helps Bernstein claim that the dialectic of public and private characteristic of nineteenth-century novels becomes internal to the language itself: the language "function[s] as family (and society) had in the nineteenth-century dramatization."[17] Language itself becomes the limit and is therefore the site of struggle.

In *The Making Of Americans,* we see Stein seizing the perceptions inexorably repeated in language through her own obsessive linguistic repetitions. The opening lines of the David Hersland chapter offer a sense of the poetic density Stein achieved when she stopped writing in the transparent language of the nineteenth-century novel and started working within the limits of language. These opening lines also provide a glimpse into Stein's thematic interest in unhinging the self from familial confines. Her character David Hersland expresses anxiety about asking people what their reaction might be if they were to realize that they do not biologically belong to their families: "I do ask some, I would ask every one, I do not ask some because I am quite certain that they would not like me to ask it, I do ask some if they would mind it if they found out that they did have the name they had then and had been having been born not in the family living

---

14 Ibid.

15 Ibid.,58-59, original emphasis.

16 Ludwig Wittgenstein, *Philosophical Investigations* (1951. New York: Macmillan, 1968), 48.

17 Bernstein, "Inventing Wordness," 59.

they are then living in, if they had been born illegitimate"[18] This dense, almost elliptical depiction of David Hersland's preoccupations and queries may suggest privacy and opacity, but with Wittgenstein's concepts of language not far in the background, Bernstein argues that it is more accurate to characterize Stein's prose as public language turned inside out: "There is no escape into a prior and hence private language, a world *outside* language. Everything we know we know *through* our shared language, our way of life is formed by it: but we must learn it and speak it for ourselves."[19] Bernstein's early poetry, to which I now turn, shows that confronting the patriarchal inheritance within language is crucial for learning the collective dimension of language and opening the possibility of "speak[ing] it for ourselves."

III. Parsing Sentences

"Inventing Wordness" shows that Stein was clearly a model for many of Bernstein's early literary interests and inclinations: the materiality of language and its unavoidably public life; the relationships among language, power, and the family; language as site of authority against which one struggles. In Bernstein's work from the 1970s, the poem became a supple place to render the irrevocability of language and family while also rebelling against them and their mutual imbrications.

Two early Bernstein poems from the 1976 collection *Parsing*, "Sentences" and "Parsing," demonstrate the impact both Stein and Wittgenstein had on Bernstein's thinking about the relationships among family, language, and power. Both poems work in a Wittgensteinian vein to simultaneously highlight and undo the pictures of reality held within language. "Sentences" is devoted to defamiliarizing sentences as habitual conveyors of meaning and is, not surprisingly, composed of sentences as well. At the beginning of the poem, each sentence begins with "It." Here is the poem's first stanza: "It's an automatic thing. It doesn't require any thought. It's a parade in and out."[20] The subject of both the poem and the sentences that compose it is unclear, and therefore actively provokes readers'

---

18 Gertrude Stein, *The Making Of Americans: Being A History Of A Family's Progress* (1925. Normal, Illinois: Dalkey Archive Press, 1995), 723.

19 Bernstein, "Inventing Wordness," 60.

20 Charles Bernstein, "Sentences," *Republics of Reality, 1975-1995* (1976. Los Angeles: Sun & Moon Press, 2000), 13.

impulse to make the "It" refer to something outside the poem. But similar to the way in which Stein turns to "wordness" in the David Hersland chapter in *The Making Of Americans,* "Sentences" seems to be a reflection on language itself. The first stanza mimes assumptions about language and its transparency. Subsequent stanzas illustrate how language functions as an unremarked upon given, naturally present to oneself, like hands or skin: "It sort of comes to you. I never look at it. The touch. My hands fit. It's the feel. I just look at them."[21] As this stanza makes clear, all the lines in "Sentences" do not begin with "It," but the ambiguity Bernstein sets up at the beginning of the poem increases rather than disappears. In fact, when Bernstein begins to use the pronoun "I," it takes on the strange and anonymous ambiguity of "It." Even the sentences that attempt to express emotion evoke anonymity and automated habits rather than heartfelt expression:

> I become very upset.
> I enjoy one thing more than another.
> I think I'm much happier.
> I have dinner.[22]

Despite or because of the poem's rote qualities, loss weaves its way into "Sentences," and this loss can be read as a response to the impediments to full understanding language places between people: "I want by now to get some clear idea of where we are in respect to each other."[23]

In the midst of this poetic meditation on language as a structure of habit, Bernstein composes a small drama in which the speaker—and perhaps the writer—of the poem appears as "Charley." However, this appearance is constructed to highlight authenticity as a guise and a particular representational mode that does not call attention to itself as such. In "Comedy and the Poetics of Political Form" (1992), Bernstein names this guise "the artifice of my authenticity."[24] We see Bernstein highlighting the artifice of authenticity in "Sentences" when he deploys a deliberately folksy, grammatically "incorrect" language: "I came up the hard way. We was treated pretty rough.

21 Ibid., 13.
22 Ibid., 16.
23 Ibid., 17.
24 Charles Bernstein, "Comedy and the Politics of Poetic Form," in *A Poetics* (Cambridge: Harvard UP, 1992), 223.

We come up at the hind and get what we can to live on. We was just children."[25] The broken texture of this passage rubs awkwardly against the previous rows of clear, clean, syntactically ordered sentences and leads into almost primal and ritualistic scene in which the poet is named and anointed "Charley" by a dying patriarch:

> He named me Charley.
>
> . . .
>
> He was dying and he called for me. He said, 'Bring me the holy bible with all y'alls names in it.' And he was dying and he said to me, 'Don't break your oath: don't   change your name don't change your name.' And I stooped over him and put his arm around my neck. And when he quit saying that he was dead. And I shook him.[26]

Enacting the ruthless interpellation of patriarchy, this passage demonstrates the power of naming: the name is an "oath" that cannot be broken and therefore weds the self to a particular place in language. The death of this father figure underscores the fact that the imperative to keep the name bestowed upon you, and all the power that naming signals, becomes internalized. Though on the next page of the poem the speaker announces his detachment from the death scene — "I'm separated./ I would put myself in suspended animation./ I was never home" — many of the lines that follow display a manic anxiety about an imperative so deeply imposed it cannot be seen: "you say to yourself let it go but you can't figure out what to/ let go."[27] Many of the issues Bernstein grapples with in "Sentences" — naming as fixity, the punitive commandments of masculinity, and the difficulty undoing them — foreshadow the following comments from "Comedy and the Poetics of Political Form." Bernstein writes that he

> felt [his] initiation into . . . a 'public voice' was the product of a profound humiliation and degradation that I had to undergo: a private-school hazing into Grammar, that once mastered I cannot unlearn, but which, like many men, I am perennially suspicious of even as it continues

---

25 Charles Bernstein, "Sentences," 21.

26 Ibid., 22.

27 Ibid., 23–24.

to inform the expression of my (most well-founded) beliefs
and convictions: the artifice of my authenticity.[28]

This reflection aligns with—and perhaps glosses—Bernstein's
"Sentences" and its depiction of patriarchal interpellation and the
difficulty of undoing the masculine self in language. In other words,
"Sentences" highlights the artifice of masculine subjectivities and
personas.

"Parsing," the second poem in the book of the same name continues the themes of patriarchal inheritance, obedience, and the internalization of authority Bernstein sets out in "Sentences." However,
the interrelation of language and patriarchy is taken up in a slightly
different form. If "Sentences" is about examining the installation of
the patriarchal order through the structure of the sentence, "Parsing"
is about the chaotic undoing of that order. The poem begins with a
compact pile of words, unhinged from the structure of the sentence:
"the reach, the middle, endless, drift, sway, hold, belie/ unfold and
furl, it makes, smack, abated."[29] The rumination on language through
the pronoun "It" continues, but in a far more rushed way:

> so its I don't want to work there you plunge in you do
> anything you can to keep from going nuts you write it
> down you go to the store with it it persists as thickness as
> shape as figments and fragments of refusal you stare at it &
> by the time you notice you have lost your comprehension
> wanting to see event k but despairing of its possibilities[30]

This manic stanza seems to address the difficulty of resisting the
ideological structure you find oneself within—even though you can
recognize the presence of its limitations. It also renders the frustration that arrives when one realizes that ideology determines the
forms of resistance: "it persists as thickness as/ shape as figments and
fragments of refusal."[31] The inadequacy of refusal emerges again as
the poem shifts from a paragraph form to these heavily enjambed
lines:

---

28 Charles Bernstein, "Comedy and the Politics of Poetic Form," 223.
29 Charles Bernstein, "Parsing," *Republics of Reality, 1975-1995* (1976. Los Angeles: Sun
    & Moon Press, 2000), 33.
30 Ibid., 34.
31 Ibid.

> it doesn't work
> too many refusals,
>   poetic
> & flat surfaceless ridgeless
>   degree zero is marked
>   ashen
>   is so many times reaching, pouring
>   in tuppats[32]

The poem then turns to a different vocabulary and world of capitalism, patriarchal lineage, and financial obligation: "a man, son, millionai:e/ 'a capital assets tax.'"[33] The fact that the line "a capital assets tax" is in quotations without attribution suggests that the language of economics "speaks" without a speaker. Following these lines, Bernstein writes: "& i sat & i listened & i behaved myself/ being in the presence of/ telling me how to live to go on."[34] Notice that Bernstein does not place anything after "of" so that an absence tells the speaker "how to live and go on." What is it that tells the speaker how to live and go on? How might the scene of patriarchal interpellation in "Sentences" help us understand this absent instructor? Does the absent presence in the lines above represent the internalization of patriarchal authority?

"Parsing" continues the theme of the thorough internalization by citing a key line from *The Making Of Americans*: "'i did not drag my father beyond this tree.'"[35] This line appears at the very beginning of Stein's novel, where she creates a graphic picture of intergenerational anger that illustrates both the violence of genealogical ties and their internalized limits: "Once an angry man dragged his father along the ground through his own orchard. 'Stop!' cried the groaning old man at last, 'Stop!' I did not drag my father beyond this tree."[36] The tree marks an inherited and conventionalized border that limits

---

32 Ibid., 39.

33 Ibid.

34 Ibid., 34.

35 Ibid., 45.

36 Gertrude Stein, *The Making Of Americans*, 3. For an extended reading of this line, see Priscilla Wald, "A 'Losing–Self Sense': *The Making of Americans* and the Anxiety of Identity," *Constituting Americans: Cultural Anxiety and Narrative Form* (Durham: Duke UP, 1995), 253–256.

the extent to which sons can rebel against their fathers, thereby containing violence and re-establishing patriarchal authority.

The appearance of this sentence from Stein's *The Making Of Americans* marks a shift in "Parsing." In the lines of poetry that follow from the citation, Bernstein deliberately relinquishes "I" as the subject of the sentence and the poem as a whole. Interestingly, this does not ponderously weigh down the poem, but frees it up: "was waiting/ was jumping around/ was giving it up."[37] It is as though Bernstein enacts the attempt to wholly reject the subjectivity that is shaped by the internalization of limits. This series of sentences without subjects culminates in a meditation on language and absence, speech and listening:

> only the talking no more than the waiting for speech,
> an emptiness I bring to it, or both together, in the interpreta-
> tion, always seeing as, & as absence[38]

These gorgeously abstract lines suggest that both language and human subjectivity are structured around absences; these absences become visible in the act of interpretation.

The citation from Stein's *The Making Of Americans* in "Parsing" reveals that Bernstein drew from Stein an understanding of the way in which the family, and the father in particular, maintains almost inescapable borders around forms of meaning and expression. Working against the imbrication of patriarchy and language highlights the abstraction and absence at its core. Bernstein's use of Stein underscores why there has been such a strong feminist investment in her work: she was not only able to characterize patriarchy as a force within language, but developed forms of writing that worked to demolish the perceptions held captive within it. This reminds us that Bernstein's exposure to Stein through a Women's Studies course at Barnard is coincident with the emergence of what came to be a rich vein of feminist theory and feminist literary criticism that centered upon and drew from Stein's work in multiple ways.

---

37 Charles Bernstein, "Parsing," 46.

38 Ibid., 47.

IV. Theorizing the Picture of Gender

Stein's work defamiliarizing the relationship between language and patriarchal authority became visible in U.S. academic feminism along with the growing influence of French Feminist theory and the Lacanian argument that patriarchal order is instituted in and through language. Catharine R. Stimpson's essay "Gertrude Stein and the Transposition of Gender" (1986) is representative of scholarship that highlights the proto-feminism at work in Stein's literary and linguistic subversions. Stein's writing, according to Stimpson, "foreshadow[s] the pulsating, lyrical polemic of much contemporary feminist theory."[39] Stimpson begins by arguing that Stein disrupts the constitutive role language plays classifying people and things according to gender: "Her poetry is a series of propositions about the possibility of transposing gender, about the possibilities of breaking up its orders, codes, and poses."[40] However, Stimpson is quick to point out that Stein's poetry "demonstrates the difficulties of such fundamental, capacious alterations."[41] So while Stimpson traces the ways in which Stein's research into "the elementary particles of language" undoes the binaries upon which gender hierarchies depends, she also unwittingly charts evidence that a full undoing is difficult to achieve: "to destabilize is not to eradicate; to dislodge is not to demolish. Traces of patriarchal message remain graven—too wispy to be laws, but chiseled enough to remind us of patriarchal longings."[42] Because it is unclear whether Stimpson sees the "residually patriarchal messages about gender" within Stein's writing and life are the result of patriarchy's ideological hold or Stein's conservative limitations,[43] I want to turn to an essay by the feminist theorist Linda M. G. Zerilli, "Doing Without Knowing: Feminism's Politics of the Ordinary" (1998). "Doing Without Knowing" draws heavily from Wittgenstein's *Philosophical Investigations* and helps us to see that the contradictions in Stimpson's argument reflect the fact that beliefs about gender are embedded in language and are therefore more difficult to "demolish" than we might want to believe. Zerilli's stress on

---

39 Catharine R. Stimpson, "Gertrude Stein and the Transposition of Gender," in *The Poetics of Gender,* ed. Nancy K. Miller (New York: Columbia UP, 1986), 10.

40 Ibid., 2.

41 Ibid.

42 Ibid., 11.

43 Ibid., 10.

this embeddedness furthers our understanding of the dialectical play
of legibility and illegibility in both Bernstein's and Stein's representations of gender identities and literary genres.

The epigraph for "Doing without Knowing" is taken from
Wittgenstein's *Philosophical Investigations*: "A *picture* held us captive.
And we could not get outside of it, for it in lay in our language and
language seemed to repeat it to us inexorably."[44] This formulation,
which vividly argues that language shapes our perception and experience of the world, serves as the premise for Zerilli's argument: claims
and counterclaims about gender draw from a set of assumptions
that we do not see but nevertheless inform our thinking. Grammar
is Wittgenstein's term for this ground of intelligibility, the forms
through which things appear as sense. Zerilli explains, "What is at
issue in grammar is not a metaphysical given but our form of representation that sets limits to what it makes sense to say and that is
held in place—I do not say justified—not through grand theories
but small acts: daily, habitual practices of speaking, acting, and
judging."[45] Zerilli wants us to see that gender is embedded in grammar and therefore more difficult to undo than we might hope or
imagine.

"Doing without Knowing" is not an essentialist argument claiming that biological difference determines gender. Rather, Zerelli
examines why arguments in feminist science studies (that the two
sexes are a myth) and feminist theory (that the category of woman
is exclusionary) seems to have forestalled rather than contributed to
feminism's political presence and vitality. In response to work such
as Anne Fausto-Sterling's, which scientifically demonstrates that the
social norms about the two sexes are repressive myths of nature,
Zerilli stresses the fact that "the powerful hold that 'the straight
mind' (Monique Wittig) has on our subjectivity and our practices
. . . is not finally dependent on a network of knowledge claims."[46]
Rather, following Wittgenstein, "the straight mind" is built through
propositions that cannot be refuted or justified. In other words, one's
gender identity is a matter of "subjective certainty" or belief, which

---

44 Ludwig Wittgenstein, *Philosophical Investigations*, 48.

45 Linda M.G. Zerelli, "Doing without Knowing: Feminism's Politics of the Ordinary,"
   Political Theory. Vol. 26 No. 4 (Aug. 1998): 442. Thanks to Robyn Wiegman for recom-
   mending this essay to me.

46 Ibid., 436.

ultimately cannot be verified through knowledge.[47] Circling back to Wittgenstein's proposition in the epigraph, Zerilli writes, "I realize that my belief (in two sexes) is groundless, but I am still captivated by a 'picture' in which the existence of two sexes constitute my world view, the frame of reference within which I act."[48] This frame of reference cannot be "unlearned." Echoing Bernstein's own description of the "private school hazing into grammar" and its connection to unrelinquished forms of masculinity, Zerilli states: "I cannot unlearn a proposition . . . 'There are men and there are women' if I never learned it as a proposition — that is, if I learned it, not in the form of hypothesis that could be proved or disproved, but as part of a world-picture that I inherited and on the basis of which I judge, that is, act."[49] In the sections that follow, I analyze how a significant strain of Bernstein's writing, shaped by his engagement with Stein, seeks to reveal and adjust the "world-picture" of gender within language while also showing that change emerges from and is connected to legible gender identities. Zerelli argues that "something must stand fast if something else is to be questioned," and Bernstein's work shows that some idea of gender must stand fast if normative masculinity is going be stripped of its punitive powers.[50]

V. "Stein's Identity" and the Dialectics of Autobiography

In the essay "Stein's Identity," published in *My Way: Speeches and Poems* (1999), Bernstein makes some of his clearest statements about why and how Stein's work informs his own. Falling somewhere between a poem and an essay, "Stein's Identity" creates its argument through associative connections. It is composed of single sentences — often quotations from Stein's "Identity A Poem" (1935) — and longer expository paragraphs. "Stein's Identity" does not, as is habit with so many analyses of Stein's work, begin with biographical statements about the modernist innovator. Instead, Bernstein poses a question that attests to how much pressure Stein's work puts on ready-made literary categories: "What is identity and why is there so much of it?"[51] This question floats above the piece without really being answered,

---

47 Ibid., 445.

48 Ibid., 449.

49 Ibid., 452.

50 Ibid., 440.

51 Charles Bernstein, "Stein's Identity," *My Way*, 141.

indirectly underscoring that Stein's work does not conform to contemporary understandings of identity. For Bernstein's next paragraph articulates the standard way that identity functions in literary studies: "Any cultural production can be viewed through the lens of its sociohistorical circumstance."[52] Bernstein does not set his argument wholly against this approach, but seeks to undo its cemented role as the primary way of reading. For in the next sentence Bernstein writes, "To ignore such contexts is to deny the social truths of the work. Yet such contexts are inadequate to establish a work's identity."[53] Bernstein wants to show how Stein's writing expands our understanding of a literary text's identity beyond positivistic reflections of socio historical circumstances.

Bernstein draws upon Stein's play "Identity A Poem" to reveal how she productively reconfigures identity. Since "Identity A Poem" is a play, but names the genre of poetry in the title, it is clear from the beginning that this text plays against the fixities of literary genres and reveals how productively and playfully they can interweave. As Bernstein explains, "'Identity A Poem' is an essay, a play, a poem; it mixes verse and prose lines."[54] This destabilization of genre manifests the play's anti-essentialist argument about identity. According to Bernstein, "Identity: A Poem," "shows identity as an acting out rather than as an inner state; externally animated, not innately fixed."[55] This expansive formulation of identity, in which the experience of self is performed in the flexible space that renders interior experiences and exterior states indistinguishable, does not easily align with identity's contemporary manifestations as a legible inscription of a historical context and a clear possession to be presented and recognized. Reiterating the relationship between identity and literary genre, Bernstein explains,

> Stein did not narrativize her otherness any more than she naturalized it and that makes her a suitably uncomfortable subject for those who would read her in terms of group-identity poetics . . . Stein's triple distance from the ascendant culture (gender, sexual orientation, ethnicity) is

---

52 Ibid.
53 Ibid.
54 Ibid.
55 Ibid.

related to her radical breaks from traditional notions of meaning, literary tradition, explanation, and linearity.[56]

Highlighting how Stein's avant-garde literary practices aligned with her anti-essentialism, Bernstein stresses the fact that her work does not consolidate identity in response to the exclusions she experienced as a Jewish lesbian in Europe. But the fact that Stein's work can be understood in anti-essentialist terms does not mean that Stein relinquished legibility, recognition, or the senses of place and cohesion one can feel in response to the listening and perceiving presence of one person—Alice B. Toklas—or a reading audience.

Stein created "Identity A Poem" for a puppet show, which attests to her interest in making her work have a broad appeal.[57] It culls lines, images, and ideas from *The Geographical History Of America Or The Relation of Human Nature To The Human Mind* (1935–36), the text in which Stein formulated her ideas about the distinction between human nature and the human mind. According to the leading Stein scholar Ulla E. Dydo, *The Geographical History Of America* and the definitions of "human mind" and "human nature" appeared after a long writing block and reflects Stein's struggle with the fame, recognition, and financial success she finally achieved with *The Autobiography of Alice B. Toklas* (1933). According to Dydo, "her distinction . . . between the human mind, which is the source of creation, and human nature, which is merely the source of personality, is one result of the preoccupation with fame . . . .What Stein calls human nature is always self-conscious. The human mind, however, is free of time, memory, identity, and free of the need for applause."[58] Reading *The Geographical History Of America,* one can begin to see the difference between the human mind and human nature when Stein defines an audience and its effects: "When a great many hear you that is an audience and if

---

56 Ibid.

57 In the introduction to "Identity A Poem," Dydo writes: "The puppeteer Donald Vestal had not heard Stein lecture when on 30 November 1934 he met her on the street in Chicago and they had a short exchange about puppets. In the summer of 1935 he wrote to ask her for a play for the marionettes he manipulated. As a result, as Stein wrote Carl Van Vechten, she 'put together the plays in [*The Geographical History of America*] for Vestal . . . .On 9 July 1936 Vestal produced 'Identity' at the National Puppetry Conference in Detroit." Ulla E. Dydo, ed. *A Stein Reader* (Evanston, Illinois: Northwestern UP, 1993), 588.

58 Ibid.

a great many hear you what difference does it make."⁵⁹ The hearing particular to an audience, Stein writes, "has nothing to do with the human mind."⁶⁰

Dydo's translation of the distinction between human mind and human nature stems from her argument about the differences between one of Stein's most difficult and illegible texts, "Stanzas in Meditation" (1933), in relation to one of her most legible, accessible, and famous books, *The Autobiography of Alice B. Toklas*. It is worth rehearsing Dydo's argument here because it helps to highlight the particularities of Bernstein's engagement with Stein. Composed during the same period (1932–34) *The Autobiography of Alice B. Toklas* and "Stanzas in Meditation" bring Stein's dialectical play with the legibility and illegibility of both identity and literary genre into high relief. *The Autobiography of Alice B. Toklas* relies on relatively stable categories of identity and genre and allows them to mirror each other. In turn, "Stanzas in Meditation" uses poetic language to radically unloosen both. But for Dydo, *Autobiography* is without question the lesser of the two: one is true and truly creative; the other: superficial, a capitulation to the market and the need for money and fame. At the opening of her magisterial study *Gertrude Stein: The Language that Rises 1923–1934* (2003), Dydo describes "Stanzas in Meditation" as the "peak of Stein's work and her last great accomplishment before she succumbed to writing to please readers, for fame and success."⁶¹ In contrast, "*The Autobiography*, written in a voice entirely different from her own, was her first book of what she came to call audience writing, created to please readers, for success, rather than writing for its own sake."⁶²

Written by Stein in the voice of Alice B. Toklas, *The Autobiography* tells a clear story of Stein's and Toklas' life together, the development of Stein's writing in Paris during the first decade of the twentieth century, and her importance in Toklas' eyes. *The Autobiography* is nothing if not charming: as Toklas tells the story of her life and testifies to Stein's genius, the prose delightfully combines the formal and familiar. Describing her first encounter with Stein, Toklas writes, "I was impressed by the coral brooch she wore and by her voice. I may

---

59 Gertrude Stein, "The Geographical History of America," in *Gertrude Stein: Writings 1932–1946* (New York: Library of America, 1998), 384.

60 Ibid.

61 Ulla E. Dydo, *The Language That Rises 1923–1934* (Evanston, Illinois: Northwestern UP, 2003), 3.

62 Ibid., 5.

say that only three times in my life have I met a genius and each time a bell within me rang and I was not mistaken, and I may say in each case it was before there was any general recognition of the quality of genius in them."[63] Passages like these, which seamlessly align voice, narrator, and story, satisfy the most basic expectations of autobiographies, and allow the reader to forget it is not Toklas but Stein who "speaks" through the writing.

In contrast, "Stanzas in Meditation" is a puzzle of words, phrases, and sentences that do not cohere into stable meaning. The reading mind gropes to make these parts of language refer to the contours of the recognizable world, but the poem creates its own linguistic universe, and language is disembodied almost to the point of abstraction. Unlike *The Autobiography*, there does not seem to be a coherent self, personality, or identity "behind" or "speaking through" the text. In "Stanzas in Meditation," everything is in question: language, reading, the selves who write and read, and, of course, the generic forms through which literature appears. The title points toward the basic organizing structure of poems—stanzas—but it is difficult to say that "Stanzas in Meditation" qualifies as poetry in any standard or expected sense. Characterizing the work as a meditation seems a far more accurate and sincere description of how the piece works and the kind of reading it requires. By meditating on the poem's form, she puts it into question, makes it stretch beyond its contained capacities. As Dydo explains, "[q]uestioning who she is and what her work is are inseparable aspects of her art in its active and reflective condition, which Stein called meditation."[64]

I take seriously Dydo's insistence that "'Stanzas' must be read as word constructions, not as concealed pieces of autobiography."[65] I do however think that "Stanzas in Meditation" can be interpreted as an exploration of what it means to think and live unhinged from the recognizable identities and literary genres *The Autobiography* represents. In other words, "Stanzas in Meditation" and *The Autobiography of Alice B. Toklas* can be seen in dialectical relation to each other: together they represent and enact the desire to make oneself illegible, which is premised upon the stability of one's legibility. Notice how this passage from "Stanzas" weaves in ideas and images from the open-

---

63 Gertrude Stein, *The Autobiography of Alice B. Toklas* (1933. New York: The Modern Library, 1980), 5.

64 Ulla E. Dydo, *Gertrude Stein: The Language that Rises*, 7.

65 Ulla E. Dydo, *A Stein Reader*, 569.

ing pages of *The Autobiography* that I cited above, Toklas' unmistaken assurance of Stein's genius in particular, while also undoing the legibility of that other narration:

> When she came she knew it not only
> Not by name but where they came with them.
> She knew that they would be while they went.
> And let us think.
> She knew that she could know
> That a genius was a genius
> Because just so she could know
> She did know three or so
> So she says and what she says
> No one can deny or try
> What if she says.
> Many can be unkind but welcome to be kind
> Which they agree to agree to follow behind.
> Her here.
> Not clearly not as no mistake.
> Those who are not mistaken can make no mistake.
> This is her autobiography one of two[66]

Set in relation to the passage in which Toklas hears Stein's voice and recognizes her genius, this excerpt from "Stanzas in Meditation" attests to the importance of Toklas' recognition, despite, but also because of, its "illegibile" form. After a strange meditation on kindness, unkindness, and an audience's capacity to "follow behind," Stein writes, "Her here": a simple assertion of what I assume to be Toklas' consistent and reliable presence, in space and time, and in the midst of Stein's creative evocation of illegibility.

Dydo may be right that fame wreaked havoc on Stein's writing life, but it seems unfair to characterize *The Autobiography of Alice B. Toklas* as only a capitulation, for I think the book registers, in various and interwoven ways, the necessity of having a self that is legible and recognizable to others. As Bernstein puts it, "Stein writes of her genius obliterating her memory and her identity . . . [b]ut she also demands recognition from the audience."[67]

---

66 Gertrude Stein, "Stanzas in Meditation," in *Gertrude Stein: Writings 1932–1946* (1934. New York: Library of America, 1998), 72–73.

67 Charles Bernstein, "Professing Stein/Stein Professing," in *A Poetics*, 49.

The work that follows "Stanzas in Meditation" and *The Autobiography of Alice B. Toklas* is preoccupied with and struggles to understand the roles recognition plays in the constitution of the self. In her piece "Henry James" (1932–34), Stein writes: "I am not I any longer when I see. This sentence is at the bottom of all creative activity. It is just the exact opposite of I am I because my little dog knows me."[68] This is a formulation Stein returns to, reformulates, and plays with in *The Geographical History Of America* and "Identity A Poem," and Bernstein picks up and plays with in his essay "Stein's Identity." This deceptively simple passage sums up the dialectic of legibility and illegibility that runs through much of Stein's work. While Stein declares that the "I" changes—and perhaps disappears—when she sees, the statement itself and its triple incarnation of "I" undermine that declaration, as the "I" who no longer sees herself in the act of looking still writes from the first-person perspective. So it is not an actual loss of the self Stein describes, but the detachment of seeing oneself in the act of looking that is particular to creative activity. The next statement refers to the previous one, and claims art undeniably requires (or inspires) the unhinging of the self from one's perceptions. Stein goes on to claim this unhinging is "the exact opposite" of the recognition one receives from those in her possession, in this case, her "little dog." Stein does not claim that recognition works against the self's potentially liberating dissolution. Indeed, this last sentence, which appears at the bottom of this passage and might be said to ground it, seems to make the erasure of the "I" in artistic production possible.

The formulation from "Henry James" that begins with the sentence "I am not I any longer when I see," attests to the dialectic of legibility and illegibility at play in Stein's work and thereby helps to complicate Dydo's celebration of "Stanzas in Meditation" at the expense of *The Autobiography of Alice B. Toklas*. It would be unfair, however, to suggest that Dydo's argument ends with this impasse. The form that straddles the poles these two texts represents is, according to Dydo, the lecture. Dydo makes the claim that Stein's *Lectures in America* (1935)cannot be described as the shallow capitulation that "audience writing" represents.[69] Rather, the essays in *Lectures in America* "became self-portraits in a new Stein voice, and they establish a

68 Gertrude Stein, "Henry James," in *Gertrude Stein: Writings 1932-1946* (1932-34. New York: Library of America, 1998), 149.

69 Ulla E. Dydo, *Gertrude Stein: The Language that Rises 1923-1934*, 5.

new balance."[70] I would claim that the balance the essays represent emerges from the dialectics of recognition Stein worked out moving between *The Autobiography* and "Stanzas in Meditation."

It is appropriate, then, to turn back to Bernstein's essay, "Stein's Identity" and not only note the differences and similarities between his representation of Stein's work and Dydo's, but to trace how his creative engagement with the essay's malleable form allows him to play with identity and its dialectics of legibility and illegibility. In "Stein's Identity," Bernstein quotes at length from Stein's "Identity A Play" to show how thoroughly she was using her linguistic imagination to understand the role recognition plays in the composition of identity:

> I am I because my little dog knows me even if the little dog is a big one, and yet the little dog knowing me does not really make me be I no not really because after all being I I am I has really nothing to do with the little dog knowing me, he is my audience, but an audience never does prove to you that you are you . . .

> No one knowing me knows me.[71]

"No one knowing me knows me": The sentence upon which Bernstein ends his citation of Stein's "Identity A Poem" enacts and attests to the excesses of the self and the crucial differences between identity, which can be known, measured, and fortified through recognition, and ontology or being. While it is certainly true that an audience, and the forms of recognition, identity, and knowledge it provides, cannot fully account for being, Bernstein's essay functions as a form of audience recognition, the ground upon which Stein's innovative articulations about identity's limitation can become visible. Indeed, Bernstein goes on to bring a supple dialectical play to Stein's categories of "human mind" and "human nature," and then lets identity play across them, which in turn gives it both a fluidity and fixity:

> Identity of/in human mind is fluid and underdetermined; forming rather than final. The human mind at play is the site of identity's continuous becoming. Grammatically,

---

70   Ibid.

71   Charles Bernstein, "Stein's Identity," 142.

identity's play is registered by the present participle (the continuous present)—an active, verbal principle. When identity enters human nature its chimerical unfolding gets boxed up as explanation, labels, naming, nouns. Human nature, insofar as it obscures human mind, is duplicitous; but when nature and mind remain at play, duplicity melts into the multiplicitous.[72]

These formulations set the stage for Bernstein to articulate his argument about what poetic language can reveal about identity. This argument manifests itself in a passage in which Bernstein mimes Stein's statements about recognition. "My doggie knows my name, my smell, but not the thought that cleaves my nature, making me part of its world, part next. Beside myself is that being that belongs neither to my past self nor to my self. This is language's tale and identity's possibility."[73] Notice how Bernstein builds upon Stein's ideas to articulate his own, and places language in the gap between ontology and self, a space that allows for the possibility of identity's play, where aspects of the self that are unknown can be revealed.

Meditating on poetry's potential for playing with identity does not mean identity can become unhinged from the world. Bernstein reminds readers of the dangerous, punitive, and frightening uses to which identity was put in Stein's time, which leads him to underscore the importance of understanding identity in dialectical terms: "Human mind represents for Stein a freedom from history from which one well might have longed in Europe in 1935. But Stein's is not an escape from determinants of self nor the self-consciousness of personality. The play is dialectical."[74] It is compelling that Bernstein's stress on Stein's dialectical play with identity leads into critique of masculinity. First Bernstein performs what we might call a feminist undoing of T.S. Eliot's status as modern literature's canonical patriarch: "*She do the identity in voices,* to turn a phrase of T.S. Eliot's." He then cites a question Stein poses in "Identity A Play" that testifies to patriarchal masculinity's obsolescence: "'What is the use of being a little boy if you are to grow up to be a man?'"[75] This question connects most clearly to Bernstein's discussion of genre, gender, and

---

72 Ibid.

73 Ibid.

74 Ibid., 143.

75 Ibid.

genealogy. Like the question the essay opens with—"What is identity and why is there so much of it?"—this rhetorical question provocatively floats unanswered; the answer is embedded in the question; it assumes a shared criticism of manhood and masculinity. The fact that this question appears just after Bernstein has set up the links and contrasts between Stein and T.S. Eliot highlights the fact that his work does not fall into a predictable line of influence: sons with literary ambitions emulating their ensconced literary fathers.

V: "The Ballad of the Girly Man"

In previous sections, I have highlighted and analyzed an aspect Bernstein's early poetry that grapples with the imbrication of genre, gender, and genealogy. In "The Ballad of the Girly Man," the last poem in his 2006 collection *Girly Man*, Bernstein takes up the feminist dimension of this pursuit with a new level of explicitness. Written in response to Governor Arnold Schwarzenegger's description of his opponents as "girly men" at the 2004 Republican National Convention, Bernstein uses a highly recognizable form—the ballad—to level a critique of the ways in which hyper masculinity and the fear of feminization operate as devices to police political dissent. While Schwarzenegger clearly had derogatory intentions for the phrase "girly man," Bernstein places it in the context of the ballad to deterritorialize its sexism. The ballad's sing-songy artificiality heightens Bernstein's denaturalization of gender. Moreover, with its predictable rhyme scheme, the ballad is the closest a poem comes to a song, and "The Ballad of Girly Man" seems to reflect a choice on Bernstein's part to create a bridge between contemporary poetry and the theater of the political culture, without capitulating to the later. One could say the poem is a bridge between aesthetic difficulty and the easily recognizable populism of the Republic National Convention.

"The Ballad of Girly Man" attempts to undo the unquestioned link between war and American masculinity. The poem begins with two end-rhyme lines that represent the repression of sadness in a post-9/11 U.S. culture and its transformation into fearful illusions and defensiveness: "The truth is hidden in a veil of tears/ The scabs of the mourners grow thick with fear."[76] In the next stanza, Bernstein

76 Charles Bernstein, "The Ballad of the Girly Man," in *Girly Man* (Chicago: U Chicago Press, 2006), 179.

expands this fear into the political rhetorics of hate, while also linking poetry to the culture's underlying abhorrence of femininity and
feminization. Notice that Bernstein deliberately misspells "rhyme" to
underscore its link in the American imagination to "crime."

> A democracy once proposed
> Is slimmed and grimed again
> By men with brute design
> Who prefer hate to rime.[77]

Bernstein continues "The Ballad of the Girly Man" by rendering an
increasingly cynical and venal political landscape almost wholly
shaped by neo-conservatism:

> Complexity's a four-letter word
> For those who count by nots and haves
> Who revile the facts of Darwin
> To worship the truth according to Halliburton.
> . . . .
> Thugs from hell have taken freedom's store
> The rich get richer, the poor die quicker
> & the only god that sanctions that
> Is no god at all but rhetorical crap[78]

To oppose a bleak and repressive state that justifies inequality with
religion, Bernstein urges his readers and his son (to whom the poem
is dedicated) to resist the rigid policing of masculinity and embrace
girlishness:

> So be a girly man
> & take a gurly stand
> Sing a gurly song
> & dance with a girly sarong[79]

The imperative to "be" a girly man quickly turns from ontology—and
perhaps the erroneous reification of ontology into the recognizable contours of identity—to acts and practices: "taking a stand,"

---

77 Ibid.
78 Ibid.
79 Ibid.

"sing[ing]," and "dancing." These activities become linked to femininity through the repetition of the adjective "girly" and its quick transformation into "gurly." Replacing the "i" with "u" gives the word a
weight and an expanse, and "gurly" is also a word to describe something as rough or someone as surly. Instead of hiding in the invisible and therefore insidiously powerful space of abstract masculinity,
Bernstein calls for men to perform and become a hyper-visible femininity. The "sarong" that dangles its ornate visibility at the end of
this stanza helps to stress this poem's investment in highlighting the
link between the feminine and visible differences. Moreover, since
the sarong is a form of clothing worn by the men and women of the
Pacific Islands, its presence in "The Ballad of the Girly Man" suggests
the relationship between feminine difference and racial difference, a
conflation that American politics has used to produce a discourse of
Islamic men's sexual pathology.

   "The Ballad of the Girly Man" makes it clear that the heroiciza-
tion of masculinity at the expense and denigration of femininity
ity — "girly" — is inextricable from the rhetorics that justify and
normalize forms of violence that take place on a national scale:

> So be a girly man
> & sing this girly song
> Sissies & proud
> That we would never lie our way to war[80]

In this stanza Bernstein points to *this* poem as the "girly song" to
sing, which suggests that the poem is performing its way into the
girlishness for which it calls. He also calls for a celebration of "sissiness," for it precisely poetry's association with "sissiness" that gives
the genre its political possibility. Following Judith Halberstam's
Female Masculinity (1998), we might say that "The Ballad of the Girly
Man" attests to the possibilities of asserting rather than repressing
minority or alternative masculinities.[81] In Halberstam's words, "The
Ballad of the Girly Man" seeks to contribute to the project of undoing
"complex social structures that wed masculinity to maleness and to
power and domination."[82]

---

80 Ibid., 180.

81 Judith Halberstam, "An Introduction to Female Masculinity," in *Female Masculinity*
    (Durham, N.C.: Duke UP, 1998), 1–43.

82 Ibid., 2.

Needless to say, "The Ballad of the Girly Man," does not approach the level of innovation at work in Stein's "Stanzas in Meditation." It is closer to the audience-centered accessibility of *The Autobiography Alice B. Toklas,* and for good reason. For Bernstein, the crises of the contemporary moment demands that the poem draws from recognizable forms that allow for a space to create a dialogue about what is at stake in the war on terror, which is not the same thing as making poetry more powerful than it is. As Bernstein writes, "Poetry will never win the war on terror/ But neither will error abetted by error."[83] Schwarzenegger threatened American men with feminization, and those threats, as Bernstein's poem begins to suggest, manifested in the deliberate feminizations and deformations of Muslim men's bodies spaces such as Abu Ghraib. In order, it seems, to contend with the cultural pervasiveness and political influence of such threats within the poem's comparably tiny scale, Bernstein chose the decidedly recognizable, accessible form of the ballad to offer an alternative model for identifying with masculinity.

It is clear that a "girly man" does not move too far beyond easily recognizable gender identities. What form gender identity is easier to conjure than girly femininity, particularly when it is used derisively to emasculate men? "The Ballad of the Girly Man" does play with strict gender difference, but scrambles the hierarchy that almost inevitably attaches to it, and flagrantly embraces "girlishness" to fly in the face of feminization as a threat. The legibility of girlishness is necessary for Bernstein to create these multiple forms of resistance.

At the opening of this essay I cited Gayatri Spivak's and Judith Butler's phrase "the necessary error of identity" in order to call attention to the importance of claiming identity so as to refute their narrow and punitive deployments. Here is the full passage from *Bodies That Matter* in which the phrase appears:

> it remains politically necessary to lay claim to 'women,' 'queer,' 'gay,' and 'lesbian,' precisely because of the way these terms, as it were, lay their claim on us prior to our full knowing. Laying claim to such terms in reverse will be necessary to refute homophobic deployments of the terms in law, public policy, on the street, in 'private' life. But the necessity to mobilize the necessary error of identity (Spivak's term) will always be in tension with the demo-

---

83   Charles Bernstein, "The Ballad of the Girly Man," 180.

cratic contestation of the term which works against its deployments in racist and misogynist discursive regimes.[84]

Acknowledging that the language of identity precedes and shapes our knowledge of ourselves, Butler argues that identitarian categories are necessary discursive and defensive weapons. She also argues that mobilizing "the necessary error of identity" is not limited to defense and contestation, and means "extending" identity's "range" and "affirm[ing] the contingency of the term."[85] Bernstein's poetry answers this call to extend identity's range and affirm its contingency. The work of Gertrude Stein, with its complicated interplay of legible forms of identity--which solicit recognition--and its artistic commitment to forms of illegibility--which undermine identity's reification–has been central to the realization of Bernstein's project and its feminist reverberations.

---

84   Judith Butler, *Bodies That Matter*, 229.

85   Ibid., 229-230.

8

LARS PALM

That Poem For Charles Bernstein

some illegal systems drawn
with one hand clapping &
one building windmills

would you chill out in a
three litre box or under
a palm tree rattling?

down on the patio things
dawn on birds who some
time later inform two humans

of the fact burning or
thundering in from the plains
on horseback

9

STEVEN SALMONI

"Spectres of Benjamin": (Re) presentation and (Re)semblance in Charles Bernstein's *Shadowtime*

Do not all the questions of our lives, as we live, remain behind us like foliage obstructing our views? (Walter Benjamin)

≈

The text needs its shadow: . . . ghosts, pockets, traces, necessary clouds: subversion must produce its own chiaroscuro (Roland Barthes)

≈

If we take eternity to mean not infinite temporal duration but timelessness, then eternal life belongs to those who live in the present.
    Our life has no end in just the way in which our visual field has no limits (Ludwig Wittgenstein)

≈

There is no parting from your own shadow (Alfred North Whitehead)

≈

Everything in the world exists to end up as an opera. (Charles Bernstein) [1]

≈

---

1 Benjamin, *Reflections*, 67; Barthes, *The Pleasure of the Text*, 32; Wittgenstein, *Tractatus Logico-Philosophicus*, 87; Whitehead, *Science and the Modern World*, 18; Bernstein, *Girly Man*, 160.

In the essay "The Impressionists and Edouard Manet," first published in 1876, Stéphane Mallarmé offers a defense of what was, at the time, a new and seemingly incomprehensible technique of painting. Rather than producing works that were "laughable to the many," if not "heretical," according to both popular and critical opinion, the Impressionists, led by Manet, reveal to the viewer "a new delight at the recovery of a long obliterated truth":

> The secret is to be found in an altogether new concept of cutting the painting that gives the frame all the charm of a completely imaginary boundary . . . Such is the painting, and the function of the frame is to isolate it, although I realize that this might run counter to preconceived ideas. For example, what is the point of portraying arm, a hat, a river bank, if they belong to someone or something outside the painting? All you have to do is make sure that the spectator . . . can reconnect with the whole [and] . . . half believe that what he is seeing is the vision of a genuine scene.[2]

This blurring of the interior and exterior marks a significant turn in the history of the "frame" as a compositional element in Western art. As Victor I. Stoichita observes, a frame that interrupts or fragments a given scene allows for a subtle, almost unnoticeable, and yet profoundly energized and fluid reimagining of the optics of painting. In a work such as Renoir's 1867 canvas *The Pont des Arts, Paris*, where the artist "depicts the bridge's shadow at the base of the scene," we see, as if for the first time, an image represent a "shadow [that] is cast by no object in the image."[3] The shadow now appears "as an extension, a projection of something that is still 'outside-the-frame,' in other words, in the real world."[4] In Renoir's image, and in Mallarmé's descriptions of Manet, the shadow "is not just a fragment, but a messenger of reality," and even more importantly, of the way in which one experiences and exists within the flow of the spatial and temporal as coordinates of reality because the shadow, as a phenomenon of nature, "corresponds to a very precise moment in the day. . . in the painting, the shadow establishes a unity between being and

---

2 Mallarmé, "The Impressionists and Edouard Manet," 42.

3 Stoichita, *A Short History of the Shadow*, 105, 103.

4 Ibid, 103.

becoming."[5] The shadow-crossing-the frame connects, and even more so, implicates, the outside world in its entirety to the image within. It invites us to imagine the entirety of the world outside the frame, concentrated, crystallized, emblematized in the interior figure(s), whereas, reversing the direction of the gaze, and moving outwards, it leads one to imagine the world constituted and reconstituted along an axis of endless possibilities. Visible only in the indeterminate spectrality of its shadow, and knowable only in its mediated form as the double of what is itself a re-presentation, the object which casts the shadow remains suspended in a virtual state of both determination and indetermination, of both actuality and potential.

This geometry of the shadow and frame is analogous to what might be called the "apparitions" of a rapidly spreading modernity that Walter Benjamin uncovers in his studies of the 19th Century. The figure of collapsed boundaries between inside and outside, of "exterior as interior" becomes, as Tom Gunning notes, "a crucial emblem for Benjamin's analysis of the nineteenth century," particularly with regard to how this figure organizes *The Arcades Project*:

> The arcade, as Benjamin frequently reminds us, is an exterior space conceived as an *intérieur*. A one line entry in the Arcades Project summons up topographical contradictions like a Möbius strip: 'Arcades are houses or passages having no outside—like the dream.' By their very nature of enclosing an alleyway, or, rather, forcing a passage through a block of buildings, the arcades present a contradictory and ambiguous space.[6]

Paris, the city that for Benjamin was the "Capital of the 19th Century," is seen taking on representative form as a space already imbued with shadows, where the visible is rendered less visible by objects—objects, moreover, which are themselves not visible. Just as one knows of "places in ancient Greece where the way led down into the underworld," in Paris, [o]ur waking existence likewise is a land which, at certain hidden points, leads

> down into the underworld—a land full of inconspicuous places from which dreams arise. All day long, suspecting

5 Ibid, 104.
6 Gunning, "Exterior as Intérieur," 105-6.

nothing, we pass them by, but no sooner has sleep come than we are eagerly groping our way back to lose ourselves in the dark corridors. By day, the labyrinth of urban dwellings resembles consciousness; the arcades (which are galleries leading into the city's past) issue unremarked onto the streets. At night, however, under the tenebrous mass of the houses, their denser darkness protrudes like a threat, and the nocturnal pedestrian hurries past—unless, that is, we have emboldened him to turn into the narrow lane."[7]

Moving forward another century or so to the present day, we can see the same sort of emboldened turn informing Charles Bernstein's *Shadowtime*, a "thought-opera," as Bernstein calls it, whose subject is the life and work of Walter Benjamin.[8] Like Benjamin's own work, Bernstein's text attempts a tracing down of these less illuminated passageways, and like Benjamin's own description of the pedagogic aims of *The Arcades Project*, Bernstein's language "educate[s] the image-making medium within us, raising it to a stereoscopic and dimensional seeing into the depths of historical shadows."[9]

As Bernstein's title might suggest, *time*, in all of its many senses, historical and otherwise, is an abiding theme throughout: "I hear the ticking of the clock," says the character of Benjamin, soon after the opera's beginning–

> the ticking of the clock
> as if I were
> on the other side of time
> staring in

---

7 Benjamin, *Arcades Project*, 84.

8 Although written as a libretto to accompany composer Brian Fernyhough's musical score, I would like here to concentrate on reading this text as *text*, independent of its relationship to Fernyhough's orchestration and to the totality of the performance of this piece as an opera. If there is a benefit to doing so, it is perhaps that we may concentrate more attentively upon its rhetorical and poetic figures and upon the philosophical implications of these figures.

9 Benjamin, *Arcades Project*, 458. In keeping the with the nature of *The Arcades Project* as a compendium of quotations, Benjamin includes this footnote to this line of his text: "The words are Rudolf Borchardt's in *Epilegomena zu Dante*, vol. 1 (Berlin, 1923), pp. 56-57." Mallarmé, for his part, uses similar language in the "Impressionists" essay: Manet's work, he argues, serves "to educate the public eye." Mallarmé, "Impressionists," 41.

—one of many moments in this text where the "life" of the person that was "Walter Benjamin" is given to, and as such gives way to, a figure (in both the biographical and rhetorical senses) derived from his writings.[10] As rendered by Bernstein, however, these writings are again, as Marjorie Perloff observes, "'written through,' ventriloquized, parodied, anagrammatized, tiffed upon, rhymed, translated both literally and homophonically."[11] *Shadowtime* as a text and "Shadow-time" as the organizing figure for the text emerge from the de- and re-arrangement of Benjamin's prior self-in-text. As a "marked translation of motifs in Benjamin," as Bernstein himself has described this work, the figure of Benjamin is "subjected to linguistic practices that, so to speak, would seem to lay bare the devices of Benjamin's own writings."[12] That they do so in a way which further obscures their already obscure objective suggests that Benjamin's writings themselves understand vision or visibility only insofar as they are in a relationship to the act of concealment.

Put another way, Bernstein's text both derives from and carries out the conceit that an illumination of Benjamin's writing requires one, or more, layer(s) of shadow. One approach, therefore, to a reading of this text is to interrogate what the title "*Shadowtime*" may suggest. What sort of shadow(s), what senses of time are at work in this text? What passages—thinking here of the importance of this term for Benjamin—of meaning are opened up by this particular compound word? How does each term in the compound inflect the other? More specifically, how, and to what consequence(s) can one trace the ways in which Bernstein explores a Benjaminian-inflected model of time and space? Throughout the opera, as is implicit in its title, these phenomenological dimensions are recast in terms of the visual, vis-à-vis the occlusions of sight caused by shadow, and, to an even further degree, to the refigurations of self and language occasioned by the world consigned to shadow, a world that only appears (if one can even call it that) under covering of shadow, inside the folds that are themselves within the seemingly visible world.

To begin, we may consider the way a shadow figure manifests itself: it is a (seemingly) immaterial projection that is the naturally occurring trace of an object in relation to light, and to the larger spaces that contain the object and the source of light, and through

---

10   Bernstein, *Shadowtime*, 39.
11   Perloff, "Constraint, Concrete, Citation," 706.
12   Ibid.

which the light travels. There is no shadow without relation of all three: object, light and space. It is a sign of perceptual and spatial relations as much as it is a sign of its (ap)parent object.

The shadow is, in this sense, a "citation," or a "quotation." Citations not only refer one specific text to another, but more universally, attest to the totally of relation between texts, just as shadows refer both to the instance and to the capacity of visual-physical relations. The quotation is intertextual, the shadow, inter-material; both signify an intersubjectivity, a figure in consciousness beyond, or more than, the singular, self-contained subject. It is here that Benjamin's and Bernstein's projects most significantly overlap, and affinity that Bernstein himself speaks to in a recent interview:

> Let me introduce Walter Benjamin here, as a good example of multipolar, rather than linear, thinking. Benjamin's form of reflective writing suggests a poetics of multiple layers or figures. A line of thought may seem to go off into one direction then drops back to follow another trajectory, only this new direction is not a nonsequitur but rather echoes or refracts both the antecedent motifs and — this is the uncanny part — the eventual ones. I mean this as a way of rethinking what is often called fragmentation or disjunction. Think of fragments not as discontinuous but as overlays, pleats, folds: a chordal poetics in which synchronic notes meld into diachronic tones . . . [into] a verbal and paraverbal echoing between interrelated motifs that, on a rational level, do not, at first, seem related. Yet, as you go into details, as you begin to listen to the essay as would a piece of music, you begin to register how intricately everything is connected.[13]

One consequence of this compositional method is an acknowledgement of the textual character of the world: the entirety of the world can be read as a single text, and the entirety of texts, as a singular, global construct. As Peter Bürger observes, a quotation that "no longer makes a specifically determinate reference to the work from which it has been taken . . . but rather by virtue of vague allusion to the themes and techniques of another author . . . determines an image or text in its entirety," causes the "opposition between text

---

13 Charles Bernstein, interview by Eric Denut, *Argotist Online*.

and quotation (to) disappear. The image is a quotation — but it no longer quotes anything determinate, for in order to do so it would have to construct a context against which all that is quoted could stand out in relief."[14] The quotation both indicates and derives from an a priori refusal of distinctions between the "inside" and "outside" of text, to the point where such geometrical categories do not apply, or if applied, do not carry their usual metaphysical significance, their usual sense of marking a spiritual/material divide. When Bernstein writes "within" or "under" the titular rubric of "*Shadowtime*," of the time and space of shadows, the resultant text also performs an exaggerative, transgressive gesture that counters, that pushes back against the spatio-temporal geometries of the inside/outside figure. A shadow-time provides "[a] way to think / Outside the self-enclosing circles / That bury us alive and make us / Deaf even to the dead."[15]

Perloff, in fact, extends this construct to *Shadowtime* as a whole, noting that "the entire documentary frame" which would provide both historical and rhetorical context for the poem "is dissolved."[16] If this is the case, then one can no longer say "within" or even "under" the title *Shadowtime*; as a controlling concept, shadow-time must be both within and without its elaborations in the text. The boundary that delimits meaning is again dissolved by that very meaning or significance that it delimits. This figure of "the controlling concept indistinguishable from what it controls" has an analogue, moreover, in the figure of "the speaking subject indistinguishable from the language spoken." If shadow-time is dissolution into itself, into the rhetorical motions of whatever is written in its name, it then *reveals* the connections between the geographical, the linguistic, and the psychological domains of subjectivity. Against a theory of writing that has a basis in the geometric reductions of an inside/outside subjectivity, a writing that, via the use of quotations, dissolves the inside/outside of text and meaning, or of text and "not-text," also liquidates that reductive figure of inside/outside with regard to subjectivity. The spatio-temporal critique of citation is at once a critique of the subjectivity of its author.

The enshadowed doubling of Benjamin by Bernstein suggests — in the form of the infinite regress — that we as readers and writers upon this text also stage an opening or fragmenting of the printed page

---

14   Bürger, *The Decline of Modernism*, 147.

15   Bernstein, *Shadowtime*, 54.

16   Perloff, "Constraint, Concrete, Citation," 705-6.

(including, or especially this page upon which I write and which you now read—itself subject to a shadowed/shadowing relationship) that provides and that contains in its space the record of the reading of *Shadowtime.* That is to say, the page upon which one writes about this text casts its own shadow, casts multiple shadows moving throughout the field of its mobility, inviting us to write upon its now immaterial surface. Then again, to write upon the shadow page materializes the shadow; that which in writing presents itself as the concreteness of the letter demands an apparent space for its imprint, for its inscription. This reverses the causality of the usual experience of the "object-that-casts-its-shadow." Here the shadow becomes object, and one cannot say which takes precedence, which is the a priori of the other.

Perhaps, then, it would not be an overstatement to say that the drama of this text is the drama of language rendered as physical space. The scene (in this shadow-time) is whiteness, an ambient field against which (and *within which*—here the two are one and the same) are placed the fragments of other poems, other fields, placed as reminders, relics of the body still present (if only in its absence) in all poetic de-compositions. In doing so, *Shadowtime* argues for the architectural, cartographical and geographical agency of words, an extension, if not a fulfillment of Bernstein's call for the "intrusion / of words into the visible" in order to heighten or maximize "writing's own absorption into the world."[17] To this early statement of Bernstein's poetics, one might add Deleuze and Guattari's observation that "[w]riting has nothing to do with signifying. It has to do with surveying, mapping, even realms that are yet to come."[18] A poem, understood in these terms, is a spatial occurrence, an act of mapping, a territorial inscription. If the meanings of the poem are the particularities of its terrain, the locale of *Shadowtime* is that of the poem questioning its own presence, its own standing.

Where does all of this leave the character of Benjamin? In the synoptic preface, Bernstein notes that the "pivotal scene in the play" occurs at the moment of Benjamin's descent into the underworld, thereby enabling the alternate history and destiny that the play envisions for his character.[19] The figure of Benjamin exists primarily as "a product of our imagination," or more specifically as a figure

---

17 Bernstein, *A Poetics*, 87.

18 Deleuze and Guattari, *A Thousand Plateaus*, 4–5.

19 Bernstein, *Shadowtime*, 21.

that both emerges from and reflects back upon "the point of view of
an American after-life for him (and maybe for the secular European
Jews whose world ended with his)." A figure come alive in death,
whose death becomes that which animates his presence, the historical Benjamin here becomes, or is reborn as "an avatar," one who
"enters the underworld or shadow world" on behalf of the living.[20]
He speaks from some alternate space, some mirrored space that both
is and is not the world that we inhabit.

    Bernstein locates the site of this entry into the shadow world in
the alternative and mirrored space of Las Vegas, the most unreal (and
thus, perhaps, the most *real* of American cities). The irony here multiplies, for while Las Vegas is hardly a random choice of location, it is
a city dependent upon, if not itself built as a kind of hyper-extended
expression of the game of chance. From a thematic point of view,
this setting encompasses one of Benjamin's most significant critical
engagements, namely his studies of Charles Baudelaire. Benjamin
locates the French poet at (or as) a nexus that joins the problem of
the alienation caused by technological/ industrial modernity to the
Freudian psycho-pathologies of trauma. This complex, in turn, corresponds with the disconnected and emptied automatism of the game
of chance, a central motif, as Benjamin notes, in Baudelaire:

> The manipulation of the worker at the machine has no
> connection with the preceding operation for the very
> reason that it is its exact repetition. Since eachoperation
> at the machine is just as screened off from the preceding
> operation as a coup in a game of chance is from the one
> that preceded it, the drudgery of the laborer is, in its own
> way, a counterpart to the drudgery of the gambler. The
> work of both is devoid of substance.[21]

So too does the matter of chance inform the underlying structure
of the author/subject relationship that is put into play here. The
text is a map of the meetings, the crossings of the two textualities
of "Walter Benjamin" and "Charles Bernstein," one that, occurring
under the sign of the shadow, is freed from the determinations of
"optical perception," and is thus itself subject to the vicissitudes of
chance. Against the reimagining of history enacted here via this alter-

20 Bernstein, interview by Eric Denut.
21 Benjamin, *Illuminations*, 177.

nate "Benjamin," the actual or "real" history of the world emerges in much greater clarity. This, in turn enables the uncovering of connections and correspondences between what had previously seemed to be disconnected events and social formations. *Shadowtime* refigures or represents this in poetic terms through Benjamin's encounters with, as Bernstein describes them, "a chorus of angels, a chorus of the angels of history," [22] who speak to Benjamin, and to whom Benjamin speaks, although it is not always (if ever) certain that each understands the other. Dialogue here unfolds (in) the paradox of asynchronous synchronicity and non-referential referentiality.

It is as if one knows what has happened because, at that exact moment, in that same space, someone else is there as well, doing something else, perhaps, even something entirely unrelated, and yet this second figure, this second act cannot help but to become continuous with the initial or primary figure/act upon which we are focused. We pass by chance, which again becomes deliberate in its passing. Drawn to the accidental crossing of events by the future inevitability of the accident's occurrence, we perform our actions because someone, or something else unknown to us will be performing actions of their own. "Real" insight, real reflection therefore comes when one stands, as it were, behind the surface of a mirror, or again "on the other side of time / staring in"—a formal pose whereby one witnesses, and again expresses a content of the fragmentations and dissolute contingencies of relation, the ephemera of forms. A moment's adjacency in space, a fleeting and accidental incidence of co-occupation of a single point, gives itself to the figure of connectedness in time.

The single point in space—which here may be that threshold between the world of the living and that of the dead, or in visual terms, that line of contact where an object adjoins its shadow—contains, conceals, reveals and yields the in-fold point in time. The singularity in space has to be, having been made necessary by the knotted and imbricate temporal topographies within it. We only see this, however, at the end, at the (anti-) climactic point of realization when the two actors cross paths with one another. With great (although at that moment, unrecognized) irony, the nameless and "quixotic" Lecturer makes this argument at the very "beginning" of the text: "the pragmatic certainty of our own death arises," he says "from the observation that advancing age often constricts the

---

22 Bernstein, Denut.

possibilities available to us often converging at the limit of a single possibility or of none at all."[23] The meeting point in space appears because it is always was required to appear, just as it appears so that appearance can itself be required. The same is true of the point's *disappearance*, keeping in mind that qualification made by the final words in the preceding quotation.

The use of aleatory methods to compose many sections of the text is itself a figure for the chance (yet determinate) crossing between Benjamin and Bernstein. How else does one meet Benjamin, except through the luminous event of concentration, a momentary brightening of a point in history, revealed through the concatenation of fragments, reassembled by an act of chance? *Shadowtime*, as an encounter between Benjamin and Bernstein, inverts, subverts, ironizes the (perceptual) faith of the logical necessity of connection. There is no connection; hence the connection. The encounter is negation, an expression of what Whitehead calls "the principle that, so far as physical relations are concerned, contemporary events happen in 'causal independence' of each other."[24]

At the same time, as Benjamin himself urges, one has to be mindful of a "notion of a present which is not a transition, but in which time stands still and has come to a stop." "Where thinking suddenly stops in a configuration pregnant with tensions, it gives that configuration a shock, by which it crystallizes into a monad."[25] What happens, in other words, when fragments of other things suddenly and inexplicably yield meaning, express a hitherto unsuspected coherence?

Shadowtime approaches and gives form to this question through the device of repetition, a device which entwines, and thus suggests coherence between the visual and auditory dimensions of the text. The text seems almost to be developed or constructed *around* signal moments of repetitive speech, of speaking itself as embedded in acts of repetition that at once have preceded and again will follow from a given moment of speaking. Nothing is said once in these moments; every phrase is rephrased, usually twice or more, each instance of the phrase given a different emphasis, a different shape, beginning or ending at different points in the line:

    Our plan is to go on

---

23 Bernstein, *Shadowtime*, 17, 27.

24 Whitehead, *Process and Reality*, 61.

25 Benjamin, *Illuminations*, 261-2.

to go on
to Lisbon
to Lisbon by train
and from there by plane
by plane from Lisbon
to America.[26]

This already is an experience of time covered by shadow. Note the persistent and insistent patterns of repetition in the above example: the second instances of the phrases "to go on" and "to Lisbon" seem to be shadows of their first; in the change of vowel sound and in the addition of the letter "e," "plane" is both a sonic and visual shadowing of "plan." The Innkeeper's speech unfolds (or rather is a speech already manifest in folds from the first moment of its utterance) in a similar homeomorphic shadowing. His words, however, are rigorously, and mechanically, robotically punctuated by the regular ticking of the names of address "Herr Benjamin / Frau Gurland" alternated with its opposite "Frau Gurland / Herr Benjamin:"

I regret to inform you
Herr Benjamin, Frau Gurland
but I must inform you
Frau Gurland, Herr Benjamin
you will understand
Herr Benjamin, Frau Gurland
it is my duty to inform you
Frau Gurland, Herr Benjamin
that your transit visas
Herr Benjamin, Frau Gurland
your transit VISAS
Frau Gurland, Herr Benjamin
Are not valid [27]

Even as this sequence is a pronouncement of authority ("We are a nation of laws, Herr Benjamin"), the law here is parasitic (read as para-sitic); it is marginal to the central "site" of being; it is the shadow devouring the parent object that cast it. This is a looped and enfolded

---

26　Bernstein, *Shadowtime*, 32
27　Ibid, 30-1.

semantic space, a space of semantic repetition, as well as an endlessly repeating semantics of space.

In such a space, it is difficult to distinguish the actual message from this pendulum-like intonation of the names. (The obvious irony that the innkeeper's message will, in fact, become Benjamin's death sentence does not undermine the necessary bluntness of this construct). This suggests that any language spoken here is already the language of shadow, the language of mortality. The clockwork pulsation of the names, a kind of extended anaphoric device which might, under other circumstances, signify the vitality of a steady heartbeat, is here refigured as parody: this is a clock whose pieces move, whose pieces register their movements with audible and repetitive beats, but that is incapable of marking, of keeping time.

Whereas for Benjamin, if exact and automatic repetition both exists within and is again productive of a featureless and uniform time, the displaced repetitions of *Shadowtime* signify the attempt to forestall time, to thicken, to estrange, to even stop time. A "shadow-time," another incarnation perhaps of Bernstein's "Time Out of Motion," is the antithesis of de-substantialized actions of mechanized repetition, if only because of its refusal to mask or hide its displacements, its self-alienation.[28] Although the shadow is simultaneous with its object, appearing in the instant of illumination, object and shadow do not have the same material status. It is not the same thing to say "the object casts its shadow" as it is to say "the shadow casts its object." The shadow in shadow-time is not simply, or solely, a consequence; rather, in its qualification of its "object" (i.e. time), it assumes the property of the name, and hence moves into its own objective existence. The adjectival (denominative) sense of 'shadowytime' hardens or solidifies in the nominative "Shadow." "The shadow-as-object," however, also becomes that which casts its own shadow. Placed within the flow of time, which is to say, within the field of potential for any and every shadow still to come, the shadow is a figure of infinite regress, of endless reproduction. It is an open question, however, whether this shadow-machine is productive of anything except (or beyond) its own reproductions.

The turn to this well-known motif of Benjamin's seems particularly appropriate for Bernstein, given the latter's own creative and innovative uses of technology to further extend the possibilities of poetry. It is possible to say of Bernstein that he is the poet of the

---

28 Bernstein, *A Poetics*, 106.

"Work of Art in the Age of Digital (Re)production." This raises the question of what sort of aesthetics this "machine" writing might entail—or, if this writing could, in fact, be understood in aesthetic terms at all as they have been traditionally conceived. In several of their works, including their studies of Kafka, Deleuze and Guattari anticipate this question when they advance their notion of the "bachelor machine." Looking back to the initial question of the spatial dimensions of the text, we can compare the movements into and within this shadow-time to the experience of deterritorialization that Deleuze and Guattari observe in Kafka, and which takes form in the image of the productive non-productivity of the bachelor.[29] One potent example of the particular kinds of spatial forms that impose themselves on the Benjamin figure comes at that moment in Scene II when the sound of the guitar is said to act as a "barrier."[30] On one hand this is a play on the barrier that prevented Benjamin's crossing into Spain, and as such, the barrier more or less directly that caused his death, but even this does not exhaust the meanings of the representation of the barrier in terms of sound, in non-representational signs. Sound as barrier, as irreducible, incommensurate to meaning here becomes a sign for the bachelor machine, the machine that does not produce, yet remains irreducible in its machine-ness. The machine (re)produces itself as machine.

While Deleuze and Guattari claim that the "production of intensive quantities in the social body, [the] proliferation and precipitation of series, [and the] polyvalent and collective connections brought about by the bachelor agent" are the definitive traits of a "minor

---

29 The "bachelor machine" has, in recent years, become central to Bernstein's thinking. He offers the following "primer" not only to trace the history of this construct, but also as a means to help understand and situate his own writings: "Bachelor machine" [machines célibataires] comes from Duchamp's "Bride Stripped Bare by Her Bachelors, Even" (the lower part of the "Large Glass," e.g., "Chocolate Grinder"). Michel Carrouges (in his book *Machines Célibataires* [Paris: Arcanes, 1954, 2nd ed. 1976] extended the term to incorporate the disciplinary apparatus of Kafka's "The Penal Colony" & also to Roussel's *Impressions of Africa*, and some of Poe's machines as well, and, crucially, to the work of Alfred Jarry. This formulation has been adapted by Deleuze and Guattari in *Anti-Oedipus* and also by Michel de Certeau in *Ars de Faire*. As a term for poetic constructions, "bachelor machine" suggests nonproductive, nonprocreative, onanistic processes, vicious (or self-enclosing/collapsing) circles, an apparatus that is unable to get outside itself. There is a connection, in my use, to délire (delirium, with special reference to Jean-Jacques LeCercle)—that which goes astray, deviates from the rational, errs, raves." Bernstein, "What, Me Conceptual?"

30 Bernstein, *Shadowtime*, 19.

literature,"[31] these seem to apply just as well to the performative intentions and aspirations of Language Poetry as Bernstein and others have described it. The character of Benjamin, in his reconstituted life-in-death and his (dis)location in a space of "endlessly refracted interstices [and] shadows of words" functions as this sort of ironically conceived writing machine. This too is an extension into the 21st Century of the Benjaminian notions of "Mechanical Reproduction" and of the "Author as Producer." What does it do to the conceit of Author-as-Producer to reframe the author as producer of nothing, as producer of "non-meaning?" A poetry in which sound has to be referred back to meaning, and in which the materiality of the letter and the word has to be referred back to the abstract, non-material, ideality of the "signified" is the natural, or normative poetry of the transcendental lyric subject—one, however, that will (from a Marxist standpoint) never be able to grasp the ideologically informed repressions that attend this subject position. The hope of Language Poetry, and of Benjamin's "Author as Producer,"[32] is to make the author/subject conscious of, and therefore able to control, the "means" of linguistic, textual production—which, for both Bernstein and Benjamin, requires that the author become aware of the corporeal, concrete reality of the "raw material," so to speak, of the industry.

Shadowtime traces these themes back even further, in both a historical and philosophical sense, to questions raised by the essay "On Language as Such, and the Languages of Man," one of Benjamin's earliest and most densely rendered works. "At issue" in this essay, as Peter Fenves argues, "is the origin of abstraction itself: the genealogy of European science since its mathematization, the becoming

---

31 Deleuze and Guattari, *Kafka*, 71.

32 Two essays in particular stand out, not only for their treatments of this connection, but also for the spatial and visual figures each uses in figuring their analyses of poetry in, and as, a system of production. In "Language Writing: From Productive to Libidinal Economy," Steve McCaffery writes: "[w]hat Language Writing is proposing is a shift for writing away from literature and the readable, towards the *dialectical domain of its own interiors* as primarily an interacting surface of signifiers in the course of which a sociological shift in the nature of readership must be proposed. For the texts of [Bruce] Andrews, Bernstein, [Clark] Coolidge, [Barrett] Watten cannot be consumed but only produced." Ron Silliman's *"Disappearance* of the Word / *Appearance* of the World" argues that while the "social function" of the poem is to "carry the class struggle for consciousness to the level of consciousness," it cannot do so unless there is "a change in the mode and control of production of material life." McCaffery, *North of Intention*, 150; Silliman, *The L=A=N=G=U=A=G=E Book*, 131. (Emphasis mine).

abstract of 'being' at the inception of the metaphysical tradition, and the retraction of language all omit the concrete and cognitive element, namely, the name."[33] If Bernstein's staging of Benjamin is also the deployment and redeployment of the name "Walter Benjamin," the text of *Shadowtime* thus engages with (or *shadows*) Benjamin's own call for a "dissolution" (dis-solution) that "has room for 'words and names,' but not for the abstract combinations of what we call 'words and names' into judgements."[34] Significantly, Fenves's use of the term "judgement" introduces Kant into the Benjamin/ Bernstein dynamic, and it points to the fact that Benjamin's "On Language" essay is itself a response to, or a refiguration of, Kantian notions space and time. Speaking to, and for, all perceiving subjects, as subjects determined by the structures of perception, Kant argues that "[o]ne can never represent that there is no space, although one can very well think that there are no objects to be encountered in it."[35] For Benjamin, however, it is language that has this same force of "transcendental ideality" that space does for Kant.[36] In the essay, Benjamin attempts to explicate such a transcendental dimension of language no longer grounded in reflexive subjectivity through the rhetoric of *analogy*, using the Kantian figures for space and time as a template or model for his figure of language. One very important consequence of such a move, both for philosophy and for poetry, is that it displaces the Kantian spatio-temporal structuring of consciousness in favor of a model that privileges language as the primary determinant of mind. Benjamin, as Fenves writes, situates phenomenological perceptions of things "within a larger domain of things as they exist and are disclosed within language." Thus for Benjamin, the world is the "experience, not of objects, but of the modes of their disclosure."[37]

Analogy, however, has a geometrical register as well, and in the mapping of shadow-time, Bernstein uses the Kantian figures of space and time to create or launch a second order analogy of poetic language based upon Benjamin's model. This, moreover, is one that displaces the transcendence implicit in Benjamin's model with a model that is *displacement* itself brought to bear upon the invisibly monolithic struc-

---

33   Fenves, "The Genesis of Judgement," in Ferris, *Theoretical Questions*, 75-93.

34   Ibid, 77.

35   Kant, *Critique of Pure Reason*, 158.

36   Fenves, 81.

37   Ibid, 81-83.

tures of language. Moving across the entirety of Benjamin's evolving career as a thinker (the "On Language" essay would be an example of his *early* writing), Bernstein displaces and fragments the figure of a singular "Walter Benjamin," much as displacement and fragmentation are, of course, devices that Benjamin himself explores as his writing develops. *Shadowtime* fractures the text of Benjamin and uses the resultant fragments against themselves, which ironically reveals the figure of fragmentary—or fragmented—whole that is the body of Benjamin's writing.

That this body of writing is one in which, to borrow another one of Bernstein's signal phrases, "the [p]arts are greater than the sum of the whole" implies that what is at stake here is the very nature of representation in language.[38] To what degree is representation contingent upon figures of analogy, and to what degree are those analogical figures always already bound up ideological (and thus imperceptible) structures of repression, political and otherwise? To what degree can poetry change the terms of representation—refuting or refusing (or rather, de-fusing) language figures that use a metrics of *substitution*, of replacement, and then again implacement, a gathering and joining of terms within a larger figure? Indeed one can read much of Bernstein's writing, *Shadowtime* included, as a fracture or disruption of the analogical mechanism. The analogy of Bernstein's shadowtime, which in turn, is built upon Benjamin's analogical extension of the Kantian figure, accomplishes this disruption of the analogical capacity through the shadow, the figure that is both joined with, and exogenous to the object which casts it. As a poetic image, "shadow" is at once metaphor and the nullity, the refusal of metaphoric resemblance. It is the sign of the visible and of the invisible, of the mutual interdependence of one to the other, and of their absolute and irreconcilable scission. The shadow, going even further, (in its hypo- and hyper-visibility) can be the site for the deliberate and comic creation of false analogies to thereby test the limit points of analogy or resemblance itself.

Such are the concerns the third section of *Shadowtime*, a scene entitled "The Doctrine of Similarity." This title itself, as Bernstein notes, "comes from an essay by Benjamin with a similar name—'Doctrine of the Similar'—in which he considers the ways that the physical sounds of language echo or mimic the primordial structures of the cosmos."[39] "Amphiboles," the first of thirteen movements that collec-

---

38 Bernstein, *My Way*, 3.

39 Bernstein, *Shadowtime*, 20

tively comprise the scene, opens this meditation upon similarity with a short lyrical text followed by two homophonic translations:

Walk slowly
and jump quickly
over the paths into
the
briar

becomes:

Fault no lease
add thump whimsy
aver
a sash onto
a
mire

which then, in turn, becomes:

Balk sulky
ant hump prick fee
clover
an ash injure
at-
tire[40]

We must ask, however naively, whether the sonic and semantic changes wrought upon the first incarnation (which is legible by normal standards of reading) represent a degeneration of the capacity of writing. Does this sequence of texts stage what can only be called a "decay," into a form which at the end still retains a trace resemblance to the original, albeit less and less so through each successive iteration? Or, is this only the illusion of decay among a series of changes in texts that nevertheless remain in stasis? That is to say, whereas the sonic variations surely alter the properties of each, these changes in the texts are only relative to one another; there is no original in the sense of a foundational or pre-text, no master text against which the others are lesser, fallen copies. The

---

40 Ibid, 62-3.

later rewritings are not regressions, and not even digressions, and certainly not transgressions, but rather coexist as in a series of movements around a circle, a shape where no point has any priority over any other. Or, as a third possibility, can we admit to an evaluative difference between the three versions, but in the opposite direction? Rather than read the third translation as the weak and degraded and fundamentally misheard rendering of the first, it is that first version itself that is the most unremarkable, the most distant from living and vital language. The Wordsworthian call to "walk slowly," and the avoidance of complex and "thorny" entanglements suggested by a "jump over the briar" echo—albeit in a parodic fashion—the "quietist" poetry so often called into question by many of the writers associated with Language poetics. From this perspective, the distortions of the second and third versions, moving as they do away from the conventional syntax and towards the greater abstractions of pure sound, make these parts of the series appear as intensifications and innovations of the language. Moreover, by forcing these syntactical irregularities and novelties to the surface, this technique suggests that these second and third versions can themselves be read as normally signifying language—although what is represented in these words is something new and transformative in its quasi-surreal imaging.

Each of the sections in Scene III are composed according to some calculation or sequence based upon prime numbers. What, then, is the significance of such a choice? Prime numbers are divisible only by themselves and by one; that is to say, they are indivisible by any quantity other than that which they already are. However, since correlation(s) of divisors/ multiples are themselves a species of resemblance, in their structural opposition to divisibility, these texts are, by implication, refusing similitude—even as they are, paradoxically, exemplars (another species of resemblance) of a "Doctrine of the Similar." Each prime number resembles one another in its resemblance to itself as an indivisible, irreducible entity—none of which admit to the larger relationship of similarities held by numbers that are divisible by one another. The similarities of prime numbers unfold under the sign of the negative, the sign of the shadow: the similarity of the dissimilar.[41] Moreover, this refusal of divisibility manifests as the refusal of *visibility*. If an object is to be visible, it must

---

41   See Perloff, "Constraint, Concrete, Citation" and Karasick, "In the Shadow of Desire" for additional approaches to this question of prime numbers.

be illuminated—i.e. it must be able to cast a shadow. As a necessary effect of visibility, the shadow is the sign for the very capacity of vision itself. Enclosed in shadow, these texts of similitude are in(di)visible except by the principle of itself: one's shadow is the not-self in self; it is the alterity in, and as, identity; it is the pure negativity of positive presence.

In their additive, if not multiplicative, redoublings and recursions of meaning, the series of texts that comprise "The Doctrine of the Similar" bear a general resemblance to the form of the serial poem. In this case, the iteration of these multiples proceeds via a principle of indivisibility, which is to say, a multiplication nullified or frozen in limbo by the absence of its mathematical complement. Here, the multiplication of meaning that is the particular capability of the serial form has no opposite. Or, rather, it has *nothing* as its opposite. But again, this is the substantive and reactive nothingness of the shadow, one that *resolves*—in every sense of the word—even as it is cast under the sign, as in Doctrine 4, of "Indissolubility": "It is never just a matter of identification but of / recognition as refiguration." Or, in the more properly (in)visible language of Shadow-time, we hear the clarified and self-reflexive act of "recognition" echoed as "see fog's mission." A metaphorical image of blindness, for the occlusions of clear sight, is given agency and purpose in these lines, which in turn allows the very "refigurative" agency of metaphor to translate into the more dramatically, ethically and politically charged act of "recuperation."[42]

These images of "recuperation" and "redemption" (a word that is also used in this section of the text) raise the question of whether we can connect *Shadowtime* to the larger progressive aspirations of Bernstein's work, and perhaps of Language Poetry itself. A poetry that is freed from the economies of reference, a poetry in which the disruptions, fracturings, misdirections, suspensions and parodies of meaning—if not a poetry that does not refer at all, a poetry of the pure signifier—at once unmasks the social, economic and political codes by which meaning is controlled and disseminated. This, in turn provides a utopian, liberated space where the reader may, to use Steve McCaffery's terms as one of many possible examples, "abandon all prejudicial perceptual reading sets" in favor of a conscious, authentic and ongoing production of "among the polyse-

---

42 Bernstein, *Shadowtime*, 67-8.

mous routes that the text offers."[43]   Whether poetry does indeed possess such redemptive or transformative capabilities has, of course, been a matter of great debate, both within and outside of what may be loosely construed as the "Language Poetry" community. One can argue, as Tenney Nathanson does, for the inability of poetry to ever accomplish these ideals—not only in a practical way, given the ever-increasing "marginalization of poetry," from most realms of public life, but as an inability that is constitutive or inherent in language itself. There can never be a pure lexeme; every utterance, no matter how gnomic, how fractured from the meaning-producing discourses of the whole, can never escape the frame of reference. The refusal of those referential horizons in fact reveals them by calling attention to their supposed absence.[44]

This problematic in Bernstein resembles one often applied to Walter Benjamin, with respect to what is perceived to be a split or tension between the materialist, or Marxist and the mystical, or Messianic strains of the latter's thinking. If this problem in Bernstein has a Benjaminian provenance, to what degree may *Shadowtime* be a later intervention or statement of this problem, one that qualifies the earlier utopian ideals with its (dialectical) opposite. Can we say that the shadow, that "shadow-time" strikes this balance between?

Bernstein's poetry, as Nathanson also observes, "might indeed be regarded as a realization by more drastic means of the dialogic project Mikhail Bakhtin assigns to the novel; rapid collage, as well as the more disconcerting strategies of interruption, exhibit a multitude of received discourses and dialogize their hegemonic claims."[45] However, where Nathanson applies Bakhtinian theory to read Bernstein as an exemplar of these "carnivalesque" qualities, *Shadowtime*'s preoccupation with time and space suggest the equally significant Bakhtinian notion of the chronotope. For Bakhtin, "it is precisely the chronotope that provides the ground essential for the showing forth, the representability of events. And this is thanks precisely to the special increase in density and concreteness of time markers—the time of human life, of historical time—that occurs within well-delineated spatial areas."[46] How does this clarity

---

43 Quoted in Nathanson, "Collage and Pulverization in Contemporary American Poetry," 310.

44 Ibid, 302-318.

45 Nathanson, "Collage," 303.

46 Bakhtin, *Dialogic Imagination*, 250.

and quality of presence in the chronotope apply to the figure(s) of shadow-time? Can we in fact label shadow-time as a chronotope? As has been argued throughout this essay, in that it "makes possible the representability of events in this text," the answer is affirmative; however, it does so — in the aforementioned play upon the in(di) visibility of prime numbers, for example — through the interjection of absence into the present and presence of the object world. The shadow, given material agency, makes absence itself present. Of all the shadows in the text, perhaps the most potent (precisely because of its self-contradiction) is: "points on a / map / that take / you back behind the stares / where shadows are / thickest at / noon"[47] — a phrasing replete with chronotopic indicators, both apparent, as in the point, the map and the dimension of the "behind," and implied: pointing to the sun directly overhead at high noon recalls, imposes the vertical *axis mundi*, that mythical line running through and joining the psychogeographic realms of heaven, earth and underworld. And, significantly, the one place where objects would not, given the angle of the sun, cast any shadow, where they would be singular and self-contained in their illumined visibility is, in fact, that place where "shadows are thickest."[48]

Shadow-time, that is to say, is as much an inversion or parody of the chronotope as it is a positive and locative marker of the spatial and temporal horizons of the text. And yet, it is this inverted or oppositional capacity that provides the means for the sorts of demystifications to which Language Poetry has aspired. Here is Bakhtin again, writing on the recuperative and redemptive potential for the comic:

> The rogue, the clown, and the fool create around themselves their own special little world, their own chronotope . . . Essential to these three figures is a distinctive feature that is as well a privilege — the right to be 'other' in this world, the right not to make common cause with any of the existing categories that life makes available; none of these categories quite suits them, they see the underside and falseness of every situation. Therefore they can exploit any position they choose, but only as a mask.[49]

---

47 Bernstein, *Shadowtime*, 62.

48 Ibid.

49 Bakhtin, *Dialogic Imagination*, 159.

The "shadow" in this text the mask behind which Bernstein writes (as) Walter Benjamin. At the same time, Benjamin—and all that he represents—is the shadow that is always apparent around the edges of the otherwise ludic and very often comic spirit of Bernstein's writing. The shadow is the visage of Benjamin rendered as a mask, just as "Benjamin-as-figure" is the visage of the shadow. It is a visible imprint or trace of that which lies outside the framed world, the world as it is enframed. By drawing one's gaze to the edges of the frame, the shadow always has the potential to hint at what must lie beyond; by virtue of being a sign within (for) something that is without, the shadow, if not breaking the frame altogether, can at the very least suggest that the frame is permeable. Rendered in language, in the language(s) that take shape in *Shadowtime*, it is a figure for a language both "continuous and discontinuous with the world, a thing that for a poet can be as plastic as transparent."[50] The shadow is the "invisible of writing" whose cast makes this writing visible and material in the world—and, *as* the world: the chiasmatic absence and presence of the frame in the shadow speaks for "language that is not something that is separable from the world but rather is the means by which the world is constituted."[51]

References

Bakhtin, M.M.. *The Dialogic Imagination: Four Essays*. Ed. Michael Holquist. Trans. Caryl Emerson and Michael Holquist. Austin: University of Texas Press, 1982.

Barthes, Roland. *The Pleasure Of The Text*. Trans. Richard Miller. Hill & Wang, 1975.

Benjamin, Walter. *Illuminations: Essays and Reflections*. Trans. Harry Zohn. New York: Schocken, 1969.

——*Reflections: Essays, Aphorisms, Autobiographical Writings*. Trans. Harry Zohn. New York: Schocken, 1986.

——*The Arcades Project*. Trans. Howard Eiland and Kevin McLaughlin. Cambridge: Belknap Press, 1999.

Bernstein, Charles. "A Brief Primer On Bachelor Machines (With Special Reference To 'Recantorium'). "What, Me Conceptual?" *PennSound*, http://writing.upenn.edu/ pennsound/x/Bernstein-Tucson.html, 2008.

---

50 Bernstein, *A Poetics*, 108.

51 Bernstein, *Content's Dream*, 61.

————. *A Poetics*. Cambridge: Harvard University Press, 1992.

————. *Content's Dream: Essays 1975–1984*. Evanston: Northwestern University Press, 1986.

————. *Girly Man*. Chicago: University of Chicago Press, 2006.

————. *My Way: Speeches and Poems*. Chicago: University Of Chicago Press, 1999.

————. "Radical Jewish Culture / Secular Jewish Practice." In Miller and Morris. 12-17.

———— *Shadowtime*. New York: Green Integer, 2005.

Bürger, Peter. *The Decline of Modernism*. University Park: Pennsylvania State University Press, 1992.

"Charles Bernstein interviewed by Eric Denut." *The Argotist Online*, http://www.argotistonline.co.uk/Bernstein%20interview.html.

Deleuze, Gilles and Felix Guattari. *A Thousand Plateaus: Capitalism and Schizophrenia*. Trans. Brian Massumi. Minneapolis: University of Minnesota Press, 1987.

————. *Kafka: Towards A Minor Literature*. Trans. Dana Polan. Minneapolis: University of Minnesota Press, 1986.

Fenves, Peter. "The Genesis of Judgment: Spatiality, Analogy and Metaphor in Benjamin's 'On Language as Such and On Human Language.'" In *Walter Benjamin: Theoretical Questions*. Ed. David S. Ferris. Stanford: Stanford University Press, 1996. 75–93.

Gunning, Tom. "The Exterior as Intérieur: Benjamin's Optical Detective." *boundary 2*, 30:1 (2003): 106–129.

Kant, Immanuel. *Critique of Pure Reason*. Eds. Paul Guyer, P. and Allen W. Wood. Cambridge: Cambridge University Press, 1998.

Karasick, Adeena. "In the Shadow of Desire." In Miller and Morris. 397-408.

Mallarme, Stephané. "The Impressionists and Edouard Manet." In *Modern Art and Modernism: A Critical Anthology*. Eds. Francis Frascina, Charles Harrison and Deirdre Paul. New York: Harper & Row, 1982. 39–44.

McCaffery, Steve. *North of Intention: Critical Writings 1973–1986*. New York: Roof Books, 2000.

Miller, Stephen Paul and Daniel Morris, Eds. *Radical Poetics and Secular Jewish Culture*. Tuscaloosa: University of Alabama Press, 2010.

Nathanson, Tenney. "Collage and Pulverization in Contemporary American Poetry: Charles Bernstein's *Controlling Interests*." *Contemporary Literature* XXXIII, no. 2 (1992): 302-318.

Perloff, Marjorie. "Constraint, Concrete, Citation: Refiguring History in Charles Bernstein's Shadowtime." *Poetics Today* 30, no. 4 (2009): 693-717.

Silliman, Ron. "Disappearance of the World / Appearance of the Word." In *The L=A=N=G=U=A=G=E Book*. Eds. Bruce Andrews and Charles Bernstein. Carbondale: Southern Illinois University Press, 1984. 121-132.

Stoichita, Victor I. *A Short History of the Shadow*. Trans. Anne-Marie Glasheen. London: Reaktion Books, 1997.

Whitehead, Alfred North. *Process and Reality*. New York City: The Free Press, 1979.

———. *Science and the Modern World. Lowell Lectures, 1925*. New York: The Free Press, 1967.

Wittgenstein, Ludwig. *Tractatus Logico-Philosophicus*. Trans. D. F. Pears and B. F. McGuinness. London: Routledge, 2001.

10

STEVE McCAFFERY

What As Poetic

for Charles Bernstein

The rain in Spain falls mainly on Mark Twain
down the drain on the plane by the window pane.
Have you ever been told this before?
That its tongue was a kilt
the night it read Burns to itself as another.
Another what? bawls the rude ontologist
spiralling modalities from elsewhere.
The halibut cat sat on the mat
thinking this should be that.
Should this hickory be chicory? trickery dock
Chicago or embargo rapes the lock
an avant garde a Kierkegaard iterability dot
the cat bit off my cock
the cuckoo came lame in French that knot
got hotter than Giotto or get off the pot
the razors are read the violins are not
you mean not blue i mean clocks tick
and ticks tock property droperty plops
(it is uncertain in this landscape which "is"
is the telling)
even Polly does the talking when you're well
and when you're walking
where the streams of Heraclitus
water Porphyrian trees which i don't believe in
        please
send me that grin-again-in-again through tocsic toothpaste
'coz i'm wiping the cheeks of my arse poetica

helvitica and dia-betica in sweet vio-
lets pretend we never happened
because the cat *is* on the mat but i don't believe it is
because they cortizoned the mutt and i don't believe they did.
"when i grow up i want to be a virgin
of a version of a brain surgeon, you mean
a drain surgeon, the brain down the drain, coming mainly
from Mark Twain" weather and wetter or knot
the cat drank up the clot of the blood stood still
of the bell rang shrill neither one knowing a lot
about the Phaedrus, or the octopus
clipperty properly schmock
Descartes is in the dock cogito ergo sum
i think he hurt his thumb sucking it
arriving in the posthumous city of vee-eye-pees
without credit cards for the final zinfandel
with Socrates (oh false, wine of the Phaedo) no
the Pheadrus, no the octopus feeding the Pheaedo
no the fido not the walrus no a walnut covered
walrus on a mattress with an octopus no
a mister and a mistress on a walrus on a mattress
pretending to be walnut trees
                    please
play it again Tom an inch from Minsk
in the non pwesence of my non awwival at
survival, severely a Tipperary tipsey juggernaut
at nipsey spurious mimesis of a snapshot ghost
in a park or is it on a moon in june in Spain
watched mainly by Mark Twain not you again
in a fuzzy festival of herbs thrown at
Biology's bigoted request for American elements
African elephants a vigilant applicant frock
eating their curds and whey which weigh
thatterway Anne Hathaway hath half a mile away
a lay-away get a better wetter way
i think i am going to sleep
because the onomatopoeia that are never really here
are here and with a temporary embargo on the itch mites
the surface of their skins becomes a lane again
the lane in Spain again Mark Twain again
polymorphous polyglottal polly put the bottle back

behind the bottle rack in the canto mentioned
in The Castle of Otranto where i happen to be reading this
in esperanto to Horace walrus Horace walnut Horace whirlpool
putting it somewhere i said
i'm writing that Stendhal's still dead.

11

MEGAN SWIHART JEWELL

Taking on the Official Voice: Charles Bernstein's Poetic Sophistry and Post-Process Writing Pedagogy

The teacher talks about reality as if it were motionless, static, compartmentalized, and predictable. Or else he expounds on a topic completely alien to the existential experience of the students. His task is to 'fill' the students with the contents of his narration—contents which are detached from reality, disconnected from the totality that engendered them and could give them significance. Words are emptied of their concreteness and become a hollow, alienated, and alienating verbosity.

—Paulo Freire, *Pedagogy of the Oppressed*[1]

Topic Sentence. However; but; as a result. Blah Blah Blah. It follows from this. Concluding sentence.

—Charles Bernstein, "The Secret of Syntax"[2]

Language poet Charles Bernstein's move from outsider poet to tenured professor in the early 1990s generated controversy at that time from the academic poetry mainstream that he opposed throughout the 1980s and poet-critics associated with the Language movement. Criticisms ranged from attacks on personal character to

---

1 Paulo Freire, *Pedagogy of the Oppressed*, trans. Myra Bergman Ramos (New York: Continuum, 2006), 71.

2 Charles, Bernstein, "The Secret of Syntax," in *Content's Dream: Essays 1975-1984*. (Los Angeles: Sun & Moon Press, 1986), 25.

nostalgia for an impossible poetic avant-garde, and they generally essentialized the nature of institutional influence while discounting the diversity of oppositional practices available within the academy.[3] While in interviews and essays, Bernstein openly addressed his so-called careerism, in his poetics he more actively engaged issues of cooptation through a characteristic sophistic ventriloquism, or direct rhetorical enactment of the discourses constructing such debates.[4] These techniques premiered in *The Sophist* (1987) largely as a critique of mainstream poetry and its associated "official verse culture." In the early 1980s, Bernstein identified "official verse culture" as the academy's predominant poetry network linking creative writing programs and major publishing venues that privilege individual expression in a conventional lyric mode.[5] Since moving into academic positions, he has since extended—through subsequent publications, conference presentations, Internet presence, and teaching—these performative engagements to other arenas of academic culture.[6] Taken together, such strategies compose a poetics of sophism that characterizes Bernstein's work as a Language poet-critic working both within and against the academy. He enacts, as Alan Golding has described it, a distinctly language-oriented and "provisionally complicit resistance" with regard to his institutional position.[7] Ultimately, Bernstein's is

---

3 For a thorough account of the controversy generated by Language Poets' academic positions, see Andrew Epstein, "Verse vs. Verse," *Lingua Franca,* (September 2000), 45-54.

4 In an interview with Jonathan Monroe, Ann Lauterbach, and Bob Perelman, Bernstein cites this nostalgia as unique to poetry: "[critiquing the professional-poet, one inside of the academy making money, receiving health benefits, a pension, etc.] is the idea that the poet is outside of history. It's the idea of innocence. All you have is innocence, outside of history. Poets can play that game very well. You want to claim that you're really somehow a special repository who is closer than everyone else to some kind of ahistorical truth" ("Poetry Community and Movement: A Conversation," *Diacritics* 26: 3–4 [1996], 199).

5 Bernstein coined this term in a 1983 Modern Language Association presentation, "The Academy in Peril: William Carlos Williams Meets the MLA," subsequently reprinted in *Content's Dream,* 244-51.

6 See Alan Golding, "Charles Bernstein and Professional Avant-Gardism," *Talisman* 36/37 (Fall 2008/Winter 2009): 28–42 for a reading of Bernstein's ventriloquistic engagement with themes of his reception and cooptation in *Dark City* (1994) and other works appearing after his hiring at SUNY Buffalo in 1990.

7 See Golding's chapter, "Provisionally Complicit Resistance: Language Writing and the Institution(s) of Poetry," in his book, *From Outlaw to Classic: Canons in American Poetry.* (Madison: University of Wisconsin Press, 1995). Golding borrows the term "provisionally complicit resistance" from poet-critic Rachel Blau DuPlessis's book

an interventionist poetics with continuing implications in terms of assessing post-avant influence on professional poetic and critical practices.

In this essay, I will focus on how Bernstein's poetic sophistry, as illustrated by his statements on teaching and his poems in *The Sophist*, represents an intervention into institutionalized writing pedagogies, specifically the Expressivist models of English composition predominant in the academy in the late 1960s and early 1970s and still evident in current practices.[8] Often associated with Process-based writing pedagogy, which articulates a model of composition carried out in distinct stages (e.g., pre-writing, drafting, revising), Expressivist writing teachers emphasize the cultivation among students of a uniquely individual voice, a private vision with access to universal truths.[9] The Expressivist method is generally considered a reaction against the Current-Traditionalist methods prominent at mid-century and concerned mostly with style and correctness. As James Berlin has characterized it, in contrast to Current-Traditional assumptions, Expressivist pedagogy "places the self at the center of communication" drawing from a distinctly Platonic rhetoric of selfhood; it therefore follows that Bernstein's poetics, aimed as it is at exposing the constructed nature of the rhetorical "I," represents a radical revisioning of the relationship of the composing subject to the written word.[10] In its direct engagement of individual voice, Bernstein's

---

of poems *Tabula Rosa* (Potes & Poets Press, 1987). Since 2003, Bernstein has held the position of Donald T. Regan Professor of English and Comparative Literature at the University of Pennsylvania.

8   Here I am agreeing with Tom Orange's observation that writing instruction in the academy hardly adheres to one particular dominant mode: "Disciplinary histories are of course rarely linear, with emergent, dominant, and residual formations (to use the *parlance* of Raymond Williams) always existing contemporaneously, and while postprocess critiques such as those by David Bartholomae and Patricia Bizzell have nuanced our notions of voice considerably they have hardly eliminated process-oriented concepts altogether" (116-117). (Tom Orange, "Performing Authority: Gysin, Bergvall, and the Critique of Expressivist Pedagogy," *ESC: English Studies in Canada*, 33:4 (2007), 115-126.)

9   The frequent conflation of Process-based and Expressivist pedagogies is largely due to the fact that both were developed at the same historical moment in reaction against post-war current-traditionalist pedagogical practices, and both were developed by three primary composition theorists: Janet Emig, Peter Elbow, and Donald Murray. The process model of writing instruction may be situated as a specific technique of writerly empowerment within an Expressivist pedagogical framework.

10   James Berlin. "Contemporary Composition: The Major Pedagogical Theories."

volume *The Sophist*, in particular, promotes a recognition of how context-specific discourses, including the academic modes in which students are frequently expected to effortlessly maneuver, necessarily serve to mediate the representation of one's writerly identity.

In this sense — given in part its critique of the unrestrained expressivism characteristic of 1970s and 80s "official," or workshop-oriented, verse — Bernstein's poetics strongly resembles current Post-process positions on writing pedagogy. A theory-informed body of approaches developed largely in reaction against Process-based instruction, Post-process methods attempt to shift writing instruction away from self-knowledge and onto discourse recognition, promoting instead students' awareness of the inherently situated nature of writing. Revisiting *The Sophist* in light of recent Post-process ideas serves to identify salient historical connections between critical and creative methods of writing instruction, particularly in terms of the varying influence of theory on both.[11] Yet, more importantly, it also has significant implications for classroom practices in that it can provide instructors of composition with essential context on the rhetoric of selfhood that is useful for teaching students to negotiate academic discourses. Therefore, this reconsideration of Bernstein's poetics in terms of post-secondary writing instruction opens up important spaces for innovative poetics' continued intervention into professional academic practices — not only within the academy, but within what is arguably the most ubiquitous of its classrooms, that of composition.

Bernstein has contributed to recent collections of essays by poets and teachers arguing the value of teaching modern and contemporary innovative poetics for its particular ability to empower readers to negotiate within cultural discourses.[12] This is a skill he believes that is fundamentally lacking in Freshman composition, which he sees as characterized by overemphasis on standardized expository-style writ-

---

In *Cross-Talk in Comp Theory: A Reader*, 2nd ed., ed. Victor Villanueva (Urbana, IL: National Council of Teachers of English, 2003), 255-70.

11   As Tom Orange points out, "there are close and distant parallels to be drawn," between the disciplinary narrative of writing instruction and "other areas of language, literature, and literacy studies: English, Creative Writing, Literature, Literary Theory, Linguistics, Communications, and so on" (116).

12   The collections to which I refer are Joan Retallack and Juliana Spahr, eds. *Poetry and Pedagogy: The Challenge of the Contemporary* (New York: Palgrave Macmillan, 2006), and Peter Middleton and Nicky Marsh, eds. *Teaching Modernist Poetry* (Basingstoke UK: Palgrave Macmillan, 2010).

ing that fails to promote critical reading. The classroom exercises and
other teaching practices that he shares in these essays, along with
other statements he has made on teaching, reflect his longstanding
concern with promoting readerly agency through a multi-generic
poetics of disruption and performance and ultimately apply to how
his own poetic experiments work to bring about an awareness of
the social nature, or situatedness, of writing in the composition
classroom. Joan Retallack and Juliana Spahr argue that "an immediately obvious pedagogical implication" of teaching such post 1960's
avant-garde works "has to do with the ways in which these poetries
demand an active making of meaning on the part of the reader—a
performative dimension that enacts a significant linguistic agency."[13]
Characterizations of the avant-garde similar to Retallack and Spahr's
have long been used to describe the political motivations of the
Language poets, most notably Bernstein, who believes that linguistic
agency is only made possible by promoting in readers an awareness
of language as a socially constructed system mediating reality. At the
time in the 1980s when Language poets were beginning to receive
critical attention by scholars of poetry and theory, Andrew Ross characterized the Language school perspective as the Wittengensteinian
belief that "language is not *about* the world, but *in* the world." [14] He
writes that language is seen by the poets as the "'constructive' fabric
of social reality," and "[t]o ignore the need to respond consciously
to that process of linguistic mediation and construction is to effectively renounce any hope of partial understanding, let alone control
of that social reality."[15] Language poets' experimentalism has always
been concerned with promoting readerly awareness of how "dominant political codes, the system of capital and the traces of its history,
are on 'display' in the language we use, and is therefore inherently
pedagogical."[16]

In his current modernist and contemporary experimental poetry
classrooms, Bernstein has replicated the pedagogical experience of
reading experimentalist works, aiming to empower his student read-

13   Joan Retallack and Juliana Spahr, eds. *Poetry and Pedagogy: The Challenge of the Contemporary* (New York: Palgrave Macmillan, 2006), 3.

14   Ross, Andrew. "The New Sentence and Commodity Form: Recent American Writing," in *Marxism and the Interpretation of Culture*, Cary Nelson and Lawrence Grossberg, eds. (Chicago: University of Chicago Press, 1987), 361-380, 372. Emphasis original.

15   Ross, 372

16   Ross, 372.

ers to uncover the social nature of language through an immersive process of active reading and writing. Although not a creative writing workshop environment per se, Bernstein in what he calls his "Writing Experiments Seminar," has students write creative responses to the poems he teaches in what he instead terms a "creative (w)reading workshop."[17] Referring to his class as "a course in anti- or para- or pluri-composition," and therefore as an "antidote to Freshman Comp," Bernstein writes that it "has its value not for budding poets only, or primarily, or exclusively, but for all writers. It's less a workshop than a lab, with experiments in mutant forms conducted on the textual body of living language."[18] His intentions toward readerly empowerment as generated through an active contact with the inner-workings of language are unmistakable. Noting that one of his students refers to the class as "abnormal writing," Bernstein writes:

> I figure the more you know how to take words apart and put them together, the more aspects of language you've turned up, down, left, right, inside out, and outside in, the better you will be able to respond to the many contingencies, screwballs and curve balls, and monkey wrenches that language will inevitably throw your way. Like my main man says, Whose in control, me or the words? (*Whose* is, that's who).[19]

He writes that "an approach like this makes for proactive readers by potentiating proactive approaches to writing" (171). While reading experimental poetics pushes readers out of their comfort zones and into a recognition of the social nature of language, creatively (w)reading/ writing in a performative classroom space only serves to multiply the benefits. Students' engagement in discursive performance is a distinct form of sophistry fundamental to the pedagogical value of Bernstein's poetics. In other words, it encourages students to examine the ways in which discourses might shape their responses —instead of the other way around—and thus represents an intervention into the expressivist "I" Bernstein has throughout his work

---

17 Bernstein, Charles. "Wreading, Writing, Wresponding" in Peter Middleton and Nicky Marsh, eds. *Teaching Modernist Poetry* (Basingstoke UK: Palgrave Macmillan, 2010), 170.

18 Bernstein, "Wreading," 171.

19 Bernstein, "Wreading," 171.

identified as a disempowering impediment to critical thinking, and that, as will be discussed, current Post-Process compositionists view as similarly problematic.

Bernstein's critique of the "I" can be traced back to his particular critique of the "official verse culture" of the 1970s and 1980s that he directly engages in *The Sophist*. This "I" as it functions in *The Sophist*, often manifests as the "official voice," representing on one level the overuse of the first person in the kinds of mainstream verse that Bernstein viewed as being promoted by the academy and major publishing houses, and, on another level, a general rhetorical device used within public discourses to maintain a conservative status quo. In this sense, the "official voice" resembles a voice-over, a controlling narrative designed to maintain unity at the expense of the disruption Bernstein sees as vital to a politically engaged poetics. Written within two years of *The Sophist*, the essay "State of the Art" explains how such rhetoric operates in both poetics and national culture, underscoring the complicity between both manifestations of the "official voice." In "State of the Art," Bernstein links the "primacy of the individual voice, fanned by a genteel inspiration," and the "well-wrought epiphany of predictable measure" characteristic of certain types of mainstream verse to political ideologies characteristic of American politics.[20] His position is that official verse edits out difference in order to provide the illusion of consensus: "As with George [H.W.] Bush's attempt to discredit special interests," he writes about mainstream poetry, "in the end we find the center is a little wizard with an elaborate sound and light show, good table manners, and preferred media access."[21] These empty rhetorics promote "social derealization."[22] They are easily-digestible narratives that gain favor due to their ability to seamlessly assimilate into the dominant culture. These narratives rely thoroughly on a representative, expressive "I," the vehicle of so-called common understanding.

In a 1996 interview, Bernstein discussed how this cultural emphasis on the expressive "I," as it has translated to the writing classroom, also does students a disservice in terms of developing a critical recognition of language and the discursive cooptation of meaning.[23] In this interview, Bernstein most explicitly links his

---

20 Bernstein, Charles. *A Poetics*. (Cambridge: Harvard University Press, 1992), 2.

21 Bernstein, *A Poetics*, 2.

22 Bernstein, *A Poetics*, 2.

23 Bové, Paul. "On Poetry, Language, and Teaching: A Conversation with Charles

poetics to composition writing pedagogy, making clear his position against what he sees as an educational overemphasis on personal expression. He argues that what is the Process-based move away from mid-century "punishment and correction" models of writing instruction to more personal, indeed lyrical, modes of expression does not work to empower subjugated students, as it once, in part, originally intended to do. [24] Instead, given the weight it places on developing one's individual voice, Expressivist pedagogy disempowers students by eliding the other rhetorical choices available to them as writers. While not arguing against completely eliminating the teaching of personal essays, which he believes can be useful for breaking down a "hegemonic, authoritative, discourse structure," particularly in terms of gender, he views their framing in the academy as "[resonating] with the precepts of official verse culture—subjectivity, lyric, authenticity, the unified voice."[25] The institutional overemphasis on "personal expression and 'creativity' as the alternative to rigorous exposition" does little to expose students to the linguistic difference he sees vital to critical thinking. Bernstein writes that he imagines instead a composition program wherein students work "in and on a series of different language projects, employing different shapes, styles, forms and exploring how these make for different meanings, where meaning is understood as something socially and aesthetically—as much logically as lexically—determined."[26] Yet, in the writing classroom, "[e]xpression has become a social safety valve that turns us from the difficulty of form to the affirmation of content, which is to say from the difficulty of thought to the manipulation of sanctioned emotions."[27] Much as he has made a case in his poetics against "official verse culture," with its endorsement of readily understood emotions, he makes a case in this interview for the benefits of teaching experimental poetry for empowering students: "Watered-down personal or scenic narrative," he asserts, is a form of "running away from the diversity of forms, structures, syntaxes, vocabularies, and sounds that make [experimental] poetry a play of, and in, linguistic difference."[28] In other words, students should be

---

Bernstein," *boundary 2* 23:2 (Fall 1996), 45-66. This interview took place with David Bartholomae, Lynn Emanuel, Colin MacCabe, and Paul Bové.

24 Bové, 50.

25 Bové, 49.

26 Bové, 51.

27 Bové, 54.

28 Bové, 54.

exposed to and immersed in a particularly abnormal writing, such as that characterizing his current Writing Experiments Seminar.

Most Post-process theorists similarly react against an institutional overemphasis on Expressivist methods and find similar pedagogical value in the written performance of difference. As mentioned, Post-process writing pedagogy developed as a response against the process-based methods of writing instruction developed in the early 1970s. While process theorists privilege the development of individual expression, those associated with the Post-process movement are unified by a belief in the social nature of writing — we are always writing in relation to others –and are more invested in its inherently interpretative, situated nature.[29] Those associated with Post-process pedagogy reject the notion that writing practices can be represented by a "generalized process or a Big Theory" and will often call attention to the extent to which process-based pedagogy has been taken for granted as the universal mode of writing instruction within the academy.[30] Further, as Gary Olson writes, "process theorists assume that we can make statements about the process that would apply to all or most writing situations," and therefore most of the time unwittingly deploy a Western cultural "rhetoric of assertion," which is "masculinist, phallogocentric, foundationalist, often essentialist, and, at the very least, limiting."[31] Olson suggests that drawing upon the works of theorists outside of composition who write from marginalized positions outside of the dominant discourse can help to "subvert such a tradition" to counter this official voice.[32] While Olson offers Donna Haraway's "cyborg writing" as a antidote to the masculinist rhetoric of western scientific rhetoric, following this line of thinking, one might also consider poet-critic Rachel Blau DuPlessis's writing "otherhow." As Jonathan Monroe points out, DuPlessis's experimental writings serve as a prime example of the kinds of "antigeneric, multigenre writings [that] offer much-needed alternatives, at once cogent and capacious, varied and various, to normative approaches to writing both within and beyond the university."[33] An exposure to

29 Kent, Thomas. "Introduction," In *Post-Process Theory: Beyond the Writing-Process Paradigm*. Thomas Kent, ed. (Carbondale and Edwardsville: Southern Illinois University Press, 1999), 3.

30 Kent, *Post-Process*, 3.

31 Olson, Gary. "Toward a Post-Process Composition: Abandoning the Rhetoric of Assertion," in *Post-Process Theory: Beyond the Writing-Process Paradigm*. Thomas Kent, ed. (Carbondale and Edwardsville: Southern Illinois University Press, 1999), 7.

32 Olson, "Toward," 7–8.

33 Monroe, Jonathan. ")Writing Writing(," in *Poetry and Pedagogy: The Challenge*

these kinds of abnormal discourses, what Roland Barthes might call "acratic" discourses—discourses outside of power—hold the key to helping students critically recognize, and, as it is implied, successfully negotiate within normative academic modes naturalized within academe.[34] As Bernstein states in the 1996 interview, the awareness brought about by more challenging modes of writing is fundamental: "if you consider the limitations of, and possibilities for, each form and each standard, you create a more open and democratic conception of language practices that does not preclude the importance of standardized forms but rather sees those for what they are—the dominant choice, which you may need as a survival skill, but which has no direct relation to truth or coherence."[35] The abnormal writing he submits in *The Sophist* serves as a prime example of the ways in which experimental poetics can bring about this critical recognition of these otherwise invisible official discourses.

Yet, helping readers differentiate between writing skillfully and writing truthfully is perhaps *The Sophist's* most crucial pedagogical lesson. Indeed, by promoting in readers a recognition that there actually exists a difference between these two kinds of writing, Bernstein's poetic sophistry represents an intervention in writing instructional methods since mid-century requiring, as it does, a radical repositioning of the self to others. As mentioned, Process-based writing instruction developed in reaction against the Current-traditionalist instructional mode, what Bernstein has referred to as the "punishment and correction" model.[36] Concerned with correct grammar and knowledge of rhetorical convention, Current-traditional rhetoric was governed by an underlying New Critical investment in the notion of literary talent and original expression. Under its rubrics, students were expected to locate and then eloquently express an external truth independent from the self.[37] In contrast, Process-oriented writ-

---

of the Contemporary. Joan Retallack and Juliana Spahr, eds. (New York: Palgrave Macmillan, 2006), 65.

34 In *The Rustle of Language*, Barthes distinguishes acratic language from encratic language, the language of power that imposes itself as natural, as Doxa. See Barthes, Roland, *The Rustle of Language*, trans. Richard Howard (Berkeley: University of California Press, 1989), 120.

35 Bové, 51.

36 Bové, 51.

37 See Berlin, James, "Contemporary Composition," for an overview of how composition theorists have viewed the relation of the writing subject to truth. He writes that reactions against Current-Traditionalist rhetoric are analogous to the differ-

ing instructors in the late 1960s and early 1970s encouraged students
to look inward to find "authentic" meaning. Individual self-expression, including the development of one's unique voice, was emphasized in "teacherless" classrooms promoting students' growth and
discovery. Such composition classrooms were not unlike the concur-
rently-developed, content-less writing workshop models where
students' primary focus remains on developing their own voices. Yet,
as much emphasis was placed on empowering the individual through
personal expression, most theorists associated with Process pedagogy
shied away from fully interrogating the role of the subject in writing.
As Sharon Crowley points out, Process pedagogy "retains the modernist composing subject of current-traditionalism—the subject who is
sufficiently discrete from the composing context to stand apart from
it, observing it from above and commenting upon it"[38] Moreover,
"this subject is able to inspect the contents of the mind and report
them to a reader without distortion, using language that represents
a well-formed composing intention."[39] Post-process theorists view
the notion of a coherent speaking subject with access to universal
truths as not only theoretically untenable, but, in terms of writing
instruction, highly problematic, in terms of its failure to account for
marginalized groups denied access to the dominant modes of expression. Bernstein similarly interrogates the notion of a unified speaking subject while enacting in *The Sophist* the very distortion that can
occur when one merely situates the writing subject, or the "I," in
terms of larger social contexts. In so doing he will often intervene at
the precise moment of Crowley's "well-formed composing intention"
in order to illustrate to readers the ways in which the private self is
constructed by public discourses.[40]

---

ence that Richard Rorty sees between hermeneutic and epistemological philosophy in *Philosophy and the Mirror of Nature* (Princeton: Princeton University Press,
1979). Berlin writes: "The hermeneutic approach to rhetoric bases the discipline
on establishing an open dialogue in the hopes of reaching agreement about the
truth of the matter at hand. Current-Traditional Rhetoric views the rhetorical situation as an arena where the truth is incontrovertibly established by a speaker or
writers more enlightened than her audience. For the hermeneuticist truth is never
fixed finally on unshakable grounds. Instead it emerges only after false starts and
failures, and can only represent a tentative point of rest in a continuing conversation" (268).

38   Crowley, Sharon. *Composition in the University: Historical and Polemical Essays.*
(Pittsburgh: University of Pittsburgh Press, 1998), 213.

39   Crowley, *Composition*, 213.

40   Crowley, *Composition*, 213.

In *The Sophist*, it is Bernstein's poetic ventriloquism that works to reveal how the concept of individual voice, or, the "guise of a coherent persona" is not only a nostalgic denial of postmodern realities, but also a meaningless rhetorical device.[41] He calls attention to the constructed nature of the "I" by inhabiting various personae and by utilizing syntactical disruption and the unrelenting de-contextualization of narrative. The poems "A Person is Not an Entity Symbolic, but the Divine Incarnate" and "Foreign Body Sensation" provide pertinent examples of Bernstein's pedagogical techniques. In "A Person is Not an Entity Symbolic, but the Divine Incarnate," Bernstein explicitly calls attention to the ideology of authentic selfhood upon which so many confessional lyrics rely by connecting it directly to the rhetorical "I." The title refers to the initial rejection of theory by some creative writing programs. The growth of theory in the academy throughout the late 1970s and 1980s created what would become a disciplinary divide between critical and creative programs housed within English departments and Bernstein's poem certainly reveals this tension. According to the poem's hyperbolic, ironic title, these poets not only reject the possibility of selfhood as a construction, a symbolic entity, or even the slightest bit vulnerable. Rather, in compensation for the theory's perceived threat, they elevate the "I," rendering it transcendent or "divine." Section seven of the 26-section poem, "Latex Dummy," illustrates just this point. Bernstein writes:

> I feel I mean I am I consider I can I wish I cut I find I
> wonder I know I lie down I saw I dream I laugh out loud I
> experience confusion I realize I slap my knee I feel closer
> I try I break lines I shrug I answer I look I get at I lift I
> choose up.[42]

This litany of "I's" and verbs-without-objects represents the obvious self-centeredness of official verse poems. In fact, these self-actualizing phrases are not unlike the mantras found in many of the self-help books first becoming ubiquitous in the mid-to-late 70s, best-selling books such as *I'm OK, You're OK*; *The Predictable Crises of Adult Life*; and *How to be Your Own Best Friend*. As Jed Rasula remarks, it is no accident that "the boom years of the Associated Writing Programs as a growth industry were the 1970s, a decade notable for the rise of the

---

41 Bernstein, *A Poetics*, 3.
42 Bernstein, *The Sophist*, 147.

self-help publishing market."[43] Indeed, by the last two lines of "Latex Dummy," the speaker becomes a poet:" I break/lines."[44] It follows then that Bernstein invites a comparison between official verse poets and conformist groups, encouraging a recognition of how an emphasis on the "I" does not convey a uniqueness of self, but instead suggests a cult of the first-person ironically privileging individual "choice." The disruptive "I," which visibly serves to break lines in the poem, thoroughly exposes itself as a construction.

In "Foreign Body Sensation," Bernstein issues the reader an "IMPORTANT NOTICE ABOUT YOUR RATES":

> *You put your whole self in*
> *You put your whole self out*
> *You put your whole self in*
> *& shake it all about.*[45]

Note how the "whole self" in Bernstein version of the children's game is never *taken out*, but always *put out* (104) indicating the absurdly confessional nature of the lyric self. The 20 or so lines following the rhyme include random corporate-style quotations ("Forget the blue./ Nobody's ever advocated blue.") that continue to disperse the concept of the "whole self."[46] The reader then encounters the following personal testimony:

> I am especially interested in the treatment of my depression. With my Lord and Savior Jesus Christ at the center of my life, I have found real Joy and Purpose in dedicating myself to the Truth of His Teaching as Written in the Bible. What gives the job it's [sic] excitement is working with Stan Richards, a nationally recognized creative wizard: *Adweek* recently named   our agency among the eight most creative in the U.S. I moved into this area after six years in the aerospace industry, which I entered after early retirement from a career as a venture capitalist and real estate developer. This has been a stimulating opportu-

---

43 Rasula, Jed. *The American Poetry Wax Museum: Reality Effects, 1940-1990.* (Urbana, IL: National Council of Teachers of English, 1996,) 421.

44 Bernstein, *The Sophist*, 147.

45 Bernstein, Charles. *The Sophist.* (Los Angeles: Sun & Moon, 1987), 104.

46 Bernstein, *The Sophist*, 105.

nity for my work on late Pleistocene and early Holocene environmental changes. Pat is currently in Sri Lanka helping organize sera collection for leprosy patients. Nowadays being a husband, father, homeowner, and Jew keeps me both busy and satisfied. I find myself immersed in a foreign but also satisfyingly tangible world of container shipping.[47]

The passage goes on for another page, accumulating more of these narratives as it progresses. Because the narratives are all framed in the first person (and lumped together in one paragraph), Bernstein intends the reader to recognize how an overemphasis on "I" leads to self-promoting discourses that eventually become indistinguishable from one another. The experiences of a depressed person undergoing religious conversion become conflated with advertising promotion, and venture capitalism, which in turn affects branches of science such as archaeology, allowing its researcher a "stimulating opportunity."[48] At one point, the discourse breaks down into the sentence, "I guess I," with the overused "I" being the only recognizable remnant of these blended-together scripts through which, ultimately, all difference is erased.[49] Juxtaposing the speakers' various appeals to commonplace authority figures, such as Jesus, a nationally-recognized "creative wizard," and the editors at a published magazine, helps readers to recognize the particularly overwrought nature of that common rhetorical maneuver.[50] The final lesson: the self is not necessarily whole, but can be easily constructed as such through various rhetorical moves. This poem essentially serves as a fill-in-the blank template for anyone writing an easily-absorbed personal testimony while exposing that mode as completely devoid of critical content.

Nearly 20 years after the publication of *The Sophist*, with the development of more rhetoric-based, post-process pedagogical techniques, current composition teachers are catching on to the usefulness of experimentalist tactics for situating writing. Gerald Graff and Cathy Birkenstein's recent textbook *They Say / I Say* (2006) demonstrates how the de-contextualization of academic discourses similar to Bernstein's

---

47 Bernstein, *The Sophist*, 105.
48 Bernstein, *The Sophist*, 105.
49 Bernstein, *The Sophist*, 106.
50 Bernstein, *The Sophist*, 105.

innovative techniques for exposing the rhetorical self in *The Sophist* can serve as a valuable pedagogical tool. Unlike Bernstein's poetics, *They Say/I Say* was written for explicit use for teaching writing, but it illustrates the same pedagogical emphasis on discursive performance. While *They Say/I Say* was influenced by Graff's 2003 book *Clueless in Academe*, wherein he emphasizes the importance of teaching students argument, one could easily suggest that in its aim to "democratize academic culture" it is as equally influenced David Bartholomae's essay, "Inventing the University" (1985).[51] Here, Bartholomae focuses on literacy issues among basic (or developmental) writing popula-tions, diagnosing students' writing problems not in terms of their unfamiliarity with grammar and mechanics, but instead viewing error in terms of their lack of access to academic discourses, or "codes."[52] (Bartholmae borrows the term "codes," from Basil B. Bernstein, whose research on class codes Charles Bernstein cites in 1996 as being fundamental to his view on the language indoctrination within the university.[53]) When reading incoming student writing diagnos-tics, Bartholomae finds that students tend to over-generalize ideas by using commonplace phrases often appearing disjointed and incon-sistent in person. For example, one student concludes an essay writ-ten entirely in the first person by suddenly shifting to direct address. After describing his work as a mechanic, the student is required by the essay's prompt to analyze the experience. Instead of a providing a technical or more "academic" discussion, the student provides a generalized truism, or "Lesson on Life."[54] The student concludes his essay as follows: "[m]ost important, worry about yourself, and keep a clear eye on everyone, for there's always someone trying to take advantage of you, anytime anyplace."[55] Rather than focusing on the essay's technical pronominal lapses, Bartholomae finds more signifi-cance in the rhetorical tendency toward generalization made by this and other students without access to academic codes. In this and in the other instances that Bartholomae cites, students lack access to

---

51 Graff, Gerald and Cathy Birkenstein, *They Say/I Say* (New York: W.W. Norton & Company, 2007), x.

52 Bartholomae, David, "Inventing the University," in *Cross-Talk in Comp Theory: A Reader*, 2nd ed., ed. Victor Villanueva (Urbana, IL: National Council of Teachers of English, 2003), 623-653.

53 Bové, 47.

54 Bartholomae,"Inventing," 626.

55 Bartholomae,"Inventing," 626.

academic authority, which requires "a special vocabulary, a special system of presentation, and an interpretative scheme," and so they invoke a commonplace form of authority, a Lesson on Life.[56] This is similar to how Bernstein's non-analytical speakers in "Foreign Body Sensation" invoke readily-available forms of authority in order to bolster their own credibility among readers. "To speak with authority," concludes Bartholomae,

> writers have to speak not only in another's voice but through another's code; and they not only have to do this, they have to speak in the voice and through the codes of those of us with power and wisdom; and they not only have to do this, they have to do it before they know what they are doing, before they have a project to participate in, and before, at least in terms of our disciplines, they have anything to say.[57]

In order to provide students with a distinctly academic authority, Bartholomae argues that teachers must define and identify academic discourse conventions so they can be "written out, 'demystified' and taught in our classrooms."[58]

Graff and Birkenstein's *They Say/ I Say* sets out to do exactly that—to provide students with the codes needed to maneuver within academic discourse and to successfully participate in scholarly conversations. In their textbook, Graff and Birkenstein provide students with a series of templates designed to both improve their writing skills, to help them to become more skilled readers of academic prose, and, as a result, to develop a more critical interpretative scheme. The textbook demystifies academic conventions while, by privileging the notion of writing as argument, simultaneously undermining the importance of individual perspective. This pedagogical impulse is the same as that which motivates *The Sophist*, and like Bernstein's poetry, the textbook helps students to recognize official discourses by exposing them in a template-like form. As Graff and Birkenstein write: "One virtue of such templates, we found, is that they focus writers' attention not just on what is said, but on the *forms* that structure what is being said. In other words, they help students focus on the rhetori-

---

56 Bartholomae,"Inventing," 626.

57 Bartholomae, "Inventing," 644.

58 Bartholomae, "Inventing," 635.

cal patterns that are key to academic success but often pass under the classroom radar."[59] Importantly, just as Bernstein in *The Sophist* is hardly encouraging the production of more cookie-cutter personal narratives within official verse, Graff and Birkenstein's goal in offering a template approach to academic writing is not to indoctrinate students into academic discourse by encouraging the rote memorization of these formulaic expressions. Noting the implicit synthesis between reading and writing, the authors defend their templates from possible detractors:

> While seasoned writers pick up these moves unconsciously through their reading, many students do not. Consequently, we believe, students need to see these moves represented in the explicit ways that writers provide. . . .The aim of the templates, then, is not to stifle creativity, but to be direct with students about the key rhetorical moves that comprise it.[60]

A popular writing manual now in its second paperback edition, *They Say/ I Say* begins by introducing students to the notion of situated writing—or the importance of what "they say," as opposed to the monologic "I say," the focus of the Process-based classroom. "To make an impact as a writer," the authors instruct, "you need to do more than make statements that are logical, well-supported, and consistent. You must also find a way of entering a conversation with others' views—with something 'they say'. . . . For it is what others are saying and thinking that motivates our writing and gives it a reason for being."[61] The authors then provide students with a series of explanations of and templates for introducing what "they say," and how to always situate the "I say," within that ever-changing context. While the rest of the textbook provides more templates for strengthening arguments, such as "simultaneously agreeing and disagreeing," "planting a naysayer in your text," and the "art of metacommentary," the emphasis is always firmly placed upon what *they* are saying. Their introduction, "Entering the Conversation," provides some models:

> She argues _____ and I agree because _____.

---

59 Graff and Birkenstein, xi.

60 Graff and Birkenstein, *They Say/I Say*, xv.

61 Graff and Birkenstein, *They Say/I Say*, 4.

> Her argument that _____ is supported by new research
> showing that _____.   He claims that _____, and I have
> mixed feelings about it. On the   one hand, I agree that
> _____. On the other hand, I still insist that _____.[62]

The authors also give examples of more elaborated templates for
acknowledging what they say:

> In recent discussions of _____, a controversial issue has
> been   whether _____. On the one hand, some argue that
> _____. From this perspective, _____. On the other hand,
> however, others argue that _____. In the words of one of
> this view's main proponents, "_____." According to this
> view, _____. In sum then, the issue is whether _____ or
> _____. My own view is that _____. Though I concede that
> _____, I still maintain that _____. For example, _____.
> Although some might object that _____, I reply
> that _____. The issue is important because _____.[63]

In essence, these templates are, as Graff has remarked, "Brechtian
defamiliarization techniques" designed as much to promote students'
recognition of the particular features of academic prose—and by
extension other discourses—as they are to improve the quality of
their thinking and writing.[64] Like the poems in *The Sophist*, such
models explicitly promote among student-readers the abandonment
of self and the recognition of discursive performance. While unlike
"Foreign Body Sensation," these templates provide an explicit "they
say," the end result is similar: students must necessarily contextual-
ize and then situate—or perform—the "I" in terms of larger social
contexts. While *The Sophist* might be said to show readers "what not to
do," in their writing, *They Say/I Say* shows them exactly "what to do"
while promoting the same important de-emphasis on the primacy of
the self.

The template-like structure of *The Sophist* serves to reinforce this
pedagogical gesture. The book is unified according to a principle of
difference, which, as Ron Silliman points out, results in a "dizzy-

---

62 Graff and Birkenstein, *They Say/I Say*, 9.

63 Graff and Birkenstein, *They Say/I Say*, 9.

64 Graff, Gerald, "A Template Approach to Academic Writing," (workshop, Case
Western Reserve University, Cleveland, OH, April 15, 2009)

ing performance."[65] As Silliman points out in detail, the works that follow the first poem include a narrative prose poem, a one-act play whose characters are Liubov Popova, Jenny Lind, and John Milton; the ventriloquist poem "Outrigger," with structured lineation; a long, single-stanza poem; another prose story; a 16-line two stanza "From Lines of Swinburne," another poem with more open lineation, a poem entirely composed of short segments divided by asterisks, and so on.[66] As Hank Lazer remarks about this structure, "Bernstein gives enough space to so many vocabularies and rhetorics that no one style or position can possibly emerge as comprehensive."[67] While Silliman reads this as a sophistic evasion of the center, "impossible to nail," one might also consider how each poem might serve as an enactment of both the performance—or abandonment of the self—necessary to successfully critically maneuver within a variety of disciplinary—in this case poetic— styles.[68] In other words, Bernstein is not only showing off his poetic versatility, but, by refusing to settle into one particular mode, he relentlessly de-contextualizes precisely in order to re-contextualize so as to model for readers the necessity of doing the same. He has discussed the pedagogical value of using imitation in the classroom as "a rhetorical exercise that pushes against the assumptions of unmediated expression or subjectivity or sincerity. Imitation can also show how difficult it is to write in a style that either you like or don't like. Encouraging students to try out do what they resistant to, is, after all, much of what we do as teachers."[69]

Again, this emphasis on discursive performance is similar to the underlying pedagogy of *They Say/I Say,* which similarly attempts to move students away from an emphasis on unmediated self-expression. As Gary Olson points out, an experimental writing of difference—or abnormal writing on the outside of dominant rhetoric—has pedagogical benefits for both teachers in terms of reconsidering their practice or for students in a Post-process classroom.[70] Following from this, one could easily make a case for the consider-

---

65 Silliman, Ron, "The Text, the Beloved? Bernstein's *Sophist*" in *The Sophist*, Charles Bernstein, (Cambridge: Salt, 2004), x.

66 Silliman, "The Text," x–xi.

67 Lazer, Hank. *Opposing Poetries: Volume 2—Readings* (Evanston, IL: Northwestern University Press, 1996), 13.

68 Silliman, "The Text," xi.

69 Bové, 65

70 Olson, "Toward,"15.

ation by composition instructors of most experimental Language writing, given the very disruption it performs into normalized writing practices and the resulting light it sheds onto the contexts requiring such standardized forms. Specifically, however, by underscoring the over-generalization that tends to occur in the absence of a critical interpretative scheme, and by emphasizing the performance of different discourses, Bernstein's poetics proves particularly useful. Most importantly—however either the poetics itself, or the ideas it promotes, are employed—*The Sophist* has the potential to encourage among the numerous instructors of university composition a (re-) consideration of the rhetorical "I" that could be radically empowering to beginning academic writers.

12

RON SILLIMAN

From *The Alphabet*

from *What*

The flower sermon:
critique is like a swoon
but with a step increase,
the awkward daughter who grows
to join the NBA. All we want
(ever wanted) was to be on that
mailing list, parties at which slim caterers
offer red, yellow, black caviar
spilling off the triangular crackers
while off on the bay
rainbow-striped sails dip and bob and
twist. The woman in the yellow raincoat sits
on a bench at the edge of the schoolyard
while two small children race
across the asphalt plaza. Too many books
sail the moth. A tooth that's lost
while flossing. A short line
makes for anxious music. Not breath
but civilization. The president
of Muzak himself says
that humming along constitutes time theft.
First snow in the Sierras = cold showers here.
The east is past. Margin of terror. The left
is where you feel it (dragging the eyes back
contra naturum). We're just in it
for the honey. Spackling paste
edits nails in wall when painted. Elbows,

shoulders jammed together on the bus.
At each transfer point, glimpse how lives
weave past. A woman with an interesting book
in her purse which I pretend not to see.
Letters crowd into a thought. Green paper
folded around long-stemmed roses
is stapled shut. Rapid winter sunset
lacks twilight. They take out the breast
and part of the lymph system. I
stare through a lens at the near world.
Hot tea sits dark in its cup.
Seeing is deceiving. Big tears
are eyes' response
to a dawn chill, first frost.
Clang of empty bottles in a paper sack.
The boulevard was a kind of free verse,
big noun skyscrapers, until the freeway
blew out the margin. Baseball cap
with the bill worn to the side or back.
Steam pours plume-like
from the roof of the new
senior tower. Thus lawn-sprinklers
sweep the air. This wool hat
itchy on your forehead, those
mysterious white sores
that dot the mouth.
New boots with Leather-Plus uppers
and waffler stomper soles. The way
gas stations dwindled overnight,
now go the banks: people
huddle in the rain
as close as they can to the wall
lined up for the automated teller.
But I just want to snuggle.
Jumping the curb on my skateboard. Even
before the war was over, vets
began to fill the J.C.s on the GI bill,
men playing rummy on the quad at lunch.
The way street folk make the sidewalk their bench.
Taking my glasses off, sensing
the muscles in the eye
flex as they refocus. Cars

at a stop light, each with its own
lone rider. Standing on the bus,
using both hands to hold on.
The sun in the trees still,
slowly rising. Beeper on a belt.
The container inverted
shall never be repeated, fungus
in a hot tub. A swamp entitled
Stanley Marsh. Black spot
on the thumbnail is permanent.
Neo-social democrat sneaks back
into Lenin closet. Not
democratic socialist. Folding chair
triangulates space. Shirt collar
as mock root for neck's trunk.
Small physical detail
enlarged (enraged)
refocuses the whole room
in the midst of the banquet.
Retrofit theory to text.
The idea of a doorstop
extends the wall. Thin palms kept trim
along commercial strip. Hollow is as
garbage truck sounds. Ghetto barber:
shop behind bars. Ask bus driver
to call out destination.
Chapped Lip Alert.
Man on a park bench
intent over crossword.
The sound of a piano
hung over the courtyard. Bliss
approximates emotional state.
Gay nerds (complex style). Drunk
on the streetcorner snaps to attention,
salutes the slow-cruising black-and-white.
Old manikin in used clothing store,
cheeks chipped, nose missing. Bin
of loose sneakers in front of shoe shop.
Dreams prod you with their skewed
pertinence. Like fingering around
in your pocket for a nickel, an

ambiguous coin, with your gloves on.
The pom-pom girl is sucking on a kiwi
as the sun rises, little startled bird.
Carved into nice pink slices, art
history is served
on seaweed-wrapped balls of rice.
At the checkout stand, the bagger
hooks the plastic sack into its wire
mould, dropping in the brown
spotted bananas before
the bottles of cider.
The close-out sale of
fiction at Dalton's
fails to attract
afficionados from their new
improved "ring" frisbees.
Please don't call it xerox.
Just because it rhymes. An absence
of form is pictured
on a milk carton. The dumpsters
are ripe. The present tense
calls up a terrific nostalgia
foreshadowing antacids.
Can you explain why Ezra Pound
and Ty Cobb were never,
not once, photographed
in the same room together?
The way cryotechnology
accounts for the Rolling Stones.
Heads of cauliflower
wrapped in plastic. Half moon rising
in the red dusk sky, streetlamps on
illuminating nothing. Twisting
the orange on
the glass juice squeezer.
Before dawn, alone
in the supermarket parkinglot,
hosing it down. Van's awning
signals catering truck. A leaf
had fallen onto the damp cement,
its image sharp years after.
Old green Norton anthology

perfect for doorstop. Albino mulatto's
curiously blonde hair. Linebreak muted
says I'm a normal guy. To generalize
a detail (use of plurals)
entails violence. Body language
at staff meeting very stiff.
Birds scatter high over
a schoolyard (asphalt
baseball diamond). My own breath
instead of a lung. Offhand,
by comments hidden in the brain,
we reiterate an old refrain.
My mind instead of an onion.
That these 20 year olds
call their shared housing
a commune seems quaint.
Old black woman with a cane
struggles to pull herself
onto the bus. I strain
to see these words. Chronicle
of Higher Medication. Learning
that I can't pick my nose when
I read, because the gesture
bumps my glasses. Our program is
compromise all positions
at all points, radical
at the cash bar. The colon swells
while the dash is but a double
hyphen. Thus paint freckles
an old ladder. Hair, combed
from the part, over the large
bald dome, barely throws
strands of a shadow. Men huddle
predawn in the vacant lot
for the grey trucks
that will carry them out
into the valley, hot day
harvesting crops. Yuppie world
where everyone's successful, everyone's
white. This guy's got great pecs,
strong deltoids, tight

abdominals, but through one nipple –
small gold safety pin. This poem,
15 lines of free verse, defining
(and as if "as spoken to") a noun
naming a common household object
has been designed
to compete successfully for space
against cartoons in the New Yorker.
Man striding down the street,
whistling loudly. Now that soft drinks
come in boxes. The Gift of
Security, the lock with 1,000
personal combinations: the only
lock in the world that let's you
set your own combination and change it
anytime, in seconds, without tools.
Because friends were coming over
for dinner, they began to think
about cooking in the early afternoon.

13

PAUL STEPHENS

Beyond the Valley of the Sophist: Charles Bernstein, Irony, and Solidarity

[Sophism] has ultimately shown itself to be right: every advance in epistemological and moral knowledge has reinstated the Sophists.
—Nietzsche, *The Will to Power*[1]

. . . every last professor teaching today benefited from the claims which shocked Plato so deeply when the Sophists first made them.
—Jacqueline de Romilly, *The Great Sophists in Periclean Athens*[2]

In some sense, the sophists were the first theorists of ambiguity.
—Ramona Naddaff, *Exiling the Poets*[3]

If someone proclaims themselves a sophist, is it possible to believe them?

By which I mean—given that "sophist" has been used for millennia as a term of derision signifying deceitfulness, artificiality, and self-interested professionalization—is it possible to be a self-proclaimed sophist? "I am a liar by nature and by profession, but I am not lying to you at the present moment [although presumably I am speaking to you in my professional capacity]" might be another formulation

1 Friedrich Nietzsche, *The Will to Power*, trans. Walter Kaufmann and R.J. Hollingdale (New York: Vintage, 1968), 233.

2 Jacqueline de Romilly, *Great Sophists in Periclean Athens*, trans. Janet Lloyd (New York: Oxford UP, 1992), 6.

3 Ramona Naddaff, *Exiling the Poets: The Production of Censorship in Plato's Republic* (Chicago: U of Chicago Press, 2003), 23.

of the problem. Charles Bernstein raises the problem of how one can believe the self-confessed sophist in his 1994 book *Dark City*:

> The debt that pataphysics owes to sophism
> cannot be overstated. A missionary with a horse
> gets saddlesores as easily as a politburo
> functionary. But this makes a mishmash of overriding ethical
> impasses. If the liar
> is a Cretan I wouldn't trust him
> anyway—extenuating contexts wouldn't amount
> to a hill of worms so far as I
> would have been deeply concerned about
> the fate of their, yes, spools. Never
> burglarize a house with a standing army,
> nor take the garbage to an unauthorized
> junket.[4]

Whereas the pataphysicist (in Alfred Jarry's terms) devises imaginary scientific solutions to nonexistent problems (thereby parodying scientific discourse), the sophist calls into question the sincerity of all discourse. The sophist and the pataphysicist cross paths in Bernsteins's writings in their refusal of literal truth and first person lyric sincerity. The answer to the question of how one distinguishes a lying sophist from a truthful philosopher, it turns out, depends not only on one's personal perspective, but also on how institutions and traditions (the proverbial "standing armies") differentiate between truth and falsehood, between art and commerce, between languages and dialects.

In his essay "Revenge of the Poet-Critic," Bernstein makes the claim that "problems of group affiliation (the neolyric 'we') pose as much of a problem for poetry as assertions of the Individual Voice (the lyric 'I')."[5] The sophist figure in Bernstein's writing, I argue, has allowed him to negotiate the gap between a "neolyric 'we'" (which would be implicit in Language writing's collective political and aesthetic project) and a "lyric 'I'" (which would constitute the mainstream notion of poetic "voice" which Language writing attempts to reject). This helps to explain why the sophist (or conman) figure

---

4 Charles Bernstein, *Dark City* (Los Angeles: Sun and Moon, 1994), 105.
5 Charles Bernstein, *My Way: Speeches and Poems* (Chicago: U of Chicago Press, 1999), 8.

has been so central in Bernstein's poetic and critical writing from his contributions to *L=A=N=G=U=A=G=E* (published from 1978-1982) to his book *The Sophist* (1987) to his most recent collection of poems, *Girly Man* (2007). Bernstein's sophist foregrounds important issues in contemporary poetic production—especially issues of audience, voice, discursive practice, and professionalization. The sophist figure, in short, continually draws attention to the rhetorical nature of poetic production and circulation, and places in doubt the personal mode of what Bernstein dubbed "Official Verse Culture" in his 1984 MLA speech "William Carlos Williams Meets the MLA." Perhaps to a greater degree than any other prominent American poet of his generation, Bernstein draws attention to issues of professionalization in his criticism and poetry, and his writings on the subject often employ an ironic humility: "I always say I am a professor of poetry, I profess poetry; think of me as a snake-oil salesman, a confidence man: I don't want to test your accumulated knowledge; I want to convince you of the value of poetry as a method, as a way of writing, as a form of vision."[6] Like Simonides, reputed to be the first poet to accept money for his poetry, and like Protagoras, reputed to be the first professional teacher of rhetoric, Bernstein must ward off charges that becoming a professional poet and critic has adversely affected his writing.[7] This essay largely sidesteps the complex question of whether or not becoming a university professor has compromised Bernstein's writing—instead I focus on how Bernstein has employed the sophist figure to discuss questions of: 1) sincerity and authorial perspective, 2) the possibility of a politically constructive version of

6   Quoted in Paul Bové, ed. "Charles Bernstein: A Dossier." *boundary 2* 23:3 (Fall 1996), 28.

7   For more on Language writing and its relation to academia, see Andrew Epstein's "Verse vs. Verse." *Lingua Franca* 10.6 (September 2000), 45-54; see also Alan Golding's "Provisionally Complicit Resistance: Language Writing and the Institution(s) of Poetry" in *From Outlaw to Classic* (Madison: University of Wisconsin Press, 1995), 144-170; and Golding's "'Isn't the avant-garde always pedagogical': Experimental Poetics and/as Pedagogy." *Iowa Review* 32.1 (Spring 2002), 64-71. For more general historical accounts of the Language movement, see Bob Perelman's *The Marginalization of Poetry: Language Writing and Literary History* (Princeton: Princeton University Press, 1996); Ann Vickery's *Leaving Lines of Gender: A Feminist Genealogy of Language Writing* (Middletown, CT: Wesleyan University Press, 2000); George Hartley's *Textual Politics and the Language Poets* (Bloomington: Indiana UP, 1989) and Barrett Watten's chapter "The Secret History of the Equal Sign: L=A=N=G=U=A=G=E between Discourse and Text" in *The Constructivist Moment: From Material Text to Cultural Poetics* (Middletown, CT: Wesleyan University Press, 2003): 45-102.

irony, and 3) Language Writing's collective understanding of itself as a movement. Correspondingly, along the lines of Richard Rorty's *Contingency, Irony, and Solidarity* (to which I suggest Bernstein offers an implicit response), this essay is divided into three sections which discuss sophistry, irony, and community in Bernstein's poetics.

1. Sophistry and Sincerity

Self-deprecatory in the extreme, Bernstein's sophist (or Bernstein-as-sophist) is fundamentally parodic. In an important essay on Bernstein's work, Susan Schultz discusses Bernstein's irony by emphasizing his concern with fashion and appearance. Schultz suggests that "what Bernstein has done throughout his nearly thirty-five year career is to critique fashions of writing that attempt to conceal their status as fashion."[8] Schultz argues that "Bernstein takes on the role of parodic poet, adman and artist combined. For Bernstein there is no paradox, or the paradox is itself a grounds for poetry and the business of advertising it."[9] Schultz chronicles Bernstein's metaphors of fashion, reading them partially as allegories of his own life as well as of his own practice. (Bernstein's father, who appears occasionally, if obliquely, in his poems, was a dress manufacturer.) Bernstein's critique of fashion is in part a meditation on gender relations and anticipates *Girly Man* in its interest in the (self-) fashioning of gender roles. The sophist can also be figured as an effeminized intellectual, as in "White Mythologies" in which Jacques Derrida suggests, "Whoever does not subject equivocalness to [the] law is already a bit less than a man: a sophist, who in sum says nothing."[10]

Bernstein's sophist, by contrast, is saying something, even if no one is necessarily listening. The sophist in Bernstein's work is not merely a self-interested ironist, he is also a defender of poetry and of political action. According to "White Mythologies," "the Sophist . . . is the very figure of that which doubles and endangers philosophy."[11] Perhaps poetry too "doubles and endangers philosophy," given that at least since Plato's attack on the sophists in the *Republic*, poets and

---

8 Susan Schultz, *A Poetics of Impasse in Modern and Contemporary American Poetry*, ed. Susan Schultz. (Tuscaloosa: Univeristy of Alabama Press, 2005), 181.

9 Ibid., 184

10 Jacques Derrida, "White Mythologies," in *Margins of Philosophy*, trans. Alan Bass (Chicago: U of Chicago Press , 1985), 248.

11 Ibid., 271.

sophists have been linked. The Sophists were "the first theorists of ambiguity," according to Ramona Naddaff in *Exiling the Poets,* her study of censorship in Plato's *Republic.* Contrary to Socrates' idealization of *eidos* (the realm of unchanging forms and ideas), the sophist Gorgias held that *logos* (in the sense of "speech" or "language") was the most powerful of all masters. The Sophists capitalized on the need of an educated aristocracy to defend itself in the public agora — working either as professional teachers of rhetoric or as "logographers" (speech-writers on behalf of wealthy patrons). Perhaps the most important characteristic of sophistry was its commercialization of knowledge. As Jacqueline de Romilly writes in her history of the movement, "The meaning of the term 'Sophist' was in principle relatively wide . . . The word itself means professionals of the intelligence. . . It could be applied to anyone thoroughly qualified to exercise his profession, be he a diviner or a poet."[12] Gorgias' fifth-century contemporary Simonides was thus a sophistical poet, having been the first to accept money rather than gifts for his talents. As Anne Carson points out in *Economy of the Unlost*, her study of Simonides and Paul Celan, this represented an epochal shift that troubled many Greek intellectuals, Socrates among them.[13] Commercialization has arguably always been more troubling for poetry than for other literary modes. Schiller's eighteenth-century denunciation of sophistry as supremely anti-poetic typifies an attempt to reconcile idea and statement, feeling and poetic utterance — in short to overcome irony and insincerity:

> At that first fair awakening of the powers of the mind, sense and intellect did not as yet rule over strictly separate domains; for no dissension had as yet provoked them into hostile partition and demarcation of their frontiers. Poetry has not as yet coquetted with wit, nor speculation prostituted itself to sophistry.[14]

For Bernstein, there is no such golden age before the intellectual division of labor between poetry and philosophy, between amateur and professional, or, more loosely, between intellect and feeling.

---

12 de Romilly, 1.

13 Ann Carson, *Economy of the Unlost* (Princeton: Princeton UP, 1999).

14 Friedrich Schiller, *On the Aesthetic Education of Man*, trans. Wilkinson and Willoughby (New York: Oxford UP, 1967), 31.

In the critique of confessional poetry set forth by Bernstein and the Language poetry movement, sincerity is not enough. In its most radical form, the critique offered by Language poetry suggests that individual lyric sincerity itself is subject to the fetish character of language under capitalism—in a sense, given the commercialization of literary production, this makes all professional poets and critics into sophists.[15]

Bernstein recognizes that the term sophist is potentially broad in its application, and in his 1986 book of criticism *A Poetics* he adopts a working definition of sophistry from Michel de Certeau:

> Sophism, says de Certeau, is the dialectics of tactics. 'As the author of a great strategic system, Aristotle was already very interested in the procedures of this enemy which perverted, as he saw it, the order of the truth [by] 'making the worse argument seem the better' [in the words of Corax] . . . this formula . . . is the starting point for an intellectual creativity as persistent as it is subtle, tireless . . . scattered over the terrain of the dominant order

---

15　In the context of the Language movement, the question of the degree to which language under capitalism takes on a fetish character was perhaps most forcefully discussed by Ron Silliman, who employed the term "referential fetish" to describe what he called "normative realism" in literature. The term "referential fetish" appears in the first version of the essay "Disappearance of the Word, Appearance of the World" (originally printed in February 1977; reprinted in L=A=N=G=U=A=G=E in 1982), but then disappears from the revised version of the essay in *The New Sentence* (New York: Roof Books, 1985). Silliman argues that "Things which appear to move 'freely,' absent all gesture, are the elements of a world of description. The commodity fetish in language becomes one of description, of the referential, and has a second higher-order fetish of narration" (126). As opposed to narrative, which is more fully inscribed in the fetish, "poetry can work to search out the preconditions of post-referential language within the existing social fact" (131). Since, as Silliman admits, "the primary institution of American poetry is the university" ("Canons and Institutions: New Hope for the Disappeared," in *The Politics of Poetic Form*, ed. Charles Bernstein. (New York: Roof Books, 1990), 157.), it is particularly incumbent upon poets to challenge the "normative realism" of English departments. It goes beyond the scope of this essay to investigate this problem in detail, or to discuss the reasons for Silliman's dropping of the term "referential fetish," and a fuller discussion would need to investigate the complex relation of Language writing to Marxism. It is important to emphasize that Silliman claims English departments have a primary role as arbiters of literary value, as well as of parameters for acceptable generic conventions.

and foreign to the rules laid down by a rationality founded on established rights and property.' [16]

As soon as he puts forward this loose definition of sophism as "the dialectic of tactics," Bernstein begins to doubt the power relation implicit in Aristotle's recuperation of rhetoric, given the latter's defense of aristocracy and the existing political system. The rhetorician, rather than being a defender of poetry, might just as easily be a defender of property:

> But isn't this just another trick of the tactician — to feign dispossession in the face of a stagnant assurance of ground? For the strategist and his 'strong' philosophy, deception is not a matter of tactics but a form of self-blindness: defending territory that belongs to no one, accumulating knowledge that would have value only in use. This is as if to say that syntax makes grammar, but grammar is only a reflection of the syntax that once was. The strategist-as-grammarian is the nomad, for he possesses his home in name only: his insistence on occupation and territorial defense precludes inhabitation. The syntactician makes her home where she finds herself, where she attends — and that is the only possession that's worth anything, a soil in which things can grow.[17]

The trick, it would seem, is how to remain nomadic in the face of a linguistic system that is contaminated by its territorialism and by its self-serving insistence on directness. Unlike the strategist with a "'strong' philosophy," the syntactician takes account of the shifting terrain of language at the level of grammar and syntax. The syntactician is not a dogmatic polemicist, but rather someone who recognizes the inherently rhetorical and grammatical nature of what he proclaims. Like the Sophist, the syntactician is an itinerant teacher of tactics rather than of unconditional truths. The syntactician merges poetic, philosophical, and rhetorical modes under the general heading of attention to the forms of linguistic usage. Bernstein refers with particular regularity to the "rhetoricality" of poetry, as in his 1979 poem/essay "Poetic Justice":

---

16 Charles Bernstein, *A Poetics* (Cambridge: Harvard UP, 1986), 164.

17 Ibid., 164.

> Not mere grids of possible worlds, as if truth were some
> kind of kicking boy, a form of rhetoric. Truthfulness, love
> of language, attending its telling. It's not unfair to read
> intentionality into other people's actions. The mocking of
> language (making as if it were a mock-up) evades rather
> than liberates. The world is in them. I can feel the weight
> of the fog. Hung. The hum is it. Touch it as it hangs on
> you. It feels good. I say so. I am not embarrassed to be
> embarrassed. My elementary school teachers thought I
> was vague, unsocial, & lacked the ability to coordinate the
> small muscles in my hands. The way it feels. The mistake
> is to think you can put on the mask at work and then take
> it off when you get home.[18]

In a sense, this passage recapitulates *in nuce* an educational experience: the mature Bernstein now wears a mask of authority unavailable to him in the restrictive environment of the elementary school
classroom. Rather than truth and rhetoric being opposed, rhetoric
is a "kicking boy." The poet comes to stand in for a whole range of
socialization processes, a whole culture of shame and indoctrination—which would presume to teach an oversimplified version of
the world where truth is truth and identity is transparent. As Schultz
points out, Bernstein is hardly reticent about including overtly
biographical details in his poems. Here, the poet comes of age not
through a withdrawal into authentic selfhood, but instead through
an appropriation of a persona analogous to that of the sophist.

Bernstein's sophist is crucially a pedagogical figure, and
Bernstein's concern with the sophistical nature of teaching, I would
suggest, is not unique. During roughly the same period (from the late
70s to the late 80s) in which Bernstein was most actively interested
in the figure of the sophist, a new movement called "Neosophism"
arose within rhetorical studies. Although I can find no evidence that
Bernstein was directly aware of the movement, his deployment of
the sophist character bears remarkable resemblances to the writings
of Sharon Crowley in particular, whose 1979 essay "Of Gorgias and
Grammatology" is usually taken as inaugurating the movement.[19]
Crowley argued from a feminist perspective that:

---

18 Charles Bernstein, *Republics of Reality* (Los Angeles: Sun and Moon, 2000), 146.

19 Sharon Crowley, "Of Gorgias and Grammatology," *College Composition and
Communication*, 30.3 (October, 1979), 279–284. The figure of the sophist seems to
have gained a particular currency in the late 1980s—not only in the neo-Sophistic

Modern teachers do not often think of themselves as professional participants in political or social issues. I want to argue that, on the contrary, those who are engaged in teaching discursive practice are always engaged in Sophistry; and, because of this, that they cannot escape the public aspect of their work.[20]

Influenced by deconstruction, advocates of Neosophism sought to ground the teaching of writing in an understanding of the radical constructedness of language, and to take into account what Bernstein would call the "positionality" of the teacher. Kenneth Lindblom summarizes the aims of the movement thus:

Neosophism. . . requires from teachers of writing attention to two principles: (1) recognition of the constructed nature of all knowledge and (2) conscious engagement of politi-cal obligations. Neosophistic teachers must themselves know their own knowledge rhetorically by working to understand the "multiplicity of truths" in their own disci-plines and by working to understand and value the public or common discourse at the heart of all forms of evidence. Neosophistic teachers must also engage their political obli-gations by recognizing and remaining aware of the politi-cal and social stakes of their every personal and pedagogi-cal choice and by making the political decision to focus their curricula on the task of encouraging students to view knowledge rhetorically.[21]

While the description offered by Lindblom bears a strong resem-blance to Bernstein's discussions of the political obligations of the poet/teacher/critic, Bernstein frames the problem of the relation of rhetoric to overlapping fields of knowledge in more dramatic terms:

---

movement—but also in works such as Roger Kimball's *Tenured Radicals: How Politics Has Corrupted Our Higher Education* (Chicago: Ivan R. Dee, 1989) as well as Stanley Fish's *Doing What Comes Naturally: Change, Rhetoric and Practice of Theory in Literary and Legal Studies* (Durham, NC: Duke UP, 1989).

20 Sharon Crowley, "A Plea for a Revival of Sophistry" *Rhetoric Review* 7.2, (Spring 1989), 330.

21 "Toward a Neosophistic Writing Pedagogy," Kenneth J. Lindblom, *Rhetorical Review*, 15.1, (Fall 1996): 93-108, 101.

The poetic — the aesthetic — the philosophic — the rhetorical: these intertwined figures dissolve into the art of   everyday life, the multiple and particular decisions and revisions, recognitions and intuitions, that make up — constitute — our experiences in and of the world. The poetic is not simply another frame of interpretation to be laid down next to the psycholinguistic and sociohistorical. The poetic is both a hypoframe, inhering within each frame of interpretation, and a hyperframe, a practice of moving from frame to frame.[22]

To question the relation of hypoframe to hyperframe is to place radical emphasis on context as well as on content. The poetic is "not simply another frame of interpretation," in that it permits greater freedom in terms of its ability to engage everyday (presumably private) life. But poetry is not necessarily a privileged form of discourse that can be considered as either truer or more ahistorical than any other genre. As Bernstein puts it in his poem "The Kiwi Bird in the Kiwi Tree":

I want no paradise only to be
drenched in the downpour of words, fecund
with tropicality.[23]

Like the title of Hayden White's *Tropics of Discourse*, Bernstein puns on trope/tropical, suggesting that poetic language might transport us to warmer figural climes — not a utopia of exact meaning, but rather a paradise of metaphor — of language in transition. The best hope of the poet-critic-teacher, then, might be to have frame (critical philosophy) and form (poetics) correspond — through inventive language, but also through community. Ironic self-identification becomes a cornerstone of ensuring that such a community remains open to recognizing itself as a linguistic and cultural construction. To (re-) appropriate a characteristically Bernsteinian (re-)use of cliché, "extenuating contexts" do "amount to a hill of worms" when it comes to pointing to the potentially sophistical nature of all communication.

---

22 *My Way*, 44.
23 Charles Bernstein, *Rough Trades* (Los Angeles: Sun and Moon, 1991), 11.

2. Irony (Metairony)

Gorgias said that one should destroy the seriousness of
one's opponent with   laughter, and his laughter with
seriousness.

—Aristotle, *Rhetoric* [24]

. . . irony, in the narrowest sense of suggesting a model
of assertion/rejection, is formally inadequate to allow for
what a mix of comic, bathetic, and objective modes might:
an intercutting that undercuts the centrality of a governing narrative or prosodic structure.

—Bernstein, *A Poetics*[25]

In its emphasis on the institutional conditions (of literature departments and professional organizations in particular) which surround
the production of literature and aesthetic value, Bernstein's irony
differs fundamentally from the high modernist irony of Ezra Pound
or T.S. Eliot. Bernstein's irony precludes any high culture dismissal
of the everyday and the popular. His term "metairony" describes this
intercutting of the everyday, the biographical, the pop cultural, the
situational, and the symbolic:

CB: Irony is simple ambiguity: ironic/iconic. What I want
is a humor that opens out onto a multivolitional field
destabilizing to any fixed meaning that can be assigned
and that persists out of context. Octavio Paz has used the
term "meta-irony": an irony that destroys its negation and,
hence, returns in the affirmative." But I wouldn't want to
stop that back flip back to the affirmative but go beyond
yes and no. Humor as destabilizing not only the negation
to mean affirmation but the affirmation also—the idea of
a perpetual motion machine that never stops pinging and
ponging off the walls, ceilings, floors. So returns to . . . let's
say "the absolute," maybe the ineffable, everywhere said,

---

24 Patricia Curd, ed. *A Presocratics Reader: Selected Fragments and Testimonia* (Indianapolis:
Hackett, 1995), 104.

25 *A Poetics*, 227.

nowhere stated. But I wouldn't want to make humor into too serious a business.[26]

Bernstein caps off this description of "meta-irony" with straightforward ironic self-deprecation. To emphasize the "multivolitional" nature of irony is to make the claim that irony is radically perspectival, but also to insist on context as fundamental to the creation of meaning. Bernstein's fullest discussion of irony appears in a 1996 interview between himself and Ann Lauterbach, Jonathan Monroe, and Bob Perelman.

> Tom Beckett once asked me what I think about radical irony in my work and in Bob's work, as opposed to the very different, anti-ironic kind of writing that he said one could see in Susan Howe, Lyn Hejinian, or Ron Silliman. I don't actually see my work as ironic in the way that irony tends to be conceptualized.
>
> BP: I don't, either.
>
> CB: I think we share this conception of the humor of it, but I've been thinking just over the past few days of the term "self-canceling irony." With irony, you're left with some sense of authoritative distance from whatever's being mocked or ironized, especially in the modernist form. I'm interested in coming back around so that you're actually where you were if it wasn't ironic. You've gone through this humorous turn, but it's self-canceling in the sense that you're not remaining at a distance from it, nor are you ridiculing it. On the contrary, you've gone through a kind of comic spin cycle. It all depends on what people's attitude toward humor is, as if humor were at odds with all kinds of things it's not at odds with, as if humor were somehow always associated with mocking and therefore with belittling.[27]

---

26 *Content's Dream*, 462.

27 "Poetry, Community, Movement: A Conversation" (Ann Lauterbach, Jonathan Monroe, Charles Bernstein, Bob Perelman) *diacritics* 26.3/4 (Fall/Winter) 1996. Accessed: http://ezproxy.bgc.bard.edu:2053/journals/diacritics/v026/26.3-bernstein01.html Ibid., n.p..

A comparison with Rorty's understanding of irony is instructive here in helping to understand Bernstein's notion of irony, as well as in understanding what Tom Beckett calls the "anti-ironic" writing of other Language poets such as Howe, Hejinian, and Silliman. If Language poets have been united in their resistance to mainstream poetry, I would suggest that they have not been as united in their attitudes toward irony. Rorty's pragmatic anti-ironism is not necessarily of a piece with that of the anti-ironism of the Language poets just mentioned. Nonetheless, I would suggest that Rorty, like more mainstream anti-ironists (a good example would be Jedediah Purdy), has little patience for what Bernstein refers to as meta-irony.[28] In *Contingency, Irony, and Solidarity* (published just two years after Bernstein's *Sophist*), Rorty defines an ironist as

> someone who fulfills three conditions: (1) She has radical and continuing doubts about the final vocabulary she currently uses, because she has been impressed by other vocabularies taken as final by people or books she has encountered; (2) she realizes that argument phrased in her present vocabulary can neither underwrite nor dissolve those doubts; (3) insofar as she philosophizes about her situation, she does not think that her vocabulary is closer to reality than others, that it is in touch with a power not herself. Ironists who are inclined to philosophize see the choice between vocabularies as made neither within a neutral and universal metavocabulary nor by an attempt to fight one's way past appearances to the real, but simply by playing the new off against the old.[29]

Bernstein's irony (or his sophistry) would seem to fulfill all three of Rorty's descriptive formulations — except for his third category. It is not that Bernstein necessarily thinks he has a "metavocabulary" better than others, but that he continually refers to himself as embedded within a community which is able to overcome the ironic

---

28 For a denunciation of irony in this vein, see Jedediah Purdy, *For Common Things: Irony, Trust, and Commitment in America Today* (New York: Vintage, 2000). For a merciless meta-ironic response to Purdy, I recommend Todd Pruzan's "Jedediah in Love," *McSweeney's* [online], October 12, 1999. Accessed: http://www.mcsweeneys.net/1999/10/12jedediah.html

29 Richard Rorty, *Contingency, Irony, and Solidarity.* (Cambridge: Cambridge UP, 1989), 73.

disavowal of public meaning and collective action. For Rorty, irony is irreducibly private and undermines any sense of community:

> But even if I am right in thinking that a liberal culture whose public rhetoric is nominalist and historicist is both possible and desirable, I cannot go on to claim that there could or ought to be a culture whose public rhetoric is ironist. I cannot imagine a culture which socialized its youth in such a way as to make them continually dubious about their own process of socialization. Irony seems inherently a private matter. On my definition, an ironist cannot get along without the contrast between the final vocabulary she inherited and the one she is trying to create for herself. Irony is, if not intrinsically resentful, at least reactive. Ironists have to have something to have doubts about, something from which to be alienated.[30]

In addition to objecting to it due to its private nature, Rorty objects to irony in that it

> unsuits one for being a liberal . . . One can make this claim plausible by saying that there is at least a prima facie tension between the idea that social organizations aims at human equality and the idea that human beings are simply incarnated vocabularies. The idea that we all have an overriding obligation to diminish cruelty, to make human beings equal in respect to their liability to suffering, seems to take for granted that there is something within human beings which deserves respect and protection quite independently of the language they speak. It suggests that a nonlinguistic ability, the ability to feel pain, is what is important, and that differences in vocabulary are much less important.[31]

In this one paragraph, Rorty grounds his vision of "liberal hope" in utilitarian, sentimental, egalitarian and human rights arguments. At the same time, he de-emphasizes the effects of ideology and of language. Twenty years later, this passage sounds somewhat high-

---

30 Ibid., 88.
31 Ibid., 88.

toned, given that liberalism has faced such difficulties in articulating its ongoing project. The ability to empathize has not by itself solved the world's social and political problems. It could be objected that Rorty's project dwells more explicitly in the realm of moral philosophy than does Bernstein's, and perhaps to compare the two is to compare very different critical projects. It should be underscored that even if the two differ markedly in seeing irony as fundamentally antithetical to community, they also share a concern that a defeatist irony might circumvent the political effectiveness of intellectuals.

The problem of a cynical irony or a passive irony which would undermine community is, I want to suggest, what Bernstein wants to avert through a metairony which would make one self-conscious of one's embeddedness in larger networks of communication and (self-) identification. Whereas irony is private, metairony is public, recycling songs, advertisements, and clichés. Metairony is inescapably rhetorical, and revels in academic battles. To overstate the case slightly: Socrates is an ironist, Gorgias a metaironist, having confessed his ironic stance from the beginning. Perhaps the New York School poets are ironist, the Language poets metaironist. But this might be taking the analogy too far—by pushing the distinction between irony and metairony, I mean not to impose well-worn categories associated with the modern and the postmodern, which would suggest that the postmodern is characterized by a greater self-consciousness. Rather I mean to suggest that Bernstein is making the case that poems convey meaning on many levels other than the literal—on the levels of sound, reference, dialect, performance, critique as well as self-critique—in short, on the levels of context and form.

Irony, it should be emphasized, has a complex relation to sophistry—just as philosophy has a complex relation to irony. Socrates after all was a great ironist—he presumes to know nothing, which is a far more skeptical position than Bernstein's or Rorty's in terms of epistemology (that is, if we take Socrates at his word). A comparison with Kierkegaard's "Concept of Irony" is useful. According to Kierkegaard, "Irony oscillates between the ideal *I* and the empirical *I*; the one would make Socrates a philosopher, the other a Sophist; but what makes him more than a Sophist is that his empirical *I* has universal validity."[32] Socrates posits transcendental ideas, and thus for Kierkegaard he overcomes the materialist skepticism of the

32 Soren Kierkegaard, *The Essential Kierkegaard*, ed. Howard V. Hong and Edna H. Hong. (Princeton: Princeton UP, 1995), 21.

Sophists. Socrates aims at the Good; the Sophist aims at the useful. Although Bernstein does not champion idealist values of the same variety as Kierkegaard, he would probably be in agreement with Kierkegaard's emphasis on irony as a tool of self-consciousness. Irony is "subjectivity raised to the second power, a subjectivity's subjectivity, which corresponds to reflection's reflection."[33] Whereas Socratic irony is implicitly founded on transcendental ideals, Bernstein's irony is often historical and polemical, and would stand to disprove Kierkegaard's claim that "irony actually is never able to advance a thesis."[34] The problem with irony may not be that it is private (as it is for Rorty), but that it is non-hortatory in that it refuses all claims to certainty.

In his discussions of irony, Paul de Man uses the term "authenticity" in lieu of "certainty," or "universal validity," but he follows Kierkegaard and Schlegel when he suggests that:

> ironic language splits the subject into an empirical self that exists in a state of inauthenticity and a self that exists only in the form of a language that asserts the knowledge of this inauthenticity. This does not, however, make it into an authentic language, for to know inauthenticity is not at the same time to be authentic.[35]

The realm where an inauthentic statement multiplied by an inauthentic statement equals an inauthentic statement is the realm of the "metaironic," a term de Man uses in "The Rhetoric of Temporality" (translated in 1983). For de Man, "Baudelaire speaks, without apparent irony, of a semimythical poetic figure that would exist beyond the realm of irony." De Man asks,

> Could we think of certain texts of that period—and it is better to speak here of texts than of individual names—as being truly meta-ironical as having transcended irony without falling into the myth of an organic totality or bypassing the temporality of all language? And, if we call

---

33 Ibid., 24.

34 Ibid., 34.

35 Paul de Man, *Blindness and Insight: Essays in the Rhetoric of Contemporary Criticism* (Minneapolis: U of Minnesota Press, 1983), 214.

these texts "allegorical," would the language of allegory
then be the overcoming of irony?[36]

As opposed to partaking of the allegorical mode which de Man associates with "organic totality," Bernstein's self-characterization is metaironic in that it rejects the notion that there can be a "semimythical
poetic figure," and instead posits a radically contingent poetic subject
who is a product of many overdetermined historical, educational,
and cultural factors. De Man seems troubled by metairony—"to
know inauthenticity is not the same as to be authentic"—whereas
Bernstein champions the metaironic. It is not that Bernstein necessarily endorses the inauthentic, but that he recognizes a radical social
situatedness involved in judging the authentic.

Bernstein's (meta-)irony, then, rather than remaining private,
attempts to interrogate the private. A Bernstein-like notion of irony
as communal and performative can be found in Kenneth Burke's
understanding of irony as inherently dramatistic. Burke sees irony as
arising not out of isolated deception or skepticism, but instead out of
competing terms and arguments:

> Irony arises when one tries, by the interaction of terms
> upon one another, to produce a development which uses
> all the terms. Hence, from the standpoint of total form
> (this "perspective of perspectives"), none of the participat-
> ing "sub-perspectives" can be treated as either precisely
> right or precisely wrong. They are all voices, or personali-
> ties, or positions, integrally affecting one another.[37]

Bernstein's irony too, I want to make the case, is inescapably public,
and represents a refusal of what Rorty refers to as a "metavocabulary"—precisely because Bernstein is ironic, and/or metaironic
about his own vocabulary. Irony, Bernstein suggests, can constitute a
mode of engaged rsistance, as well as constituting a mode of cynical
complacency:

> . . . the comic is anything but a unitary phenomenon, and
> the range of comic attitudes goes from the good-humored

---

36 Ibid., 223.

37 Kenneth Burke, *On Symbols and Society*, ed. Joseph R. Gusfield (Chicago: U of
Chicago P, 1989), 255-256.

to the vicious, from clubby endorsement of the existing social reign to total rejection of all existing human communities: Poet as confidence "man," deploying hypocrisy in order to shatter the formal autonomy of the poem and its surface of detachment; the sincere and the comic as interfused figure, not either/or but both and. For our sincerity is always comic.[38]

In other words, the self-proclaimed conman in a classroom is far less dangerous than the conman with an army and a navy. To be truly communal is to accept responsibilities, and to be part of a community, it goes without saying, precludes a "total rejection of all existing human communities," whether those communities take themselves seriously or not.

3. Solidarity (Situatedness)

> I am a language
> poet wherever people try to limit the modes of
> expression or nonexpression. I am an experimental poet
> to those who value craft over interrogation, an
> avant-garde poet to those who see the future
> in the present.
> —Charles Bernstein, "Solidarity Is the Name We
> Give to What We Cannot Hold."[39]

This is Charles Bernstein speaking . . . from the Upper West Side of Manhattan, home of Zabar's and Barney Greengrass, the Sturgeon King. With thanks to Jerry, Marjorie, Jackson, Pierre, Rachel, and the rest of the Poetics "Jews" and Protest-ants (irregardless of ethnic origin) who insist on debating what they/we cannot understand. & now for some further sophistry: "the critical activity that destroys faith"[40]
> —Bernstein, "Pound and the Poetry of Today"[41]

---

38 Charles Bernstein, "Comedy and the Politics of Poetic Form" in *The Politics of Poetic Form: Poetry and Public Policy*, ed. Charles Bernstein (New York: Roof Books, 1990), 242.

39 *My Way*, 34.

40 Ibid,, 155.

41 Ibid., 155.

Particularly significant about Bernstein's sophist is that it is not, for
the most part, a figure of alienation or despair. Rather, as in the case
of Bernstein's discussion of Pound's anti-semitism "Pound and the
Poetry of Today," the sophist admits his own prejudices and limitations, and continually describes himself as a member of a community. In this way, the sophist gets beyond private irony through situatedness, complexity, and "positionality." In connecting the figure
of the sophist to the figure of the Jew, Bernstein rejects a Poundian
poetics that would take insufficient account of the dangers of taking
oneself too seriously, or of isolating oneself from one's friends (as
in the case of Pound's troubled friendships with Jews such as Louis
Zukofsky). "Pound and the Poetry of Today" begins with a quotation from Pound: "What Greek logomachy had in common with the
Hebrew poison was debate, dialectic, sophistry, the critical activity
that destroys faith."[42] In redeploying Pound's attack on sophistry as
"the critical activity that destroys faith," Bernstein both parodies and
supplements Pound's views of Jews as essentially sophistical in the
challenge they present to a unified—i.e. "sincere"—culture, which
would conceal its own rhetorical and even philosophical underpinnings. As if in answer to Eliot's famous statement that "reasons of
race and religion combine to make any large number of free-thinking
Jews undesirable," Bernstein summons a provisional community of
Poetics "Jews" and "Protest-ants."[43] Crucially, "Jews" is in quotation
marks and "Protest-ants" is hyphenated. The community Bernstein
constructs is inclusive; rather than being exclusive and based in race
or ethnicity, it is based in a shared insistence on tolerance for debate
and ambiguity.

Pound's and Eliot's poetics presume that it is possible to get
beyond logomachy (or polemic); Bernstein's poetics presume that
logomachy is an inescapable dimension of poetic production, and
that the writer is implicated within literary and cultural movements
which make their appeals through rhetorical means. Bernstein's
comedy is contextual (rather than situational) in that it uses irony in
the service of larger polemics:

> Making claims is an aspect of a poet's work that has vast
> potential—staking out ground to inhabit—especially

---

42 Ibid., 155.
43 T.S. Eliot, *After Strange Gods* (New York: Harcourt Brace, 1934), 20.

insofar as these claims preempt or needlessly complicate subsequent, ostensibly more accurate, critical approaches. (They often have the opposite effect.) This means speaking for yourself in different tongues, even if other people might speak for you more accurately: for it is just this accuracy that you might with to contest. That is to say, you might wish to make claims for your work and the work you support that are inaccurate and need to be put out in order to misrepresent that work properly. *Now is that remark ironic or his humorous or is it comic?* What I'm emphasizing is the provisional quality of the enterprise of poetics. In other words, I think that the activities such as this one have to be understood as situational.[44]

An irony that admits its own artifice, and that emerges from a ventriloquist rather than from a confessing voice, cannot be private, nor can it reinforce a view of private life where the emotive experiential life of the poet is paramount. Bernstein's irony is neither of the situational variety, nor of the cynical solipstic variety.

So, again, I do not propose some private voice, some vatic image of sincerity or the absolute value of innovation, as an alternative to the limitations of the voices of authority I can never completely shake off. For I am a ventriloquist, happy as a raven to preach with blinding fervor of the corruptions of public life in a voice of pained honesty that is as much as a conceit as the most formal legal brief for which my early education would have prepared me. If my loops and short circuits, my love of elision, my Groucho Marxian refusal of irony as an effort to explode the authority of those conventions I wish to discredit (disinherit), it constantly offers consoling self-justification of being Art, as if I could escape the partiality of my condition by my investigation of it. But my art is just empty words on a page if it does not, indeed, persuade, as it enters into the world of self-justification or self-flagellation or aesthetic ornamentation rather than as interaction, as conversation, as provocation (for myself and others).[45]

---

44 *A Poetics*, 156.
45 "Comedy and the Politics of Poetic Form," 239-240.

The irony of all ironies, it would seem, is that Bernstein's "positionality" frames him within a context of peers; thus it counteracts private
irony, but may result in something like a semi-private irony—or
what James Joyce (borrowing from the medieval writer Michael of
Northgate) might have referred to as "inwit," an inside joke variety
of irony primarily available to a specific community of like-minded
intellectuals. This does not in my view fundamentally blunt the theoretical force of Bernstein's response to high modernism's rejection of
an irony that would undermine a "homogenous" (Eliot's term) tradition. But it may be the case that avant-garde literature is fated to
a semi-private irony. It may also be the case that poetry need not
always be apologetic about its limited audience (as Bernstein makes
the case in his essay "Against National Poetry Month as Such").[46]
   For Bernstein, to make his "positionality" continually apparent
through ironic self-presentation becomes a kind of talismanic precondition for communicative action. This does not mean, however,
that his writing is uniform in its ironic modes. Bernstein's most
recent poetry has arguably become much more direct in its social
criticism. There is no irony in "The Ballad of the Girly Man" (with the
possible exception of the poem's title):

> Things from hell have taken freedom's store
> The rich get richer, the poor die quicker
> & the only god that sanctions that
> Is no god at all but rhetorical crap.[47]

The poem is unapologetically direct in its scathing indictment of the
current political order. But a poem like "Thank You for Saying Thank
You" is supremely ironic (or metaironic):

> This is a totally
> accessible poem.
> There is nothing
> in this poem
> that is in any

46 See Charles Bernstein, "Against National Poetry Month as Such." [Essay which
    first appeared on the University of Chicago Press web site, April 1999]. Accessed:
    http://www.press.uchicago.edu/Misc/Chicago/044106.html
47 Charles Bernstein, *Girly Man* (Chicago: U of Chicago P, 2007), 180.

way difficult
to understand.
All the words
are simple &
to the point.
There are no new
concepts, no
theories, no
ideas to confuse
you. This poem
has no intellectual
pretensions. It is
purely emotional.[48]

The poem is a performative parody of popular conceptions of poetry as emotional expression with few prospects for innovation, and fewer prospects for political or philosophical content. The poem ends:

[This poem] follows
no fashion. It
says just what
it says. It's
real.[49]

As Bernstein's writing has repeatedly shown, there is no stepping outside of fashion, even on dress-down-at-work day (or even for the proponents of the "Nude Formalism").[50] Nothing says exactly what it says, and to proclaim that one is uniquely able to "keep it real" is simply to fall into a different register of cliché. The title "Thank You for Saying Thank You" is an instance of epanalepsis: To thank someone for saying thank you is to fall into a hermeneutic circle of the everyday and the banal, but it is also to establish a communicative reciprocity, even if that reciprocity is constrained by cliché and convention.

In his most recent work, Bernstein finds a way to get beyond irony by placing himself within an increasingly familial poetics.

---

48 *Girly Man*, 7.

49 Ibid., 9.

50 Susan Bee and Charles Bernstein, *The Nude Formalism* (Los Angeles: Sun and Moon, 1989).

To champion the oxymoronic "girly man" is to redeploy Arnold Schwarzenegger's campaign remark about his opponent—which in itself was the politician Schwarzenegger quoting the actor Schwarzenegger. Like the Sinatra title of Bernstein's collection of essays and poems, *My Way*, "girly man" is cliché diverted to new ends. In fashioning himself as a man with an unmanly profession, a man in solidarity with his son, his wife, and with feminism in general, Bernstein is tapping into a new kind of irony, an irony of clarity or even satire, premised on an examination of codes of masculinity. This would be a communal irony of a type not described by Rorty. Given his interest in Hegel in *Contingency, Irony, and Solidarity*, it seems odd that Rorty omits mention of Hegel's famous assertion that women are "the everlasting irony [in the life] of the community."[51] For Hegel, women threaten to undermine the public sphere by introducing private irony. Seyla Benhabib offers a succinct account of Hegel's view of women and their relation to the ironic moment of the dialectic:

> Spirit may fall into irony for a brief historical moment, but eventually the serious transparency of reason will discipline women and eliminate irony from public life . . . . Hegel's Antigone is one without a future; her tragedy is also the grave of utopian, revolutionary thinking about gender relations. Hegel, it turns out, is woman's gravedigger, confining them to a grand but ultimately doomed phase of the dialectic, which "befalls mind in its infancy."
>
> What about the dialectic then, that locomotive of history rushing on its onward march? There is not way to disentangle the march of dialectic in Hegel's system from the bodies of the victims which it treads. Historical necessity requires its victims, and women have always been among the numerous victims of history. What remains of the dialectic is what Hegel precisely thought he could dispense with: irony, tragedy, and contingency. He was one of the first to observe the ironic dialectic of modernity: freedom that could become abstract legalism or selfish pursuit of economic satisfaction.[52]

---

51 Quoted in Seyla Benhabib, *Situating the Self: Gender, Community, and Postmodernism in Contemporary Ethics* (New York: Routledge, 1992), 288.

52 Ibid., 256.

Hegel's association of irony with the feminine produces a number of expected misogynistic tropes (or is produced by them). Irony for Hegel emerges within the privacy of the family and discourages the active male from participating in public life. Women introduce deception, arbitrariness, and superficiality into the community. By means of her private irony, the female restrains the active heroic spirit of the male:

> Womankind—the everlasting irony [in the life] of the community—changes by intrigue the universal end of the government into a private end, transforms its universal activity into a work of some particular individual, and perverts the universal property of the state into a possession and ornament for the Family. Women in this way turns to ridicule the earnest wisdom of mature age which, indifferent to purely private pleasures and enjoyments, as well as to playing an active part, only thinks of and cares for the universal. She makes this wisdom an object of derision for raw and irresponsible youth and unworthy of their enthusiasm.[53]

Woman-as-ironist is much like a sophist—"something less than a man" in Derrida's terms. Irony represents, in this view, a fundamental untruthfulness on the part of an other, a moment of falsehood that must be overcome. The female ironist, like the sophist, threatens to undermine the confident project of the State. Claire Colebrook suggests, by contrast, that we not think of irony as a defining feature of any particular social group. For Colebrook, if there is a private irony, it can only be overcome through a recognition of the collective performativity of language. The potentially ironic nature of all language makes it impossible to oppose an inauthentic private irony to an authentically open and transparent public speech:

> Irony, for writers like Butler and de Man is not a figure of speech that "we" can choose to use or not use. There is no such thing as faithful and literal speech, which is at one with its world, and then ironic or distanced speech, which

---

53 G.W.H. Hegel, *Phenomenology of Spirit*, trans. A.V. Miller (New York: Oxford UP, 1979), 188.

would speak with a sense of distance, quotation or otherness . . . . We cannot, as Richard Rorty suggests, adopt our
language with a recognition that it is merely a language.
Such a hope would rely on a notion of language as other
than ourselves, as something we might have to use, but
which "we" would always recognize as provisional and
arbitrary.[54]

By placing "we" in quotations, Colebrook acknowledges that irony
often misidentifies subjects, and yet irony in itself does not threaten
the social any more so than any other linguistic formation. Perhaps
the effeminized irony described by Hegel constitutes a sub-language,
while post-Romantic irony (a sublation of a sublation) is a metalanguage that overcomes inaction. Bernstein's irony could be read as
bridging the gap between irony as sub-language (the language of a
community of poets) and irony as meta-language (the language of
the larger community of intellectuals in the face of their increasing
marginalization within political life as a whole).

Bernstein's poetry thus addresses not only the misrepresentations
of private irony, but also the misrepresentations of public lying—in
the purportedly unironic speech of the "war on terror," for instance.
In "The Ballad of the Girly Man," Bernstein advocates a communitar-
ian ethic, without placing much hope in faithful and literal speech:

> Poetry will never win the war on terror
> But neither will error abetted by error
>
> We girly men are not afraid
> Of uncertainty or reason or interdependence
> We think before we fight, then think some more
> Proclaim our faith in listening, in art, in compromise
>
> So be a girly man
> & sing this gurly song
> Sissies & proud
> That we would never lie our way to war[55]

---

54 Claire Colebrook, *Irony* (New York: Routledge, 2004), 129.
55 *Girly Man*, 180.

Perhaps with this passage the Cretan liar has come full circle. Through absolute directness, the poet-as-sophist makes public a counter-faith in compromise. The self-professed liar is hardly as dangerous as the liar who never comes clean, so to speak. Specifically addressed to his son, Bernstein's poem is hardly ambiguous in connecting masculine self-representation to "the war on terror." Like much of Bernstein's verse, from the "Artifice of Absorption" to "A Defence of Poetry," *Girly Man* is self-consciously essayistic, as if to reinforce Adorno's claim that "the essay salvages a moment of sophistry."[56] This is a poetry that forces us to rethink didacticism and experimentalism, irony and sincerity, individual and community. In the "Athenaeum Fragments," Friedrich Schlegel poses the question: "The poetry of one writer is termed philosophical, of another philological, of a third rhetorical, etc. But what then is poetical poetry?"[57] Bernstein's poetry, I want to suggest, is rhetorical—but it is also philological in its concern with literary history, as well as philosophical in its concern with language and ethics—not to mention poetical, in that Bernstein continually returns to poetry as his central medium, as an unapologetic defender of its role within the larger intellectual culture.

Language writing in general, I am arguing, should be situated within the crowded and constantly shifting geography of post-1960s American cultural politics. One recent critic of Language writing, Oren Izenberg, has suggested that the Language movement has little or no collective coherency aside from its opposition to mainstream poetry. Izenberg pays particular attention to Bernstein's notion of "uncommunity":

> Bernstein's resolution on a negation—an "uncommu-nity"—is the result not of a rich anthropology but of a theoretical dead end. If there is one thing about which the Language poets seem certain, it is that a meeting of poets, whether at the pastoral First International Summer School or the subterranean Composers Union, must entail the formation of groups organized on some other princi-ple, but what that principle is they cannot say. The poetic effort to construct a nonparodic version of collectivity in the wake of the fall of historical communism--one that

56 Theodor Adorno, "The Essay as Form" in *Notes to Literature, vol. 1*, trans. Shierry Weber Nicholsen. (New York: Columbia University Press, 1992), 1.

57 Friedrich Schlegel, "Athenaeum Fragments" in *Classic and Romantic German Aesthetics*, ed. J.M. Bernstein (Cambridge: Cambridge UP, 2003), 243.

would allow full autonomy not only for the poem but for the poet, not only for the poet but for the person--that effort is relegated to fantasy by an inability to imagine that poetry could offer anything other than another set of conventions that come to look oppressive as soon as they are understood to be conventions. Thus, despite their great pains to manifest themselves as engaged in a group enterprise, despite the manifest similarity of their texts, Language poets are theory-bound to represent themselves as a group that is not just pluralist but internally differentiated almost to the point of nonexistence. Almost, that is, but not quite. For there is at present no claim more characteristic of the uncommunity of Language writing than the claim that Language writing cannot be characterized.[58]

Although I think Izenberg is right that Language writing has difficulty characterizing itself as a cohesive community, I think he draws an excessively literal conclusion from this difficulty, and I would take exception to several of his formulations. It is true that Language writing has always encompassed a variety of poetic styles and aesthetic philosophies, and that, if anything, the group was mostly united by its opposition to prevailing poetic modes, as well as by its suspicion of the influence of late capitalism on language. That Language writers as a community may have problems articulating a cohesive theoretical platform beyond these shared concerns can be considered an ongoing problem. I would maintain, however, that Izenberg misunderstands what Bernstein means by "uncommunity," and that Bernstein does not mean for Language writers to be understood as resistant to being identified as a community. An uncommunity is an inherently undefinable, ironic term—it is neither a formal grouping, nor an anti-grouping. In its original context, it is clear that Bernstein does not mean for us to take the notion of uncommunity literally. As far as I can tell, Bernstein first uses the term in a 1996 essay titled "Community and the Individual Talent," which is an account of his involvement with the SUNY Buffalo Poetics List. Bernstein describes the Buffalo online discussion group (or listserv) as an uncommunity, and suggests "my hope for electronic communication is that it engenders not virtual communities, but rather virtual uncommunities."[59]

---

58   Oren Izenberg, "Language Poetry and Collective Life." *Critical Inquiry* 30.1 (Fall 2003): 132-159.

59   Charles Bernstein, "Community and the Individual Talent." *Diacritics* 26.3/4, (Fall-

Bernstein begins his essay by emphasizing the tentative, performative context of online discussion groups:

> I had a number of thoughts, over these past weeks of posts, about community, but I've misplaced them.
>
> Every time I hear the words literary community I reach for my bivalent autocad simulation card emulator.
>
> Poetry is (or can be) an aversion of community in pursuit of new constellations of relationship.
>
> In other words, community is as much what I am trying to get away from–reform–as form.[60]

Rather than reading the uncommunity — or the ironic community — as a "theoretical dead end," I would submit that pluralism of voices and pluralism of styles within Language writing is part of the theoretical point. To read a plurality of voices as constituting the project of Language writing suggests an open-endedness rather than a "theoretical dead end." To read Bernstein too literally is to fall into a trap of expecting an absolute coherency from a community of diverse interests. Izenberg suggests that the goal of Language writing is "to construct a nonparodic version of collectivity in the wake of the fall of historical communism — one that would allow full autonomy not only for the poem but for the poet, not only for the poet but for the person."[61] This, it seems to me, underestimates the theoretical sophistication of the Language poets (few, if any, of whom put much faith in Soviet communism, for instance). Or rather, perhaps Izenberg's formulation underestimates the *sophistical-ness* of Language poetry. It is not that there are no solutions, but that there are no easy solutions; it is not that there is no literary form, but that literary forms must be continually re-formed; it is not that there is no autonomy, but that there is no "full autonomy"; it is not that there is no possibility of sincere communication, but that there is no genuine communication without community.

Winter 1996): 176–195. Accessed: http://ezproxy.bgc.bard.edu:2053/journals/diacritics/v026/26.3-4bernstein01.html

60   Ibid., n.p.

61   Izenberg, n.p.

In other words, if someone proclaims themselves a sophist, it is possible to believe them — but not without context and not without irony.

14

RAY CRAIG

Poem for Charles

"KISS, BUS"

"MIND'S ARRANGEMENT WITH
REGARD TO
'CERTAIN

OBJECTS" ⊡ 'ANDRE BRETON,'
NADJA ⊡ "DISTANCE,
RATHER

THAN ABSORPTION. IS

THE INTENDED

EFFECT " ⊡

BARRETT WATTEN, TOTAL

SYNTAX ⊡ KISS,

BUS,

SO " ⊡ CHARLES BERNSTEIN,

ISLETS⌒ IRRITATIONS

⊡ "LETTERS

|OCCUR |ON THE
  PAGE AT
    INTERVAL'S "

BOB PERELMAN, A.K.A.
  " THEY WILL
    SIT

BESIDE ME RATHER
    THAN STAND
    UP

|ON THE BUS "
    RON SILLIMAN,
    T/J/ANT/IN/G'

15

JASON LAGAPA

To Think Figuratively, Tropically: Charles Bernstein's Post-9/11 Grammar and Pragmatist Lessons in the Age of Baudrillard

His writing looks for a grammar that will do the work of what he would later called radical empiricism. The grammar would make us aware that the relations between things are as important to experience as the things themselves. It is necessary to stay loose. His ideal grammar leads to his politics, and not the other way around.
—Richard Poirier on William James in *Poetry and Pragmatism*[1]

Having already written an article entitled "The Gulf War Did Not Take Place" in the French newspaper *Libération* after the Iraq War, Jean Baudrillard composed the essay "The Spirit of Terrorism" for *Le Monde* in November 2, 2001 to weigh in on the terrorist attacks of September 11th, 2001. Baudrillard's earlier argument in 1991 centered upon an claims that what was leading up to the Gulf War was a "soft war" of continual deterrence and that the media coverage, including the obligatory and omnipresent guest military experts, advanced the idea of a "clean war," a "pure electronic war without hitches" once military action had actually started. [2] Baudrillard's statements about

---

1 Richard Poirier, *Poetry And Pragmatism* (Cambridge, M.A.: Harvard University Press, 1992), 152.

2 Jean Baudrillard, *The Gulf War Did Not Take Place*, trans. Paul Patton (Bloomington: Indiana UP, 1995), 40 & 34. Though both "The Gulf War Did Not Take Place" and "The Spirit of Terrorism" were originally published as newspaper articles, the quotations here are taken from the essays that were subsequently published in

the Gulf War and his critique of the news coverage in "The Gulf War Did Not Take Place" are, of course, consistent with his theories of simulacra, as Baudrillard warns that media images and the endless expert commentary will eclipse the real, original event itself. "We are left with the symptomatic reading on our screens of the effects of war, or the effects of discourse about the war . . .We must learn to read symptoms as symptoms, and television as the hysterical symptom of a war which has nothing to do with its critical mass" (41).

By way of contrast, Baudrillard in "The Spirit of Terrorism" appears initially to be taken aback by the sheer magnitude of the destruction by the terrorist attacks of September 11th and acknowledges the pure reality of what occurred. Baudrillard posits early in the essay that, if the Gulf War had been a non-event, then the 9/11 attacks signaled a return of *the* event, or what he called "the absolute event, the 'mother' of all events."[3] However, even this testament to the realness of events quickly returns to an argument in line with Baudrillard's critique of simulation. Indeed, despite the sobering effects of the collapse of the Twin Towers, Baudrillard's theories of simulacra soon find their way into his analysis of September 11th, particularly as the proliferation of media images prompts Baudrillard to write: "the spectacle of terrorism imposes the terrorism of the spectacle" (30). By this, Baudrillard means that that spectacle will begin to supersede the reality of the terrorist attacks, and in turn, the images of 9/11 will become themselves instruments of terror. The repeated televised image — the spectacle — then functions in such a way as to "substitute, for a real and formidable, unique and unforeseeable event, a repetitive, rehashed pseudo-event" (34). Such a substitution of the repetitive, rehashed spectacle for the real implies a merging of reality with the televised image and a corresponding impairment of the ability to comprehend fully and clearly the events of 9/11. Baudrillard writes that the "image consumes the event, in the sense that it absorbs and offers it for consumption. Admittedly, it gives it unprecedented impact, but impact as image-event" (27).

Charles Bernstein, in a series of poems entitled "Some of These Daze" from his book *Girly Man*, also addresses the terrorist attacks on September 11th and similarly raises questions about the problem-

---

books.

3 Jean Baudrillard, *The Spirit of Terrorism and Other Essays*, New ed. Trans. Chris Turner (New York: Verso, 2002), 4.

atic nature of televised images and the ability to represent what has happened. Bernstein speaks as well to the difficulty comprehending the magnitude of the terrorist attacks and the corresponding destruction. Though Bernstein and Baudrillard share similarities in their response to September 11th, the two ultimately diverge in their larger arguments about the nature of representation: while Baudrillard asserts that our collective ability to apprehend the terrorist attacks has been impaired due to the onslaught of media images and effects of spectacle, Bernstein affirms his belief in being equal to the task of addressing reality. Though Bernstein admits to being overwhelmed in the wake of 9/11 and nonplussed by the barrage of televised images surrounding the event, he also sees language and poetry as the very means with which to work against any paralysis in the face of what seems impossible to comprehend or represent about September 11th. In this manner, rather than succumbing to what is debilitating about the task representing history in the postmodern age, Bernstein will adhere to a poetics—what I will call the grammar of pragmatism—that reveals the degree to which language provides a means for comprehending our age and method for practical action within the contemporary world.

Bernstein's initial focus in "Some of These Daze" is his and his fellow New Yorkers' stunned responses in the aftermath of the attack on the Twin Towers. The title of the first poem of the series, "It's 8:23 in New York" echoes Frank O'Hara's "I do this, I do that" poems and conjures the immediacy of O'Hara's improvisations written on his lunch hour. Uncannily absent from Bernstein's poem, however, is O'Hara's capricious and campy appreciation of his life in Manhattan, yet Bernstein does maintain the elegiac notes evoked in such O'Hara poems as "A Step Away From Them." The loss in Bernstein's poem is not, of course, for Jackson Pollock or the building where the Armory Show was held but for the reference points of the World Trade Center and the skyline of Manhattan itself: "I can't imagine Manhattan without those two towers looming over the south end" (GM, 17).[4] In subsequent lines, Bernstein registers the traumatic shock of what

---

4 Quotations from Charles Bernstein's works are cited in the text with the abbreviations listed below.

GM: *Girly Man* (Chicago: The University of Chicago Press, 2006).

AP: *A Poetics* (Cambridge, M.A.: Harvard University Press, 1992).

DM: *Dark City* (Los Angeles: Sun & Moon Press, 1994).

MW: *My Way: Speeches and Poems* (Chicago: The University of Chicago Press, 1999).

has occurred through a negative utterance, acknowledging all that resists articulation: "What I can't describe is the reality; the panic; the horror" (GM, 19). The repeated avowals of loss and the failure of the imagination and powers of descriptions squarely situate "It's 8:23 in New York" within the sublime tradition and testify to an experience of extreme magnitude, one that outstrips articulation.

These sentences about the diminished capacity for representation refer back to the very first line of "It's 8:23 in New York" and Bernstein's initial invocation of the sublime, where the poet struggles to express the beauty of New York: "What I can't describe is how beautiful the day is in New York; clear skies, visibility all the way to the other side of wherever you think you are looking" (GM, 17). However, whether Bernstein invokes the splendor of Manhattan on a clear day or addresses the traumatic commotion after the planes hit, each sentiment is a testament to the sublime. In Greek antiquity, the sublime was, for Longinus, an attribute of a great writer whose skillful writing could abundantly convey a beautiful or magnificent experience: "We become aware of a writer's inventive skill, the structure and arrangement of his subject matter, not from one or two passages, but as these qualities slowly emerge from the texture of the whole work. But [the sublime] appears suddenly; like a thunderbolt it carries all before it and reveals the writer's full power in a flash."[5] Longinus' emphasis was on the writer and the stylistic techniques constituting "great" — or sublime — writing, yet in eighteenth-century aesthetics, a shift in emphasis occurs so that the sublime, "the writer's full power in a flash," now becomes associated with a power in nature so magnificent that is frightening. Edmund Burke famously aligns the sublime with an object that produces feelings of terror:

> Whatever is fitted in any sort to excite the ideas of pain, and danger, that is to say whatever is in any sort terrible, or is conversant about terrible objects, or operates in a manner analogous to terror, is a source of the *sublime*; that is, it is productive of the strongest emotion which the mind is capable of feeling. [6]

---

5 Longinus, *On Great Writing (On the Sublime)*, trans. G.M.A. Grube (Indianapolis, I.N.: The Bobbs-Merrill Co., 1957), 4.

6 Edmund Burke, *A Philosophical Enquiry into the Origin of Our Ideas of the Sublime and Beautiful*. ed. J.T. Boulton (Notre Dame, I.N.: University of Notre Dame Press, 1968), 39.

A consequence of this feeling of terror, Burke further explains, is the disruption of the mental faculties by the sublime: "the mind is so entirely filled with its object, that it cannot entertain any other, nor by consequence reason on that object which employs it" (57).

For Bernstein, the sublime in "It's 8:23 in New York" thus initially stems from a positive interaction with nature—the assessment of beauty on an extraordinary day—and yields to a negative, overwhelmed reaction to a terrorist attack far too horrific to register and more in line with what Burke designates as sublime terror. By acknowledging his inability to describe "the reality; the panic; the horror," Bernstein could also be said to participate in a new era of sublime, one that functions analogously to what Rob Wilson has called the nuclear sublime. In the Cold War era, Wilson argues, American poetry frequently exhibited "the sense [that] the nuclear sublime [had] become the American commonplace or common sense of an *unspeakable* force that cannot be—by any power of the imagination, however transcendental—overcome."[7] The condition or sense of the ineffable that Wilson charts in the nuclear sublime arises as well on September 11th, as the terrorist attacks—while certainly not stemming from destructive capacity of thermonuclear force—nevertheless present a large-scale, unimaginable catastrophic scene.

Faced with the unspeakable and unimaginable, Bernstein turns to what is immediately at his disposal, popular culture and its endless array of disaster movies, as he grasps for a context or a conceptual category to make sense of what he has witnessed. In doing so, Bernstein notably approximates Baudrillard's tenets of simulacra and hyperreality: "It was hard not to feel like it was a movie, and one with an unbelievable plot at that. All the airports closed in; the Pentagon bombed; four commercial jets hijacked on suicide missions" (GM, 17). Bernstein constructs his sentences here with the clipped, truncated phrasing of a spy-thriller plot synopsis, rendering actual history with the simulated feel of the hyperreal. The flight of people out of Manhattan in subsequent lines is also reminiscent of a disaster movie in which evacuees form an exodus to safety: "The bridge was overflowing with people streaming out of Manhattan, a line as wide as the bridge and as long as Manhattan itself" (GM, 17-8). Though the immediate context is Hollywood cinema, there are echoes of T.S. Eliot's reference to London Bridge in "The Waste Land," and the

---

7   Rob Wilson, *American Sublime: The Genealogy of a Poetic Genre* (Madison, W.I.: University of Wisconsin Press, 1991), 232.

lines convey Bernstein's disbelief, not that death, but a terrorist attack, "had undone so many."[8] The location of New York, more-over, certainly also recalls Whitman whose crowds traverse from one borough to the next in "Crossing Brooklyn Ferry." The fused Eliot-Whitman references point to the epic proportions of Bernstein's poem, yet absent from "It's 8:23 in New York" is any sense of deep chronological time, whether it would be Eliot's postwar London func-tioning as a palimpsest of Greek antiquity and Medieval Rome or Whitman's extension of his present into an immortal and everlasting future, where "time nor place—distance avails not."[9]

Instead, time seems trapped in a continuous present, an elongated "now," that offers no recourse for critical understanding or distance. "I keep turning on the TV to hear what I can't take in and what I already know. Over and Over. I don't find the coverage comforting but addictive" (GM, 19). Coming after this pronouncement about the deleterious, addictive effects of news coverage of September 11th, the last line of the poem, "It's 8:23 in New York," is a repetition of its title and refuses to resolve into a single, static meaning. Indeed, shed-ding its initial echo of an O'Hara lunch poem, the line can be read alternately: Bernstein—a witness to the day's historical events—is resignedly "signing-off" from his own broadcast, *or*, more emphati-cally, he isolates this moment as the marking of historical time itself, a pragmatic starting point from which to proceed. These readings thus speak to two divergent reactions, one of a dismayed finality or one of urgency, signaling a moment in need of response.

The next poem of the "Some of These Daze" series, "Today is the next day of the rest of your life," appears initially to surrender to feelings of being incapacitated, as Bernstein expressly adopts Baudrillard's terms and his concept of simulation:

> the image is greater than the reality
> the image can't approach the reality
> the reality has no image" (GM, 22).

To affirm "the image is greater than the reality" is to concede that media images—like the serial images of the planes hitting the Twin

---

8   T.S. Eliot, *Selected Poems* (New York: Harcourt Brace & Co., A Harvest Book, 1936), 53.

9   Walt Whitman, *Leaves of Grass*, ed. Sculley Bradley and Harold W. Blodgett (New York: W.W. Norton & Co., 1973), 160.

Towers — have superseded the actual terrorist attack, constituting, in Baudrillard's formulation, "the terrorism of the spectacle." The subsequent two lines, furthermore, extend Baudrillard's hyperreal into its nightmarish conclusion, such that images have no bearing on reality and reality itself seems occluded: ("the image can't approach the reality / the reality has no image"). With this statement about the incommensurability of images and reality, Bernstein reiterates the sublime attributes of an historical moment that resists representation. Bernstein thus sounds perilously close to expressing Fredric Jameson's contention about the "waning of historicity" in our cultural period. The predominant postmodern aesthetic of the image, Jameson argues, impairs any meaningful rendering of history: "This approach to the present by way of the art language of the simulacrum . . . endows present reality and the openness of present history with the spell and distance of a glossy mirage." Jameson consequently concludes that, in the era of late capitalism, "we seem increasingly incapable of fashioning representations of our current [historical] experience."[10]

However, it is important to recall that in *A Poetics* Bernstein famously contested Jameson's argument about contemporary historical representation and postmodernism as a cultural dominant. Bernstein writes: "The pernicious fallout of postmodernism understood as an all-permeating cultural condition is that we are asked to either take it or leave it, or asked to imagine that there is no difference whether we do it or not . . . But seeing these *differences* is the source of our social power to intervene, to agitate, to provoke, to rethink, to take sides — using all of the formal and cultural rhetorics at our command" (AP, 97). With Bernstein's call to intervene and take sides in mind, one can readily recognize that the initial similarity between Baudrillard and Bernstein is merely a step towards Bernstein's ultimate resistance to postmodernism as an entrenched cultural force and his rebuttal of the simulacrum-constituted sublime.[11] Rob Wilson

---

10 Fredric Jameson, *Postmodernism, or the Cultural Logic of Late Capitalism* (Durham, N.C.: Duke University Press, 1991), 21.

11 Not to be overlooked is Jameson's own remarks on interventions into the cultural dominant of postmodernism. Jameson, himself, is not indifferent to questions of agency and addresses possibilities for subversive aesthetics, community politics and collective action. See, for instance, the conclusion of *Postmodernism* (408-18), where Jameson discusses the art installations of Hans Haacke and also the potential of local, grassroots political movements to work on a national or international scale.

offers a relevant line of reasoning when he seeks a poetics equal to the sublime in the nuclear era: "That is, even within this recycled discourse of the sublime, can't we find new formations and affects commensurate with (if not resistant to) this space-age threshold of nuclear force?" (236). For Wilson, there is indeed an appropriate poetic response to what would otherwise be debilitating about the nuclear sublime. "The hope of such cultural work, it seems to me, is that by employing the means not of technological production but of semiotic, the poet can offer symbols of discursive resistance" (241).

Bernstein's own efforts at resistance to the hyperreal in "Some of These Daze" correspond to the techniques he has used throughout his career: his adoption and adaptation of Brecht's *Verfremdungseffekt*, or defamilarization, which breaks the reader's full absorption into, or empathic identification with, the poetic text. The defamiliarizing techniques and devices that Bernstein employs thus include the use or quotation of heterogeneous voices, the invocation of multiple discourses (whether business, academic, or the colloquial, etc.), the serial repetition of phrases, the pronounced use of typographic marks (like the asterisk and ampersand), the quotation and revision of clichés and platitudes, the use of puns and word play, unconventional spacing, line breaks and stanzaic structures, and of course, Bernstein's characteristic humor. These poetic techniques continuously work to foreground the process of representation and constitute Bernstein's grammar of pragmatism: a pragmatic politics and poetics whose foundation is an ever more keen attention to the operations workings of language and grammar. The result of Bernstein's grammar of pragmatism in the serial poems from "Some of These Daze" is a practical slowing down, and an intense focus on language, undertaken so as to engage with, and represent, what would otherwise seem unrepresentable about the terrorist attacks of September 11th in the age of the simulacrum.

Bernstein's grammar of pragmatism has its roots in the American pragmatist philosophical tradition of William James and Ralph Waldo Emerson. Conceiving of pragmatism as a method of arriving at the truth in philosophical inquiry, James writes that the pragmatist endeavors "to interpret each notion by tracing its practical consequences" and therefore asks: "what difference would it practically make to any one if this notion rather than that notion were true?" [12]

---

12 William James, "Pragmatism and Four Essays" from *The Meaning of Truth* (New York: The World Publishing Co., Meridian Books, 1970), 42.

Due to such a philosophical method focused on practical outcomes, James identifies an entire attitude that corresponds to pragmatism. He thus characterizes a pragmatist as one who turns away from "fixed principles, closed systems, and pretended absolutes and origins. He turns towards concreteness and adequacy, towards facts, towards actions and power . . . . It means open air and possibilities of nature, as against dogma, artificiality, and the pretence of finality in truth" (45). Though James outlines his pragmatic method and attitude in terms of philosophical inquiry, pragmatism equally has applications for poetry, as Richard Poirier has so ably demonstrated in his pioneering book *Poetry and Pragmatism*. Correlating pragmatist beliefs with a group of poets he calls the "tribe of Waldo," including Whitman, Frost, Stein and Williams, Poirier isolates in Emerson's view of language a key pragmatist tenet with special pertinence towards poetry. Poirier observes that language for Emerson was an evolving and dynamic—not closed—system: "more than any of the others, [Emerson] offers himself as a truly sacrificial figure, the one who in his writing creates ever more ponderable, ever enlivening, ceaselessly vibrant energies of language . . . " (31). The emphasis that Emersonian and Jamesian pragmatism places on eschewing "fixed principles" and "closed systems" and also on embracing an open view of language and "action" in the battle "against dogma" certainly lends itself to Bernstein's work as well.[13]

Poirier, in *Poetry and Pragmatism*, raises two fundamental concepts of pragmatism—troping and action—that are particularly relevant to Bernstein's poetics. An enemy of pragmatist thought is an uncritical acceptance or obedience to dogma and tradition, yet the past and its traditions are not to be wholly given up either. Pragmatism, instead, advises a thorough understanding of the past, though one that does not wholly defer to the thought of prior generations. Emerson indeed

---

13 It should be noted that Stanley Cavell, with whom Bernstein studied philosophy at Harvard, has questioned recent work that characterizes Emerson as a pragmatist. See for example, Stanley Cavell, "What's the Use of Calling Emerson a Pragmatist?" in *The Revival of Pragmatism*, ed. by Morris Dickstein. (Durham, N.C.: Duke University Press, 1998). Cavell identifies Emerson's call for patience in the essay "Experience" as a refutation of pragmatist emphasis on action: "It is hard not to take this plea of Emerson's for suffering and waiting as pretty flatly the negation of the primacy of practice" (78). For Cavell, what distinguishes the pragmatists from Emerson is the pragmatist dismissal of skepticism and Emerson's appeal to "mourning [as] the path to human objectivity in the world, to separating the world from ourselves, from our private interests in it" (73).

challenges in "The American Scholar" the static nature of cultural knowledge based on the past: "The book, the college, the school of art, the institution of any kind, stop with some past utterance of genius. This is good, say they,—let us hold by this . . . .They look backward and not forward."[14] However, Poirier contends that it is possible to achieve a proper relation to the past through the act of troping: "Writing can show us, nonetheless, how instead of trying to revoke or revere or repeat the past we might, to a limited degree, renew it by troping [our inherited] language . . . " (39). The pragmatist principle of remaining open to the "mutations and superfluities of meaning," to what Poirier calls the "aboriginal power of troping, of turning or changing the apparently given," is, of course, not foreign to Bernstein (39). Bernstein's own privileged terms for troping and its aboriginal power would be language's "radical morphogenerativeness" or its "unsettling and polydictory logics" (MW, 189). To highlight the relevance of pragmatism to Bernstein's poetics, one might note, moreover, that "morphogenerativeness" and "polydictory" are themselves playful neologisms that enact the very concepts they are meant to designate: both terms encapsulate a view of language that repudiates ossified meanings of words in favor of change, linguistic innovation and polysemy.

The troping of language can have real world implications, and this corresponds to the second pragmatist term, "action" that Poirier uses that is pertinent to Bernstein's poetics. Outlining a vision of how a change in language could have social and political import, Poirier sounds a note that is modest and, at the same time, quite ambitious: "Any inflection of language is thus a small gesture of freedom. It cannot accomplish wonders; it will not change the world. But it may ever so slightly make some persons feel like changing the world" (39). Though such claims about changing the world, however qualified or attenuated, may appear utopian to some, the relation between language and thought is not so extravagant, particularly if social change—if action—is predicated upon an alteration in society's conventional thought process. As Poirier observes, Emerson "tries hard to persuade himself, and us, that the kind of work that goes on in writing might change the way we manage our inheritance of language to a point where it might also change our habits of thinking" (113).

---

14 Ralph Waldo Emerson, *Emerson's Prose and Poetry*, ed. Joel Porte and Saundra Morris (New York: New York: W.W. Norton & Co., 2001), 59.

It is at this nexus of language, thought and action that Bernstein's own pragmatism conspicuously manifests itself, for throughout his writings, he advocates for a politically inflected poetry:

> By refusing the criteria of efficacy for determining the political value of the poem, we confer political value on the odd, eccentric, different, opaque, maladjusted—the non-conforming. We also insist that politics demands complex thinking and that poetry is an arena for such thinking: a place to explore the constitution of meaning, of self, of groups, of nations,—of value. The politics of poetry for which I speak is open-ended; the results are not assumed but discovered in the process and available to reformulation. (MW, 4)

To speak of an "open-ended" politics of poetry that "demands complex thinking" and is arrived at through "process" and "reformulation" is to articulate a pragmatist poetics consistent with James's definition of a pragmatist.[15] Bernstein does indeed take the political implications of poetry seriously, yet it is a perspective that is especially comprehensible when one considers that Bernstein construes the act of writing poetry and its politics widely: "The poetic is not confined to poetry but rather is embedded in all our activities of critics, teachers, researchers, and writers, not to mention citizens. When we use figurative language, which is just about whenever we use language at all, we are entangled in the poetic realm" (MW, 43).

Such claims for the politics of poetry have often been dismissed as utopian, and the Language poets own beliefs about the liberating, utopian dimensions of their work ought to be scrutinized carefully. Along these lines, Tenney Nathanson has questioned the more radical utopian pronouncements in Language poetry manifestoes of the seventies as well as some assertions about utopian content in

---

15 For a related discussion Bernstein's relation to pragmatism in terms of community, selfhood and friendship, see Andrew Epstein, *Beautiful Enemies: Friendship and Postwar American Poetry* (New York: Oxford University Press, 2006). Though his primary focus is on the poets Frank O'Hara, John Ashbery and Amiri Baraka, Epstein briefly addresses how Bernstein's work along with other Language poets share a similar pragmatist strain: "Much like Emerson, the pragmatists, and the poets I have discussed, Bernstein never denies that the self is socially indebted and compromised and never idealizes an impossible autonomy from other people or institutions" (284).

Bernstein's more recent essays as being "theoretically problematic and at odds with the textures of the poems themselves."[16] However, Nathanson ultimately comes to an assessment that sounds very close to Poirier's modest claims for Emersonian pragmatism, where the potential for action—borne from a resistance to prevailing social thought—arises. Nathanson argues that "[Bernstein's] poems do not embody a language that would escape symbolic constraint, but instead register, in their straining against received discourse and normative syntax, the desire for such apocalyptic liberation. Unrealized and perhaps unrealizable, this desire may nonetheless energize political practice" (316). Framed as a poetics that employs innovative, experimental writing and draws on the mutability of language to usher in new ways of thinking and, thereby, a political practice, Bernstein's poetry embodies the pragmatist method, recurrently seeking to demonstrate how "troping" language can lead to "action."

The impulse to trope, to pursue the polysemous or "morphogen-erative" qualities of language, is something that Bernstein has consistently fostered in his poems. The use of metaphor, metonymy and synecdoche to transform conventional thought would all satisfy the conditions of pragmatist troping, yet Bernstein also adopts other rhetorical figures and forms of verbal play, like puns, that are in line with comedic sensibilities. Hank Lazer has remarked upon this primacy of puns in Bernstein's poetry and underscores the poet's aim for a provisional aesthetic: "Humor (often of the pun, the replacement [of one word for another similar word], and of association) and a perceptual shifting of perspective become Bernstein's vehicles to an absolute contingency."[17] One witnesses such an appeal to contingency, for the mutability of words, in "The Lives of the Toll Takers" from *Dark City*, for example, when Bernstein writes that "The things I / write are / not about me/ though they / *become me*" (DC, 15). Bernstein here puns on how his works come into being *and* are suited to, flatter, or become him. Relating that his poems are less about himself than about his poetics, Bernstein mocks poetry that would solely flatter his own or another poet's sense of self, and the pun of becoming thus reinforces both his anti-confessional stance and his aversion to the primarily self or voice-based poetry of official verse culture.

---

16 Tenney Nathanson, "Collage and Pulverization in Contemporary American Poetry: Charles Bernstein's *Controlling Interests*," *Contemporary Literature* 33, no.2 (1992): 309.

17 Hank Lazer, "Charles Bernstein's *Dark City*: Polis, Policy, And The Policing of Poetry," *The American Poetry Review* 24, no. 5 (1995), 42.

To return to *Girly Man* and the poems *Some of These Daze*, one sees that troping can also manifest itself as parapraxis, or the disruption of a person's conscious intentions, like a slip of the tongue. The particular parapraxis in question occurs in "Aftershock," and as Bernstein readily acknowledges his error, the blunder itself even becomes incorporated into the poem:

> By mistake I first wrote "Word Trade Center."
> Tuesday morning I rouse my friend Stu from a profound slumber to tell him what has happened to the twin towers. — "They're ugly," he says, after a pause, "but they're not that ugly" (GM, 23).

By foregrounding his errant substitution of *word* for *world* in the phrase "World Trade Center," Bernstein reminds us of the materiality of language and refuses to treat words as a transparent medium with which to represent reality. Bernstein's pragmatist troping here—the simple subtraction of the letter *l* from *world*—forges a direct relationship between the words one uses and the world one lives in, underscoring the degree to which humankind's comprehension of reality is necessarily language based. This instance, and acknowledgement, of parapraxis also functions as an intervention into the unrepresentable, sublime nature of images that earlier left Bernstein at a loss in "It's 8:23 in New York." If seeing repeated images of planes flying into the twin towers conditions the viewer to the tragedy and leads one to see the attacks as unreal, Bernstein persists in calling attention to language in order to lay bare the very act of representation. Bernstein furthermore recognizes that errors like parapraxis are in fact productive. As Bernstein has argued in the essay "Optimism and Critical Excess," poetics "must necessarily involve error. Error in the sense of wandering, errantry, but also error in the sense of mistake, misperception, incorrectness, contradiction. Error as projection (expression of desire unmediated by rationalized explanation: as slips, slides" (AP, 153-54). Such an attitude or stance towards error coheres with pragmatism in both determining the usefulness of missteps and recognizing how the embrace of mistakes can lead to openness and a rejection of the "fixed principles, closed systems" which William James abhorred.

Bernstein's grammar of pragmatism—his will to trope—also finds expression in "Aftershock" with the conjugation of the verb "to bomb" at the poem's end. Though the recourse to the elementary form of verb conjugations seems to communicate simplicity, the lines actually function with a great deal of complexity when one takes into account Bernstein's irony and humor. Bernstein thus strives yet again to foreground the basic operations of language and thereby also deftly scrutinizes subject positions in individual, communal and global politics:

> I bomb
> you bomb
> he/she/it bombs
> we bomb
> you bomb
> they suffer
> We're ugly, but we're not that ugly
> & hey, Joe, don't you know —
> We is they.   (GM, 25)

The conjugation of "to bomb" works through repetition — as do the looping images of the world trade center attack — but unlike the serial televised images, Bernstein significantly introduces change. His permutations shock the reader out of the position of a passive viewer. Moreover, the deceptively simple conjugation of "to bomb" requires U.S. citizens to consider not only the loss of life on September 11th and in other terrorist attacks internationally, but also the United States' own bombing missions in Iraq and Afghanistan: "We is they." At the same time, the line "We is they" does not reduce down solely to a message of the United States' own culpability in war activities in the Middle East but additionally registers a common humanity, an insistence on Bernstein's part, that "we" are no different than "they" as human beings. The line from earlier in the poem ("they're ugly, but they're not that ugly"), which was an utterance that relied on both repetition and a comedian's sense of timing, is altered as well, and the pronominal shift, from "they" to "we," asks us to consider not an aesthetic, architectural dilemma of ugliness but an ethical one, in the eagerness to wage war.

Repetition of lines and the permutation of repeated phrases constitute a key aspect of Bernstein's poetics and efficiently illustrate the principles of pragmatism: a line of poetry can readily stand for a received way of thinking, that, once repeated or altered slightly by permutation, enacts the pragmatist tenet of troping or actively changing entrenched thought. A paradigmatic example of the effects of repetition arises in "Report from Liberty Street" when Bernstein invokes the phrase *"They thought they were going to heaven"* as a refrain. The phrase most immediately refers, of course, to the motivation of the terrorists who hijacked planes on September 11th, 2001, yet occurring eleven times throughout the poem, the italicized refrain also shifts in meaning, particularly in juxtaposition with other lines. The torque exerted on words and phrases to mean more than they say—or to mean differently and variously—begins with the title "Report from Liberty Street" itself and also the first line, as Bernstein assesses Manhattan in the days following the Twin Tower attacks, registering with irony the very name of his location: "I took a walk on Liberty Street today. Only it was not the same place as I had known before" (GM, 26). The first instance of the refrain *"They thought they were going to heaven"* occurs in the following line, and it remains unclear in whose voice the words are uttered: the words could be Bernstein's interior thoughts interrupting his report, the sentiment of public opinion, or a contemporary equivalent to an ancient Greek chorus.

In the subsequent instances, the refrain's initial meaning as the mindset of the highjackers no longer obtains:

> Across the way, the sign on the almost completed "The Residences" at the Ritz-Carlton Downtown says: "Live in Legendary Luxury / Occupancy Fall 2001 / Spectacular Views."
>
> *They thought they were going to heaven.*   (GM, 27)

Though the refrain is repeated verbatim, the lines that precede the refrain color its meaning. The very act of repetition itself, as Lyn Hejinian has observed, can also alter the meaning of the line being repeated: "Where certain phrases recur in [a] work, recontextualized and with a new emphasis, repetition disrupts the initial apparent meaning scheme. The initial reading is adjusted; meaning is set in motion, emended and extended, and the rewriting that repetition becomes postpones completion of the thought indefinitely."[18] The idea of getting to heaven here changes in meaning and relates to the aspirations of those who would purchase luxury in the form of new residences, as Bernstein muses sardonically upon the desire for

---

18 Lyn Hejinian, *The Language of Inquiry* (Berkeley, C.A.: University of California Press, 2000), 44.

opulence and "spectacular views" that must be dramatically revised like the skyline of Manhattan itself in the context of September 11th.

The next instance of the refrain also takes on a different meaning due to the contiguous lines:

> Because the park is closed, it's impossible to get to the Museum of Jewish Heritage: A Living Memorial to the Holocaust. *They thought they were going to heaven.*
> (GM, 27)

Bernstein's irony is present in these lines as well, though more contemplatively and less acerbically so than in the previous instance. The Museum of Jewish Heritage should serve as a reminder for humankind to be vigilant against collective acts of hatred, and Bernstein laments the occurrence of another incident of atrocity and mass killing. Such a contemplation of historic tragedy and senseless murder and the consideration of the victims of the Holocaust summon a corresponding thought of the victims who died on September 11th including those in the Pentagon, at the World Trade Center and on the hijacked airplanes as well as those who first responded to the attacks. The refrain's repeated reference to heaven, then, becomes almost prayer-like, expressing a compensatory logic in hope that the victims' suffering would be short.

If at the beginning of "Report from Liberty Street" Bernstein questions a street's name to underscore the loss of freedom in the wake of September 11th, he continues to show in the rest of the poem how words and the ideas that they represent can, and perhaps ought to, be contested. In his street side report, Bernstein remains vigilant about the ends towards which words are mobilized, remarking, for example, on the slogans which soon crop up: "So it's almost no surprise to see someone with a T-Shirt that says "What Part of Hatred Don't You Understand?" (GM, 28). Though steeped with implication, the question's rhetoric is hardly nuanced and jingoistically infers that the only thing that needs to be understood about September 11th is the enmity with which the attacks were conducted. Bernstein, though, counterbalances his rebuke of chauvinistic patriotism as a reductive mindset with a challenge to an equally reductive perspective that sees an imperial United States as fully culpable and deserving of attack:

> *They thought they were going to heaven.*
> "We got what we deserved," a shrill small voice inside

some seems to be saying. But surely not *this* person, nor
this one, not *this* one, nor *this* one.

Nor *this* one. (GM, 29)

The repetition and italicization of the pronoun *this*—the highlighting
of the act of deixis—points to the particularity of words and emphasizes that language (not to mention politics) is always embedded in
context. It may be arguable that the U.S. global dominance—its will-
fulness as a sovereign power to engage in actions and underwrite poli-
cies that have had deleterious effects on poorer, less powerful regions
of the world—somehow precipitated the September 11th attacks, yet
Bernstein forcefully affirms that an abstract proposition ("We got
what we deserved") cannot hold true when actual people—including his neighbors, friends, family, or even strangers—test the truth-
value of the statement.

In a self-reflexive moment at the end of "Report from Liberty
Street," Bernstein asks "the question isn't is art up to this but what
else is art for?" (GM, 30). Though the context of war and the historical
event of the terrorist attacks are unprecedented subject matter, the
purpose of *Some of These Daze* is no different from that of Bernstein's
work prior to September 11th. Bernstein has continuously sought a
politically engaged poetry that questions the world as it is and the
ideas expressed within it. In "Comedy and the Poetics of Political
Form," first presented as a conference talk in 1988, Bernstein states:

> For every aspect of writing reflects its society's politics and
> aesthetics; indeed, the aesthetic and the political make an
> inseparable *poetics*.
>   Poetry can bring to awareness questions of authority
> and conventionality, not to overthrow them, as in a certain
> destructive intent, but to reconfigure: a necessary defigu-
> ration as   prerequisite for refiguration, for the regenera-
> tion of the ability . . . to think figuratively, tropically. (AP,
> 227)

In the aftermath of September 11th, at the historical moment of wars
in Iraq and Afghanistan, and within the context of the Patriot Act
and its restrictions on civil liberties, the poems of *Some of These Daze*
illustrate the connection between politics and poetry is as pressing as

ever and in Bernstein's view, ever reliant on pragmatist troping and reformulation.

William James, in the essay "The Moral Equivalent of War," exposes the logic—and the words—of those who supported a strong military in 1910. James writes, "'Peace' in military mouths to-day is a synonym for 'war expected.' The word has become pure provocative, and no government wishing peace sincerely should allow it ever to be printed in a newspaper. Every up-to-date dictionary should say that 'peace' and 'war' mean the same thing, now *in posse*, now *in actu*."[19] In lieu of war, James seeks war's moral equivalent by finding a different outlet for humankind's bellicose drives and what he sees as the reasonable appeal of the military itself: including an outlet for patriotism and the honor of serving one's country, a means for collective action, and the dignity of hard work and activity. As Poirier observes, the idea that James has in mind is the type of organized and collective effort of the Peace Corps applied to the domestic concerns of the United States (115). James, himself, describes his equivalent in this manner: "If now—and this is my idea—there were, instead of military conscription, a conscription of the whole youthful population ... enlisted against *Nature* ... numerous goods to the commonwealth would follow" (359). An army of young people directing their energy into public works rather than to the war effort is utopian, something that James readily admits at the end of his essay, yet James also sees his ideas as an important recasting of well-entrenched sentiments of pro-war writers. James directly quotes in his essay the words of these war advocates for the very starkness of their message, first citing General Homer Lea, who argues "War is, in short, a permanent human *obligation*" and then summarizing S. R. Steinmetz's opinion that "War ... is an ordeal instituted by God, who weighs the nations in balance" (353, 354). It is precisely against such definitions of war that James offers his moral equivalent and thereby seeks to challenge and to reformulate the war sentiment.

Whether functioning as a direct allusion to James' essay "The Moral Equivalent of War" or not, Bernstein employs a similar strategy of pragmatist reformulation in "War Stories" from *Girly Man*. Bernstein, adapting Carl Von Clausewitz's formula that "war is the extension of politics by other means," urges a reconsideration of the arguments for military conflict in the immediate context of the Iraq

---

19 William James, *William James: The Essential Writings*, ed. Bruce Wilshire (New York: Harper & Row, Harper Torchbooks, 1971), 351-2.

War. Using the rhetorical figure of anaphora, Bernstein proceeds with ninety-five newfound definitions of war, of which these are the first four:

> War is the extension of prose by other means.
> War is never having to say you're sorry.
> War is the logical outcome of moral certainty.
> War is conflict resolution for the aesthetically challenged.
> (GM, 149)

Again, Bernstein will use repetitions and introduce permutations, and the cumulative effect of the lines works to undercut a single, privileged understanding or definitive statement about war. The lines also traverse territory familiar to Bernstein's poetics: irony and humor are present, and so too is elision of line between politics and poetry, if war is, as Bernstein suggests, for those who cannot create art or can communicate only prosaically.

The majority of Bernstein's equivalent definitions of war are decidedly anti-war. However, several of Bernstein's definitions cut against the grain of a pacifist sentiment; Bernstein, for instance, writes: "War is the right of a people who are oppressed" (GM, 151). Bernstein is not interested, though, in a single political perspective however variously or multiply stated, and the rights of the subjugated to engage in war are also challenged: "War is unjust even when it is just" (GM, 152). Such viewpoints are incommensurable, and Bernstein endorses the contradictory meanings, as this might productively lead to a provocation — rather than unquestioned congealing — of thought about the nature of war and its politics.

One entry of "War Stories" returns squarely to Baudrillard and the question of images, as Bernstein writes: "War is the desecration of the real" (GM, 152). Bernstein here not only alludes to Baudrillard and his invocation of the hyperreal in this post-9/11 poems, but he also remains consistent with remarks he made about combating the omnipresence of simulacra in a lecture at The Poetry Project 1990 Symposium entitled "State of the Art" (a version of which appears in *A Poetics*): "Our images of each other, and of other cultures, seem to go from ignorance to sinisterly deluded fabrication, almost without any middle ground. Poetry can, even if it often doesn't, throw a wedge into this process of social derealization" (AP, 3). To achieve such an end of combating derealization, Bernstein advises to be attentive to the language we use and thereby to the reality we experience. At the end of "War Stories," Bernstein's definitions get shorter:

> War is here.
> War is this.
> War is now.
> War is us. (GM, 154)

With a tone both quiet and direct, Bernstein urges us to be practical and implores us into action, as he seemingly asks: what now will we do with this reality and these truths?

16

PETER MONACELL

Charles Bernstein's Anti-Suburban Poetry

On the first page of *A Poetics*, Charles Bernstein emphasizes the dictum that "*Poetry is aversion to conformity*" (1). Contemporary poets would generally agree with this statement, though many would maintain that the crucial factor in this "aversion" is the establishment of an individual voice. For Bernstein, poetry does not distinguish itself in the world through voice, but through "new forms" that "[swing] wide of this culture's insatiable desire for, yet hatred of, assimilation" (*A Poetics* 1). A "new form" does not mean an original prosodic mode or an innovative way of configuring text on a page. It means an understanding of the world that departs from conformity, on the one hand, or the hatred of it, on the other. (In Bernstein's view both are versions of the same thing.) "Official verse culture" is Bernstein's term for the conformist poetry featured in the majority of poetry anthologies and circulated by "all the major trade publishers [and] the poetry series of almost all university presses."[1] Bernstein first used this term in print in 1986's *Content's Dream*, but his clearest description of "official verse culture" may appear in a footnote to his essay "In the Middle of Modernism in the Middle of Capitalism on the Outskirts of New York." After summarizing his 1986 definition, he adds that "the bulk of this poetry tends to be blandly apolitical or accomodationist [*sic*], neoromantic, and (often militantly) middle-of-the-road, or as it is now called, 'suburban'" (*A Poetics* 4). Bernstein places *suburban* in quotation marks, but his source for the adjective remains unspecified; he

---

1 Bernstein, *Content's Dream: Essays 1975-1984* (Evanston, IL: Northwestern University Press, 1986), 247.

therefore implies that one or more previous critical works have aptly described conformist poetry by using this adjective.

Bernstein's footnote refers simultaneously to critical texts by Jerome J. McGann and Robert Von Hallberg. Most immediately, Bernstein's footnote recalls McGann's 1988 article "Contemporary Poetry, Alternative Routes," which defines language poetry as an historical counterpart to "personal (not confessional) or localized verse" (625). Unlike language poetry, this verse is "marked stylistically by a moderated surface urbanity and, substantively, by an attempt to define 'social' and 'political' within a limited, even a personal, horizon (626). Although McGann himself calls this homogenous body of work "the poetry of the suburbs" and "suburban," he cites Von Hallberg as the origin of such a characterization (626n.). In the conclusion of 1985's *American Poetry and Culture, 1945-1980*, Von Hallberg conceptualizes the poetry of the suburbs: "In the last decade, several important poets have tried in particular to accommodate the middle and lower-middle classes resident in the suburbs and represented through television, movies, and tabloids." This has been the case, he argues, because, "the actual audience for poetry is suburban only insofar as college and university towns are suburban." Von Hallberg claims to examine the poetry of the suburbs so that he might understand how poets have looked "searchingly and fairly at the national culture."[2]

By calling "official verse culture" "suburban," Bernstein joins McGann in expropriating Von Hallberg's original term.[3] Whereas Von Hallberg admires the poetry of the suburbs, the two latter critics use "suburban" in a derisory way. The conformist poetry that Bernstein dubs "official verse culture," and which McGann criticizes in "Contemporary Poetry, Alternative Routes," is suburban inasmuch as suburban Americans themselves are politically uncommitted and preoccupied with personal affairs. But this analogy cuts both ways. If a body of poetry is suburban, then a large segment of the American population can fairly be described as *like* the poetry of the

---

2 Robert Von Hallberg, *American Poetry and Culture, 1945-1980* (Cambridge, MA: Harvard University Press, 1985), 228-229.

3 In an interview archived in SUNY Buffalo's Electronic Poetry Center (Seminary Co op Bookstore, 1999), http://epc.buffalo.edu/authors/bernstein/interviews/SemCoop. html, Bernstein recalls a conversation that he had with Von Hallberg about "Official Verse Culture." This conversation points to Von Hallberg as a source for Bernstein's conception of this poetry as "suburban."

suburbs: politically uncommitted and preoccupied with personal affairs. In his highly polemical 1998 book *The American Poetry Wax Museum*, Jed Rasula offers insight into where this second analogy leads. Rasula claims that suburban Americans think in the same way in which suburban poetry operates. He theorizes the so-called "suburban epiphany," which results from a suburbanite's "strong dose of fantasy, compensating for the professional obligations and social maladjustments endemic to late capitalism."[4] According to Rasula, such epiphanies have become the lamentable aspiration of too many contemporary poets. He associates the abundance of suburban poetry with the rapid institutionalization of the American poet in academia: "The white collar subject of Whyte's *Organization Man* in the 1950s has, in the 1990s, become the Organization Poet, studiously and obediently working up *curriculum vitae* itemizing the published 'McPoems'. . . by which such careers are profiled."[5] These "McPoems" churn out suburban epiphanies in response to the perception that suburbia oppresses its inhabitants, including its resident poets.

To employ Bernstein's terminology, suburban poetry is an "old form," which fails to provide a new way of making sense and reiterates an objectionable worldview. But even if Bernstein does not use "old forms," suburban imagery still comprises an important component of his work. The poems in which Bernstein portrays suburban people and environments are not "suburban" in the sense that he expounds in *A Poetics*, but in the sense that they are to an extent *about suburbia*. As might be expected, Bernstein mounts a Marxist critique of suburbanites and their commonplace perceptions of disenfranchisement and oppression. However, Bernstein does not automatically make "suburban" synonymous with "bourgeois." In "The Klupzy Girl" (1983) he succinctly evaluates the bourgeois worldview:

> To stroll on the beach is to be in
> the company of the wage-earner and
> the unemployed on the public way, but
> to command a view of it from a vantage
> both recessed and elevated is to enter
> the bourgeois space; here vantage and view

---

4 Jed Rasula, *The American Poetry Wax Museum: Reality Effects 1940-1990*. (Urbana, IL: National Council of Teachers of English Press, 1996). 428.

5 Ibid., 433.

become consumable.[6]

In "The Klupzy Girl" the elevated, bourgeois perspective turns a stroll on the beach, an activity weighted with romantic associations in both the literary and emotional realms, into a commodity. Bernstein portrays suburbanites not as inhabitants of this elevated "bourgeois space" but as one of the populations among "wage-earners . . . on the public way." His work attests that suburban lifestyles can contain aspects of proletarian experience, including an inarticulate resentment against "the system." White-collar labor, like blue-collar labor, appears in Bernstein's work as a form of bourgeois dominance.

Bernstein situates suburban imagery and themes into the "new forms" of his poetry in order to portray suburbia as a complex cultural phenomenon. Three of his poems—from three different decades—represent suburbia in especially overt and incisive ways. "Force of Habit" (1983), "Foam Post" (1991), and "The Throat" (2001) take outwardly lyric shapes, seeming from a distance much like the representative poems of "official verse culture." Within their lines, however, these poems contain various fragments and acute disjunctions. If the uniformity of lineation in these poems corresponds to social restraints, then Bernstein's difficult syntaxes and esoteric diction challenge these restraints. "Force of Habit," "Foam Post," and "The Throat" each fantasize about personal autonomy and model that autonomy through language play. In these poems Bernstein demonstrates how language might be used to assert freedom, even within suburbia, an environment that encourages orthodoxy.

"Force of Habit," from 1983's *Islets/Irritations* (the same collection that includes "The Klupzy Girl"), features a description of white-collar labor and a solitary worker's declaration of rebellion against that labor. The poem begins by evoking the anesthetic routine of a morning commute out of the suburbs and into the workplace. Bernstein focuses on the commute's diminishment of a driver, who represents just one individual amidst a crowd of people following a common routine:

Freckle motorizes bejesus spanking tall
tarpaper. Along then, brain in hands, sail
the mechanism three times beyond sight of house, rolling

---

6 Bernstein, *Islets/Irritations* (New York, NY: Roof Books 1983), 49.

unconsciously in chaos of already presupposed forces,
winding way into the all the more inappropriate
breach of already insufferable
attitudes.[7]

As this passage begins, a "Freckle motorizes" by "spanking tall /
tarpaper." In other words, a car moves along the roadway; it becomes
like a sailboat in the windy "chaos of already presupposed forces."
These forces propel the car well beyond the driver's residential space,
"three times beyond sight of house." Amid a sea of other drivers, the
commuter relinquishes independence, seeming to himself like an
automaton with "brain in hands." The rewards for this relinquish-
ment are not heroic. This passage parodies the famous monologue
in *Henry V*, Act III ("Once more unto the breach, dear friends . . .").[8]
Through this comical allusion, Bernstein juxtaposes the commuter's
entrance into traffic against a soldier's brave entrance into battle.
Far from intrepid, the inhabitants of the commuters' realm exhibit
"already insufferable / attitudes" that seem to typify their mundane,
white-collar lives.

The main thematic thread running through this poem is the
dehumanization caused by sustained mental labor. Several epithets
characterize white-collar workers as lifeless; for example, they are
"comatose cryptographers," "tulips, inlaid with enameled frost," "a
protein substance."[9] In an extended pun Bernstein suggests the back
pain caused by sitting in an office chair: "Lumbar from antiquated
/ resistance, concoct what seeing fells."[10] The workers' lower backs
feel to them like wood ("lumber"), owing to an absence of ergonomic
support, the "antiquated / resistance" of their desk chairs. On another
semantic level, the office workers "lumber" through their work in
a wooden way. Later in the poem, the time-clock antagonizes their
efforts. Bernstein writes, "Time / the measured sustenance, becomes
/ all more alert to maze like hat / of bemused focus."[11] These lines
describe the experience of "watching the clock," even while seeming to continue working. Given the poem's description of their jobs,

---

7 Ibid., 10.

8 See William Shakespeare, *The Life of Henry V*, Act III, scene i, in *The Riverside
   Shakespeare*, ed. G. Blakemore Evans, (Boston: Houghton Mifflin, 1974), 947.

9 Ibid., 10-11.

10 Ibid., 10

11 Ibid.

no one could blame the workers for becoming impatient. Sitting at computers, they perform "guileless manipulation" and "shock tabular spacing," and their work seems mathematical, a "horn rimmed metrics." Another line asserts that they "Target to presuppose umpteen incineration."[12] Each time the workers perform one of their logarithmic functions, they imagine the utopian "incineration" of their workplace.

"Force of Habit" proceeds to fantasize about individual resistance to the grind of mental labor. About midway through the poem, a first person voice appears to reclaim the sense of autonomy lost in the poem's first half:

> . . . I take hat
> in hand, by hand announce
> a sequel logic, steady
> against the line of the shore, pushes
> back as keeps coming, dote on
> pressurized feed grain, wells it shut.[13]

Doing anything "by hand" contrasts the automation that the poem attributes to white-collar labor. Presumably, the commuter himself takes "hat in hand," and as a result deviates from workplace conformity. He resists the system in which he labors by declaring his understanding of it as "a sequel logic, steady / against the line of the shore." This description visualizes the poem itself, which is both "a sequel logic" and also a tide of words, pushing against the recalcitrant "line of the shore." (Textually, the straight left margin represents this shore, whereas the undulating right margin resembles a series of crashing waves.) The poem constitutes an act of resistance, in which the commuter perceives himself as an unruly cow in a feed lot. He imaginatively wells shut the "pressurized feed grain" that sustains life under such conditions. This obstruction produces images of bursting; suddenly there is a "gush / with parting stem," as if a succulent branch is snapped off of a plant. The poem continues, "Springs / redress, funneled cue note to lost dominance."[14] Bernstein implies the commuter's assertion of raw human nature, over against his feeling of "lost dominance."

---

12 Ibid.

13 Ibid., 11.

14 Ibid.

When compared to the domineering forces of capitalism, the commuter's autonomy seems a mere intrigue. His will is "discarded remittance," comprising a "Fund for the city of the unincorporated, / the scattered talk in the apricot park."[15] These lines depict the commuter's rebellion as a pastoral fantasy that transpires within a carefully circumscribed setting. They also suggest mounting proletarian resentment towards those human cogs that are fully "incorporated" into the machine. Workers that remain "unincorporated," at least psychologically, can only express their autonomy as "scattered talk" instead of an organized movement. "Force of Habit" ends by asserting the impossibility of a white-collar revolution:

> . . . Given, a protein
> substance neither panicked enough nor
> wary enough to take the cow by the tail
> and lip read limericks to the assembled labels—
> false warning of the make believe
> embroglio, hand painted summation.[16]

Finally, the commuter has neither the fear nor the awareness necessary to control his own destiny. He cannot "take the cow by the tail"—a pun on "taking the bull by the horns" that recalls the feed lot imagery appearing earlier in the poem. In addition, he cannot make light of his situation, or "lip read limericks to the assembled labels." Because of these inabilities, the commuter conveys only the "false warning of the make believe / embroglio." His plot against the system is, from the beginning, a fantasy of independence and cooperation among workers. Even so, the poem itself exhibits his "hand painted summation," his intricately crafted language that starkly contrasts the automation obliged by white-collar labor.

"Foam Post," which appears in Bernstein's 1991 collection *Rough Trades*, also celebrates the freedom that language play can provide. A much more aleatory poem than "Force of Habit," "Foam Post" elaborates on the sense of impotence that accompanies masculine domesticity. Such a unified meaning may at first seem unlikely because, as Pierre Joris observes, in *Rough Trades* the majority of poems "are constructed from a cornucopia of found (read, overheard) phrases &

15 Ibid.
16 Ibid.

sentences: they are a collage of discourse-fragments from extremely heterogeneous origins."[17] "Foam Post" clearly furnishes such a collage; however, the poem also unifies its various components to suggest the theme of impotence. This theme initially appears in the poem's title, which evokes a sheath of protective foam placed around a post to ensure safety (such as those found in athletic stadiums), and with this title, Bernstein presents an image of emasculation that resonates later in the poem:

> Tinsel of titularly vague versions
> Verging behind programmable dual
> Dipsticks. Everything seen so far
> Away and more produce on other
> Seismographic orifice bundle branching
> Toxemia inadmissible as to stuck-up
> Steam stadium circuits bored cauldron.[18]

Because the "programmable dual dipsticks" resemble remote controls, this passage suggests television watching. Indeed, Bernstein creates the perception of flashy movement at a distance: "Tinsel of titularly vague versions" that are "seen so far / Away." The television itself becomes a vaginal "seismographic orifice" that the viewer, with his "bundle branching," wants to penetrate. Frustratingly, he is "inadmissible." The poem mentions toxemia, or pre-eclampsia, a medical condition in which a pregnant woman's body accumulates toxins. By extension, the television is already pregnant, and dangerously so. Were the viewer actually to penetrate the television (the poem does suggest as much), its "circuits" would electrocute him, causing a bodily emasculation in which the phallus becomes a violently feminized "cauldron."

Television watching is endemic to suburban life, but the poem's suburban content really materializes near the end of the poem. In a seemingly narrative passage, Bernstein connects impotence with suburbia:

> . . . Rain, rain
> Raining inside my tailored suit. "Twelve

---

17 Pierre Joris, "Bernstein's *Rough Trades*," *American Book Review*, 14(6), Electronic Poetry Center, http://epc.buffalo.edu/authors/bernstein/reviews/abr-joris.html.

18 Bernstein, *Rough Trades* (New York: Sun and Moon, 1991), 56.

> Yards, only twelve yards over, at the
> Intersection of Vein and Vine—another
> Lawn being mowed! Another
> Gracious day!"¹⁹

Owing to Whitman's *Leaves of Grass*, the very image of a lawn being mowed carries castrative overtones. Bernstein reinforces these overtones with his location of the lawn mower at the intersection of "Vein and Vine." Both terms euphemize the penis, but in combination they suggest that the rigid "vein" has become a flaccid "vine"—a reimagined "foam post." What causes this sexual diminishment? Stuck inside of his "tailored suit," the speaker feels alienated from his workaday life. With mock-enthusiasm he observes "another / Lawn being mowed!" on "Another / Gracious day!" The yard work communicates a blind sense of purpose that the suited man cannot share. He interprets the lawn mower "only twelve yards over" as a symbol of his impotence. Instead of the nursery rhyme "rain, rain, go away," he recites, "Rain, rain / Raining inside my tailored suit," and with this image, he conveys his inescapable gloom. However, by alluding to a nursery rhyme, Bernstein implies that the suited man's thinking is playful. In the larger context of *Rough Trades*, rain symbolizes language play. Bernstein establishes this symbolism in the opening poem of the volume, "The Kiwi Bird in the Kiwi Tree," which begins with a desire "to be drenched in the downpour of words."²⁰

"Foam Post" celebrates its own irreducibility as a private utterance, and conceives of the free use of language as empowerment. The poem ends with a sort of "rhapsody" on privacy:

> . . . Not to have to
> Not to say, not to have to have
> To, not to have to prey, not to
> Have to, not to have to feel
> Not to, not to have to have to
> Say. Pink lemons on the orange

---

19 Ibid., 57.

20 Ibid., 11. "The Kiwi Bird in the Kiwi Tree" also contains the image of a tailor and the word "versions." The semantic parallels among this poem, others such as "Riddle of the Fat Faced Man" and "Wait," and "Foam Post" suggest that Bernstein develops complex symbolic motifs in *Rough Trades*.

Lime tree.[21]

The litany of "not to's" and "have to's" extols willful disengagement from public expression, from exploiting other people ("to prey"), and from sentimentality ("to feel"). The poem does not "have to say," or even "not have to not to say," anything at all. Although it may appear to evoke one set of meanings, like the suited man, its outgrowths are ultimately surprising. Within its lineated boundary, the poem presents a "new form," yielding "pink lemons on the orange / Lime tree." This imagery refers to the heterogeneous materials contained within a poem that looks relatively conventional, or "suburban." Similar to many instantiations of "official verse culture," "Foam Post" takes on the stichic, left-justified form of an individual lyric. However, unlike those poems, it exhibits an unwillingness to operate in an orthodox manner. "Foam Post" ends with a riddle that reasserts the suburbanite's masculinity. The enigmatic tree has a phallic virility about it, and also conceptualizes masculine strength as rigid taciturnity.

As a whole, the poem meditates on the resemblances between sexual impotence and the suburban male's social disempowerment. Just prior to its "TV" passage, "Foam Post" describes the viewer as having a "Notable / Inclination: 'Too much belly an' no' / Eno' brain."[22] He has grown fat and sedentary, and he feels a complete lack of personal fortitude in his daily life. Using a second-person address, Bernstein writes to this subject, "as agent you / Devolved and basically are / Spunk in a minute reprobated / Adverse elemental approbation gelatinous."[23] These lines envision his reduction to a biological element, "gelatinous" semen ("spunk"), and admit to his feelings of "reprobated" sexuality. The imagery here is masturbatory, a preamble to the suburbanite's bizarre desire for his television. "Foam Post" contains several passages that attribute the suburbanite's lack of masculine agency to financial anxiety. He feels the "guarantee" of "cleaned / Out pockets" and ponders a "Rant about owing restricted / Tributary and wakes on / These stupid tires."[24] In other words, he regrets his dependence on an unserviceable car, which drains his money and keeps him awake. As a "Pede-like" individual (in part,

---

21 Ibid., 57.
22 Ibid., 56.
23 Ibid.
24 Ibid.

because forced to walk), he worries about "piquant insolvency."[25] The poem portrays him as a proletarian mired in debt. An earlier passage imagines his "implements / Trashed in an overgrown bestiary / In a vest of tiers."[26] These "implements," representing both his phallic *tool* and his masculine agency, languish under the confinement of a class system, or "vest of tiers." In summary, "Foam Post" ascribes the suburbanite's sense of emasculation to his social position, but nevertheless demonstrates his empowerment through language play, which yields "Pink lemons on the orange / Lime tree."[27]

"The Throat," a poem that appears in Bernstein's 2001 collection *With Strings*, seems to eschew such empowerment in favor of a more conventional, "suburban" form. The poem differs from "Force of Habit" and "Foam Post" because it does not delve into social issues related to suburbia, such as white-collar labor and masculine gender roles. Instead, it imagines suburbia as a bourgeois space that harbors bourgeois forms of utterance. Much of the poem transpires in an affluent neighborhood: "Goethe Avenue's sprawling / stone mansions."[28] Its protagonist remembers his mother's suicide, which occurred in one of these mansions, his childhood home. The bourgeois setting complements several passages that resemble "official verse culture." Consider, for example, "A dense gauze of grayish silver light / parted as we passed through /and into it, reforming itself."[29] The diction and rhythms in this passage seem poetical, as though "workshopped." As a whole, "The Throat" exhibits linguistic concision and narrative progression much like the "suburban poetry" that Bernstein so stridently criticizes. According to his essay "In the Middle of Modernism in the Middle of Capitalism on the Outskirts of New York," such poetry conceives of language as an "instrument that [can] be used neutrally and transparently to 'transmit' a pregiven communication." Its authors instantiate the "bourgeois, liberal, patriarchal space of a rhetoric-free discourse that aspires to be unitary, causal, linear, dialect-neutral, imperious/impersonal, unambiguous."[30] "The

---

25 Ibid., 57.

26 Ibid., 56.

27 See also Ibid., 80, where Bernstein opens his long poem "Pockets of Lime" with an image of suburban men tending to their lawns: "The lawn engages / Its constituent appraisers."

28 Bernstein, *With Strings* (Chicago: University of Chicago Press, 2001), 40.

29 Ibid.

30 Bernstein, *A Poetics*, 94-97.

Throat" meditates on poetry as "pregiven communication" partly by situating its speaker in suburbia. At the midpoint of the poem, he recalls approaching his childhood home: "I walked blindly across the lawn, / then, without thinking, started / moving back through the bright vacancy."[31] Shortly thereafter, the protagonist envisions his mother's body.

"The Throat" uses an "old" form: it depicts a private journey as a passage into self-knowledge. The protagonist narrates his walk along Goethe Avenue and eventual descent into "the other / side of the absolute darkness."[32] Modernism has predisposed readers to recognize, even to privilege, the metaphorical fusion of exterior spaces with interior ones. Sigmund Freud bears much of the responsibility for this, but so do Joseph Conrad and T. S. Eliot. In addition to its allusion to Conrad's *Heart of Darkness* (1902), "The Throat" alludes to Eliot's early poems "The Love Song of J. Alfred Prufrock," "Portrait of a Lady," and "Rhapsody on a Windy Night," which were published in *Prufrock and Other Observations* (1917).[33] Like these poems, "The Throat" employs a crepuscular setting and contemplates the relationship of the speaking subject to the author. Bernstein evokes a surreal atmosphere, using fog in much the same way as both "Love Song" and "Portrait." He alludes to "Rhapsody on a Windy Night" by including street lamps in his poem. After the protagonist passes three of these civic installations, the meaning that he wishes to convey dissolves. ("Rhapsody" uses street lamps to punctuate and inspire its speaker's bizarre fantasies.) The most apparent similarity between "The Throat" and Eliot's poetry is the profusion of symbols that Bernstein presents. Near the end of the poem, the protagonist encounters four objects relating to his mother's death—a bottle, glass, gun, and suicide note—which strike him with their rich significance: "For all their differences, / each seemed crammed with possibilities, / with

---

31 Bernstein, *With Strings*, 40.

32 Bernstein, *With Strings*, 41. Bernstein refers to the Vietnam War in the next line of his poem "The Throat." The protagonist of Peter Straub's *The Throat* (New York: Signet, 1994), from which Bernstein draws fragments of language, is a Vietnam veteran. In addition, Bernstein evokes Francis Ford Coppola's movie *Apocalypse Now* (1979), which transplants the narrative of Joseph Conrad's *Heart of Darkness* (1902) into Southeast Asia.

33 See T. S. Eliot, *Collected Poems 1909-1962* (New York: Harcourt Brace, 1963), and especially *Prufrock and Other Observations* (1917), which is included in this volume on pages 1-26 and includes "The Love Song of J. Alfred Prufrock" (3–7), "Portrait of a Lady" (8-12), and "Rhapsody on a Windy Night" (16-18).

utterance."[34] These lines might as well describe symbols in any of Eliot's poems, which communicate meaning through constructing intricate symbolic matrices.

By alluding so clearly to Eliot, Bernstein points out similarities between Modernism and the bulk of contemporary poetry. He echoes Marjorie Perloff, who establishes many such similarities in both *The Poetics of Indeterminacy* and "Pound/Stevens: Whose Era?" Perloff observes that modernist symbolism, despite its fragmentation and allusiveness, actually lays the groundwork for the contemporary prevalence of self-contained, first-person lyrics.[35] Eliot's early poems "The Love Song of J. Alfred Prufrock," "Portrait of a Lady," and "Rhapsody on a Windy Night," each an example of modernist symbolism, do finally qualify as such poems. Refracted through the more recent critiques of McGann, Rasula, and Bernstein himself, Eliot's poetry anticipates "suburban poetry." It follows that "The Throat" harkens back to its own origins in Modernism, even while Bernstein imitates "official verse culture." His psychological narrative goes so far as to incorporate several italicized "epiphanies" (to use Rasula's term); for example, the protagonist seems suddenly to realize of his dreamlike suburban setting, "*this is where I dip my buckets, where I | fill my pen.*"[36] But these phrases are not what they appear to be. In the notes to *With Strings*, Bernstein reveals that "The Throat" takes as its source Peter Straub's 1994 novel also entitled *The Throat*.[37] Straub's novel is a thriller about a murder investigation. The popular, prose form employed by the novel stands in stark contrast to Eliot's definitive illustrations of Modernism, and to the profound, personal utterances that the audience for "official verse culture," or "suburban poetry," has come to expect.

In "The Throat" Bernstein observes how this poetry obfuscates its own conformity to "old" forms. He imitates "official verse culture" in order to emphasize its similarities to prose works like Straub's *The Throat*. He further implies that, whereas these popular novels make no secret of their commodity status, "suburban poetry" essentially pretends to be high culture—the continuation of Modernism. This

---

34 Bernstein, *With Strings*, 41.

35 See the introduction to Marjorie Perloff, *The Poetics of Indeterminacy: Rimbaud to Cage* (Princeton, NJ: Princeton University Press, 1981), especially pages 29-38, and Perloff, "Pound/Stevens: Whose Era?" *New Literary History*, 13, no. 3 (1982): 485-518.

36 Bernstein, *With Strings*, 40.

37 Ibid., 131.

poetry is lineated, narrative, even nominally fragmented and allu-
sive, but finally homogenous. It follows that "The Throat" surprises
readers, ultimately producing "Pink lemons on the orange / Lime
tree." In view of both its concern with suburbia and its formal dissim-
ulation, the poem is of a kind with "Force of Habit" and "Foam Post."
However, *With Strings* contains other poems that resemble these ante-
cedents even more closely. "Today's Not Opposite Day," for example, features a lengthy "block" of suburban incidents apparently
culled directly from local newspapers. For instance, "An injured cat,
still alive in the road, was sighted in the vicinity of Goose Lane."[38]
Another poem in *With Strings*, "Low Regrets," recalls the quotidian
content of "Force of Habit." The alienated speaker of this 2001 poem
lives surrounded by products such as "The Club antitheft device."[39]
He laments, in a similar manner to the self-pitying suburbanite in
"Foam Post," "I should have wasted my life."[40] The presence of these
poems in *With Strings* shows that Bernstein's concern with suburbia
has continued well into the twenty-first century.

In conclusion, this recurrent concern with suburbia distinguishes
Bernstein among practitioners of language poetry, and criticism
that focuses on such recognizable content deviates from the *pars pro
toto* way in which these literary figures are usually discussed. The
frequency with which Bernstein writes about suburbia comprises a
crucial aspect of his "signature." In her 1998 article "Language Poetry
and the Lyric Subject," Marjorie Perloff coined this term as an alternative to "voice," which Bernstein has disavowed.[41] Ten years earlier,
in his *The Utopian Moment in Contemporary American Poetry*, Norman
Finkelstein suggested why individualizing language poets among
their artistic collective is even necessary:

---

38 Ibid., 75.

39 Ibid., 82.

40 Ibid., 82. Compare this poem to James Wright's "Lying in a Hammock at William
Duffy's Farm in Pine Island, Minnesota" (1963), collected in *Above the River: The
Complete Poems* (Middletown, CT: Wesleyan University Press, 1990), 122.

41 Perloff, "Language Poetry and the Lyric Subject: Ron Silliman's Albany, Susan
Howe's Buffalo" (Electronic Poetry Center, 1998), http://wings.buffalo.edu/epc/
authors/perloff/ langpo.html, 1. See also a quotation from Bernstein's 1981 interview with Tom Beckett in *Content's Dream*, 407. The poet states, "To try to unify
the style of work around [the] notion of self is to take the writing to be not only
reductively autobiographical in trying to define the *sound* of me but also to accept
that the creation of a persona is somehow central to writing poetry . . . . I don't
have a voice."

The taboo against the author as a fundamental unit of criticism has, in the case of the language poets, success-fully concentrated attention on the political principles of an alternate literary collectivity, and on the formal prin-ciples of an alternate poetic language. But the extent to which these principles operate in a number of increas-ingly mature and distinct (though still related) personal styles remains to be explored.[42]

As of 2010, such explorations have only just begun. By and large (and with the exceptions of McGann and Perloff), critics have read Bernstein and the language poets through the lenses of language poetry's own manifestos, and the continental theory that undergirds these manifestos: Derrida, Foucault, Althusser, Adorno, and others. This way of reading has a few corollary effects on Bernstein's work. First, poems that already appear esoteric are made doubly so by pronounced associations with writing that is also difficult, requiring a large measure of initiation into its matter and methods. Second, such criticism risks arriving at reductive descriptions, however conceptu-ally complicated, of Bernstein's writing—descriptions which focus on his indebtedness to received constructs and vocabularies. And finally, the theoretical abstraction of Bernstein's poetry mitigates against its exciting linguistic performances, which play out in the material world that surrounds us.

---

42 Finkelstein, Norman, *The Utopian Moment in Contemporary American Poetry* (Cranbury, NJ: Associated University Presses, 1988), 118.

17

DONALD WELLMAN

Some Nouns

for Charles and Susan

The smell of horehound, crushed and rolled in the palm
Yarrow, tansy delight my friends
turning a leaf
The wind exposes silver under straw- bay- black-
berry, laurel

Lambkill has narrow leaves, Rhodora
Names confuse the species
Balsam and red cedar are stories From the hill
the sweet air disposes blue, sea, sky

Near and far, the mountains: Penobscot, Pemetic
Roofs of mansions, meadows, proper
and inappropriate
nouns, knowing The sense
is gray rose rock
yellow

Points, estuaries, simply shorelines
divide the panorama, suspending odor and taste
between water and not-water, surfaces
in the voluminous light

18

CARLOS GALLEGO

From a Philosophy of Poetry to Poetry as Philosophy: The Dialectical Poetics of Charles Bernstein

> I am engaged in a process, in questioning, not in offering solutions.
> —Charles Bernstein, "A Conversation with Charles Bernstein"

Critical debates regarding the aesthetic value and political significance of Charles Bernstein's poetry and poetics have continued now for approximately three decades, fueled by ongoing distinctions drawn between linguistic-aesthetic interpretations and politico-philosophical readings of his work. As a result of these distinctions, Bernstein's writing is usually analyzed in terms of either poststructuralist experimentalism or Marxist political aestheticism. As Paul Naylor observes, "Critical discourse has characterized Bernstein in particular and the group of poets with which he is associated—the 'language poets'—in order to contain them under the rubric of either Marxism or poststructuralism" (119). As an alternative to this "containment," Naylor follows Marjorie Perloff's suggestion in "Toward a Wittgensteinian Poetics," where she proposes a Wittgensteinian approach to the Language poets' understanding of language and meaning-production.[1] Being "wary of any attempt to equate [Bernstein's] position with poststructuralism," Naylor instead reads "his poetry and poetics in terms of the work of Ludwig Wittgenstein in order to show

---

1   See Marjorie Perloff, "Toward a Wittgensteinian Poetics," *Contemporary Literature* 33 (summer 1992).

that Bernstein's concepts of language and the self are not reducible to either Marxism or poststructuralism" (120–122). While I applaud this commitment to not "contain" Bernstein's poetics, I nonetheless find the distinctions drawn between Wittgenstein, poststructuralism, and Marxism problematic in two regards: first, it implies that Wittgenstein is in no way affiliated or associated with poststructuralism, which seems strange considering Wittgenstein's influence on theorists like Foucault, Lyotard, and Derrida.[2] Second, the unquestioned distinction drawn between Marxism and Wittgenstein's philosophy of language seems overstated, especially when one considers the similarities between the Marxist concepts of exchange-value and use-value and Wittgenstein's theory of language-games.

Rather than privilege any one of these popular interpretive models, I instead propose a more dialectical approach that highlights the ways in which these critical theories intertwine to create a more comprehensive understanding of Bernstein's work. It is important to remember that, when analyzing Bernstein's poetics, one must remain open to the possibility of critical reexamination and epistemic risk, since his poetry demands the type of anti-identitarian thinking advocated by the Frankfurt School and Lacanian psychoanalysis. As Henry Sussman observes, "'Language poetry' and critical theory . . . share a certain commitment to the explicit, to rendering overt and subject to question conceptual and operational underpinnings which in the context of dominant culture are hidden, occulted, sublimated, and a prioritized" (1203). Viewing Bernstein's work through these theoretical traditions does not limit or contain his poetics, but rather helps locate it within a modernist legacy of ideological struggle and sociocultural resistance.

In what follows, I attempt to demonstrate how form, historicity, and ideological critique dialectically interact to build a dynamic tension in Bernstein's poetry, particularly through his strategic use of materiality. I argue that materiality is central to Bernstein's poetics, guiding his theory of antiabsorption while giving his poetry a philosophical quality reminiscent of avant-garde modernism. This antiabsorptive approach enables Bernstein to accentuate the inher-

---

2 See Bernstein's remarks concerning Wittgenstein and Derrida in "The Objects of Meaning," in *Content's Dream* (Los Angeles: Sun & Moon Press, 1986). For a brief discussion concerning Wittgenstein's influence on Deconstruction, see Mark Taylor, introduction to *Deconstruction in Context* (Chicago: University of Chicago Press, 1986). For a longer study, see Henry Staten, *Wittgenstein and Derrida* (Lincoln: University of Nebraska Press, 1984).

ent tensions between subject and object, content and form, reader and text, thereby calling attention to the process of meaning-production—the situatedness—that constitutes a poem. Moreover, I maintain that, while poststructuralism and Wittgenstein's theory of language-games may help us better understand Bernstein's manipulation of poetic form, Marxist theory and Lacanian psychoanalysis need to be equally considered since they illuminate the sociopolitical significance of Bernstein's aesthetic experimentation. The theories of Theodor Adorno, Jacques Lacan, and Alain Badiou help elucidate how Bernstein's poetry continues in the avant-garde tradition of counter-ideological aesthetic production—that is, a poetry that aims at encouraging thinking and revaluation, particularly of what constitutes the subject (self, individual, voice, identity, etc.) and how this subject relates to its world (environment, nation, community, etc.). I regard this modernist influence as being of utmost importance, especially when considering how critics like Fredric Jameson have interpreted the politics of Language poetry as more aligned with the ostentation and "discursive schizophrenia" of postmodernism than the avant-garde concerns of modernism.[3]

The first section of this essay addresses the question of poetic style, and how Bernstein manages to distinguish himself from an "official verse culture" that continues to uphold a lyric paradigm founded on traditional notions of identity. The second section examines the philosophical implications of antiabsorption, specifically how this poetic technique aims at absorbing the reader in the text through formal-experimental means, and how such antiabsorptive absorption differs from traditional lyric-based poetics that rely heavily on the content-based transparency of an expressive "I." In conclusion, I argue that the defamiliarization created by antiabsorption elevates the reading process from passive consumption to an exercise in re-cognition, thus transforming that which is "simply" aesthetic into a politico-philosophical experience. The eventfulness produced by the dialectical formalism of Bernstein's poetry thus encourages a critical engagement that goes beyond the identity thinking and the exchange-value logic so prevalent in contemporary American culture. It is this emphasis on the sociopolitical significance of aesthetic experimentalism that I believe locates Bernstein's poetics in a critical

---

3   See Fredric Jameson, *Postmodernism or the Cultural Logic of Late Capitalism* (Durham: Duke University Press, 1991), 28–31.

modernist tradition, more so than the postmodernism with which he is popularly associated.

Identity and Its Discontents: Contemporary Poetry and the Lyric Paradigm

The idea of language—as knowledge, discourse, or ideology—permeating the totality of our existential reality, even our deepest, most personal thoughts, complicates the aesthetic idealism of "self-expression." The problem is even more pertinent to poetry, which is traditionally associated with the communication of abstract ideas (be they emotional, intellectual, experiential, etc.) via efficient expression and formal precision. As a discursive formation, poetry occupies a tenuous space in our contemporary world. While still the bastion of self-expression, voice, and authenticity, modern poetry has also developed into a discursive practice that questions its own foundations, its own belief in the stability of a referential infrastructure. In contemporary American poetics, this complex issue of free expression and discursive institutionalization gained recognition with the publication of the journal L=A=N=G=U=A=G=E (1978–1981), edited by Charles Bernstein and Bruce Andrews. Originally intended as a forum for poetic experimentation, the journal quickly became associated with a movement known as Language poetry, a school of writing that overtly dismisses the poetic "aura" of traditional formalism. As Kevin McGuirk notes, Language poetry is "based, negatively, on a rejection of the dominant voice model for poetry—that is, the expressive lyric organized around an individual and putatively authentic self—and related paradigms of authentic experience and unitary knowledge" (206).[4] Language poets thus challenge conventional poetry by decentering the traditional, ego-centered model of "voice" and "authentic-

---

4 Some of the poets usually associated with Language poetry are Susan Howe, Ron Silliman, Lyn Hejinian, Steve McCaffery, Leslie Scalapino, Bruce Andrews, and Bob Perelman. Though the poets usually grouped under the umbrella term "Language poets" do agree on many basic, aesthetic principles—for example, the need for experimentalism—they do not necessarily agree on any specific political platform. The politics of Leslie Scalapino, for example, differ significantly from those of Bruce Andrews, even though both are regarded as "Language poets." For a theoretical account of the Language poets and their respective views concerning the intersection of poetry and politics, see *The Politics of Poetic Form: Poetry and Public Policy*, ed. Charles Bernstein (New York: ROOF Books, 1990) and *Artifice & Indeterminacy: An Anthology of New Poetics*, ed. Christopher Beach (Tuscaloosa: University of Alabama Press, 1998).

ity" and replacing it with a renewed focus on the various ways in which discourse affects our understanding of the subject and subjectivity.[5]

In order to understand how Bernstein stands against the postmodern mainstream, it is helpful to briefly summarize the characteristics of what remains conventional in contemporary poetry. Marjorie Perloff, for example, begins "'Modernism' at the Millennium" with an analysis of the lyric paradigm and the "official verse culture" still dominant in the United States. She analyzes three poems spanning the twentieth century: Delmore Schwartz's "Tired and Unhappy, You Think of Houses" (1938), Anthony Hecht's "Message from the City" (1968), and Edward Hirsch's "How to Get Back to Chester" (1981). As Perloff accurately observes, the "poetics in question are remarkably constant," even when disregarding the cultural commonality among the three poets (male, white, Jewish). Perloff's point is that the "premises that govern the form these poems take" is what binds them together:

> First and most obviously, it is assumed that "poetry" involves lineated verbal — and only verbal — text (no mixed media permitted). Second, lineated though it is and orderly as it looks on the page as a text column with white space around the stanzas, the "modern" poem must avoid meter and fixed rhyme scheme — sound features too rigid to represent the phenomenology of individual consciousness. Third, lyric is understood to be the expression of a particular subject (whether designated as "I" in Hecht and Hirsch or "you" in Schwartz), whose voice provides the cement that keeps individual references and insights

---

5   Although co-founder of the journal from which the term "Language poetry" emerged, and usually considered the central and most recognized member of the group, Bernstein views the label as misleading and limiting. Having founded the journal precisely to avoid the rigidity of aesthetic labels and styles, Bernstein rejects not only the idea of a "Language School" but also of any aesthetic idealism that would transform something potentially radical into something dogmatic: "'Language poetry' is a term I prefer not to use. . . . There isn't one kind of form, one kind of style, or one kind of approach that interested us in L=A=N=G=U=A=G=E. . . . I would say that the interconnectedness among the poetic styles attended to in L=A=N=G=U=A=G=E has to do with the rejection of certain traditionally accepted techniques for poem-making and an openness to alternative techniques, together with a distrust of the experimental as an end to itself — i.e., theatricalizing the processes of poem generation rather than making poems" (*My Way*, 63–64).

together. Fourth, "modern" language should not be stilted
or formal (shades of "poetic diction") but rather "natural"
and colloquial, even as (fifth), a poem conveys its feelings
and ideas only by means of indirection—which is to say,
by metaphor and irony. (*21st- Century Modernism*, 158)

Perloff's list of governing principles does not restrict itself to the
New Critical poetry of the early twentieth century, as Hirsch's *For
the Sleepwalkers* (1981) exemplifies, but rather permeates, in an almost
sardonic manner, the very center of postmodern poetics.

Consider, for example, the "revolutionary" ethnopoetics of Gloria
Anzaldúa, as represented in her 1987 work *Borderlands/La Frontera: The
New Mestiza*. Regarded as a postmodern classic in Chicana/o poetics,
the text examines the multicultural complexities of being a "new
Mestiza"—a postmodern subject born of modernist divides, such
as sociopolitical borders and gender roles. The poem "To live in the
Borderlands means you" examines the intricacies of this subject posi-
tion, which differs considerably from that of Schwartz, Hecht, or
Hirsch. It begins by asserting that living in the borderlands "means
you

> are neither *hispana india negra española*
> *ni gabacha, eres mestiza, mulata, half-breed*
> caught in the crossfire between camps
> while carrying all five races on your back
> not knowing which side to turn to, run from."
> (194–195)

The poem continues in this prescriptive manner, not only showing
how the borderland subject transcends traditional boundaries such
as gender ("half and half"), geographic division ("you are the battle-
ground / where enemies are kin to each other;"), and even culinary
taste ("put *chile* in the borscht"), but also outlining some of the basic
characteristics that would endow one with "new Mestiza" consciousness. Cultural markers of difference aside, the poem shares many, if
not all, of the mainstream principles outlined by Perloff: (1) it does
not stray from the tradition of lineated verbal text, (2) it avoids fixed
meter or rhyme, (3) it expresses the voice of a particular subject
("you"), (4) it relies on natural or colloquial language, and (5) it uses
both metaphor and irony to describe the complexity of the subject
position it represents. Aside from the linguistic "crossover" (mix of
Spanish and English), the poem offers no significant variation from

the lyric paradigm criticized by Perloff and noted by McGuirk. In fact, the only glaring difference is that the poet in question is a Chicana lesbian of indigenous descent, a feature that differentiates the poem in terms of biographical content but not necessarily in terms of formal expression. Thus, although considered experimental and revolutionary in some academic circles, such poetry fails to escape the haunting influence of conventional lyric subjectivity, remaining stiflingly traditional despite claims to the contrary.[6]

The persistence of the lyric subject in contemporary poetry serves as an example of what Bernstein terms "poetic dramatization." In contrast to an "official verse culture" that still celebrates lyric paradigms founded on the identitarianism of the Cartesian *cogito*, Bernstein's complicated relationship to tradition offers a refreshing alternative. His suspicion of the lyric "I" is evident in poems like "Solidarity Is the Name We Give to What We Cannot Hold" (*My Way*, 33–35). Using himself as an example of definition and its discontents, Bernstein goes through an expansive and comic variety of labels in an effort to undermine the theatricalization of poetic identity and "style":

> I am a nude formalist poet, a sprung
> syntax poet, a multitrack poet, a
> wondering poet, a social expressionist poet,
> an ideolectical poet. I am a New York poet in
> California, a San Francisco poet on
> the Lower East Side, an Objectivist poet
> in Royaumont, a surrealist poet in New Jersey,
> a Dada poet in Harvard Square,
> a zaum poet in Brooklyn, a merz poet
> in Iowa, a cubo-futurist poet in Central Park.
> (34–35)

In an ironic exemplification of the poem's title, Bernstein satirizes the desire for existential and aesthetic solidarity, exponentially

---

6 It should be noted that Anzaldúa's work, while highly influential in various disciplines, does not represent the totality of Chicano/a poetics. Poets like Heriberto Yepez, though in agreement with some of the poetic principles espoused by Anzaldúa, belong to an entirely different poetic tradition, one more aligned with avant-gardism than "new Mestiza consciousness." See, for example, his "definition" of ethnopoetics in "Ethnopoetics and Globalization" (http://www.ubu.com/ethno/discourses/yepez.pdf).

multiplying the details and labels he uses to describe himself in order to complicate the assumed simplicity of poetic "style" and the unified self. Although the poem resembles Anzaldúa's work in many ways, such as in the use of colloquial language and traditional lineated verbal text, the poem differs on one important point: the use of irony. Whereas Anzaldúa utilizes irony thematically, combining "*chile*" and "borscht" to communicate a multicultural experience, Bernstein uses irony formally, undermining the discursive-existential stability of the declarative statement "I am" through repetition. This formal use of irony-as-repetition helps locate the poet's not-so-unconscious anxiety concerning the permanence, and performance, of identity and style.

Yet, for the reader who approaches the poem with a conventional understanding of definition, a perturbing question remains unanswered: "what?" What type of poet is Bernstein? Can he be both a "parent poet" and "a sleepy poet at night"? Can he be a "sad poet" and a "detached poet" simultaneously? More importantly, are these descriptions valid or relevant to our understanding of Bernstein's poetry? The tempting and more accessible answer to these questions is "yes"—Bernstein is everything he claims to be. His poetic identity comprises all of those traditions and situations he lists. The labels are not irrelevant but rather serve as markers of all the various aesthetic theories and situations that influence Bernstein's poetics.

The simplicity of this "yes," however, is not to be accepted uncritically, since it is undermined at the conclusion of the poem, where Bernstein adopts a different, more philosophical tone: "& I am none of these things, / nothing but the blank wall of my aversions / writ large in disappearing ink—" (35). The phrase "nothing but the blank wall of my aversions" can be read as a commentary on the descriptive chaos and exorbitant denomination that precedes it. Here the irony is thematic, referring to the logical impossibility of a person being "nothing but [a] blank wall of aversions." When simplified, Bernstein's multifaceted qualities equal the "blank wall," the plain "nothing" at the end of the poem, which makes the details following the conjunction "but" seem even more redundant and unnecessary—the wall remains blank despite his "aversions." Even with this multiplication or extension of "nothing," Bernstein's aversions—the descriptive excesses that characterize the poem, noted in the phrase "writ large"—set up the climactic "disappearing ink" at the end. Serving as a metaphor for the impossibility of permanence, the image is exemplary of both discursive limitations and denominative excesses, reminding us how we cannot define the total "truth" of the

world because it transcends our understanding, and how we tortu-
ously attempt to define it nonetheless.

   Accordingly, the answer to the question "what type of poet is
Charles Bernstein" is stated in the poem itself: he is the chaotic and
complex "everything" that makes up the majority of the poem, as
well as the simple "blank wall" at the conclusion. In essence, he is
the embodiment of poetic conjunction, of a dialectical tension that
connects being and nothingness, element and void, allowing for
an ontological negativity that stands against the lyric paradigms of
identity, presence, and self-sameness. The poem does not pretend
to resolve the problem of solidarity with philosophically appealing
generalities or poetic idealizations; instead, the arduous cataloging
demands a reexamination of the immanent tensions pertaining to
identity, location, individual talent, and aesthetic tradition. This, of
course, leaves the ending perpetually "open" in that Bernstein does
not provide a ready-made answer to the question of poetic identity,
but instead exposes such identity thinking—which functions on
the idea of closure, however false or manufactured—as hysterically
narcissistic. He multiplies and extends particularity to the point of
fragmentation, thus satirizing the possibility of any one subject position—or prescribed combination of positions—capturing the material reality, the historicity, of "Charles Bernstein." Rather than posit
an identity, however complex and multifaceted, godlike or multicultural, we are instead presented with a bewildering instance of non-
identity "writ large in disappearing ink."

   The main feature that thus distinguishes Bernstein's work as
simultaneously aesthetic and philosophical is his attention to form,
as well as his poetic manipulation of what Foucault termed "one of
the most dangerous elements" in discourse—its awesome materiality: "I am supposing that in every society the production of discourse
is at once controlled, selected, organized and redistributed according
to a certain number of procedures, whose role is to avert its powers
and its dangers, to cope with chance events, to evade its ponderous,
awesome materiality" (Foucault 216).[7] Materiality in this instance

---

7 It seems appropriate at this point to clarify the difference between "materiality" and "materialism." As opposed to the concept of "essence," materiality refers
   primarily to the material or physical nature of any given object, subject, or situation. One can speak of the materiality of a particular table, of a family relative, or
   of a sporting event. Materiality applies equally to everything that exists in physical
   form. The philosophical tradition of materialism, on the other hand, has an extensive and complicated history, going back to Democritus in the fourth century B.C.

refers to the ways in which language impacts and transforms real people, places, and situations—the type of discursive materiality theorized in Marxist studies of ideology and psychoanalytic accounts of the unconscious. As Foucault explains, society is obsessed with constructing rules and barriers to contain the material dimension of language—its ability to impact the world beyond transparent signification. One reason for this is that the materiality of language undermines the sovereignty and selfsameness of identity—it underscores the fact that our notion of "self" is in large part a linguistic construct and therefore fallible to "dangers" and "chance events."

However, even if materiality serves to undermine conventional notions of identity and selfhood, Bernstein is still careful not to romanticize its revolutionary possibilities. Though materiality is central to Bernstein's poetics, he is wary of simply exploring it as some abstract theory, and chooses rather to view it as an existentially and historically grounded practice by which one can understand the interconnectedness of individual and collective being: "The social grounding of poetry cannot be evaded by recourse to a purely intellectual idea of the materiality of language since the materiality of language is in the first instance a social materiality and, at the same time, a materiality not of selves and identities but of bodies" (*My Way*, 9). The dialectical interplay between the social and the personal informing Bernstein's understanding of materiality is equally important to his theory of "antiabsorption," which emphasizes the symbiotic relation between the social production of meaning and the presence of the social in all self-expression.

Antiabsorption and the Politico-Poetics of Materiality

In "Artifice of Absorption" Bernstein explains how "antiabsorption"—his approach to formal experimentation—though at times ruptured and disjunctive, can function as a means of "absorbing" the reader in the text:

Whereas the concept of materiality has gained in popularity, particularly in postmodern discussions concerning the materiality of "the body" or the materiality of "the gaze," the concept of materialism is strictly limited to an Enlightenment-Modern tradition going back to ancient Greece. The Marxist concept of materialism, which is the one referred to here, emphasizes the concrete relations of production behind any given object, subject, or situation. For the purposes of this paper, materialism can be understood as the critical study of the materiality of social relations.

There is, then, a considerable history
of using antiabsorptive techniques
(nontransparent or nonnaturalizing elements)
(artifice)
for absorptive
ends. This is an approach
I find myself peculiarly
attracted to, & which reflects my
ambivolence
(as in wanting multiple things)
about absorption & its converses.
In my poems, I
frequently use opaque & nonabsorbable
elements, digressions &
interruptions, as part of a technological
arsenal to create a more powerful
("souped-up")
absorption than possible with traditional,
& blander, absorptive techniques . . .
This is the subject of much of my work . . .
. . . For one thing,
the more intensified, technologized
absorption made possible by
nonabsorptive means may get the reader
absorbed into a more ideologized
or political space . . .
(*A Poetics*, 52–53)

As Bernstein states, antiabsorption is a poetic strategy founded on the manipulation of aesthetic forms. Although its primary purpose is to create a greater ideological effect on the reader, its experimental quality may also confuse and alienate, prohibiting not only political or ideological sympathy but also identification and understanding in general. Such confusion, however, takes place when one reads for a *particular* meaning in Bernstein's poetry. In other words, if one reads his work for a crescendo of recognizable knowledge communicated through traditional forms and themes, cognitive frustration is almost an inevitable result. The reader is then presented with a hermeneutic dilemma: how *is* one to be "absorbed into a more ideologized or political space" if one cannot understand the content or idea because of the form—the means—of expression?

The answer to this question lies in the fact that Bernstein's understanding of absorption is not characterized by sentimentality or transparent realism, but rather by a type of formalism that Edgar Allan Poe defines in terms of "effect." This aesthetic philosophy demands reciprocity between content and form, where the form not only expresses the content but also supplements it actively as elaboration, exemplification, or contradiction. Poe describes such reciprocity as "combinations of tone and incident":

> I prefer commencing with the consideration of *effect.* Keeping originality *always* in view . . . I say to myself, in the first place, 'Of the innumerable effects, or impressions, of which the heart, the intellect, or (more generally) the soul is susceptible, what one shall I, on the present occasion, select?' Having chosen . . . a vivid effect, I consider whether it can be best wrought by incident or tone—whether by ordinary incidents and peculiar tone, or the converse, or by peculiarity both of incident and tone—afterward looking about me (or rather within) for such combinations of event, or tone, as shall best aid me in the construction of the effect. (480–81)

As Poe explains, the communication of effect is grounded in the delicate negotiation of both content (incident) and form (tone). In Bernstein's poetry, this reciprocity is embodied in the words themselves, which fluctuate from vehicles of communication (i.e., couriers of content) to things in themselves (i.e., materialized forms), thus adding to the reader's interpretive challenge. If the reader is not discouraged by the initial confusion produced by antiabsorption, then the experience of reading may evolve into a cognitive event that transcends conventional literary imbibing. In other words, the defamiliarization produced by antiabsorption aims at transforming the text into something radically "other," thus adding to the poem's materiality—its being experienced. The poem is not, then, presented for passive consumption but formally manipulated to challenge rather than reinforce the reader's epistemological foundations. This results in an entirely different, more profound form of absorption than possible with transparent techniques that aim at formal harmony.

As most critics note, Bernstein's appreciation for materiality and formal experimentation is partly attributable to his understanding of Wittgenstein's philosophy of language. In his essay "The Objects of

Meaning: Reading Cavell Reading Wittgenstein," Bernstein describes Wittgenstein's philosophy as concerned primarily with "the activity of knowing, which has its meaning only in *use* in the *context* of language" (*Content's Dream*, 170). According to this view, the method by which meaning comes into existence is always contingent on the particularity of a given linguistic situation. That is, meaning is determined by the way words are *used* in a particular context. Consequently, a word may produce significant meaning in one situation while remaining completely nonsensical or irrelevant in another. Wittgenstein terms these linguistic situations "language-games," implying that each particular context, like a game, has its own rules governing the use of language. Wittgenstein argues that, for the most part, the production of meaning is completely dependent on the rules of usage: "For a *large* class of cases—though not for all—in which we employ the word '*meaning*' it can be defined thus: the meaning of a word *is its use in the language*" (20). For both Wittgenstein and Bernstein, meaning can never be absolute or transcendental because it can never exist outside the language-game from which it originates. Context is therefore what grounds the potential chaos of signification and allows for a specific meaning to emerge.

Through the use of antiabsorption, Bernstein succeeds in bringing to light the processes of meaning production, the language-games, in order to unmask the transcendental idealism found in most discursive practices. Bernstein follows Wittgenstein's critique of "the desiring impulse in rationality for certainty, for a world of representation beyond the world" by shattering idealized notions of signification and grounding the process of meaning strictly in terms of usage (*Content's Dream*, 177–78). Moreover, both Bernstein and Wittgenstein remind us that, politically, this desire for certainty "beyond the world" leads to a dangerous logic of domination and control:

> "It is not the slumber of reason that engenders monsters, but vigilant, insomniac rationality" [*Anti-Oedipus*, pg. 112]. A rationality that starts with the idea of representation ("universal" "underlying") and constantly translates the world back into this shadow world: just the picture Wittgenstein wishes to exorcise by starting *Investigations* with a quote from Augustine in which he imagines learning a language as a child to be like learning a second language, translating from the old already-given names,

as if he came into the world with an already full-blown
language. (178)

As evidenced by Bernstein's comparison, the desire for fixed meaning
is directly related to an "insomniac rationality"—a totalizing logic
that functions on categorization and labels, precisely the "fascist
thinking" that Foucault warns against in the preface to Deleuze and
Guattari's *Anti-Oedipus*. The fact that Bernstein links Wittgenstein's
theory to a post-Marxist-Freudian study of modern alienation is a
clear example that his interest in the materiality of language is motivated by political concerns.

Unfortunately, most criticism ignores or devalues this aspect
of Bernstein's work, opting instead to keep any political discussions at an abstract, undefined level. Naylor, for example, ends his
Wittgensteinian analysis at the first mention of politics, concluding, "Bernstein's politics are not expressed as overtly as some might
like" (136). Although it is true that Naylor's purpose is not to define
or investigate the "political space" of Bernstein's poetics, but rather
to liberate Bernstein's poetry from Marxist and poststructuralist containment, he nonetheless feels compelled to raise the issue
of politics, even if only in regard to language: "For Bernstein, as for
Wittgenstein, the necessity as well as the ability to choose among
language games not only distinguishes their concepts of language
and the self from most versions of poststructuralism; their insistence on the act of choosing also locates us squarely in the social and
political dimension of language" (136). Curiously, the last sentence of
Naylor's article includes a quote from Bernstein's "The Dollar Value
of Poetry," in which he calls for a "breaking off" from the "economic
and cultural—social—force called capitalism" (*Content's Dream*, 57).
It is interesting that Naylor ends the article at the first mention of
any specific political-economic practice. Prior to this quote, Naylor
describes the targets of Bernstein's critique vaguely—as "coercive
social strategies" and "contemporary culture"—thus avoiding the
complicated issue of connecting Bernstein's critique of capitalism
with his Wittgensteinian view of language (136–37).

Rather than dismiss this issue as irrelevant, being that the relation between Wittgenstein and Marx is usually considered dubious
at best, it is important to understand that their respective theories
interact reciprocally in Bernstein's poetry. Perhaps the most striking similarity between Wittgenstein's theory of language and Marx's
theory of labor is their shared suspicion of abstraction as a means of

determining value.[8] In the first chapter of *Capital*, Marx describes the mystical quality of the commodity as a "process of abstraction" that permeates the totality of the capitalist system, especially as it relates to the concepts of exchange-value and use-value (164). According to Marx, the abstraction underlying the commodity-form transforms the creative and active work of living human beings into an abstract economic category called "human labor-power." Similar to the ways in which words lose their material significance and become mere symbols of predetermined meaning, so too does capitalist abstraction devalue the worthiness of human activity: the usefulness of tangible work becomes a commodity that can be bought and sold, and thus an expression—a representation—of exchange-value.

It should be noted, however, that the relationship between Marx and Wittgenstein is not based on an agreement concerning specific political-economic practices. Marx does not commit himself to a philosophical investigation of language, nor does Wittgenstein analyze the fundamental contradictions inherent in the capitalist mode of production. As Bernstein himself states, Wittgenstein was generally "silent . . . on the political and economic level" (*Content's Dream*, 181). However, both Marxism and Wittgensteinian linguistics, as critical theories, share a weariness of abstraction, which both judge as dysfunctional in its "decontextualized codification." As Bernstein reminds us, such abstraction can lead to reified thought and totalitarian politics: "Language is thus *removed from the participatory control of its users* & delivered into the hands of *the state*. . . . *Decontextualized codification* of the rules of language enforces a view that *language operates on principles apart from its usage*" (26, emphasis added). To "operate on principles apart from usage" is the problem that both Marx and Wittgenstein analyze in political economy and linguistics respectively. Not only does the desire for transparent meaning reinforce the social tendency toward abstraction—a desire Wittgenstein warns against—but our capitalist infrastructure, the material basis for our social interaction, also reinforces cognitive repression and dangerous generalizations. Such abstraction or reification distorts our understanding of the production of meaning. This is exactly how ideologies become entrenched in mass society, and why Bernstein's critique of abstraction takes into account capitalism's totalizing effects, whether

---

8 This is not meant to suggest that the connections between Wittgenstein and Marx established here are unique. See, for example, Ferruccio Rossi-Landi, "Wittgenstein, Old and New," *Ars Semeiotica: International Journal of American Semiotics* 4 (1981): 29–50.

it is the unreflective thinking of television programming, the predominately superficial or transparent communication of modern advertising, or the doublespeak of political values.

Exploring the inherent tensions between an individual's understanding of his/her sense of "self" and the socio-capitalist production of meaning is one of the many themes Bernstein examines through antiabsorption. As previously noted, the concept of identity—being a theme that is of particular interest to Bernstein—usually functions as a vehicle for the exploration of these issues. Bernstein's poetry negates the compulsion toward the false totality of the unified "self" by presenting instances of what seem to be "complete subjects," and immediately undermining them by highlighting their artificiality, as evident in this passage from the often-cited poem "Standing Target":

> Ralf D. Caulo, Deputy Director of the
> HBJ School Department, arrived in New York
> via Dallas. He spends much of his
> time on the road, however, talking with
> sales managers in all HBJ sales regions,
> and visiting school districts and
> school personnel around the country
> to discuss trends in education, curricular
> changes, and new programs. When
> not involved with his job, Caulo enjoys
> sporting events, and keeps in shape
> by playing tennis and racket ball. He
> also maintains an interest in history,
> especially American history, and is
> currently focusing on the period of
> industrial expansion between the 1870's
> and 1900. (*Controlling Interests*, 43)

This short biographical sketch attempts to capture the totality of the individual by offering fragments of personal information—occupational responsibilities, intellectual interests, and leisurely pursuits. Bernstein's sketches "characterize 'model' citizens in a capitalist economy" that exemplify "what it means to be a well-balanced, successful person" (Naylor, 132). Ralf Caulo, for example, is presented as an efficient individual who has achieved success by remaining active in all facets of his life. His time is carefully budgeted with a variety of socially productive activities, ranging from the scholarly to the recreational. Overall, it seems that he is a "model citizen" worthy of emulation.

The unaffected manner of presentation, however, alerts us to the irony of Bernstein's biographical sketches. Contrary to the seriousness of the lyric, the "personalization" or intimate feeling in Bernstein's example comes across as prepackaged and generic. The language used to describe "the real person" mimics the drab and dreary discourse of television talk show introductions, popular magazine profiles, and company biographies. Such transparency underscores the distance or gap between person and portrait, making it more difficult to identify with the individual represented. Although strategic details are included in order to neutralize the packaged existentiality of the biographical description, the information given only helps to intensify the feeling of artificiality, thus disproving the notion that discourse is capable of representing the "real" person. In fact, what Bernstein's corporate bio-description demonstrates is how discourse is used to actually *produce* the "individuality" of the individual—to manufacture the humanity of the person.

The link between capitalism's need for packaged individuality and the Enlightenment-inherited obsession with categorization is made most apparent in the summer camp "character evaluations" of a young Charles Bernstein (i.e., "Charlie"):

> Last spring Charles put himself on record
> that he didn't like crafts. We soon
> came to understand his feelings
> when we worked with him. Charlie
> is not strong in manual dexterity. (This
> may be part of a mixed dominance
> situation Mrs. B. and I discussed in
> relation to tying shoes.) Fortunately,
> what he lacks in developed skills
> he makes up for in
> patience, determination, and
> knowledge of what he wants as
> results.
> (*Controlling Interests*, 45)

Such passages come eerily close to Foucault's haunting suggestion that it is the institutions of discourse that produce the subject, not vice versa. In this passage, we see how Charlie is being repaired as a

discursive entity only to be fitted into a larger socioeconomic structure. There is mention of "tests" and evaluations of character and
abilities. The statements "put himself on record," "not strong in
manual dexterity," and the reference to a "mixed dominance situation," all suggest a psychological profile of Charlie, an institutional
effort to "understand his feelings." Again, the result is an inten-
sification of alienation, a sense of being objectified in order to be
examined and categorized. Regardless of intention, the therapeutic
gaze supports a panoptic ideology, as well as the institutional need
for constant evaluation. Such examinations epitomize the "vigilant,
insomniac rationality" that aspires to gain an encyclopedic knowledge—and thus absolute control—of the world.

Bernstein immediately responds to this reification by exploding
the false totality of the gaze and giving us a more "realistic" representation of the same condition:

```
        fatigue
                of              of
                  open for
      to                  , sees
      doubles
      glass                        must
          are                      for
        in       :  they
                                  , her
                  that it
      watches, leaves,
                            days that
                    made
      and the
                      The
```

(45–46)

The ideological need for a unified subject is here represented in a
negative manner. The realism of the portrait lies not in its clarity but
in its frustrated attempt at totality. Every line is fractured, "pulver-
ized" as Tenney Nathanson has observed, prohibiting not only the
completion of thought but the presumption of a unified subject as

well. [9] However, as stated earlier, Bernstein's purpose in using antiabsorptive technique is not simply to alienate potential readers — it is not a poetic act of whimsy intended to obfuscate meaning for purposes of academic rigor or to satisfy an intellectual pretension. In fact, as Bernstein himself notes, such antiabsorptive moments are not meant to establish poetic impermeability whatsoever: "'Artifice of Absorption' is sometimes characterized as being against poetry that absorbs attention and for poetry that's impermeable or antiabsorptive. But that's not the argument I make" (Caplan, 140). Contrary to claims of impenetrability, passages like the one above are very much grounded in the experience of the poem — its situation or language-game — and are very much "readable" in the traditional, literary sense of the term. A close reading of such an antiabsorptive passage helps elucidate this point.

The first noticeable detail in this passage is the spatialization of the words, which underscores the fact that they produce meaning both individually and relationally. The first word, for example, implies an existential "fatigue" with the process of classification that characterizes the poem. We do not know if the word refers to a state or an action, or if it is a verb, an adjective, or a noun. What is apparent, however, is that it communicates an exhausting and frustrating condition. For a young boy like Charlie, such institutional efforts at categorization can prove scarring, if not traumatic. This is further implied with the repetition of the preposition "of," which connotes an inability to label. Fatigue of what? Of summer camp? Of counselors? Of "tests" and "records"? Whereas the preposition "of" usually functions as an indicator of specificity, its total lack of clarification underscores the poem's inability to name or locate the source of Charlie's problem, here emphasized by a failure to communicate despite repetition ("of of"). The next line, "open for," suggests an opening up, perhaps to the possibility of a different experience, yet the poem refrains from situating this possible "openness" in anything specific. Openness seems a direct response to fatigue, yet we do not know toward what (implied by the preposition "to") or whom (implied by the preposition "for"). Moreover, the strategically placed comma that comes afterward functions as a visible break, implying some sort of transition, most likely in thought. This is reinforced by the verb "sees," which definitely suggests an action and an actor.

---

9   For a more detailed account of pulverization in Bernstein's poetry, see Tenney Nathanson, "Collage and Pulverization in Contemporary American Poetry: Charles Bernstein's *Controlling Interests," Contemporary Literature* 33 (summer 1992).

In fact, the lines following the action "sees" seem to describe a Lacanian mirror-stage experience, first suggested by the verb "doubles" and further reinforced with the noun "glass." Indeed, a mirror is a "glass" that "doubles" appearances, and as Lacan reminds us, such a doubling is exactly what humans do as a means of coping with existence. We must double our "self" as a means of creating a social "I."[10] This sense of necessity, of having no choice in the matter, is represented in the commandment "must." Consequently, the socioeconomic propensity for packaged and marketable identities, like that of "Ralf D. Caulo," is here shown to originate with a structural psychological phenomenon. This suggests that capitalism—as an economic system that thrives on the psychological manipulation of consumer desire, as evident in advertising—perpetuates an instinctive and narcissistic form of thinking that serves to repress critical and self-reflective reasoning, thus minimizing the capacity for independent thinking. This is represented in the passage with the words "are" and "for," which in combination suggest a Sartrean "bad faith" of being("are")-"for"-an-other.

The lines that follow seem to be attempts at clarification, specifically of locating this "other." The preposition "in" sets up this effort, but it is quickly undermined by the strategically placed colon, which neither explains, clarifies, enumerates, or proves what precedes it. It is simply floating, as if intended to separate the "in" from the "they" or perhaps signify an abstract confinement, where the "I" is lost "in" the "they." The introduction of "they" ushers in the first pronoun in the passage, and thus reiterates the "not-I" which underlies Charlie's existential angst. The pronoun "her" that follows is interesting in that it further qualifies the "they" without necessarily clarifying the vagueness (who is "her?" Mother? Counselor? Examiner?). The singularization of "they" is further complicated with the next line, which reads "that it." Has the "her," which was deducted from the "they," become an object ("it")? Is the impersonal pronoun meant to suggest a lack of humanity, an example of reification in an institutional setting? The thought seems to be completed with the following line, which describes two actions, "watches, leaves"; though the action of the "they"-"her"-"it" is clarified, who exactly is watching and leaving is left undefined. One possibility is that "it" reminds Charlie of his mother, who also "watches" and "leaves" him at camp, as so many

---

10   See Jacques Lacan's essay on the "Mirror Stage" in *Écrits* (New York: W.W. Norton, 2004).

other parents do during summer. The themes of the passage are thus detachment (the scene is impersonal, despite the pronouns), examination (whether academic or psychological), and abandonment (by examiner or relative). It is obvious that Charlie is not happy, that he is alienated and that his surroundings do not present him with opportunities for closure and identity-reinforcement, but rather with compounded instances of otherness and incompletion, traits that are communicated by the fragmentary form of the passage.

Following this fragmented attempt at locating the "other," the passage switches focus, from people to the "days that" characterize Charlie's experience. The use of the verb "made" (as the past participle of "to make") coincides nicely with "days that," except that the thought remains incomplete. We are not certain what exactly was "made" during those "days," and the ineffability of the experience is probably the reason why. What exactly do discursive formations make of us, except abstract "subjects," the definition of which is highly contested? And how does a child, sensitive enough to experience the process of interpellation, rationalize the experience? We can be certain, from the passage, that time has elapsed and that this passing of time has resulted in something — has had some form of impact or consequence — but *what* exactly is left unspecified. In an ironic elaboration on nothingness, reminiscent of the final lines in "Solidarity Is the Name We Give to What We Cannot Hold," Bernstein recalls Wallace Stevens's famous declaration at the end of "The Man on The Dump": "Where was it one first heard of the truth? The the" (Stevens, 163). Bernstein modifies this famous poetic statement by fragmenting it, thereby highlighting the ineffability of the truth that Stevens poeticizes. The addition of the conjunction "and" implies an unnecessary supplementation to "the / The." The "The" is meant to signify the impossible truth of being, which recalls Badiou's thesis concerning the inexpressibility — the unnameability — of truth, the infinite and the void.[11] The passage thereby suggests the impossible reality of the real, which transcends both subject and signification.

Thus, while the first bio-sketch of Charlie attempts to reconstruct his condition through generic psychological diagnoses and therapeutic clichés, the second explodes the assumption of identity by showing us the *effects* of institutionalization, the fragmentary reality that a subject experiences upon such reification and alienation. As demon-

---

11   See Alain Badiou, *Being and Event* (New York: Continuum, 2005).

strated, this reality-effect is further established with the abundance of prepositions and articles in the passage; as opposed to the "straightforwardness" of traditional poetic statements, the experimental use of words like "the," "for," "in," and "of" suggests incompleteness and creates a sense of cognitive frustration. In this manner, Bernstein is able to represent the "truth" of alienation in a capitalist society—the reality of not being an independent subject with free will, but rather an object manipulated by different discursive practices.[12]

Conclusion: Poetry as Philosophy

Bernstein's formalist experimentation with materiality thus aims at ideological revaluation, which is consistent with the modernist tenets characterized by Theodor Adorno in *Aesthetic Theory*. According to Adorno, art attempts to negate society by substituting historical reality with an imaginary construction that transports us from the immediacy of our historical condition to an imaginary space and time. However, and this is Adorno's main point, the historical tensions of the present persist in the chosen medium of expression—the *form* of the artwork. In other words, the form always contains, and refers to, external pressures that cannot be avoided by simply resorting to an alternative reality: "The tension in art . . . has meaning only in relation to the tension outside. . . . The unresolved antagonisms of reality reappear in art in the guise of immanent problems of artistic *form*. This, and not the deliberate injection of objective moments or social content, defines art's relation to society" (8). Similar to Poe's theory of effect, Adorno explains that the dialectical tension of art is best communicated through the material effect of form, and not by intentionally representing reality at the level of content, as in most lyric poetry. This emphasis on form, in turn, encourages a more active involvement on the part of the reader, who is compelled to integrate

---

12   When referring to the "alienation of a capitalist society," I am simply calling attention to the context or situation of the poet Charles Bernstein. As a New Yorker, Bernstein's experience of capitalism is one that informs the poem, not the experience of agrarian reform in Latin America, say Brazil or Mexico. Although the latter examples are considerably different from a first world experience, alienation is not specific to any culture, nation, or economy. The psychological condition outlined in this poem is one that can be attributed just as easily to an American from New York as it could be to an indigenous farmer in Australia or a bureaucrat in the old Soviet Union.

the otherness of the poem, thus transforming the simple act of reading into a "socio-historical event":

> The other defines the work, completes the process and
> makes it definite. No matter how heterogeneous I try to
> make a poem, no matter what incommensurabilities I
> attempt to rend my writing with, it becomes absorbed
> in that self-same project stipulated by the limits of my
> name: my origins & residencies, my time & language, what
> I can hear & see enough to contain by force of *form*. Yet
> it is precisely what I have contained but cannot identify
> that the other, being other, makes palpable, lets figure,
> & (hopefully) flower. It is only an other that, *in the final
> instance*, constitutes the work, makes it more than a text
> (test), resurrects it from the purgatory of its production,
> which is to say its production of self-sameness.
> (*A Poetics*, 186)

Highly aware of the "limits of [his] name," Bernstein incorporates
the otherness of the reader as a means of avoiding communicative and ideological "self-sameness." This dialectical interaction
between reader and poem ensures the latter's openness, as well as
the potential transformation of the former. By confronting the reader
through antiabsorption, Bernstein compels him/her to participate in
the productive process of the poem, thus changing an instance of
consumption into a moment of possible enlightenment.

In order to fully appreciate Bernstein's work, one must understand that his poetic project aims at offering an alternative method
by which various issues — cultural, political, philosophical, social,
and economic — can be critically reexamined. In this regard, not only
does Bernstein's experimental poetics exemplify many of the tenets
put forth by Wittgenstein and Marxist aestheticians like Adorno,
but his poetry also captures the essential philosophical quality that
makes poetry such a revered and time-honored discourse — it makes
one *think*. Alain Badiou, though far from sharing Adorno's pessimism
concerning the possibility of art after Auschwitz, does agree on the
philosophical capacities inherent in modern poetry:

> [The] modern poem identifies itself as a form of thought.
> It is not just the effective existence of a thought offered up
> in the flesh of language, it is the set of operations whereby

this thought comes to think itself. . . . [The] role of the poem is to engineer the sensory presentation of a regime of thought. . . . [This] move results in a crucial displacement of philosophy's relation to the poem. From this moment onward, this relationship can no longer rely on the opposition between the sensible and the intelligible, the beautiful and the good, or the image and the Idea. The modern poem is certainly not the sensible form of the Idea. It is the sensible, rather, that presents itself within the poem as the subsisting and powerless nostalgia of the poetic idea. (20–21)

Responding to the Platonic differentiation of poetry and mathematics, Badiou explains how modern poetry enacts the thinking that Plato reserved for scientific logic. In fact, Badiou argues that Plato himself is compelled to utilize poetic speech when attempting to explain the thinking of thought itself: "In short, when what is at stake is the opening of thought to the principle of the thinkable, when thought must be absorbed in the grasp of what establishes it *as* thought, we witness Plato himself submitting language to the power of poetic speech" (19–20). As both Badiou and Adorno note, poetry has the potential to inspire a sort of Nietzschean revaluation of values—a re-cognition of how meaning, identity, or value comes into being.

Although Bernstein's poetic experimentalism and his deconstruction of identity may seem in accordance with his postmodern label, his use of antiabsorption transcends the political detachment commonly associated with postmodernism. Bernstein is skeptical of the Enlightenment project of total rationalization, but he does not abandon the use of reason. He does not critique notions of unification and agency in order to discredit them as unfounded concepts, but rather examines these ideas in order to understand the basis of their dysfunctional condition. He does not favor the "end of history," but rather an active history that is capable of change and redirection. Accordingly, the goal of his poetics is not simply to deconstruct utopic aspirations, but instead to analyze how we have failed in their implementation, thereby beginning a process of reconstructing our "common ground of signification" and social interaction. This reconstruction can only come about by removing those ideologies that perpetuate our communicative failure, such as our tendency toward simplistic totality and unproblematic closure. Bernstein's poetry breaks this ideological bind by undermining such tendencies, revealing their dangerous ubiquity. This makes his work political in that it engages in active social transformation, and historical in that it intentionally draws from its historical moment for dialectical tension. As Perloff observes, Bernstein's poetic enterprise can be seen through a modernist lens, concerned with establishing "certain truths . . . to study the relation of literary to so-called ordinary language, to determine the respective role of author and reader in the interpretation of a given text, and to establish the ways in which individual texts speak for their culture."[13] Or as Benjamin says of Baudelaire: "[His] poetic output is assigned a mission. He envisioned blank spaces that he filled in with his poems. His work cannot merely be categorized as historical, like anyone else's, but it intended to be so and understood itself as such" (162). Bernstein also seems to be a poet of history, of experience, encouraging us to look at the discursivity of contemporary existence from a different—and ironically, more traditional—standpoint.

References

Adorno, Theodor. *Aesthetic Theory*. London: Routledge Press, 1984.
Anzaldúa, Gloria. *Borderlands/La Frontera: The New Mestiza*. San Francisco: Aunt Lute Books, 1987.
Badiou, Alain. *Handbook of Inaesthetics*. Stanford: Stanford University Press, 2005.
Benjamin, Walter. *Illuminations*. New York: Schocken Books, 1969.
Bernstein, Charles. *A Poetics*. Cambridge: Harvard University Press, 1992.
———. *Content's Dream*. Los Angeles: Sun & Moon Press, 1986.
———. *Controlling Interests*. New York: Roof Books, 1980.
———. *Girly Man*. Chicago: University of Chicago Press, 2006.
———. *My Way*. Chicago: University of Chicago Press, 1999.
Caplan, David. "A Conversation with Charles Bernstein." *The Antioch Review* 62 (2004): 140-41.
Foucault, Michel. *The Archaeology of Knowledge*. New York: Pantheon Books, 1972.
Lacan, Jacques. *Écrits*. New York: W.W. Norton, 2004.
Marx, Karl. *Capital*. New York: Penguin Books, 1990.

---

13 Marjorie Perloff, "After Language Poetry: Innovation and Its Theoretical Discontents," http://epc.buffalo.edu/authors/perloff/after_langpo.html (accessed June 1, 2006).

McGuirk, Kevin. "'Rough Trades': Charles Bernstein and the Currency of Poetry." *Canadian Review of American Studies* 27 (1997):206.

Naylor, Paul. "(Mis)Characterizing Charlie: Language and the Self in the Poetry and Poetics of Charles Bernstein." *Sagetrieb* 14 (1995): 119, 136–37.

Perloff, Marjorie. "After Language Poetry: Innovation and Its

Theoretical Discontents,"accessed June 1, 2006, http://epc.buffalo.edu/ authors/perloff/after_langpo.html.

———. *21st-Century Modernism:The"New"Poetics.*Malden, MA: Blackwell Publishers, 2002.

Poe, Edgar Allan. *The Fall of the House of Usher and Other Writings.* New York: Penguin Books, 1986.

Stevens, Wallace. *The Palm at the End of the Mind.* New York: Vintage Books, 1990.

Sussman, Henry. "Prolegomena to any Present and Future Language Poetry." *MLN* 118 (2004): 1203.

Wittgenstein, Ludwig. *Philosophical Investigations.* New York: Macmillan, 1953.

19

MICHAEL ANGELO TATA

Content's Profusion: Noise, Interruption and Reverse Peristalsis in the ~~poetics~~ of Charles Bernstein

" . . . Before the dream
was the sleep, punctuated by endoscopic rigmarole."

—"Explicit Version Number Required"

" . . . I'm (that nostalgic
notion) at pains (I don't mean this metaphorically
but synecdochically) to say that the context-
dependence of meaning (meaning is addicted
to context) rules out neither
truth not trust, knowledge nor
bicarbonate of soda
in these difficult to get a take on (make
on) circumstances everybody's always
riffing off of."

—"Whose He Kidding"[1]

---

1 "Explicit Version Number Required" appears in *My Way: Speeches and Poems* (191) along with "Whose He Kidding" (268).

Flash Point

For the Charles Bernstein of *Content's Dream: Essays 1975-1984, A Poetics* and *My Way: Speeches and Poems*, among other adventures in theoretical poetics (the closest writerly analogue to theoretical physics), language presents itself as a rich surface whose materiality eclipses and overdetermines its semantic value, producing a ripple pool of meanings where denotation and connotation, signifier and signified, matter and antimatter crash against one another sportively in the infinite play of sense and nonsense. Whether or not we confront extended or thinking matter (Descartes' dualism in the *Meditations on First Philosophy*), word machine or thought machine (Breton's automatism in his *Manifestoes of Surrealism*), we have no choice but to entertain this excess, as it erodes the stabilities and respective durabilities of ego and personality in the creation of a postmodern self resonant with Deleuze and Guattari's schizoid *Corps Sans Organes*, an entity whose defiance of organicism and Oedipalism speaks to the paranoia and ecnoia of this novel species of the self and its attendant poetries.[2] Pushed to the point of absurdity, Bernstein's approach to words and the constellations and configurations they both assume as well as presume, an enterprise I have labeled ~~poetic~~ in deference to Bertnstein's radical socialization of form, which, like the human subject of civilization in Rousseau's *Social Contract* and Freud's *Civilization and Its Discontents*, aligns itself with dis-content, does not so much liquidate fixities as much as it opens cliché, conceit and convention to the productive possibility of their unraveling—for, as Bernstein never tires of elucidating and demonstrating:"FORM IS NEVER MORE THAN AN EXTENSION OF MALCONTENT," a surplus

---

2 Bernstein first discusses *ecnoia*, a psychological term of his own creation, in the essay "Thought's Measure" as a response to Ron Silliman regarding the Wittgensteinian problem of a *langue privée*: "So I do maintain the value of the perspective of broken-off-ness (inherent in aspects of both 'privacy' and 'idleness') as central to a genuine social revelation. If I rest on a term like 'poetry' it is to allow for the (talismanic? ecnoid?) power the medium itself has acquired through its history to emerge: revealing the adherence of individuality and collectivity, binding and unbinding and rebinding" (*Content's Dream*, 86). Bernstein continues this thread in "Writing and Method": "To be aside, to be next to (para/noid), is at least a significant break from a practice which places one outside, out of (ec/noid—out-of-one's-mind); it is the position of being in history, conditioned by time and place and body; and it is true that my relation to 'things-in-themselves' is more accurately described by this account of experience of a self than by one that simply presumes such experience as impartial" (*Content's Dream*, 232).

uselessness flapping vestigial wings ("Introjective Verse," *My Way*, 111). While the aspiration of content is to a form able to give it expression, and the secret wish of language is to revolutionize the very ground of its articulation and, in the case of the printed word, inscription, or the digital enunciation, coding, these dreams can only be accomplished through a primary dysraphism that is the polar opposite of accord and motor coordination alike and a dyssemia according to which signals (not signs) are launched yet never received in quite the right way. Inside a lung, we feel a misdirected ball of hair and teeth bounce about like a Lotto ball in a pneumatic tube, while through a neon Plexi-straw we catch what we can of a semaphore flag blowing in a particularly amped lunar wind—and yet even with this discomfort, and this failure of communication, there is comfort, and the possibility of community (Maurice Blanchot's $n \geq 1$).

Bernstein defines dysraphism most closely in "Blood on the Cutting Room Floor," his essay on the technics of writing as it passes through both Gutenberg revolutions (first the haecceic printed word, then the virtual, digital word). In this essay, Bernstein illuminates his theory of the suture, the seam connecting thought to thought in the production of a social garment made primarily of smooth muscle:

> Dysraphism may be a useful term in this context. Medically, it would mean a congenital misseaming of embryonic parts—*raph* means seam, a rhapsodist being one who stitches parts together, that is, a reciter of epic poetry. So different parts from the middle, end, and beginning—it's a 4D image—are fused together to become one entity (*Content's Dream*, 359).

What dysraphism and its Einsteinian spacetime structure are to organs, dyssemia and its depth are to perception, and proprioception, as it is this "disorder" or disordering which elevates the accidental and the erroneous to the status of the aleatory or the fortunate, a critical category within Language production (for example, the chance operation, *sgraffito* of texts percolating through one another).[3]

---

3 In her essay "*Bernstein's 'Dysraphism': Dysfunction and Thrombolysis*, Béa Aronson analyzes Bernstein's poem "Dysraphism," from the collection *The Sophist* with the precision of a neurosurgeon: "Language is sick, incontinent. Meaning leaks" (*Found Object*, 89). Throughout, Aronson is acutely attentive to the presence of diseases throughout the poem, making it a sort of *Modern-Medicine*–meets-Eliot's-*Wasteland*-in-the-belly-of-Gertrude-Stein.

Bernstein introduces dyssemia in the context of a *New York Times* article regarding children who are unable to communicate effectively and the orthopedic means of smoothing out their language:

> While I both identify with and try to attend to such differences, peculiarities, and idiosyncrasies of perception, the article predictably prescribes the psychological orthodontics of correction and behavioral modification to obliterate the dis-ease, which is given the high-fallutin' name of dyssemia (flawed signal reception), a suitable companion discipline to my own poetic preoccupation, dysraphism ("An Interview with Manuel Brito," *My Way*, 31).

Through dyssemia, signs, recast as signals, are lobbed and launched, yet their reception is at odds with their production and intention; in short, as poets, we are these "out-of-sync" kids, these beings whose existence challenges what Bernstein terms the Conduit Theory of Communication, or that paradigm according to which message passes from speaker to spoken-to transparently, and with a minimum of semantic friction and *frisson*. Oddly, Bernstein's implicit distrust of that arbitrariness in the sign first identified and thematized by Ferdinand de Saussure in his *Course in General Linguistics* and used as a basis for deconstruction by Jacques Derrida in his *Writing and Difference* cuts against his love of the dyssemic, which resists nostalgia and *kenosis*, as no loss of plenitude is ever experienced, an important misreading of Saussurian whim and Derridean mourning mis-seaming Bernstein and potential allies.[4]

Much like the Rimbaudian imperative that a derangement of the senses give birth to poetry through the systematic and intentional

---

4   Comically, it is Barrett Watten who voices the most frustration from within the Language school regarding Bernstein's misreading of Saussure. In "Characterization," structured around the death of advertising giant Bill Bernbach, Watten cannot suppress his discomfort with Bernstein's total rejection of the Saussurian tradition: "When Saussure wanted to talk about the arbitrariness of the sign what he meant was that it was not mystic. He was trying to get rid of undue concern with etymology in nineteenth century linguistics, and that's exactly what that means, and it doesn't mean *anything else*. I wish somebody would put it on a billboard someplace" (*Content's Dream*, 442). Watten goes on to insist: "Okay, Charles. I really think you should purge your vocabulary of phrases like 'structuralist linguistics from Saussure to Derrida" (443), because "it's not only a provisional construction, but it's an illusory and unexamined construction that you in fact know better of. And so in fact you can *do* better" (444).

pulverization of sensation, Bernstein's gumming up of linguistic process through an identification of language with material surface removes transparency from the equation and condemns glibness to the reliquary, as it is no longer possible to make any denotative or declarative assumptions without taking into account the social conditions of their utterance. Placing metonymy above metaphor, *glissement* and hoarding above *phanopoiea* and the Surrealist empty-ing of imagination, this ethos culminates in the re-materialization of language not unlike Jackson Pollock's rediscovery of paint *qua* paint or Gertrude Stein's proffering of a grammar that is first and foremost grammatology, total syntaxes of sight and sound breaking through complacency and complicity with the heralding of audience as audi-ence. Within his worlds, it is the opacity of language which pushes it in the direction of chaos, as trope disintegrates and tropism takes surprising objects of gravitation, all according to an obscene logic of polysemy. In the zone of the ~~poetic~~, language is not easy, nor is it transparent—translucent, perhaps, but with these strange photons that are particles and waves and membranes not always making it through the picture window of our Levittown homes where pitch-ers of dirty martinis make the afternoon fly. Resisting absorption, language thus facilitates a politicization of syntax based almost entirely on obfuscation and disorientation. If the new combinations marking this novel syntax are something like the language of robots or future perfect Cro Magnons, it is because they are in a sense unut-terable, a fact marking their actual utterance as shocking, disorient-ing and toxic. Who could speak these words? Who could create an *écriture* of these pottery shards from a dig on Io? For whom could this delirious hypersense in the guise of nonsense compute to any sum outside of the amassing of imaginary numbers on imaginary numbers, so many mystical *i*'s throwing into disrepair the cathedral of mathematics? Only impossible creatures in search of possibilities through whose slits they can push the mass of their nonbeing, their stops and stutters a Lacanian *lalangue* recapitulating the scissions of selfhood.[5]

Since Bernstein's praxis and theories are integral to the flowering of a L=A=N=G=U=A=G=E aesthetic form the plastic 80s through a post-

---

5   Lacan presents his theory of *lalangue* in *Encore*, his seminar on the limits of love and knowledge. For Lacan, only the master signifier, or S1, exerts linguistic mastery, as it is the Representing-representation through which an order is insti-tuted via self-grounding. See also my essay "objet petit a as *je ne sais quoi*" in the forthcoming "Psychoanalysis and Literature," edited by Alvin Henry.

postmodern present in which 'neural lyres' continue their strumming and so much poesis has become advertising, their influence on our present and its presence cannot be understated.[6] Bernstein's language, which unfolds like an alien topography over whose crevasses the tongue skids wildly, takes the Steinian hypothesis of a language of middles to its limit, transcending baby-talk and luxurious nonmeaning through the production of an apoetic poetics committed to reorganizing the world of referents such that they begin to denote more than mere objects or contents. In fact, their reference is to the act of reference itself, the precondition for denotation, connotation, demonstration, and all other language-games connecting designation with thing and making language exhibit its "handiness," or *Zuhandenheit*, to employ the word linking being to usefulness within Heidegger's lexicon. Without handiness, there can be no care (*Sorge*), as there is no way for interest to flower, and Bernstein is nothing if he is not a handyman tinkering with discarded motors and cuckoo clocks whose birds have stopped singing "Edelweiss": his mechanisms make us care, refreshing our alliance with a world capable of sustaining interest and in doing so, engaging thrownness or *Geworfenheit* at the source of its ejection. To paraphrase and twist the Wittgenstein of the *Tractatus Logico-Philosophicus* " Language is all that is the case," a phenomenon dividing into things, not facts.[7] And the encasement, the skin of thought, the skein from which all macramé flows. Through language, the matrix for thought, expres-

---

6 The New Formalist theory of the neural lyre is presented by Frederick Turner and Ernst Pöppel in their essay "The Neural Lyre: Poetic Meter, the Brain, and Time" in *Poetry* (October 17, 2001). Apart from the theory's uses within what Bernstein terms Official Verse Culture (OVC), it does open the field of writing to *neuropoiesis*: for example, as when pentameter is timed at 3.30 seconds. A pattern such as this brings pleasure and beauty (*kalos*) to the organism through which it pulses: "The human nervous system has a strong drive to construct affirmative, plausible, coherent, consistent, parsimonious, and predictively powerful models of the world, in which all events are explained by and take their place in a system which is at once rich in implications beyond its existing data and at the same time governed by as few principles or axioms as possible."

7 A more productive way to view the relation between Wittgenstein's *Tractatus* and his *Philosophical Investigations* than to posit the second as diverging from the first and in essence from Analytic Philosophy is that the *Tractatus* presents a world that divides into facts, while the *Investigations* presents a world that divides into things, as per 1.1: "The world is the totality of facts, not of things," and 1.11: "The world is determined by the facts, and by their being *all* the facts." In this interpretation , the two works hang together, hinging on whether we take the world as a logical or material entity.

sion, communication (even when that communication is intraper-
sonal), handiness and care produce motivated form, this shaping
of content into socially legible structures which are also strictures:
as with Rousseau, freedom requires chains. For, as Bernstein reiterates throughout *Content's Dream*, the subject of poetry is limitation,
and as his psychology proves, the subject of thought, emotion and
expression is a being best categorized as liminal. When asked by Tom
Beckett, interrogator of an "Ongoing Interview," in what sense limitation enters into his work, Bernstein replies:

> Well, completely — that there's no limit to limits and
> blockages, stoppages, jam as depth of field, as the abstrac-
> tion/condensation of poetry, as if a dam were the poem's
> hydroelectric power/intensity source. So it's both a subject
> matter and a formal concern. What, after all, is the subject
> matter of poetry? Certainly limitation is right up there, *as*
> the body, time, place (*Content's Dream*, 406).

Subjectivity is limitation, form this limited subject's selection of an
outerwear matching and optimizing an environment and a climate.

Shedding the meanings which time has adhered to their surfaces
through habit and reiteration, objects and the words which describe
them precipitate a crisis in lyricism caused primarily by the dissolution of voice and the disconnection from its task of confession: how
can the self sing of these things that have ceased signifying, these
items and emotions and sensations which have become synonymous
with the discursive value they have been assigned by the greeting
card industry, the talk show circuit, magazine culture, MySpace,
Twitter, when its very uniqueness and originality are called into
question? No longer sung, yet aspiring to a time when they can once
again fuse with melody, words wrest themselves free from sono-
rousness and *melopoiea* because the time is not yet right for song,
nor is it the hour to devour peaches, ripe and juicy as they may be.[8]

---

8 My reference is to T.S. E. Eliot's "The Love Song of J. Arthur Prufrock," in which
   the tandem questions, the first an issue of senescence, the second a problem of
   sensual consumption, "Shall I part my hair behind? Do I dare to eat a peach?",
   refer back to the quantum "Do I dare" of "Do I dare/ disturb the universe?". Here,
   peach-eater and *pécheur* are synonymous, as it is the sin of beginning which is ever
   deferred, washed out to sea with the insular dreams of mermaids singing among
   themselves. See T. S. Eliot, *Prufrock and Other Poems*, West Valley City, UT: Waking
   Lion Press, 2007.

Where love resides within this economy becomes another point of confusion, especially as regards O'Haran Personism, a tendency that Bernstein retains, despite the unitariness of O'Haran voice and ego: but to whom can the heart address itself in this space where the inhuman lurks behind every syllable, where poetry becomes so many elements and sets, naturally fantastic geodes summed up in a poetry of the mineral? Between a benign Steinian situation in which even buttons achieve tenderness and a vicious Lacanian circle of demand and disappointment, there lies the rare opportunity for people to connect to other people through a fractured O'Haran program in which egos have been redefined as functions and desire has become amperage, yet double happiness is still held out as a promise, much in the way that, via desiring-production (a function that, curiously enough, Bernstein never hyphenates, despite the fact that Deluze and Guattari link them via the embrace of the cleaving hyphen), the CSO converts knowledge (*Numen*) to voluptuousness (*Voluptas*). It is these strange proclivities for mechanization and synchrony that are the felicitous side effects of a language reborn as language on a human plane where words still have to do things and performativities of language carry Wittgensteinian urgency nonetheless, whether we have to orchestrate the transport of concrete slabs or undertake an act of mourning. Here, play accomplishes work, as do structure and sign, but how? Here, even Pac Man undertakes acts of poesis, his path through a Minotaur's labyrinth tracing out an invisible collection of near misses and snappy saves leading ultimately to his demise, but buying time nonetheless (in the lingo of performance artists Kiki and Herb, we are always "playing for time," whether we maul a cabaret classic, convert our soul into a lyricism-generator, or spirit Pacman away from hostile ghosts with names like Blinky, Pinky, Inky or Clyde). Thickening into a matter that is also *dura mater*, language undertakes an internal dialogue risking autism and lunacy in the interest of novelty and all that it can usher in via the poetic event, whose ruptures rip through us repeatedly.

The Absorption Spectrum of Iridium

In January 2010's installment of the — *empyre* — Forum, an online discussion where luminaries and moonwalkers convene cybernetically to discuss a pre-arranged topic, poet and historiographer of the printed letter Johanna Drucker tells the following vignette, all to illustrate a compelling point about art and complicity, the month's theme, as set by Nicholas Ruiz III, author of *The Metaphysics of Capital*:

> Once, when I was teaching at Columbia, I had occasion to attend a talk by a very famous architect and theorist whose name I honestly do forget, though someone else will no doubt remember. He was talking about the then recent renovation of Parc de la Villette in Paris. He took issue with the design that had been developed-which was created to make a recreational, pleasant outdoor space in a high density neighborhood whose demographic was working class and at the lower end of the economic scale. He suggested instead that the park should be made as *unpleasant* as possible, disagreeable, difficult to use, grating on the senses because then and only then would the working classes rise up and overthrow the capitalist masters (posted January 4, 2010).[9]

While I have never had the good fortune to pass through Parc de La Villette myself, wasting my Parisian time sitting along the Beaubourg waiting to catch a glimpse of local celeb Sonia Rykiel, I immediately found Drucker's tale to bear critical relevance to Bernstein's approach to language; and so I replied:

> I wonder: what would it be like to design difficult and treacherous parks in the best 'hoods, making CPW a spike garden with acid pools, or converting Kensington Gardens into a field of Venus Fly Traps? This could be an interesting twist, and might inspire something marvelous. True, discomfort and displeasure do get the gears of a coup turning, reminding me of Charles Bernstein's theory of language, indeed, his own 'complicity,' if we might call it that, with regard to Analytic Philosophy, whose currency he is quite smart to trade: here, opacity makes us stumble,

9 Drucker continues: "This from a person whose yearly income had long since topped out the salary scale at the University and who lived a life of security and relative luxury. I found this appalling, but the colleague I was with told me to hold my tongue because the audience was in thrall—all thought this was the most brilliant and radical talk they had heard in ages. This seems to me to be a completely different thing from teaching students Foucault, for instance, to give them tools for critical thought" (posted Jan 4, 2010).

and stutter, as absorptions are refused and the necessity for action surfaces, calling us to make language into something more than transparency machine. On the other side, the silence of Wittgenstein and Laura Riding Jackson await, complicities with quiet, renunciations of community and convocation. Ladders take us so deeply into this world that we leave it.

I will return to the theme of Analytic Philosophy and its installation at the heart of Language Poetry in the next section of this essay; for the moment, I remain with the theme of poesis and pleasure, and the de-coupling of form from content in order to re-align content with narratives of social progress. For, as Drucker's very rich and fraught story demonstrates, there is a productive connection between industriousness and suffering consonant with Rousseau's critique of indolence in his *Essay on the Origin of Languages*—only with Drucker's park, it is not latitude recast as Southernness which prevents development, and which interferes with the gears of historical necessity, but the opiate effect of public art that lulls a potentially rowdy population into a slumber quashing rebellion, insurgence, change.

For Drucker herself, it is her emphasis on the visual dimension of language that prevents what Bernstein terms the Transparency Effect from disrupting the *Verfremdungseffekt*, her hyptertextual hijinks producing texts in which the legible is rivaled by the sensuous, it being no longer possible for poem to collapse to voice and diffusion to condense into confession. In his essay "Alienation Effects on Chinese Acting," Bertolt Brecht discusses the theatrical value of alienation, a method " . . . most recently used in Germany for plays of a non-aristotelian (not dependent on empathy) type as part of the attempts being made to evolve an epic theatre. The efforts in question were directed to playing in such a way that the audience was hindered from simply identifying itself with the characters in the play" (91).[10] For Bernstein, the application of Brecht's prescription is a particular dream of content, producing dis-identification, *méconnaissance*, and the ecstasies of entropy. In the context of Brechtian alienation, popularly known within cultural studies as the V-effect, Bernstein views Drucker and Jenny Holzer as taking diametrical stands on Aristotelian (capital 'A,' unlike Brecht's deflated spelling)

---

10 The essay "Alienation Effects in Chinese Acting" appears in the collection *Brecht on Theatre: The Development of an Aesthetic*, trans. and ed. John Willett (New York: Hill and Wang, 2001).

spectatorship, Drucker syncing up with his project of disrupting
reading and reading disruptively, Holzer digitalizing texts he views as
insipid, inferior and exuding a failed irony indicative of the different
paths that postmodernism has followed in the literary and visual arts.
Specifically, Holzer fails poetically, her diodes zipping by bathetically
and anaesthetically, facilitating smugness and superficiality among
viewers when they should be having their minds shaken violently:
" . . . --I wonder why she doesn't collaborate with a writer, or set
already existing texts, say by Leslie Scalapino or Hannah Weiner or
Kathy Acker, to lights. She's like a great composer who insists on
writing her own libretto but only knows about one type of sentence
structure and has never, apparently, read any other librettos" ("The
Response as Such," *My Way,* 184). While Holzer's works, such as her
Truisms, "disenfranchise" their audience, Drucker's energize them:
"She has visually troubled the transparency of letters, giving way
to contents, so that you cannot help but see and be exhilarated by
the many ways that letters and their sizes and shapes or ordering
allow for, are a necessary prerequisite of, the aesthetic dimension
of the verbal domain" (180). As a result, videopoiea and logopoiea
are trumped by linguistic materiality, words leaping into visibility
and sabotaging their subsumption by message, yet another way that
experimental writing has made its medium a part of its content (179).

  Apart from the productive juncture between poetry and the plastic arts, there is a second hotspot where artifices of absorption lull
consumers to sleep: the cinema, its moving images so often demanding little of its audience, perhaps a pre-programmed act of cathar-
sis, or the re-creation of emotion as kitsch. While I am not entirely
sure that the cinema demands and commands the kind of passivity
attributed to it by Bernstein, who, in contradistinction to Marshall
McLuhan's prognosis in *Understanding Media*, views it as a cool, rather
than hot medium, I credit Bernstein with using his experiences as
cinemagoer to develop a theory of the image as amoeba wrapping
its pseudopods around the unsuspecting, as they drift off, immersed
in plot and character making their own behavior and selfness disappear. To make his point, Bernstein coins the term *imagabsorption* to
describe the suction of the image, its pull on a psyche all too happy to
lose itself in a medium which has done the most to popularize representation, much as the 'e' of 'image' slides beneath absorption's 'a.'
In response to a screening of *Mad Max*, Bernstein comments:

  What's involved doesn't feel like a *willing* suspension

of disbelief, as if I actually had to work at conjuring the images, as you do in reading this sentence: Max's world imposes itself on me, all I have to do is slip into neutral. *Absorption*: the unwilling (that is, passive) suspension of disbelief. Not imagination (the act of forming a mental image out of something not present to the senses), but *im-position* of the image on the mind — *imagabsorption*" ("Frames of Reference," *Content's Dream*, 90).

If Lacan's great contribution to a theory of the visual is his unearth-ing of an individuative and counter-anamorphic, scopic drive through which the invidious makes itself known and felt, then for Bernstein, the new loop of desire brought to light is something like the subject's drive to de-individuate, eye flowing out of I: "The need to respond to situations seen is numbed, satisfying an intense craving for passivity. Film is infinitely more technically adept at defeating self-consciousness than theater" (91). Taken as such, the image neutral-izes its viewer, who experiences the pleasures of drowning itself in the flesh of others, their giant features playing across the screen in this dark place where all that is expected is that I abandon myself to the same Hollywood machinery that for Adorno and Horkheimer is the obscene outpost of Enlightenment thinking. Into this mael-strom I throw myself, taking a temporal break from the project of my spatialization, as *imagabsorption* causes me to be sucked into the game of representation, a ludology not without its stakes.

In this vein, it is the essay "Artifice of Absorption" in the collec-tion *A Poetics* which delves deepest into the critical role that dissolu-tion plays in constructing spectators and wedding content to a form that will create docility, domestication and rest rather than foment revolution or force an ideology into showing itself, therein disarming it: "From a compositional point of view/ the question is, What can a poem absorb?," but also: what absorbs its content, how do trans-parency and absorption come together, what is the history of the naturalization of various writerly devices (22)? Absorption is always artificial, for example, as when the letters of advertising copy in a publication like *Modern Medicine*, the one Bernstein edited and whose editorial demands are the site of a certain trauma continuing to exert an effect, foster an act of reading through which time disappears and I am not tempted to search behind the letters on the page for mean-ing because I am satiated by transparency. As Bernstein later explains in the highly gratifying "An Autobiographical Interview," the one spot where, for just a moment, we get a glimpse of the man behind the curtain:

> In New York, I worked initially at the United Hospital Fund, writing the scintillating *Health Manpower Consortia Newsletter*, which Susan and I designed in exactly the same format that we would use, a few years later, for L=A=N=G=U=A=G=E, then briefly for the Council on Municipal Performance, a public interest group where I primarily worked on mass transit issues and against the subway fare hike of that moment, and then for a couple of years as abstracts editor for the Canadian edition of *Modern Medicine*, where I wrote about 80 medical abstracts each month. This immersion in commercial writing and editing—as a social space too but more in the technical sense of learning the standard compositional roles and forms at the most detailed, and numbingly boring, level of proofreading and copyediting—was informing in every way (*My Way*, 246).

From both the look of L=A=N=G=U=A=G=E to his genuine fear that writing is erasing subjectivity, these years of commercial work impact the Language project at the level of its surfaces (cover, design and layout) and running themes of absorption and counter-absorption, even as these shift within the same piece of writing: "The oscillation of attentional focus,/ and its attendant blurring,/ is a vivid way of describing/ the ambivolent switching, which I/ am so fond of, between absorption &/ antiabsorption, which can now/ be described as redirected/ absorption" (78).[11]

For example, in the masterpiece of disjointedness that begins *Content's Dream*, the poem "Three or Four Things I Know about Him," the demands of economics force a writing that can only produce a highly socialized form of mental illness and en ethics known as Toilet Paper Consciousness ("keep yr ass clean," 23):

> It goes like this. "Clear writing is the best picture of clear thinking." Providing a clear view. (An imperial clarity for

---

11 Ambivolence is a combination of ambivalence and volition, a willful ambivalence used for antiabsorptive ends; as a term, it traces back to Steven McCaffrey, and is an important part of his social-poetic lexicon. For Bernstein, it functions as a cornerstone of Language Poetics.

an imperial world.) An official version of reality, in which ethics is transformed into moral code & aesthetics into clean shaving, is labeled the public reality & we learn this as we would a new landscape (Orthography & expository clarity are just words for diction & etiquette.) (25).

Despite the fact that even the most insipid ad-speak, as in the obituary for Bill Bernbach around which a conversation among conspirators flowers at the end of the catechesis of *Content's Dream*, conceals complex and varied readings, the point remains solid: there is great danger in letting the medium obscure its existence as medium, presenting itself as invisible in an effort to put the breaks on interrogation, deconstruction and dislocation. But does medium's massage come with a happy ending? What has been concealed is the fact that absorption is not an effect of nature, something given, a *donné* among *donnés*; rather, inspiring a spectator or reader to vanish is a complicated affair bearing all the weight of prestidigitation and thaumaturgy, as well as something of the apotropaic, even the charming, as art tames reality via the act of re-presenting it:

> Charm melos depends on
> "artificial", jaggedly rhythmic
> prosodic elements to create a centripetal
> (or vertical)
> energy in the poem that is
> able to capture and hold the attention (not
> just conscious attention, but the imagination
> or
> psyche). The power of charm melos is *technical*
> in the precise sense of Rothenberg's title: the
> superficially antiabsorptive elements
> (disjunction,
> repetition, accentuated stresses, nonlexical "scat"
> sounds) are the basis for this
> souped-up poetic
> engine (47-48).

What needs to appear is something like what Drucker terms the *metalogics* of the text, the hidden choices, decisions and movements that hide behind the Reveal Codes function in standard computing; preferring a poetry which no longer hides behind its conventions and inventions, Bernstein forces language to reappear as medium, therein breaking with Official Verse Culture's tradition of confession, voice, clarity and the naturalness of speech, as it bathes tympani in a gentle acid with just the right pH to cause a damage that can only be perceived gradually, yet whose effects are irreversible.[12]

Poetically, as well as politically, writing is thus quite simply defined as an act of marking, it falling upon the poet, an unacknowledged legislator of the world, to find a way to make these marks resonate, since otherwise they might be put to other uses in the interest of commercial gain. As system of series of marks, things that may be read serially, sequentially, syntactically, writing is more than simple chain of differences:

> The "mark" is the visible sign of writing.
> But reading, insofar as it consumes &
> absorbs the mark, erases it—the words disappear
> (the transparency effect) & are replaced by
> that which they depict, their "meaning". Thus
> absorption is the "aura of listening" destroyed
> in this writing: Antiabsorptive
> writing recuperates the mark by making it opaque,
> that is, by maintaining its visibility
> & undermining its meaning, where "meaning" is
> understood in the narrower, utilitarian sense
> of a restricted economy" (64).

The invocation of Georges Batailles' concept of a restricted economy, as compared with a general economy, carries the text toward the anthropology of the potlatch, privileged seat where the gift convenes with waste and excess, revealing an obscene core to the act of giving, which can come to mean something closer to evacuating. For Bernstein, the restricted economy is the space of *Modern Medicine* and the *Health Manpower Consortia Newsletter*, as well as Official Verse Culture, popular cinema, and the cryogenically preserved mind of Bill Bernbach, the place where we demand of subject and subjectivity a voice capable of confessing secrets, and of making the interior exterior, the private, public, while the general economy is the locus

---

12 In Drucker's and Jerome McGann's SpecLab project in speculative computing, one desire is to expose textual dark matter, the invisible scaffolding around which writing coils, making it able to appear as writing in the first place. See her *SpecLab: Digital Aesthetics and Projects in Speculative Computing*, Chicago: The University of Chicago Press, 2009.

where language does not content itself with delivering trivialities or bolstering a social order hegemonically, but where it frees itself from inherited form in order to give back a kind of freedom. Hence if for Derrida in *Given Time* and *The Gift of Death* the problem of generosity becomes an issue of the ontology of the gift, and is inherently a deconstruction of what giving has meant to sociologist Marcel Mauss and his heirs, then for Bernstein the question becomes one of what can and ought to happen in the realm of writing, of how the textual excesses represented by antiabsorption and impermeability—" . . . artifice, boredom,/ exaggeration, attention scattering, distraction,/ digression . . . "—can be used to re-mark the billboards and pages and screens and skins of the social, alerting it to wild nights and brash possibilities and the flash of flesh as novelty enters the world in a burst challenging the Neils Bohr model of the atom (29).

Wittgenstein's Ladder at the Home Depot

Although we use, abuse, inhabit and ultimately take leave of language as we progress toward a post-mortal future where only table-tilting and visits from Madame Blavatsky await, its open system of marks is something we can only make ours provisionally in the space of the today; as Lacan points out in his seminar *Encore*, language is subject to the laws of usufruct, that body of rules governing how a political and civil subject is able to benefit from—literally, use and enjoy—the property of others (for example, as when one rents land and is able to grow fruit trees there, in essence paying a price that allows him to profit from what that land is able to produce). A line that Bernstein quotes from Abraham Lincoln Gillespie's poem "Expatracination" in his essay "Poetics of the Americas" makes playful reference to this governing code, albeit with a neologistic twist typical of Gillespie's hyperactive *spieltrieb*: " . . . THEN—the/ The American Spirit will commence-sing as naïve-direct-elimgoalpur-/ sue-clearly as its present FolkMelod—"PopularSong," frequently as/ blare-OutréFruct-freely as its dynaSaxophoneyc . . . "(*My Way*, 133). Gillespie's playful operation on usufruct, rendered far-out (outré) and potentially unreachable in its existence light years away from present realities, makes the problem of use—a pragmatic concern which Bernstein will examine primarily through the lens of Wittgenstein's *Philosophical Investigations* but which, in a parallel universe, might have passed through Willard van Orman Quine's ideas on translation, inscrutability and indeterminacy—a game of telepoiesis, as we attempt to contact a future society to ask questions about the trafficking of syntagms and sinthomes. Since language is ours only provisionally, even if we factor in the effect we may continue to exert upon it after death, as the words we leave behind enter the eyes, ears and imaginations of future generations, there are inherently problems of solipsism and private language, collapse of meaning and correspondence of thought with world, performativities of the spoken word and constants of constativity, and the greatest bugbear of all, the meaning of silence not as mere stop between sounds or syllables, or marker of sonic difference, but as the pre- or extra- or post-discursive, whether or not these regions are identical or represent different terrains where words fail us, as Meena Alexander reminds us in works like her *Poetics of Dislocation* where, floating on the Indian Ocean between India and Sudan, she feels her words turn to liquid and flow away from her in this zone of radical speechlessness.[13]

Bernstein installs Wittgenstein at the center of his poetics, focusing most closely on his *Philosophical Investigations* and placing the *Tractatus* under relative erasure, losing sight of the fact that the one could not exist without the other, their complementarity creating a particularly rich vista of what language can do, whether we adhere to a correspondence theory according to which language works when it is able to draw clean lines bijectively between logical structures and states of affairs among signifieds (*Tractatus* Ludwig), or step away from the visual metaphorics of language and its 'pictorial' quality in order to examine how words function within social structures irrespective of the injections and surjections of correspondence (*Philosophical Investigations* Ludwig). Ultimately, the *Philosophical Investigations* is Language Poetry's passport to theoretical vigor, the gold standard ensuring that the luxe nonsense of colliding discourses and genres is relevant even at its most gratuitous moments, when reference becomes irrelevant. If there is a philosophical currency here, it is printed with the face of Ludwig Wittgenstein, a state of affairs allying poetry with Analytic Philosophy and, implicitly, logic:

---

13 Alexander explained this perspective in a reading of her *Poetics of Dislocation* held by Kate Moss' Postcolonial Studies Group at the CUNY Graduate Center, March 26, 2010. In "Crossing the Indian Ocean," Alexander writes: "The sea cast me loose. The sea tore away from me all that I had. In doing so, it gave me an interior life far sooner than I would have had otherwise, but at great cost. I was forced to enter into another life, the life of the imagination. But it was not as yet the life of language" (178). As such, the sea, "unselving," casts her adrift upon an expanse of linguistic liquidity where she cannot be at home, a "wordless poet" caught up in these incomprehensible dual surges (179).

hence the marvelous resistance of Bernstein's work to the sclerosis of certainty as it embarks upon what he terms "Gertrude and Ludwig's Bogus Adventure, " a voyage from which he never returns, his poetry a never-ending travelogue through indeterminacy:

> Vienna was cold at that time of year.
> The sachertorte tasted sweet but the memory
> burned in the colon. Get a grip, get a grip, before
> The Grippe gets you. Glad to see the picture
> Of ink—the pitcher that pours before
> Throwing the Ball, with never a catcher in sight (*My Way*, 109).

At some level, the adventure of these twin Steins, however bogus it is, carries Bernstein beyond identity—"My doggie knows my name, my smell, but not the thought that cleaves my nature, making me part of its world, part next. Beside myself is that being that belongs neither to my past nor to my self"—and beyond the idea of language as an entity dissipating the arbitrary by creating a factual portrait of the world encouraging us to pass over the unspeakable in the reticence Wittgenstein recommends with the coldness of an 'ought' ("Stein's Identity," *My Way*, 142). Curiously, while there is never a catcher in this, Jack Spicer's baseball game, as appears to be present in the *Tractatus,* there is catching: " . . . sometimes a catch, or/ A clinch or a clutch or a spoon" (109). Which language-game are we playing? What counts as speech or writing or reading here, as we immerse ourselves in these words we can never grasp with any Cartesian-Leibnizian surety, but which we can turn to our advantage, if only after we step out of both the suffocating shell of solipsism and the cold grey of a logic which tricks itself into thinking that it is the axiomatic ground of art and science alike?[14]

From the far side of Wittgenstein's hinge, Bernstein imports three critical themes that in their own way anchor the Language project: (1) language-games and their relation to pragmatism (the wordness of words, thingness of a thing language, equally parts Carnap and Spicer), (2) the idea of the Logopolis (language as City); (3) aspect blindness (the rabbit-duck mirage). Using these three fundamental moments within the *Philosophical Investigations*, Bernstein is able to wrest content free of form, giving it *carte blanche* to construct its

---

14 "5.64 Here it can be seen that solipsism, when its implications are followed out strictly, coincides with pure realism. The self of solipsism shrinks to a point without extension, and there remains the reality co-ordinated with it."

own Golgonooza, the place where we never lose money on Emily
Dickinson, where Cenozoic life rids itself of a nostalgia for Gondwana
and the Tethys Ocean, and where mistaking a duck for a rabbit, or
an eye for an I, count as felonies punishable with tickle torture. In
Bernstein's account, there is a marvelous before and after to the
Wittgenstein story, a divide separating Analytic Philosophy from
pragmatism, Bertrand Russell from Charles Sanders Pierce, language
as logical monolith ("2.141 A picture is a fact") to language as multiplicity of language-games, with their dissonance of aims, ambitions
and payouts ("You seem to be thinking of board games, but there are
others," §3). In the dialogue "Characterization," Bernstein answers
a comment of Tom Mandel regarding John Ashberry's history:
"Well, yes, you have a lot of artists who progress. But I agree with
Barry on Ashberry. On the surface you could say it seems like early
Wittgenstein versus later Wittgenstein, where the latter is a psychoanalysis, almost, of the early work, showing its limitations" (*Content's
Dream*, 434). Hence while the arctic quality of *Tractatus'* meticulously
numbered propositions will lead to silence and a sort of alienation
from one's tools, the *Philosophical Investigations* will multiply language
into language-games and in doing so make it possible for words to do
so much more than mirror, ape or reflect. Wittgenstein's farewell is
as legendary as that other refusal of words, Laura Riding Jackson's,
as she lurches forward into the silence of one disillusioned with the
necessary artifices of any poetry which, as we know from Wilde, is
concerned with anything but truth: "6.54 My propositions serve as
elucidations in the following way: anyone who understands me eventually recognizes them as nonsensical, when he has used them—as
steps—to climb up beyond them. (He must, so to speak, throw away
the ladder after he has climbed up it.). He must transcend these propositions, and then he will see the world right." (74). Hence although
Bernstein sees the one work as superseding the other, it is clear that
Wittgenstein prepares the way for his later work in the earlier, allying himself with nonsense and encouraging his readers to obviate
him, his ultimate lesson being to discard him, along with his tool
belt. And then there is the clincher, which I read as an unnumbered
proposition, a thought beyond enumeration, rather than a part of
6.54, a premise I am reading as penultimate: "What we cannot speak
about we must pass over in silence" (74). For Bernstein, these dual
moments of ladder-retraction and quiet open Wittgenstein to post-
positivist life: hence the quasi-psychoanalytic quality of the relation

that obtains between the two Wittgensteins, the sublation of the one by the other, at least in Bernstein's alluring and influential myth.[15]

In the *Philosophical Investigations,* Wittgenstein presents one very important and loaded metaphor of language: language as City, or what I term the Logopolis. Bernstein paraphrases this image in "The Dollar Value of Poetry": "—Any limits put on language proscribe the limits of what will be experienced, and as Wittgenstein remarks, the world can easily be reduced to only the straight rows of the avenues of the industrial district, with no place for the crooked winding streets of the old city. 'To imagine a language is to imagine a form of life'—think of that first *imagine* as the active word here" (*Content's Dream,* 59). Wittgenstein expresses himself as such:

> . . . for these [chemistry, calculus] are, so to speak, suburbs of our language. (And how many houses or streets does it take before a town begins to be a town?) Our language can be seen as an ancient city: a maze of little streets and squares, of old and new houses, and of houses with additions from various periods; and this surrounded by a multitude of new boroughs with straight regular streets and uniform houses" (§18).

For Wittgenstein, the point is the radical openness of language: for example, even among the logical positivists and analytic philosophers, or those who, like Plato or Leibniz, view geometry or mathematics as the purest philosophical language, there is the paradox of invention, development and fallibility, his instances of the notations of chemistry and calculus forcing the question of the fundamental completeness of mathematics when taken as a total language (and as we know from Quine, even geometry can be reparsed as a skeletal logic supplemented with vacuities like 'spherity').[16] It is this radical

---

15 Even in the *Tractatus,* we sense Wittgenstein's epistemological exhaustion: "I therefore believe myself to have found, on all essential points, the final solution of the problems. And if I am not mistaken in this belief, then the second thing in which the value of this work consists is that it shows how little is achieved when these problems are solved" ("Preface," 4).

16 Specifically, in "Truth by Convention" (*Quintessence*) Quine hypothetically denotes geometry, as branch of mathematics, by the elliptical expression 'Φ (sphere, includes)', the implication being that, "it involves the expressions 'sphere' and 'includes' inessentially, in fact vacuously, since the logical deducibility of the theorems from the postulates is independent of the meanings of 'sphere' and 'includes' and survives the replacement of these expressions by any other grammatically

and fundamental openness of the Logopolis which attracts Bernstein, the conclusion being that, if language is indeed citylike, then it, too, must be open to the ages, who will deform and reform it time and time again as they renegotiate their own materialities and instrumentalities, language's *Zuhandenheit* once again coming to the fore. And yet I wonder: can I experience what my language denies me, is there a linguistic outside where I may feel what I cannot utter, speak what has been denied existence *tout court*, or is language the limit of sensation, perception, proprioception, introspection (the Meena Alexander question)? In Wittgenstein's Logopolis, the fact that language lives as City seems to indicate that we only must reorient ourselves to the fantastic urban sprawl at our feet in order to begin our itinerary anew, walking through these streets as Michel de Certeau recommends in his essay "Walking in the City"—that is, using our feet to create an ambulatory poem in the *art de faire* of simple locomotion. New Bernstein City is no different: all we are obligated to do is to open our eyes and let sensation rush in.

If the Logopolis spatializes language in a way that allows us to understand its temporal structure, then it is the dual figure of the duck-rabbit that undercovers the limits of perception as these inform our sense of what is and what can be. In Bernstein's thought, the optical illusion of the duck-rabbit ties to themes of ideational mimesis and frame lock, ideational mimesis being the normalized, inert prose of clarity, descriptiveness and composition, frame lock the ways in which our matrices of interpretation dictate exactly which kinds of reality are perceivable and processable. Frames, or aspects, become locked into place, facilitating certain vistas while foreclosing others:

> Frame fixation bears a family resemblance to aspect blindness, as described by Wittgenstein in part 2 of *Philosophical Investigations*, where the single figure that can be interpreted as a duck and a rabbit is discussed. Different contexts may suggest the appropriateness of particular interpretative systems, some of which may then seem determining. That is, once viewed through a particular frame, it becomes difficult to recognize alternate readings. A gaze freezes into a stare; only one aspect of an ambigu-

admissible expressions whatsoever" (8). As such, geometry is closer to sociology or Greek mythology than to logic proper, which is less subject to the involvement of vacuous terms. Still, logic does not quite escape the close shave of Quine's razor, as evidenced by his assault on analyticity and flirtation with nominalism.

ous figure is visible. The projection overwhelms the text
without exhausting the work ("What's Art Got to Do with
It?," *My Way*, 43).

Epistemology is thus never a pure or unmotivated endeavor, as
previously demonstrated with the dangers of form, content's BFF,
and also its nemesis, and frenemy, Paris Hilton to its Lindsay Lohan.
Responding to the ambiguous figure, Wittgenstein remarks: "The
change of aspect. 'But surely you would say that the picture is altogether different now!' But what is different: my impression? my
point of view?—Can I say? I *describe* the alteration like a perception;
quite as if the object had altered before my eyes" (Part II, XI, 195), for
". . . the flashing of an aspect on us seems half visual experience, half
thought" (II, XI, 197). Similarly, a triangle floating on the space of the
page might be seen as so many things: " . . . as a triangular hole, as
a solid, as a geometrical drawing; as standing on its base, as hanging
from its apex; as a mountain, as a wedge, as an arrow or pointer, as
an overturned object . . . " (II, XI, 200). Like the City whose older, less
regimented streets escape us if we remain behind with the newer
condos being built on the carcasses of leveled developments, the
duck-rabbit will not quack if we deem it a bunny, and can't procre-
ate wildly if we insist on calling it Daffy. Here, content's dream is of
an infinitely finitizable negative capability which does the greatest
honor to the habitation of murkiness first championed by Keats:

> I don't think I manage to achieve as many different
> possible interpretations as I might like [laughter]. I'm
> very limited by what makes sense to me, because of this
> horribly mistaken but nonetheless ongoing concern for
> the poem to sound right. I have a desire for an infinitely
> negative capability, and yet I am always coming upon
> very concrete forms of stabilization, characterization, that
> make patterns in respect to one another, which is what
> you notice at the level of the book ("Characterization"
> 458).

This dwelling within indecision and ambiguity Bernstein cherishes,
wishing the impossible wish of remaining within it while somehow
creating some kind of order from its nebulized particles: mathematically, we might call it Bernstein's Paradox in deference to other
famous oxymorons (Russell's Paradox, for example).

And yet, despite this great love of Wittgenstein carrying Bernstein forward from his senior thesis at Harvard to the present borders another tale, one which may one day be told: the potential influence on his work of analytic philosopher W.V.O. Quine, with whom he became acquainted at Harvard. Reading Bernstein's account of their interactions in his "Autobiographical Interview," what becomes clear is how closely he allies him with determinacy, this despite the fact that much of his philosophy concerns itself with linguistic indeterminacy at the level of radical translation. Back in Cambridge, Quine inspires Bernstein to have an oneiric adventure: "I had a dream one night in which I was haphazardly trying to stuff all my clothes into a suitcase and Quine came over to show me how they would all fit if neatly folded. I shot him" (241). Wittgenstein suffers no such symbolic fate, becoming abscissa to Gertrude Stein's ordinate, the two comprising the axes on which so much of Bern(stein)'s work is graphed with magenta chalk, neon green antifreeze, and bloodstains traceable to thrombolytic ADD, he being the Third Stein in this one-act play I lovingly call *Three Steins*.[17] Ludwig is never shot, but is injected into a gas tank and used to speed a perspective to the stars, but Willard falls to the floor, a portmanteau fatality. As he falls, he might say something excoriating about the distinction between analytic and synthetic statements, or give a dying insight into the life of Pegasus, perhaps even being so kind as to explain why the failed project of translation is no cause for alarm, even for the staunchest logician. He might say: "To exist is to be the value of a bound variable," leaving Hamlet's predicament open to questions of existential quantification.[18] And just where was Bernstein headed with this suitcase: was he running away from Quine, which is why he must be punished for his intrusion? Did it contain only tutus and whirly skirts, or maybe fencing costumes and chain mail tunics? I wish for the reality of a parallel universe where this scene blossoms into a Broadway hit, and where the indeterminacy at the center of Bernstein's infinitely negative negative capability meets the indeterminacy revealed to Quine by acts of translation and feats of refer-

---

17 Originally, Bernstein had wanted to title his Harvard thesis "Three Steins," not "Three Compositions on Philosophy and Literature." It is for this reason that I refer to Ludwig, Gertrude and Charles as the Three Steins (almost as it they formed an East Village rock group).

18 My references are to the following Quine pieces, all in *Quintessence*: "Two Dogmas of Empiricism," "Two Dogmas in Retrospect," "Reference," "Translation and Meaning," and "On What There Is."

encing, these two intense pryings-open of language setting up waveforms that level buildings and cause tuning forks to melt, all for the impersonal gaze of the logician and language poet, the two people who have done the most work deconstructing wordness. My own valise in hand, I outrace magma flows and fall into a poetic wormhole, taking leave of Charles if only for a moment as a poem escapes me, the way a brave particle makes it out of a black hole, going on to alight on Stephen Hawking's shoulder. It reads:[19]

Envoyage: Charlotte Corday in Corduroys

In the mental ward
of meaning, there are
metallurgic assays of
Mexican candy and
the smashed glass of
Jim Dandy sundae cups
from an ice cream social
fiasco and the surreptitious
chatter of astrolith matter
spilling secrets of cosmic
glamour to a throng of
screeching howler monkeys
in skorts and Cha-cha heels:
oh, the clanging and clamour.

"Diagonal stripes for everyone!"
urges one who fancies himself
a sociologist, his shovel digging
through the strata of a sandbox
at angles curiously acute.

In the hydrotherapy room,
a figure who has escaped
the clutches of his keepers

---

19 Here, I think of Bernstein's engagement of Peter Weiss' *Persecution and Assassination of Jean-Paul Marat as Performed by the Inmates of the Asylum of Charenton under the Direction of the Marquis de Sade* in the capacity of director: a role causing me to die, for just a moment, when I discovered it ("An Autobiographical Interview," 244). And so I end with Charlotte Corday, the play's heroine, in my poetic recapitulation of the themes of my essay.

reclines in a tub of ice water,
pondering the addition of
months to a calendar charting
incipient wonders-to-be.

Will she stab him? Will this
revolution continue to revolve?
Letter openers have so many
uses, not all of them epistolary.

A lunch of Lobster Thermidor
leaves her satiated and strangely
incensed, a burning freesia
cone. If time is to march on, it
is she who must twirl the baton.

A slice can be so nice, the
promise of her head in a bucket
the fruits of fame. History will
befriend her. Songs will be sung,
bells rung. Yes, she's the one.

References

Alexander, Meena. *Poetics of Dislocation*. Ann Arbor: University of
Michigan Press, 2009.
Aronson, Béa. "Bernstein's 'Dysraphism': Dysfunction and
Thrombolysis." *Found Object*: CUNY, Fall 2000.
Bernstein, Charles. *My Way: Speeches and Poems*. Chicago: University
of Chicago Press, 1999.
_____. *A Poetics*. Cambridge: Harvard University, 1992.
_____. *Content's Dream: Essays 1975-1984*. Evanston, IL:
Northwestern University Press, 1986.
Brecht, Bertolt. "Alienation Effects in Chinese Acting," in the *Brecht on
Theatre: The Development of an Aesthetic*. Trans. and ed. John Willett. New
York: Hill and Wang, 2001.
Callois, Roger. "A New Plea for Diagonal Science" and "The Natural
Fantastic," in *The Edge of Surrealism: A Roger Caillois Reader*.
Ed. Claudine Frank. Durham: Duke University Press, 2003.
de Certeau, Michel. *The Practice of Everyday Life*. Trans. Steven
Rendall. Berkeley: University of California Press, 1984.

Derrida, Jacques. *The Gift of Death*. Trans. David Wills. Chicago: University of Chicago Press, 1995.

_____. *Given Time I: Counterfeit Money*. Trans. Peggy Kamuf. Chicago: University of Chicago Press, 1992.

_____. *Writing and Difference*. Trans. Alan Bass. London: Routledge, 1978.

de Saussure, Ferdinand. *Course in General Linguistics*. Trans. Roy Harris. Peru, Illinois: Open Court, 1986.

Drucker, Johanna. *SpecLab: Digital Aesthetics and Projects in Speculative Computing*. Chicago: University of Chicago Press, 2009.

Eliot, T. S. *Prufrock and Other Poems*, West Valley City, UT: Waking Lion Press, 2007.

Lacan, Jacques. *Book XXIII Le Sinthome*. Trans. Luke Thurston. As yet unpublished.

Lacan, Jacques. *Book XX Encore: On Feminine Sexuality, the Limits of Love and Knowledge*. Trans. Bruce Fink. New York: W. W. Norton & Company, Inc., 1975.

McLuhan, Marshall. *Understanding Media: The Extensions of Man*. Cambridge: MIT Press, 1994.

_____. *The Gutenberg Galaxy: The Making of Typographic Man*. Toronto: University of Toronto Press, 1962.

Quine, W.V. *Quintessence*. Ed. Roger F. Gibson, Jr. Cambridge: Belknap Press, 2004.

Rousseau, Jean-Jacques. *Essay on the Origin of Languages*. In *First and Second Discourses, Together with the Replies to Critics and Essay on the Origin of Languages*. Trans. Victor Gourevitch. New York: HarperCollons, 1986.

_____. *The Social Contract*. Trans. Maurice Cranston. New York: Penguin Classics, 1968.

Turner, Frederick, and Pöppel, Ernst. "The Neural Lyre: Poetic Meter, the Brain and Time." *Poetry*, October 17, 2001. Available online: http://www.cosmoetica.com/B22-FT2.htm

Wittgenstein, Ludwig. *Tractatus Logico-Philosophicus*. Trans. D. F. Pears and B. F. McGuinness. London: Routledge and Kegan Paul, 1977.

_____. *Philosophical Investigations*. Trans. G.E.M. Anscombe. New York City: Macmillan Publishing Co., Inc., 1968.

Mixed Media

Brook, Peter. *Marat/Sade*. United Artists, 1967.

-empyre-. *The Art of Complicity*. Moderated by Nicholas Ruiz III. January 2010. https://lists.cofa.unsw.edu.au/pipermail/empyre/2010-January/002288.html

Kiki and Herb. *Playing for Time*. Fez, March 19-Sept. 3, 2000.

20

KRISTEN GALLAGHER

Charles Bernstein in Buffalo 1999–2004

When Dominique Fourcade was unable to make it to Buffalo due to illness, he rescheduled. In the interim period, he wrote a book-length poem dedicated to the students in the poetics program called *Everything Happens,* a truly remarkable poem full of great lines. In preparation for Fourcade's visit, we discussed the book in Charles' seminar. His favorite line at the time, or the one he kept coming back to, was "be ready, not prepared."

≈

Charles' office

When you entered, you were in the left rear corner. The office unfolded approximately 14 feet to the right, and 24 feet ahead. All along the far right wall were large contiguous windows, filling the upper half of the wall. They looked out onto the fake pond and unused fake rolling-hill commons of the North Campus of the University at Buffalo.

The approximately 24-foot length of the room was divided in two, with the seminar space closest to the door, and in the distance, Charles' desk and bookshelves. Separating the seminar space and the desk/books part of the office was a long couch, facing and therefore part of the seminar space. Some people I asked remember the couch as slate blue, some as bright orange, one person as black or black with white pinstripes. You could sit on it and be at the farthest point from the center of the seminar, and sitting there also meant you were at a lower vertical point in the room than everyone else. It was a good place to hide when you didn't want to deal with everyone.

The table at the center of the seminar space was really 4 tables: large, cheap, rectangular, institutional, state school style tables, which some people remember as blue, some others as gray, and one person as black. They were pushed together to make one giant square table space, so large you could not reach the center. Chairs of the same institutional style were placed around the table, and a row of them back along the left wall nearest the doorway.

At the end of this row of chairs was Charles' cassette tape collection, hundreds of tapes of poetry readings and interviews with poets, artists, and musicians from throughout the twentieth century. He encouraged us to use the office as a listening space when he was out of town from Friday through Tuesday. Marilyn, the poetics secretary, would let us in.

An aisle formed between the chairs along the left wall and the chairs at the seminar table facing toward the windows. That aisle continued through the tape collection to the left and the couch edge to the right, leading straight to Charles' desk, which also faced the windows, so that when you walked toward the desk you were approaching it from its right side. I rarely found Charles sitting at the desk; my experience was that he was often standing and talking to someone. Well, not exactly standing, but with his right foot about a foot in front of his left, rocking back and forth, forward to back on his Saucony sneakers, as if he were getting ready to run but kept reconsidering, or starting over, while his upper body engaged primarily in gesticulating and talking, sometimes leaning forward, propelled back and forth with all the rocking. This was often done either at the right edge of the desk, with Charles facing the window, or by the left edge of the couch, with Charles facing the cassette tapes. These two conversational positions are what I most remember, though I suppose there were other positions (were there?). There was a regularly employed third position for when he met with small groups of students at the seminar table to formally (though always informally) practice for orals.

To the right of the entrance, along the wall connecting the door to the wall of windows, hung one giant piece of art, Susan Bee's To The

Lighthouse II, a hilariously phallic painting of a lighthouse with a town gathering where the balls and pubic hairs would be, and the head with a little yellow window that seemed, sweetly and cheerfully, to say "hello." During seminar in my first year, which began in fall 1999, Charles always sat directly in front of that lighthouse, so that if you sat directly across from him, the upper half of the lighthouse seemed to extend directly from his head. But then during my second year, he switched, and began sitting with his back to the window, all the way at the corner of the table farthest from the door. Why did he move? What did this mean?

~

A Typical Charles Bernstein Outfit

Comfortable, practical, non-fancy pants
Tee-shirt or button down shirt
Blue blazer
Saucony sneakers

~

Charles' Saucony History 1999–2004

1999–2000—dark gray with a light gray Saucony swirl
2000–2001—navy blue with a gray leather Saucony swirl
2001–2002—light gray with a royal blue insignia outlined in silver
2002–2003—a much more complex shoe, light gray with a light blue stripe around the side of the sole, with orange shoelaces and orange Saucony swirl
2003–2004—black with a black felt Saucony swirl

~

The last time I saw Charles out and about in Buffalo, we were at a mediocre restaurant (not much choice near campus) he used to take us to after Wednesdays at 4 readings. He was standing by a large rectangular serving dish of dry meatballs with sterno under it. He said, "I assume you've heard what's happening."

~

A Meal for Charles, who loves steak

One brontosaurus-sized steak, bigger than any plate
A cartoonishly giant martini, requiring a fistful of olives
No vegetables

≈

All the drinks I saw Charles drink

Martini
Martini
Martini
Martini
Martini
Martini
Martini
Martini
Martini
Martini
Martini
Martini
Martini
Martini
Martini
Martini
Martini
Martini
Martini
Martini
Martini
Martini
Martini
Martini
Martini
Martini
Martini
Martini
Martini
Martini

Martini
Martini
Martini
Martini
Martini
Martini
Martini
Martini
Martini
Martini
Martini
Martini
Martini
Martini
Martini
Martini
Martini
Martini
Martini
Martini
Martini
Martini
Martini
Martini
Martini
Martini
Martini
Martini
Martini
Martini
Martini
Martini
Martini
Martini
Martini
Martini
Martini
Martini
Martini
Martini
Martini
Martini
Martini

Martini
Martini
Martini
Martini
Martini
Martini
Martini
Martini
Martini
Martini
Martini
Martini
Martini
Martini
Martini
Martini

~

Charles commuted to Buffalo from New York City. Every Tuesday night, his flight would arrive and he would stay in his little apartment near campus, an area with one highway, several strip malls, and the occasional lonely, scruffy tree. He taught his undergraduate class on Wednesday mornings, attended the Wednesdays at 4 reading series that afternoon, and we all went out to dinner and drinks with the visiting poets after the readings. On Thursday he met with students preparing for their orals in the morning, and taught his graduate seminar in the afternoon. He flew back to the city every Thursday evening, weather permitting. I always imagined him arriving home in time for dinner.

It may sound like he was absent, but his presence and attention were so complete it felt like much more than two days' worth. The times I think we missed him most were on the weekends, when we had our own curated reading series, often inviting each other and poets from out of town to read at various peoples' houses. It would have been fun to hang out with him in that context, and perhaps to have his opinions on our work. But it may have been just as well that we fended for ourselves, that we had the weekend to apply what we had learned during the week.

◇

When planning a reading list for my oral exam, we decided it would be best if I chose only authors whose last name began with the letter B. This was not an act of self-promotion on his part, but his taking seriously an offhand joke I made. I already had, by chance, a significant number of authors whose last names began with B, and joked that this should be my guiding principle. Charles was so excited by this idea. He strongly encouraged it and also asked me to announce it to everyone that day in seminar.

◇

Charles' car

Sometimes on a Wednesday or Thursday morning, driving around looking for parking in the triple-football-field-sized parking lots of the University at Buffalo, one would pass by Charles, also driving around looking for parking, in his station wagon with the wood paneling. (The wood paneling of station wagons, so iconic.) I want to remember it as a 1967 Ford Country Squire, but I think it may actually have been a Buick Roadmaster. What I remember is the wood paneling. I thought it represented how out of his element he was, we all were, in a town like Buffalo. Even if I am wrong about the car, I am right that we were, most of us, lost.

◇

We thought it would be a good idea to have a goodbye party. A surprise would interrupt that final hour of his final seminar. It seemed like a good idea as we prepared it, but in actuality, at the point of interruption, we were just starting to get into a really good conversation. A twinge of loss mixed with cake and wine and laughter. That was probably fitting.

◇

Seminars, with memorable moments

Fall 1999—Material Poetics
listening to cassette tape of Frank O'Hara reading "Lana Turner Has Collapsed"

Spring 2000—Poetry, Music, Performance
looking at a Morton Feldman score

Fall 2000—The Blank Seminar
some graduate students attacking Nick Piombino for being a psycho-
analyst

Spring 2001—Modernisms
that one could organize a course entirely around authors' birth years

Fall 2001—Second Wave Modernism
who Michael Bloomberg is

Spring 2002—sabbatical
C returns to Buffalo for orals and dissertation defenses

Fall 2002—Textual Conditions 2002
no memories; I took Neil Schmidt's "Literature of Confederacy,"
which met at the same time

Spring 2003—New American Poetries (Modernisms 3)
the goodbye party

Fall 2003-Spring 2004—no seminars
C's final return to Buffalo for orals and dissertation defenses

21

THOMAS FINK

Charles Bernstein's
Catalogue Poetry

According to Charles Bernstein, no poetic form possesses "a wholly intrinsic meaning" or "a priori superior[ity],"[1] and he has utilized a wide variety of forms throughout his poetic career. The catalogue form, a device often associated with Walt Whitman and employed with some frequency by New York School poets, may seem less hospitable to the kind of disjunctive (or, in his words, "dysraphic" and "anti-absorptive") poetry for which Bernstein is known than sprawling texts like "Standing Target" and "Log Rhythms" that assemble widely divergent modes. However, a catalogue poem, "Gradation," which consists of small narratives of violence or consequential duplicity, appears as early as 1983 (in *Islets/Irritations*),[2] and the mode assumes a rather prominent place in *Girly Man* (2006).[3] In fact, as an analysis of several catalogue poems will indicate, this use of the "list" (with or without anaphora) as an organizational principle provides a strong platform for the realization of crucial aspects of Bernstein's poetics.

A foe of "frame fixation," Bernstein champions "context sensitivity" through "the art of parataxis"; he wants poetry (and criticism) to allow "different contexts to suggest different interpretive approaches

---

1 Charles Bernstein, *My Way* (Chicago: University of Chicago Press, 1999), 4.

2 *Islets/Irritations* (New York: Jordan Davies, 1983; rpt. New York: Roof Books, 1992) 24–28.

3 *Girly Man* (Chicago: University of Chicago Press, 2006).Tim Peterson considers "Self-Help" (171–174), a catalogue poem that I will not be discussing here, as part of a strategic shift in Bernstein's aesthetics that Peterson locates in *Girly Man*. See Peterson's "Either You're With Us and Against Us: Charles Bernstein's *Girly Man*, 9–11, and the Brechtian Figure of the Reader," *Electronic Book Review* (2008), Web.

[269]

while at the same time flipping among several frames, or. . . acknowledging the provisionality of any single-framed approach" because
"poetry" can encompass "incommensurable elements without
getting locked into any one of them. . . ."⁴ While catalogue poems
may seem to have a single context, organized either by the title or
by anaphora, the "themes" that Bernstein chooses afford a relatively
open field where widely divergent frames can interact with and
displace each other.

For example, in "Solidarity Is the Name We Give to What We
Cannot Hold," a poem in *My Way* (1999), a version of Charles Bernsein
himself as a poet with identity/identities is the starting point for the
catalogue, but the poet's unity as a speaking subject is undermined,
not just by the diversity of his sub-categories, but by the unresolv-
able contradictions that emerge in their "dialogue." While he praises
how Gertrude Stein "celebrates her suspension of identity, this hold-
ing off naming, to see what otherwise emerges," so that "her writing
becomes a state of willing, of willed, unknowingness,"⁵ Bernstein in
"Solidarity. . ." performs a plethora of identifying, perhaps, implicitly,
to will a condition of "unknowing." The poem is not a Whitmanian
boast about containing multitudes; to a large extent, it demonstrates
that multitudes (of interpreters with differing agendas) frequently
constitute representations of the poet-self. As Bernstein puns in the
essay, "Frame Lock," "I've only just begun to contradict myself. But I
contain no multitudes. I can't even contain myself."⁶ To convey this
failure of self-containment near the beginning of "Solidarity . . . ," the
poet resorts to a thicket of allusions:

> I am a New York poet in
> California, a San Francisco poet on
> the Lower East Side, an Objectivist poet
> in Royaumont, a surrealist poet in Jersey,
> a Dada poet in Harvard Square,
> a zaum poet in Brooklyn, a merz poet
> in Iowa, a cubo-futurist poet in Central Park.
> I am a Buffalo poet in Providence, a London
> poet in Cambridge, a Kootenay School

---

4 *My Way*, 44-45.
5 *My Way*, 144.
6 *My Way*, 97.

of Writing poet in Montreal, a local poet
in Honolulu . . .
I am a capitalist poet in Leningrad
and a socialist poet in St. Petersburg;
a bourgeois poet at Zabar's, a union poet
in Albany; an elitist poet on TV,
a political poet on the radio.[7]

Understandably, because of the historical circumstances of particular affiliations in the seventies and eighties, Bernstein is labelled a "Language poet." However, in the passage above from "Solidarity. . .," the use of the New York/California binary questions the notion that "Language" writing is a unitary entity. Ron Silliman's important "Language" anthology, *In the American Tree* (1986), places the poetry of the "West" and "East" in separate sections, and he justifies this division as a way of "foreground[ing] the particular distinctions that occur within this writing," not only due to "who lives where and the important, but informal, influence of face-to-face interaction," but the idea that "poetry. . . is a much more highly visible art form in San Francisco than in New York" and that poets on the two coasts manifested "very different orientations toward such issues as form and prose style (especially with regard to syntax). . . ."[8] The recent *The Grand Piano: An Experiment in Collective Autobiography San Francisco 1975-1980*[9] confirms that the so-called Language writers of California had a strong sense of themselves as distinct from New York based fellow-travelers like Bernstein and Bruce Andrews and from those who formed a community in Washington, D.C. All of the "Pianists" spent most of the time-period in the subtitle in the San Francisco area, and their relatively infrequent references to the New York

---

7 *My Way* 33. Further quotations from "Solidarity Is the Name We Give to What We Cannot Hold" will be followed by a page-citation for purposes of identification. For a playful reading of this poem, interspersed with a general consideration of wordplay in Bernstein's work, that indicates what the poet does *not* include in his catalogue, see Javant Biarujia, "CHARLES BERNSTEIN: Creating a ive disturbance,"*Boxkite* 3 (2004), Web.

8 Ron Silliman, "Language, Realism, Poetry," *In the American Tree* (Orono, ME: National Poetry Foundation, 1986), xxi-xxii.

9 Rae Armantrout, Steve Benson, Carla Harryman, Lyn Hejinian, Tom Mandel, Ted Pearson, Bob Perelman, Kit Robinson, Ron Silliman, Barrett Watten, *The Grand Piano: An Experiment in Collective Autobiography San Francisco 1975-1980* , Part 1-9 (Detroit: Mode A, 2006-2009).

based group members place heavy emphasis on letters written and received. Therefore, whatever influence his living in New York exerts on Bernstein is perceived in California, whereas Manhattan's Lower East Side poetry community, heavily influenced by the New York School and Nuyorican and other performance poetries, may view him as someone whose work has absorbed the characteristics of San Franciscan "Language" poets like Lyn Hejinian, Ron Silliman (who now lives in Pennsylvania, where Bernstein teaches), and Barrett Watten.

While Bernstein has written appreciative essays on Oppen, Reznikoff, and Zukofsky, few in the U.S. would see him as a latter day Objectivist. "Oppen's syntax," he writes, "is fashioned on constructive, rather than mimetic, principles,"[10] but Bernstein's "constructivism" usually disrupts the mimetic so thoroughly and variously that one could not confuse one of his poems with those of Oppen or his contemporaries. However, "in Royaumont," where Reznikoff worked on a major volume and where conferences have been held on this poetic movement, French scholars, insisting upon Objectivism's centrality and abiding influence, may not care about distinctions between the poetics of its proponents and that of "Language" writers. Further, since Bernstein was, until his move to the University of Pennsylvania, a central figure in the Poetics Program at the State University of New York at Buffalo along with Susan Howe and, more recently, Myung Mi Kim, that association may be the most important feature for those involved with the creative writing program at Brown University (staffed by innovative poets who are not associated with "Language" writing) in Providence, Rhode Island, even if both programs might be lumped together by members of mainstream poetry communities as (dangerously or foolishly) "radical." French-speaking Montreal innovators like Nicole Brossard might focus on their own differences from the Vancouver-based Kootenay School of Writing, seeing the school and the area as a Canadian "Language" enclave, while many in the U.S. would not detect such distinctions. By whimsically calling himself "a local poet/ in Honolulu," Bernstein envisions Hawai'i as a place where aesthetic—as well as racial/ ethnic—heterogeneity is accepted, or perhaps alluding to the presence of his fellow travelers Susan Schultz and (his former student) Juliana Spahr in the 50th state as evidence of his "local" status.

---

10 *My Way*, 193.

Various "Language" writers have had substantial contact (in visits to the Soviet Union, which continued after its fall) with innovative Russian poets, and this experience resulted in Michael Davidson, Lyn Hejinian, Ron Silliman, and Barrett Watten's publication of *Leningrad: American Writers in the Soviet Union*.[11] Bernstein might be suggesting that, the poets of Leningrad, still accustomed to Soviet ideological perspectives even after 1991, will see him first as an American, hence a capitalist. Thus, they will consider his efforts to be a left cultural/ political critic and "a serial poet, a paratactic poet, a/ disjunctive poet, a discombobulating poet,/ a montage poet, a collage poet" using these defamiliarizing techniques for "social expressionist" (33) effects to be subsumed by this context, or he might attribute this perception of the inescapability of a national frame to his friends, the writers of *Leningrad*. Of course, in St. Petersburg, *Florida*—not the Soviet Union or Russia or even liberal New York City—Bernstein's rhetoric will brand him as a "socialist" and perhaps a "pinko commie."

In a direct expression of distaste for the label that has plagued him and many of his associates, Bernstein writes, "I am a language/ poet wherever people try to limit the modes of/ expression or nonexpression" (34). Right before this sarcastic utterance, he reproduces the gist of virulent negations of the poetry he and his cohorts write that have sprung up since the early eighties: "I am a fraudulent poet, an incomprehensible poet, a degenerate/ poet, an incompetent poet, . . . / an infantile poet, . . . / an egghead poet, a perverse poet," yet he ends the extremely long sentence with phrases that may call the denunciations into question: "an emotional poet, a (no) nonsense poet." One criticism of "Language" poetry is that it lacks emotion, and another holds that it is not only "incomprehensible" but meaningless. Bernstein strives for poetry in which emotion is not cheapened by obvious, worn out signifiers of emotion. By putting the "no" in parentheses to modify/not modify "nonsense" and to produce a pun, he emphasizes how nonsense and sense, humor and seriousness, can mutually frame one another and liberate new possibilities of referentiality.

Bernstein ends the poem by seeming to negate the entire two-plus-page catalogue with a forceful closure: ". . . & I am none of these things,/ nothing but the blank wall of my aversions/ writ large in disappearing ink—" (35). The poet frequently breaks the rules of

---

11 Michael Davidson, Lyn Hejinian, Ron Silliman, and Barrett Watten, *Leningrad: American Writers in the Soviet Union* (San Francisco: Mercury House, 1991).

decorum in traditional Euro-American poetry, and these mixed (up) tropes threaten to undermine any clear message about the "nothing but" of poetic identity. How can a "wall" simultaneously be "blank" *and* have writing in "ink"? And when the ink disappears, the wall is blank, but is it still a "wall of. . . aversions"? Yes, a wall is put up so that "aversions" can occur, but even the material traces of those aversions are blanked (made to evaporate), and so we are left with "nothing" to say that the poet "is." However, even if Bernstein as a poet cannot be accurately represented by any single group of adjectives and/or noun in a philosophical sense or be "held" "in solidarity" with a single aesthetic or community, as the title has it, there is no pure ideal realm where he can be eternally free of others' characterizations, and the catalogue poem gives us a sense of the experience of an actual, contested social arena. As a reader of his own status, Bernstein can repetitively practice "aversion" to those characterizations, but he cannot leave the arena.

"In Particular," one of the catalogue poems in *Girly Man*, reflects Bernstein's preoccupation with and constitutes a response to the inadequacies of a paradoxically homogenizing, corporation-inflected multiculturalism. In the essay "Poetics of the Americas," first published in 1996, he expresses his misgivings about how "the challenge of multiculturalism. . . has entered U.S. arts and education in the past decade," finding

> many of its proponents more interested in reinforcing traditional modes of representation than allowing the heterogeneity of forms and peoples that make up the cultural diversity of the Americas to transform poetic styles and personal and group identities. Yet it is hardly surprising that static conceptions of group identity represented by authentic spokespersons continue to ride roughshod over works and individuals whose identities are complex, multiple, mixed, confused, hyperactivated, miscegenated, synthetic, mutant, forming, or virtual.[12]

Pointing to such complexity and multiplicity in "In Particular," Bernstein explores "this unrepresentable yet ever presenting collectivity"[13] in ways that make "poetry" about cultural identity "a

12 *My Way*, 115-116.
13 *Ibid* 116.

process of thinking rather than a report of things already settled; an investigation of figuration rather than a picture of something figured out."[14] In this case, the word-pictures supplied trigger "an investigation" of their figurative energies and limitations.

In the poem's first two lines, the references to race and gender may seem irrelevant, since the objects of attention are performing extremely ordinary activities that are not associated with any particular group: "A black man waiting at a bus stop/ A white woman sitting on a stool"[15]. However, in the almost chiasmically reversed last two sentences, the elimination of the concluding indefinite articles has no impact on the final one but an effect of ambiguity on the penultimate one, suggesting that the white man could be engaging in an act of abjection: "A white man sitting on stool/ A black woman waiting at bus stop" (6). Between this beginning and end, none of the sentences mimic stereotypes, except perhaps a possible reference to Saddam Hussein or Monica Lewinsky ("A barbarian with beret"), but they tend to disrupt culturally conditioned expectations in differing ways:

A Filipino eating a potato
A Mexican boy putting on shoes
A Hindu hiding in igloo
A fat girl in blue blouse
A Christian lady with toupee
A Chinese mother walking across a bridge
An Afghanastani eating pastrami
A provincial walking on the peninsula
A Eurasian boy on a cell phone
An Arab with umbrella
A Southerner taking off a backpack
An Italian detonating a land line
A barbarian with beret
A Lebanese guy in limousine
A Jew watering petunias
A Yugoslavian man at a hanging
A Sunni boy on a scooter (3)

---

14 *Ibid* 117.

15 *Girly Man*, 3. Further quotations from "In Particular" will be followed by a page-citation for purposes of identification.

Anyone assuming a the member of a particular ethnic group would
confine themselves to their native cuisine would be judged ignorant
of contemporary mores; furthermore, the potato is not just "Irish"
but is a part of Philippine cuisine. The second item above seems ridic-
ulously ordinary, unless one realizes that some people might associate the term "Mexican boy" with poverty, forgetting about the privileged class in that nation.

Various lines in the poem are generated by sonic effects, but this
does not limit their signifying potential. In reading the seventh line
above, one may assume that a (Muslim) Afghanastani would not
eat a European-Jewish sandwich-meat, but in actuality, Northern
Afghanistan has the same delicacy—probably with a different
name.[16] The third line in the passage includes internal slant-rhyme,
four short "i" sounds in five words, and alliteration, and even if it
seems one of the most unlikely items in the entire catalogue, I should
note that there is a Hindu temple in Anchorage, Alaska, although a
Hindu Alaskan or tourist would *visit* an "igloo" (or perhaps a commercial simulation) rather than "hiding" in it, "hiding" here can be
considered a trope for finding sanctuary by appropriating another
culture's prop. Indeed, in the next two lines, a girl labeled "fat" (but
not assigned an ethnic marker) may be seen as taking refuge in her
"blue blouse," and the "lady" identified only by her religious faith
hides her alopecia with a hair-piece generally identified as male
rather than female, perhaps because her hair had been short before
she lost it. Her religion has no appreciable connection with her use of
the "toupee," just as in a later line, the fact that a person is "Jewish"
seems to have no relation to the kind of flowers s/he is "watering"
or to the fact of the watering itself. People do all sorts of things that
cannot and should not be explained by their perceived or self-avowed
subject positions.

Nevertheless, a reader can register any represented event as
a trope or assign it a positive or negative connotation, and some
lines seem to sustain such a reading more easily than others. Is the
"Chinese mother" crossing a literal "bridge," or is she crossing from
the constraints of traditional patriarchal Chinese culture to greater

---

16 See M. Elmali, H. Yaman, Z. Ulukanliz, and A. Elmali, "Determination of some
chemical and microbial parameters of experimental Turkish pastrami during
production," *Archiv fur Lebensmittelhygiene* 56.6 (2005), 139-43. The article, though
published in a German publication, is written in English.

freedom and opportunity in "the New China" (whether Mao's or post-Mao) or elsewhere in the world? The "Yugoslavian man at a hanging" recalls the ethnic violence among Serbs and Croatians after the fall of the Soviet Union; those who do not appreciate the political complexities of the Bosnian conflict in the nineties might stereotype Yugoslavians as "primitive" or "barbaric." There are so many advertisements that sell products with multicultural images, and so the "Eurasian boy" may be depicted on TV to promote the "cell phone" that he is "on" — and so, to promote multinational corporate influence. The line suggests that "we" can impose first-world technology on you no matter where you are in the world, and we can make "a Sunni boy" think he needs a motorcycle. Of course, Saddam Hussein, the leader "with beret," was the most famous Sunni in the West, so whoever tars all Sunnis with his brush might assume that the "scooter" is a vehicle for terrorist activity. Five lines prior to the "Sunni boy," the line about the "Italian" is a parody of the evocation of terrorism; the man does not "detonate" a land mine but "a land line," and so "detonation" probably entails "exploding" in verbal rage or changing emotional tone (de-tonat-ing) on the phone or even angrily hanging up the phone rather than physically destroying telephone wiring.

One of the most prominent features of "In Particular," evidence of the experiential hybridity that arises from the complex encounters that characterize American history and especially from the transnational migrations and global capitalist penetrations of the (post) modern era challenge simplistic notions of identity and provide a shorthand for how multiple subject-positions can operate: "A Quinnipiac girl with a bluesy drawl"; "An adolescent Muslim writing terza rima"; "A Mongolian imitating Napoleon" (4); "A Peruvian French hornist sipping Pernod" (6). The Native American girl is not necessarily demonstrating assimilation into mainstream U.S. culture; her "bluesy drawl" can mark a point of contact between resistance to the oppression of her people and African-Americans' development of the Blues as a means of protest and psychological survival. Though co-optation is always a risk, many sub-continental and Caribbean poets have demonstrated that the utilization of canonical European aesthetic forms does not always mean tacit acceptance of European political domination and cultural superiority. Appropriating Dante's form, the "adolescent Muslim" not only imports local, non-Christian content but language that has the potential to de-form Dantean mastery and to signify upon it.

The brevity of the narrative and/or descriptive fragment comprising each line ensures that the "particularity" of each depicted individual in "In Particular" is extremely limited. Many imaginable contexts are excluded, and this makes a sense of a full range of a single individual's multiple subject-positions impossible. The poet's choice of the catalogue form has dictated this strategy; each line stands both as a synecdoche for a multiplicity that readers may try to construct for themselves and as a potential misrepresentation with ideological consequences.

For Bernstein, poetry affords a place to explore the complex interactions of differing ideologies so that expedient simplifications do not induce readers to ignore the complexities of political issues. Therefore, he rejects "the criteria of efficacy for determining the political value of the poem," since "poetry can interrogate how language constitutes, rather than simply reflects, social meaning and values,"[17] and, in doing so, the reader will make strong use of her own critical faculties before taking a position. "War Stories," situated in the concluding title-section of *Girly Man* and Bernstein's most ambitious catalogue poem to date, is a strong example of such interrogation.[18] One frame in which the poet entertains ideas about war involves the category of aesthetics:

War is the extension of prose by other means.

War is never having to say you're sorry.

War is the logical outcome of moral certainty.

War is conflict resolution for the aesthetically challenged.
. . .

"War is beautiful because it combines the gunfire, the cannonades, the cease-fire, the scents, and the stench of putrefaction into a symphony." (149)

---

17 *My Way*, 4.

18 *My Way*, 149-154. Quotations from "War Stories" will be followed by a page-citation for purposes of identification.

. . . . War is a poem that is afraid of its shadow but furious in its course. (150)

. . . . War is poetry without song. . . .

War is the ultimate entertainment. . . .

War is an excuse for lots of bad anti-war poetry. (151)

. . . .War is Surrealism without art. (152)

. . . . War is not a metaphor.

War is not ironic. (153)

In the first sentence above, which is the first sentence of the poem, Bernstein is playing on Prussian military philosopher Carl von Clausewitz's famous assertion about war in relation to politics/policy; he substitutes "prose," evidently to support the implicit assertion in several of Emily Dickinson's poems that poetry (to put it simplistically) constitutes an opportunity for imaginative liberation while prose is a dull prison. (We should remember that, for Bernstein, Silliman, Hejinian, and many of their associates, prose-poetry involving "the New Sentence," Silliman's coinage, is not "prose" in this context, but poetry.[19]) If we take "poetry with song" to consist of active, emotionally engaged, exploratory thought and "prose" or "poetry with song" to refer to lifeless received thought and unbridled "moral certainty" cherished by "the aesthetically challenged," this point is indirectly supported in the second sentence by the poet's revision of the cliché, "All's fair in love and war," via an allusion to the biggest cliché in Erich Segal's smarmy seventies pop novel, *Love Story*. Whereas Segal's line, which begins with "love" rather than "war," signifies what humanist psychologist Carl Rogers would call "unconditional positive regard," a trust, in this case, between lovers that transcends the need for apology, Bernstein's revision parodies a blanket excuse for atrocious behavior. Lest one assume that "poetry with song" is any aesthetic product that has anti-war views, Bernstein cites the existence of "bad anti-war poetry." Rigid, dogmatic verse — and he was

---

19 See Ron Silliman, "The New Sentence," *The New Sentence* (New York: Roof Books, 1987, rpt.1995), 63-93.

probably thinking of some "New American" or "naked" poetry written to protest the Vietnam War—stems from "moral certainty" and
the neglect of linguistic inventiveness.

Author of the 1909 "Futurist Manifesto," which glorifies the
machine age, fascism, anti-feminism, and aggressive energy in
general, F.T. Marinetti also wrote a manifesto cited extensively by
Walter Benjamin and partially re-cited by Bernstein in the sentence
beginning "War is beautiful . . ." about his support for the Italian
campaign in Ethiopia. (In fact, he enlisted as a soldier in that war.)
For Marinetti and other Italian futurist artists, war is a fundamental source for aesthetic breakthroughs because it disrupts the
complacency of conformist society. In "The Work of Art in the
Age of Mechanical Reproduction," Benjamin quotes the primary
Futurist theoretician's paean to war, which is close in meaning to
"war is the ultimate entertainment" yet insists upon a high seriousness that "entertainment" cannot deliver, as an acute example
of the pernicious aestheticization of politics—indeed, how fascism
operates in Germany and Italy prior to World War II: "All efforts to
render politics aesthetic culminate in one thing: war. War and war
only can set a goal for mass movements on the largest scale while
respecting the traditional property system."[20] Benjamin attributes
"the virtue of clarity" to Marinetti's manifesto, and "Fascism, . . .
as Marinetti admits, expects war to supply the artistic gratification
of a sense perception that has been changed by technology. This is
evidently the consummation of *"l'art pour l'art."*[21] For Benjamin, then,
"mankind's" "self-alienation has reached such a degree that it can
experience its own destruction as an aesthetic pleasure of the first
order," and whereas Fascism aestheticizes politics, "communism
responds by politicizing art."[22] Recognizing the seductiveness of the
Futurist and Fascist manipulation of aesthetics, Bernstein includes
sentences rejecting the treatment of military devastation as "metaphor" and "irony," since such a contextualization could easily make
one forget that "war is men turned into steel and women turned into
ash" (150) and "war is never more than an extension of Thanatos"
(151).[23] War's "surrealism," the way its "furious . . . course" violates

---

20 Walter Benjamin, *Illuminations,* trans. Harry Zohn (Frankfurt: Suhrkamp Verlag,
     1955; translation, New York: Schocken Books, 1969), 241.

21 *Ibid* 242.

22 *Ibid.*

23 Bernstein is parodying Robert Creeley's statement, "Form is never more than an

normal experience, is not an occasion for aesthetic celebration, as it is for Marinetti, but for a refusal to view it as "art"; this refusal attests to its potential destruction of justifiable aesthetic possibilities and all else. Therefore, Bernstein's foregrounding of the interpenetration of the aesthetic and the political neither devalues the former realm nor seeks to locate its "pure" "essence."

In justifications for and denunciations of war, binary oppositions of realism/ idealism, pragmatism/irresponsibility, and morality/ immortality almost always appear, and often, they intertwine. This poem was written relatively early in the first decade of the twenty-first decade, during George W. Bush's Iraq War and his and Dick Cheney's promulgation of their pre-emptive strike doctrine, whereas Barack Obama gave his justification for U.S. escalation very close to the decade's end in his Nobel Peace Prize acceptance speech. Despite substantial differences in the rhetoric of Bush/Cheney and Obama's foreign policy statements, distinctions that helped the 44th President to garner his Nobel laurels, the presence of these binaries is a common thread. The juxtaposition of various sentences in "War Stories" constitute Bernstein's interrogation of the argument that it is realistic and pragmatic to wage particular wars, that it is foolishly idealistic to shrink from such action, and that the most cherished ideals must sometimes be realized by war:

> War is the legitimate right of the powerless to resist the violence of the powerful. (149)

> . . . .War is the reluctant foundation of justice and the unconscious guarantor of liberty.

> War is the broken dream of the patriot.

> War is the slow death of idealism.

> War is realpolitik for the old and unmitigated realism for the   young.

> War is pragmatism with an inhuman face. (150)

---

extension of content," presented by Charles Olson in his 1950 essay, "Projective Verse," *Selected Writings* (New York: New Directions, 1966), 16.

. . . . War is the opiate of the politicians. . . .

War is the world's betrayal of the earth's plenitude.

War is like a gorilla at a teletype machine: not always the best choice but sometimes the only one you've got. . . .

War is moral, peace is ethical. . . .

War is capitalism's way of testing its limits.

War is an inevitable product of class struggle. . . .

War is the right of a people who are oppressed. (151)

. . . . War is the principal weapon of a revolution that can never be achieved. . . .

War is two wrongs obliterating right.

War is the abandonment of reason in the name of principle.

War is sacrifice for an ideal.

War is desecration of the real.

War is unjust even when it is just. . . .

War is no vice in the defense of liberty; appeasement is no virtue in the pursuit of self-protection. (152)

War is tyranny's greatest foe.

War is tyranny's greatest friend. . . .

War is the death of civilization in pursuit of civilization.

War is the end justifying the meanness. . . .

War is tactical violence for strategic dominance. (153)

War is international engagement to cover domestic indifference. . . .

War is our obligation.

War is justified only when it stops war.

War isn't over even when it's over. (154)

In some sentences, pragmatism/realism as a justification for war is exposed as an excuse for corporate and/or national economic interests and "strategic dominance" at the expense of any other parties' rights or as a government's "cover" for "indifference" to a domestic crisis. "Realpolitik" is an abstraction that "old" leaders, affluent and generally well protected from threats of violence, use to distance themselves from the significance of their act of inflicting horrible realism on "young" soldiers thrust into battle. Politicians' rhetoric of realism in promoting war is not only "justifying [their own] meanness" but stands as "a desecration of the real"—that is, it creates "real" negative effects in the experience of the politically powerless while non-violent political processes could create a much more favorable actuality for those people.

To the extent that the pursuit of armed conflict is interpreted as "pragmatic," Bernstein insists that the bureaucratic neutrality or "objectivity" often associated with the term "pragmatism" be challenged; he exposes the "inhuman face." Before the Soviet Union bulldozed its way into Czechoslovakia in 1968 to assert its absolute control of the country, Czech leaders instituted the refreshingly liberal "Prague Spring" with the slogan, "Socialism with a human face." Bernstein suggests that war is a pragmatic way to impose a particular ideology on those who do not want it and to allow a select group to reap the benefits of that imposition. The sentence about the "testing" of "limits" by "capitalism" alludes to how some economic theorists, never questioning any tenets or structures of monopoly capitalism, consider war the only "cure" for a prolonged recession.

Some sentences above indicate that war, in fact, is not pragmatic, but irresponsible, unrealistic, and foolish. Troping on Marx's famous declaration, the poet paints "the politicians," not common people, as "stoned" on the "religion" of war. The political "world" wastes "the earth's plenitude" on destruction, and how can "the death of civilization" bring about realization of "the pursuit of civilization"? The articulation of war's justification, stopping war, is followed immediately by the sense that the temporary termination of hostilities is merely a period of suspension before further conflict. Victory is an illusion: "War is not won but survived" (152). And "a gorilla at a teletype machine," far from being "the best choice," is never "the only one you've got," thus casting doubt on the pragmatic argument for war as necessary in a desperate situation.

Though Bernstein makes an interesting distinction between what is "moral" (war) and "ethical" (peace), allowing for the separation of dangerously abstract idealism (which suffers "a slow death" in war) and careful assessment of a complex array of consequences, there are sentences where it would be much harder to differentiate the two. "War" *can be* perceived as "the . . . foundation of justice and," whether "unconscious" or conscious, as "guarantor of liberty," since despotic regimes use violent force to destroy the practice of these ideals. Not only is self-defense generally considered a legitimate and ethically sound reason for military action, but the engagement of "a people who are oppressed" in armed resistance is not, for Bernstein, in the same category as the powerful who "cover domestic indifference" with imperial adventures: "War is the legitimate right of the powerless to resist the violence of the powerful" (149) Yet the poet speaks of war as the main "weapon of a revolution that can never be achieved"; it seems necessary but is an inadequate solution, as so many sentences indicate. Indeed, even for those with a just cause, circumstances can make "war . . . unjust even when it is just." It can easily turn into "revenge on the wrong person" (152). Even if "war is no vice" when "liberty" is at stake, and "appeasement" of tyranny "is no virtue," battle does not encourage the overall development of virtuous action: "War is two wrongs obliterating right."

Though, a handful of times, Bernstein's sentences suggest that war is inevitable, many other sentences in the poem indicate the centrality of human motives and the implication that negotiation is an alternative to war, and so hard determinism does not hold sway. Thus, it is hard to take sentences like "War is our inheritance" and "War is us" (154) seriously. As for the Marxist truism, "War is the inevitable product of class struggle" (151), this aphorism has been an accurate characterization of innumerable historical situations, yet the first adjective in the sentence speaks as though a particular causal chain is absolutely and perpetually applicable. Overgeneralization de-historicizes what is supposed to be a historicizing political philosophy.

"War Stories" was written during and in opposition to George W. Bush's Iraq debacle, and it was placed in a book, *Girly Man*, containing "Some of These Daze," a lengthy, diaristic prose-section on the aftermath of 9/11 in Manhattan and a poem, "The Ballad of the Girly Man," that directly critiques the U.S. incursion in Iraq. What is interesting, though, is that quite a few sentences in "War Stories"—most notably, the ones about the right of "the powerless" and "oppressed" to fight back—do not necessarily pertain to that contemporary context. In staging a "war" of aphorisms about war in general and not always making it clear which are to be regarded ironically and which are not, Bernstein achieves the aim of developing a multi-perspectival collage of social, political, ethical, and economic attitudes toward the subject, of investigating social dimensions of language, and of allowing the reader to perform her/his own complex ideological analysis.

Given the ample evidence of left-liberal positions that can be gleaned from Bernstein's social/poetic criticism, most readers would take "War Stories" (predominantly) as a multi-faceted critique of various kinds of war, yet I believe that the one element that resists a totalizing reading is the implied possibility that war may be a *valid*, if always deeply lamentable and problematic course of action. The poet does not present the kind of elaborate argument—difficult to make fully in the poem's format and perhaps difficult to make altogether—that would either justify or discount this possibility, and so "War Stories" leaves a challenging remainder of political contemplation for the reader to tackle on her own. Those who want President Obama to succeed in implementing some portion of the domestic, foreign, and ecological agenda featured in his 2008 campaign might hope that he will be able to think past the rhetoric of justification presented in "War Stories" and either develop a thorough rationale for the validity of continued military intervention in Afghanistan that would, miraculously, persuade the "doves" among his supporters to "give war a chance" or find that reason cannot support continued intervention and choose entirely peaceful "conflict resolution for the aesthetically" enabled.

Each of Charles Bernstein's catalogue poems open its "theme" to a multiplicity of contexts that demand an ever-widening adaptation to the clash or, at times, unsettling confluence of divergent claims, gestures of perception, and pressing questions. For his readers, the catalogue provides a means for thinking dialogically, without a fixed end-point, more than it is a means for arriving at a thesis or solution or a gathering of "experience."

22

ALLEN FISHER

Readdressing Constructivism and Conceptual Art: aspects of work factured by Charles Bernstein[1]

> I . . . feel drawn to note that there is a way to
> conceptualize language with meaning as the passenger
> and the words as the vehicle (or conduit)."
> —Charles Bernstein, "A Conversation
> with David Antin," (2002: 36).

It is probably obvious to most readers that the early work of Charles Bernstein found its springboards in the works and procedures of Constructivism and Conceptual Art. What stating this makes evident is that perhaps this combination has been seldom remarked upon. It is also evident that these namings are not precise terms. Bernstein's work in the 1970s was on the leading edge of what might be named the fourth phase of Constructivism and the first wave after the development of Conceptual Art. A range of artistic practices that contributed to them preceded these modes of twentieth century operation. The focused use of numeracy and geometry, proportions, repetition and sequence, have long traditions in European practice, in music, poetry, architecture, and visual art.[2] The use of song in poetry, the visual design decisions for page layouts, and the complexities of

---

1 An earlier version of this paper was first given for the Faculty of English, University of Cambridge, in May 2009.

2 Philip Steadman's *Form* magazine, 1-8 (1966-68) and the magazine *0-9*, issues 1-6 (1967-69) edited by Vito Acconci and Bernadette Mayer, exceptionally show the contemporary range from poetry to music and the visual arts. The issues of the latter, with miscellaneous additions, were collected and republished in 2006.

connectedness can be said to contribute to all poetry worth attending to. What is restored and innovated in Bernstein's work has been the emphatic use of particular twentieth century procedures, both early *Cubist* as well as subsequent *Constructivist*, which has been given emphasis by the practice of Conceptual Art that he makes explicit in his poetry and poetics. This paper simply pays attention to some of the precedents and earlier activities of this range of his attentions.

In 1919 and 1920, in response to Marxist materialism, an austere form of technical inquiry, a so-called "laboratory art", overlaps with the "international constructive tendency". This can be largely exemplified in the "Programme of the First Working Group of Constructivists", published in 1922, in which the Constructivists established three disciplines: *Tectonics, Faktura* and *Construction.* These can be summarised as (i) building from expedient use of industrial material; (ii) *facture of* material consciously worked and expediently used; (iii) Construction understood as an organizational function. All of these disciplines were implicit in early *Cubism,* and to a lesser extent, some aspects of *Dada;* the *Constructivists* make the schema more explicit.

Under this schema, *the poet is an expert in her own business,* knows the needs of those for whom she is working. Studying poetry means studying the laws of linguistic processing. Content and Form are not divided. An indicative list of the canon of contemporary American writers would include: Gertrude Stein, William Carlos Williams, Ezra Pound, Louis Zukofsky, and subsequently Charles Reznikoff, Jackson Mac Low, Hannah Weiner. These writers were taking on language as a "material", presenting poetry with visual as much as a semantic acumen. This theoretical legacy of linguistic semiology was adopted into Conceptual Art in 1966.

Hypertextually, the indicative canon given above both precedes and follows the Constructivist moment, the 1922 programme. What is recognised in this paper is the particularity of constructual elements in Bernstein's works, without interest in whether or not they are part of any *movement*. Similarly, the dates above for *Conceptual Art* may be varied according to whether you take the gallery and dealer system to be the initiators of Conceptual Art, as Richardson does, or not. Many of the poets and musicians involved are absent from all histories so far presented to the public. Tony Godfrey notes, "that some form of Conceptual art has existed throughout the twentieth century." (Godfrey 1998: 6)

Art-Language, an analytical form of Conceptual Art, problematised the convention of art's visuality and used language to question the status and framing conditions of the art object that led to a second-order practice explicitly concerned with the status of the modern art object. Conceptual art was both an aesthetic and a cultural reassessment.

An early example of Conceptual Art was recognized in Sol LeWitt's work, characterized by the use of repetition and permutation and by the systematic exclusion of any individuality of touch. Sol LeWitt wrote "Paragraphs on Conceptual Art" in 1967. His typical works were open-framed, rectangular structures presented in series. In 1968 he began formulating proposals for wall drawings, to be executed, not by him but according to his instructions.

Douglas Davis talking to Elaine Sturtevant says, "I am sure that you have often noticed that visitors to your apartment—like the visitors to our loft—shrug off the Warhol or the Stella before you tell them that it is Sturtevant [that is work by Elaine Sturtevant]. Watch how their eyes roll! Their hair stands on end! Their palms collect sweat! Over and over they fall to fighting, arguing, debating. If this isn't the shock of the new, then the term is meaningless. Art is involved with so much more than visual appearance, as television has very little to do with the eye, or radio with the ear." (Douglas Davis in Eugene W. Schwartz and Davis, "A Double Take on Elaine Sturtevant," *FILE*, December 1986. n.p. in Thomas Crow, 'Unwritten Histories of Conceptual Art' in Alberro 2006: 53)

"Charles Harrison, editor of *Art-Language,* laid down the requirement for any Conceptual art aspiring to critical interest that it conceive a changed sense of the public alongside its transformation of practice. But on precisely these grounds, he finds the group's own achievement to be limited: 'Realistically, Art & Language could identify no *actual* alternative public which was not composed of the participants in its own projects and deliberations.'" (Harrison, "Art Object and Artwork" in Claude Gintz (ed.), *L'art conceptual: Une perspective,* 63, in Alberro 2006: 56)

Thomas Crow notes, "In Jeff Wall's view, that isolated imprisonment was the cause of the pervasive melancholy of early Conceptualism: both 'the deadness of language characterizing the work of Lawrence Weiner or On Kawara' and the 'mausoleum look' embodied in the gray texts, anonymous binders, card files, and steel cabinets of Joseph Kosuth and Art & Language. 'Social subjects,' he observes 'are presented as enigmatic hieroglyphs and given the authority of the crypt,' pervasive opacity being an outward betrayal of art's rueful, powerless mortification in the face of the overwhelming political and economic machinery that separates information from truth." (Crow 2006: 56)

The development of Conceptual Art was contemporaneous with the investigative works of Michel Foucault. In a 1966 interview (in *La Quinzaine littéraire*, April 15, 1966) Foucault says, "We have experienced Sartre's generation, as a generation that was certainly brave and generous, one that had a passion for life, politics, and existence. But as for us, we have discovered something else, another passion: the passion for concepts and for what I will call 'system'." (Eribon 1991: 161) In the following year Georges Canguilhem noted that Foucault was said to be reactionary because he wanted to replace the bourgious or over-blown idea of humankind with "system". "But was not this the task set by the logician Jean Cavaillès, the eminent epistemologist, twenty years earlier, for philosophy: 'to substitute for the primacy of a lived, or reflected, consciousness, the primacy of concept, system, or structure'? (Eribon 1991: 165). It was already evident, from much of the work of Michel Foucault, particularly, from the opinion gathered here, *The Order of Things* (1966), his inaugural lecture, "The Discourse on Language" (1971) and *The Archaeology of Knowledge* (1972), that Structuralist ideas derived and developed from the work put together by the students' notes of lectures given by Ferdinand de Saussure, and the subsequent work in semiotics by Roland Barthes and Roman Jakobson, particularly regarding the arbitrary and representation, needed a new understanding. It was no longer viable to conflate language with visual demonstration, even if it was a poetic stance to break the boundaries between them. The relationship between discourse and images, for Foucault, are in inexact, but reciprocal presuppositions, that consist of heterogeneous potentials for performances. It was a discussion in the 1960s that poetry and image and sound were heterogeneous processess that operate situations of mutual grappling, overlap and capture.[3] It had been evident, at least since 1951 (through the work of Norbert Wiener and the artists at Black Mountain College in that year), that many of the shifts of interest on the boundaries between these manifestations, issues of genre and disciplines, had become amorphous or sometimes cohesive. Conceptual Art's efforts to justify its shifting of "dematerialized" written pieces as exhibits in exhibition spaces are unnecessary. The shift from visual to verbal to aural and their over-

---

3 Many of these ideas have been discussed by Gilles Deleuze in his work on Michel Foucault and by Ricardo Basbaum in his work on Lygia Clark (Alberro 2006: 96 *passim*).

lapping can be assumed as part of any aesthetic investigation worth salt.

In New York the response of the poetry and art community in the 1950s (in, for instance, the work of Frank O'Hara, Grace Hartigan, Jasper Johns, and Larry Rivers) to collaborations and into the '60s was contemporary with the beginnings of and then the announcement through the documents of Conceptual Art, for instance the early work of Henry Flynt and the subsequent work of Sol De Witt. Lucy Lippard noted that "While it has become feasible for artists to deal with technical concepts in their own imaginations, rather than having to struggle with constructive techniques beyond their capacities and their financial means, interactions between mathematics and art, philosophy and art, literature and art, politics and art, are still at a very primitive level."

Charles Bernstein's developed work in the 1970s, and in the immediately subsequent period, participated in this milieu in which the renewed premises of Constructivism (what is sometimes by then named contructionism) and the developing theses of Conceptual Art were established; a milieu in which, in America, the work of Jackson Mac Low, Armand Schwerner, Jerome Rothenberg, and David Antin coexisted with work from musicians, dancers, film-makers and other artists. Systematic works, works in series, critiques of poems as objects and collaborations contributed to a growing and developing culture in New York and California, in Toronto, and in Washington. Charles Bernstein and Bruce Andrews' New York magazine *L=A=N=G=U=A=G=E*, contemporary with Robert Grenier and Barrett Watten's *THIS* and Bob Perelman's *HILLS* in California, demonstrated the energy pools of the various interactions. Two examples of work by Charles Bernstein may begin to make this understanding clearer.

The first example is Charles Bernstein's poem in a volume entitled *LEGEND* (a copy of which has been appended to this paper). *LEGEND* was published in 1980 by Bruce Andrews and Charles Bernstein's L=A=N=G=U=A=G=E press in association with James Sherry's Segue and supported by the National Endowment for the Arts. It has been factured by five poets: Bruce Andrews, Charles Bernstein, Ray DiPalma, Steve McCaffery and Ron Silliman. Much of the work has been published previously in small press magazines, but the cohesion of the book suggests a project at the outset that has been concluded in this book form. The book is printed using offset-lithography; the typesetting in the book has been kept as a manuscript document and uses an IBM electric typewriter with a *Courier New* 11-point golf-ball.

Of the 26 pieces of work in the book, 21 have been factured collabo-
ratively by different groupings of the five poets into pairs and larger
sets. Five of the pieces are by the single authors indicated above. All
of these pieces are comprised of list-like, aphoristic-like forms, and
comprise 100 items each; all but one of these are numbered 1 to 100;
one (the piece by Bruce Andrews) has been initially numbered 1–3,
then not numbered until 98–100; there are however still 100 items.

The first work in *LEGEND* is "My Life as a Monad" and is by Charles
Bernstein. It is one of the five numbered list-like forms. The items in
his list vary from sentences, such as at numbers 1 and 2, to phrases,
such as 13 and 14 and a few single words, such as at 5, 11, and 14. Items
45 and 55 are empty. Some of the items (we might call these stanzas)
appear to be out of place as if randomly present. Many stanzas are
thematic, descriptive of structure or method. The use of potentially
figurative language has been sandwiched, as if between interlocutors.

Stanza 1 appears to let the reader in, into the poem, the book, the
whole conceptual package, "The door, yellowed from the sun, stands
open." Stanza two announces the method, "No nonsense now, just
steady nerves, clear thinking." Stanza 3, inside speech marks, implies
a self-questioning or conversation with another about the project, "I
can't see it." What follow are a number of descriptions or metaphors
describing the form and content, such as stanzas 5 and 6, "Slant"
and "Curvaceous". Stanza 35 announces Gertrude Stein's canonical
work *The Making of Americans* and, so to speak, places it as a crucial
or indicative precedent. Stanza 37 announces monad from the title
"discussed" and stanza 46 introduces Leibniz, the author of *On the
Art of Combinations* (1666) and the *Monadologie* (composed in 1714 and
published posthumously); the latter consists of 90 aphorisms.

Stanza 47, "The haecceity of a hover", shifts the debate with
Charles Bernstein's work here and Leibniz's proposals against Gilles
Deleuze and Felix Guattari's semiotics towards what Jamie Murray
names "a semiotic of law through a discussion of the intensive semiotics of the field of emergence and pragmatic semiotics of social
power. Within the framework of the pragmatic semiotics, it is argued
that the crucial tension is how social machines and their regimes of
signs operate with the intensive semiotics of the field of emergence.
The signifying regime of the State social machine constructs itself on
the excluded foundation of the field of emergence, and what is lost
are the real ontological and social conditions of emergence, intensity and affect." Murray argues for a counter-signifying regime of the
war social machine which actively operates with the intensive semiotic of the field of emergence, and develops an image of legality and

regime of signs that taps the field of emergence for social organisa-
tion and expression. Returning to the issue of emergence and legality, Murray notes that "the concept of Emergent Law is developed as
a war social machine, abstract machine, assemblage, and regime of
signs, that operates a semiotic that is developed in terms of an intensive semiotics that is open to and taps the forces of the field of emergence." Charles Bernstein's work precedes Gilles Deleuze's *The Fold.
Leibniz and the Baroque,* but his allusion, through "haecceity", provides
a necessary prediction of post-flamboyance.

At stanza 53, again with monad, the themes of boundary and
perception produce a refrain. The refrain of boundary recurs from
stanza 1 into 14, 15, 20, and onto 66 and 86. Visual perception persists
after stanza 3 at 9, 11, 12, 13, 24 and at 54. Stanza 59 then names
the tension: "Is it a possible danger that philosophy will take over
the poetry, could it, & if it could would that be a bad thing?" This
recalls Joseph Kosuth's proposal titling his collected works, *Art
After Philosophy and After.* Monad is again referenced at stanza 62.
Philosophical thought can be directly noticed at stanzas 18, 19, 46,
64, 83, and indirectly at 23, 53 and 62. Do they link to the naming
of fruits after nutshells, grapefruit, pears, apple juice. Deleuze notes
that Leibniz's nutshells theory of appurtenance "leads to a fundamental inversion that will forever begin over and again. Monads that
have a body must be distinguished, and monads that are the specific
requisites of this body, or that belong to parts of this body. And these
second monads, these monads of bodies, themselves possess a body
that belongs to them, a body specifically other than that whose requisites they are, and whose parts in their turn possess crowds of tertiary
monads" (Deleuze 1993:108.)

Perception is the datum of the prehending subject, to the degree it
fulfills a potential or objectifies it by virtue of its spontaneity: thus, as
Deleuze puts it, "perception is the active expression of the monad, as
a function of its own point of view." (1993: 79)

At stanza 68 the materiality of the work overtly surfaces: "Can
sentence fragments count as sentences?" Stanza 98 names and
spreads this difficulty, What is "To suage"? a shortened form of
sausage and archaic for sewage, a fragment from assuage, to soften,
to mitigate, to abate, to diminish, not unlike usage or swage rope
fittings, a method to bend or shape using a swage. Questioning
language itself is evident at 36, 58, 68 and 73.

If aphorisms are concise statements of a principle or a terse formulation of a truth, the brevity can sometimes undermine this. As 42

notes "Weight upon weight" and 81, "It always seems to take on so much weight".

"Conceptualism administered a rebuff to the Modernist demand for aesthetic confections. 'Nonreferentiality . . . was central to the discourse of the journal [L=A=N=G=U=A=G=E]." "*Legend* demonstrates new formal possibilities of writing in the dialogic, the collective practice of its five authors. The counterhegemonic discourse asserted in *L=A=N=G=U=A=G=E* by virtue of the missing referent of the work . . . is enacted in *Legend* in various forms of language-centred texuality—generating a wealth of technical innovations, formal possibilities, and new meanings within a space of reflexive dialogue. If a series like and unlike author positions are drawn together by the equal signs of *L=A=N=G=U=A=G=E, Legend*'s demonstration of complex modes of writing necessarily entails a riskier, more difficult negotiation of group politics as it enacts the revolution of avant-garde poetry in new and productive forms." (Watten 2003: 63-64)

Charles Bernstein, in "Semblance" for Reality Studios "Death of the Referent?" symposium, written in 1980, the year *LEGEND* was published, states:

> Not 'death' of the referent—rather a recharged use of the multivalent referential vectors that any word has, how words in combination tone and modify the associations made for each of them, how 'reference' then is not a one-on-one relation to an 'object' but a perceptual dimension that closes in to pinpoint, nail down (*this* word), sputters omnitropically (the in in the which of who where what wells), refuses the build up of image track/projection while, pointillistically, fixing a reference at each turn (fills vats ago lodges spire), or, that much rarer case (Peter Inman's *Platin* and David Melnick's *Pcoet* are two recent examples) of 'zaum' (so-called transrational, pervasively neologistic)—'ig ok aberflappi'—in which reference, deprived of its automatic reflex reaction of word/stimulus image/response roams over the range of associations suggested by the word, word shooting referential vectors like the energy field in a Kirillian photograph." (Bernstein 1986: 34–35.)

Barrett Watten notes five devices in *Legend*, "in Jakobson's sense, they are: (1) thematic argument; (2) the exploration of the signifying potential of specified linguistic levels: sentence, phrase, lexeme,

morpheme, phoneme; (3) the exploration of the signifying potential of graphic signs, both linguistic and non-linguistic; (4) forms of
intertextuality created by mixing modes of signification that suspend
authorial intention as they explore the pace between subject positions; and (5) dialogic argument . . . Bernstein's section, 'My Life as
Monad,' which opens the book, is a decentered portrait that juxtaposes irreducible units of language ('Nutshells') with autobiographical accounts . . . " (Watten 2003: 64)

    SHADE, Charles Bernstein's main second book, first published two
years earlier than *LEGEND* in 1978 begins with "Poem". The first seven
lines read:

>   here. Forget.
>   There are simply tones
>   cloudy, breezy
>   birds & so on.
>   Sit down with it.
>   It's time now.
>   There is no more natural light.

The occasion is realist description, sitting down and writing and
reflecting on figurative language. The occasion is decisive, the time is
to facture, to construct to re-understand and affirm Conceptual Art.

Line 28 reads simply "unassuaged", this is followed at 29, 30 and
31 as if in homage to the constructionist aspects of William Carlos
Williams' work by:

>   which are things
>   of a form, etc
>   that inhere.

The refrain, to retro-lift a set of themes from the book to come:
boundary in lines 11, 'this thing inside you'; 33–34, 'becomes space
between/ crusts of people'; 53, 55, "ruffling edges" and ''The distance
positively entrances"; 61–62, "detach, unhinge/ beyond weeds . . . "
and perception at 12, "this movement of eyes"; 49–50–51, "Your eyes/
glaze/ thought stumbles, blinded"; so that, in the cause of language,
almost without allusion to W.C. Williams, from 12 to 14: " . . . this
movement of eyes/ set of words/ all turns, all grains".

The social stance towards production, the analytical praxis of facture and the re-addressed comprehension of the poem object, as commodity shifted into the poem as interactive after Conceptual Art's sojourn, are made manifest and partly explicit in these works and in many that were to follow.

References

Acconci, Vito and Mayer, Bernadette. *0-9. The Complete   M a g a z i n e 1967-1969.* Brooklyn, New York: Ugly Duckling Presse, 2006.

Alberro, Alexander and Buchmann, Sabeth (eds.). *Art After Concepual Art.* Cambridge, Mass. & London and Vienna: MIT Press and Generali Foundation, 2006.

Andrews, Bruce; Bernstein, Charles; DiPalma, Ray; McCaffery, Steve; Silliman, Ron. *LEGEND.* New York: L=A=N=G=U=A=G=E, 1980.

Antin, David and Bernstein, Charles. *A conversation with David Antin,* with *Album Notes* by Antin, David. New York City: Granary Books, 2002.

Atkinson, Terry; Bainbridge, David; Baldwin, Michael; Hurrell, Harold; Kosuth, Joseph. *Art & Language.* Köln: Verlag M. DuMont Schauberg, 1972.

Bernstein, Charles (2000) *Republics of Reality, 1975-1995,* Los Angeles: Sun & Moon Press.

Bernstein, Charles. *Contents Dream. Essays 1975-1984.* Los Angeles: Sun & Moon Press, 1986.

Bernstein, Charles *Shade.* College Park, Maryland: Sun & Moon Press, 1978.

Deleuze, Gilles. *Foucault,* translated by Sean Hand. Minneapolis: University of Minnesota Press, 1988.

Deleuze, Gilles. *The Fold. Leibniz and the Baroque,* translated by Tom Conley. London: The Athlone Press, 2001.

Eribon, Didier. *Michel Foucault,* translated by Betsy Wing. Cambridge, MA: Harvard University Press, 1991.

Foucault, Michel. *The Order of Things. An Archaeology of the Human Sciences.* London: Tavistock Publications, 1970.

Foucault, Michel. *The Archaeology of Knowledge and The Discourse on Language,* translated by A.M. Sheridan Smith. New York: Pantheon Books, 1972.

Gintz, Claude (ed.). *L'art conceptual: Une perspective,* exhibition catalogue. Paris: Musée d'Art Moderne de laVille de Paris, 1989.

Godfrey, Tony. *Conceptual Art.* London: Phaidon Press, 1998.

Harrison, Charles and Wood, Paul. *Art in Theory, 1900-1990, An Anthology of Changing Ideas*. Oxford UK and Cambridge, MA: Blackwell Publishers, 1992.

Leibniz, Gottfried Wilhem. *Philosophical Writings*, translated by Mary Morris and G.H.R. Parkinson. London & Rutland, Vermont: J.M. Dent & Charles C. Tuttle Co., 1992.

Lippard, Lucy. *Six Years: the dematerialization of the art object*. New York and London: Praeger, 1973.

Richardson, Sophie. *Unconcealed. The International Network of Conceptual Artists 1967-77. Dealers, Exhibitions and Public Collections*. London: Ridinghouse, 2009.

Steadman, Philip; Weaver, Mike and Bann, Stephen (eds.). *Form, A quarterly magazine of the arts*, issues 1-8, Cambridge: Philip Steadman, 1966-1968.

Wall, Jeff. *Dan Graham's Kammerspiel*. Toronto: Art Metropole, 1991.

Watten, Barrett (2003) *The Constructivist Moment, From Material Text to Cultural Poetics*, Middletown, Conn.: Wesleyan University Press.

APPENDIX

Charles Bernstein's "My Life as a Monad"

1. The door, yellowed from the sun, stands open.
2. No nonsense now, just steady nerves, clear thinking.
3. "I can't see it."
4. The ordering of pears.
5. Slant.
6. Curvaceous.
7. Perspicuity his middle name.
8. Peek o boo.
9. The feel of the reel.
10. So mangled pure, so dust encrusted, so self encumbered: shellacked reminisces, sheets of firmness, straight grapefruit & mocks & splits, pity, mercy, &c, crisper, louder, sharper . . . .
11. Tunnels.
12. Tunnel vision.
13. A mixed gaze.
14. Nutshells.
15. Outward demeanor: looks, sound, stance.
16. Transfixed dream state between 9 & 10 where I am just about awake & only the power of this dream unreeling in my head

keeps my eyes shut as if saying 'shut up & listen to this' as I struggle to get up.

17. What's to be insecure about?

18. I mean for the first time I felt the very corpuscles of my mind.

19. The 'absolute', so to say, is nothing.

20. I'd outskirted my welcome.

21. Double the work pace, no raise schedule, less holidays and sick days, no overtime.

22. "Ashes asleep."

23. While I was in college I'd always be answering all kinds of questions by saying "it's unclear" & that became characteristic of me though it remained for the most part a spontaneous answer.

24. He investigated the subcutaneous portions of his reticulum.

25. I remember poetry readings in which the drone of the reader's voice would drive me up the wall until I began to take a certain pleasure in the drone, constant as it was.

26. It's just a passing antagonism.

27. He had to let himself go because he couldn't take his own dictation fast enough.

28. Resentment has done me no good.

29. He done done done.

30. You know, people don't like to have their lives reduced to a pithy paragraph.

31. I can't help wishing.

32. Jesus, what do you think this business is, playtime pallies?

33. It's better to soar in ordinary skies.

34. "We're out of pheasant under glass but would you like to try our spaghetti meat, very good?"

35. What *The Making of Americans* got me to see was that regardless of how puzzling people & events often seem, you can still know them—a whole cloud of concern about truthfulness and false selves disappeared with that.

36. Swish, swash, swap.

37. In much of my work (is there any reason not to be explicit about this? does explicitness really dissolve any ambiguity?) 'opal' has the sense of 'monad'.

38. "Do you think if you could inspect if there's some apple juice?"

39. It's justice not charity that's wanting.

40. Forget about underbellies.

41. This is getting totally out of foot.

42. Weight upon weight.

43. And you say to yourself I can learn to take that.
44. I would to expand on this point.
45.
46. Leibniz defines a monad as having every one of its properties essential to it, its contingencies, its accidents, its timeliness and shapeliness, its erraticism & irrelevancies, essential to it.
47. The haecceity of a hover.
48. Far in.
49. Awful sadness, green & sticky.
50. "You're being a silly."
51. Is it that I want contradictory things?
52. Are they mind forged or not?
53. The bounds of each monad the boundaries of the world, each containing—"mirroring"—all times & all spaces.
54. Joe saying well maybe it was true reality more & more seems to be what we accustom it to be.
55.
56. I wonder what the others are doing & if they will like what I'm doing?
57. I was immediately put off.
58. Why does it seem easiest to make a particular, a description, into a sentence by making a question?
59. Is it a possible danger that philosophy will take over the poetry, could it, & if it could would that be a bad thing?
60. This place is a past hole.
61. "They don't make any decisions, really, but we let them think they do."
62. The difference between one monad & another is simply but actually its point of view, & for each only its particular perspective is illuminated.
63. Grinding your teeth, you stare straight ahead.
64. As each city looked at from its different sides seems different, multiplied by each new perspective, so for each one of an infinite possible number, there are as many different worlds, which are only the perspectives of a single one.
65. They ran out of the carriage and down the slope to the water.
66. People always seem to be falling off the edge of the earth.
67. In a single bound he leapt tall buildings.
68. Can sentence fragments count as sentences?
69. A kind of involuntary & unconscious memoir.
70. Kneejerk, want of stomach, giddy.

71. It's a muddiness that interests.
72. How nicely wrapped.
73. Capital letter blah blah blah period.
74. So we can only get a view of it.
75. It's 'us'.
76. I'm trembling but it's not cold outside.
77. This goddamn middleness.
78. Lists listing every facet, nugget, & ocean cranny.
79. Music to my eyes.
80. You might say we were slow but it would be unfair, we honestly thought we had lead in our shoes.
81. 'It' always seems to take on so much weight.
82. Search me.
83. Is the insistence that each one is separate the manifestation of a self-generated antagonism principle arising from a fantasy of its own division by a oneness conscious of its solitude?
84. Isn't it really that I'm afraid I don't make myself clear & as a result (though it doesn't follow) imagine I'll be passed by?
85. It's showing.
86. The delusion of between.
87. A floatsom of her whimsey.
88. I'm embarrassed to be embarrassed.
89. "Pass them by boys & girls."
90. Apart from the social—commodity—value of being a "poet" and writing "poetry", wouldn't it be more likely that writing, unlike painting, would be self-viewed not as a specifically art-creating activity but rather as part of a more general, non-writing-centered, activity—the investigation and articulation of humanness?
91. Tie your shoes & read the paper.
92. I will tell you & not 'once upon a time' or 'once for all time' but once & again & again.
93. Cash in your tokens.
94. And you keep saying 'all in a good time' 'soon' 'one day'.
95. If I sang it would it make more sense to you?
96. As shape, as sound, as buzz & click & spit.
97. Bounds not out but in.
98. To suage.
99. It is self-sameness in being.
100. Don't bank on it.

Andrews, Bruce; Bernstein, Charles; DiPalma, Ray; McCaffery,

Steve; Silliman, Ron. *LEGEND*. New York:
L=A=N=G=U=A=G=E, 1980. pp.1-5.

23

MAGGIE O'SULLIVAN

circles from which

this   then,   There   is   it   .   Is   it
           it *here*
       ~~severing~~ - - ----- ----   --- -----

Dis*figure*ment mans**ions** voice
taboo "in"versely, escape),
At" vocabulary sotto boundary .
nuance avowals error - - - - - -   - - - - - - - -

lapsed
quietness is - *a* -   *a* -   "
outside, ones, "ONE!"   tissue defile .
bird slang
Givenmutinies;
angles " broken
chromatic plateaus
misdeeds, ("marked") -- **or** -   **or** - - - **or**
refusal
dances, "pulled" failure
circles from which

24

JAMES SHIVERS

Visual Strategies: a Line, a Verse, Something on Paper

"Hang there, my verse, in witness of my love"
— Shakespeare, *As You Like It*

The act of making public one's verse on paper is nothing new. Once scripted and framed, what isn't visual about writing? For Bernstein, as he makes public his verse, the visual is not merely a secondary carrier of meaning, but a vital malleable materiality of *a p o e t i c s*. In this chapter we will see how his visual strategies are avenues for innovation in criticism, philosophical inquiry, and poetics. Although he does employ methods similar to other visual poets, Bernstein's visual work transforms former collage, shape, and concrete techniques into vivacious forms. His visual work also includes the illegible, an aesthetic use of punctuation, collaborations with visual artists, and an investigation of page design and layout. In each context Bernstein redesigns the terrain of words and this innovative praxis opens up not only the textual and graphic semantic domains but also areas of syntagmatic production and reception. For him the spatial, the linear, and the material sign-on-the-page are all essential elements in shaping and inventing a writing that attempts to explore as much as possible the technology of the word on the page. He remains unbound to one set design for his critical, poetic, or editorial work. As design itself becomes and is a mode of aesthetic procedure for Bernstein, the possibilities of what can be produced abound. What also increases is the difficulty of reading and interpreting his work.

Should we resist a poet who moves beyond normal visual expectations? What shall we do with a poet who crosses border expectations? Many readers of Bernstein's works have confessed to their difficulty.

Linda Reinfeld in *Language Poetry* writes to persuade readers not to dismiss Bernstein's work because of these difficulties. Rather, she beckons readers to read Bernstein through "the experimental writing and critical theory of our time—Derrida and Barthes and Adorno as well as Stein and Beckett and Joyce" (51). She offers this vision of reading instead of "academic criticism" which according to her would lead a reader towards dismissal instead of engagement. [1] Golding groups Bernstein with 'Language' writing and argues the difficulty of reading stems from a redress of "three sets of conventions: narrative conventions, the grammatical and syntactic conventions governing the sentence, and the convention of lyric univocality."[2] Furthermore Golding argues these writings adopt the tradition of twentieth-century avant-gardes for whom "rupture" has always been a central trope (149). Not only are conventions redressed through rupture these works also resist the idea or expectation of what poetry is supposed to be (145). According to Golding, the pattern of reading promoted within certain academic practices can only be a partial guide if we are enter into a 'reading' of 'Language' writing. The texts place a demand of rupture on the reader: are these differences a deficiency in reading, in quality, in purpose of a poetics? By yes, do we say as has been said 'no good poems' has come from this group?[3] Lazer argues that Bernstein "resists reductive recuperative reading strategies".[4] Notice the alliteration. And the effect. Perelman also argues that Bernstein's work is not "governable by a normative poetics" and that his poetry demands "changes in reading".[5] These supportive critics illuminate

---

1 Linda Reinfeld, *Language Poetry: Writing as Rescue* (Baton Rouge and London: Louisiana State University Press, 1992), 50.

2 Alan Golding, *From Outlaw to Classic: Canons in American Poetry* (Madison, Wisconsin: University of Wisconsin Press, 1995), 145

3 Here is the full comment from David Bromwich in 1987: "Jerome McGann's subject comes closer to home for an American. There is a big problem, perhaps a minor one, about "the L=A=N=G=U=A=G=E poets", the heroes he selects to represent radicalism today. They do not appear, as yet, to write good poems. McGann allows as much space, however, to their manifestos as to their poems: understandably, for in a movement of this kind, there is apt to be a high proportion of manifestos to poems. In dealing with any "school" whose aims and theories have been well publicized, a sympathetic critic stands in peril of taking the wish for the deed. This tendency is always part charity and part convenience." *Politics & Poetic Value*, ed. by Robert von Hallberg (Chicago: University of Chicago Press, 1987), 327.

4 Hank Lazer, *Opposing Poetries, Volume 2: Readings* (Evanston, Illinois: Northwestern University Press, 1996), 142.

5 Bob Perelman, *The Marginalization of Poetry: Language Writing and Literary History*

a defense of Bernstein's apoetics/*poesis* as an act where "destruction and creation are simultaneous". Looking through Williams via these critics we can say the close reader is called into a process of *poesis*. Nothing new here. But how does this new reading work?

Most recently, Bruns constructs another broad perspective on reading Bernstein. Using Adorno's voice he suggests that Bernstein writes in a time where all language is open to the poet: "there is no criteria by which anything can be set aside as non-poetical. We live in an anarchic state of affairs in which poets like Charles Bernstein have for a seemingly endless number of years."[6] To prove his point Bruns cites multiple passages from *Poetic Justice* (1979). He argues that Bernstein has made a point of expanding "the standard received model of a (unitary) speaking voice. This is the form *his* iconoclasm takes" (74). A writing of moving beyond is seen as iconoclastic. This breaking of likeness — the breaking of an image of poetry is done through an extension of poetry's image. As Sydney long ago wrote, poetry, metaphorically speaking is a speaking picture. Although critics argue that Bernstein's praxis is one of 'dis', I want to explore his poetics as one of 'ad', addition, expansion that calls upon creative investigation to enact. We all work with a definition of poetry. Can we collect, catalogue, definitions? Can we look at how a poetry is made, and then surmise, value, critique? Do we have unspoken images of poetry? We do. Filling our landscape these icons inform our readings of any image of poetry. Closely reading Bernstein's extension of poetry's image will show more not less of poetry's ability to transform, translate, and transliterate the world of sights and sounds.

Tom Beckett and Earel Neikirk began the journal *The Difficulties* in 1980. Throughout the decade it served as a public forum for process-oriented and/or language centered writings. Several issues were devoted completely to poets like Bernstein, Susan Howe, and Ron Silliman. Recalling an earlier avant-garde, the over-arching project returned from Olson and Cid Corman: They wanted to "provide for the 80's the kind of kick that Olson and magazines like "Origin" gave to the 50's and 60's."[7] Importantly, they wanted to keep a "level of

---

(Princeton, N.J.: Princeton University Press, 1996), 80, 85.

6   Gerald Bruns, "Should Poetry be Ethical?", *SubStance* #120, Vol. 38, no. 3 (2009): 74–75.

7   Tom Beckett and Earel Neikirk, *The Difficulties* (Kent, Ohio: Viscerally Press, 1980): 1.

provocation which keeps the difficulties in" (1). The first issue was a symposium on "language environment" and the following proposal was sent to all the contributors:

> Is it meaningful to you to speak of locating yourself in your work in terms of a 'language'? If so, please respond to what constitutes a 'language environment' and what you consider the relationship between you and it to be. If not, what sense of language would you oppose to this and why? (1)

Included in this first issue were statements and manifestos from many poets who had been associated with the L=A=N=G=U=A=G=E journal (1978-1981, 1982). Tom Raworth's submission the last one in the volume is called "Loose Alphabet (an excerpt)". Taped to the page with a black background are the letters f, h, s, s.[8] Dick Higgins writes: "I think that 'language environment' can only be a meaningful concept to me if 'language' is taken in its Saussurian, linguistic sense of a 'langue', a sort of landscape of the work and/or the life, constitute the individual 'word' or 'parole'" (38).[9] Susan Howe submits a poem beginning with the lines, "maybe// words and things among us go///wherever your end is" (27). Rosmarie Waldrop submits the poem "The Tongue Around the Mouth" for Claude Royet-Journoud with a lines, now to repeat my theory:/what use/the categories of attribute and head//block/egg/knuckle/copper" (46). The brilliance of the prompt gives readers in 1980 a viewing of 'language' in relation to a writing practice. No two submission are alike in form. Each response merits further critical investigation. The journal as a whole does create as the editors desired a "new context for the creation of art" (1).

Bernstein's submission unlike any of the others can neither be classified as poetry or as a critical essay. Some writers filled their pages with words giving either a look of poetry or of an essay. In contrast, Bernstein has a framed language space filled with traces of both genres (Fig. 1.1.).[10]

---

8 Tom Raworth, "Loose Alphabet (an excerpt)", *The Difficulties* (Kent, Ohio: Viscerally Press, 1980): 59.

9 Dick Higgins, "Dick Higgins", *The Difficulties* (Kent, Ohio: Viscerally Press, 1980): 38.

10 Charles Bernstein, "Charles Bernstein", *The Difficulties* (Kent, Ohio: Viscerally Press, 1980): 54.

We have an image of a box working a fullness of letters, line, and logos. Black ink invades the space of words, exploring the word as an object from the technology of the typewriter. Stein's invention, "satisfaction in language made present"[11], is one way of seeing meaning developed. As the discursive line is embraced, the lines burst ink into the illegible and perusable difficulties. Narrative epistemology spills into syntagmatic production and a phenomenology of the typed sign, sentence, and semantic space. The shape shapes an intentional state, where reoccurring choices are made to fit within a chosen frame. Quotation requires iconic editing. Icons temper substances. Meanings abound, unbound. Environs adjudicate.

"I became a consultant to the world outside"
"for those who understand the long range poi/nt of American foreign policy"
"lets put an end to us hegemony all over the world"
"there are lots of easier ways of putting it than this"[12]

As readers we agree: "there are lots of easier ways of putting it than this". Bernstein, in almost a tribute to the journal, leaves in the diffi-

---

11 Bernstein in "Professing Stein/Stein Professing" argues that her contribution to writing was the invention of 'wordness'. Her work was to see words not simply as a medium of exchange for something else, but as a revelation of something in and of themselves. See *A Poetics* (142).

12 These are lines taken from Figure 1.

culties. As we see, and will see, his response to the editor's question employs an innovative visual strategy.

If by "putting it" is a political critique of the new Reagan era, then we can ask: is this the best way to criticize a new government? Bernstein was asked a similar question at the Institute of Policy Studies in Washington, D.C. in December of 1981. In the last session of eight on politics and language, Bernstein was critiqued from the audience for his views on language. He was unwilling to describe writing as a basic one to one communication exchange. This move upset a member of the audience who pushed Bernstein's position. He questioned Bernstein's obscurity, and suggested that he was not fulfilling his "responsibilities as a writer".[13] He went further to state that the simple comic book *Marx for Beginners* had done more to further the "class struggle than anything Gramsci wrote in his prison cell late at night in pain" (*CD* 421). Bernstein's response can be seen as a defense of what he calls a "utopian content". Political responsibility contrary to the speaker's suggestion is larger than any one kind of writing. Mass communication may seem productive but is embedded with in a certain value laden discourse which is not neutral, nor the only kind of discourse that can change the world. In contrast, he argued as he responded to the challenge, reading and writing alternatives offer a potent critique of dominant discourse. "Moreover, there is an instructive value in working with—reading *and* writing—texts that offer alternatives to the directional, unifunctional, hierararchialized structures that dominate both Capitalist and Communist societies" (*CD* 422). The instructional value of working with reading and writing forms outside the dominant norms on both the left and the right is to see and envision alternatives. Bernstein offers a different formalism: the formal dimensions of a discourse form its values and are its values. It is clear to him how dominant forms of discourse create values. If values are going to change, the values, being built in language, demand a set of alternative ideas *and* practices. Bernstein does not simply back into a leftist position as he is critiquing the right. Admitting that both positions contain errors changes the landscape and allows for reform. He is not willing to simply overlook the form because of the content. The inability to examine the ethical and aesthetic nature of the dominant forms of discourse requires a further formal investigation.

---

13 Charles Bernstein, "Socialist Realism or Real Socialism?", *Contents Dream* (Los Angelos: Sun & Moon Press, 1986), 421, 411-427. Hereafter referred to as *CD*.

Marxism as a literary approach has been plagued with difficulties since the 1920s. Graff and Leitch have argued that it was unable to take hold in the past because it ignored the aesthetic quality of the work.[14] Bernstein rebukes the audience for ignoring or underestimating form. Approached from this angle, the "opening" line of his statement becomes more meaningful.

$^{i"}$I became a consultant to the (w(or)ld outside"

To read this statement we must work through a visual density that is rooted in past semantic marks. To quote this line changes its environment, and is not a simple slice of its meaning. We cannot just read his position; we must also view it through typographical density and its object/formal status. The semantic field occurs in a space where meaning is not simply contained in linear discourse. The method of over-typing lines and words leaves the reader with historical residue and limited accessibility. Does this fit into Bernstein's way of reading? Do we come away thinking of more alternatives, and a different kind of exchange? "WE'VE GOT TO DO SOMETHING AND SOON-" can be extracted. The message is fused in architectural space, altering any political reading. The man in the audience, unable to see another view of language beyond a simplistic mass communication model, questions Bernstein's responsibility as a writer. Bernstein's form, like the content, is political.

Any reader unable to think about the language environment in a new combination of the visual and semantic will be at a loss as to how to proceed. Reading this piece depends upon a knowledge and acceptance of visual poetics: that poetry can be built within the whole page and use numerous aspects of the material sign. Yet this piece is different from other visual strategies. Its form, instead of being inspired by the handwritten form as were many of the first visual poetries, looks to the typewriter.[15] Others in the volume responded with a poem. Is

---

14   See Vincent Leitch, chapter one, "Marxist Criticism in the 1930s", *American Literary Criticism from the Thirties to the Eighties* (New York: Columbia University Press, 1988), 1–23. See also, Gerald Graff, "Scholars Versus Critics: 1915-1950", *Professing Literature: An Institutional History* (Chicago and London: University of Chicago Press, 1987), 121–161.

15   Willard Bohn, *The Aesthetics of Visual Poetry: 1914–1928* (Cambridge: Cambridge University Press, 1986), 3. "Although the invention of the typewriter would also seem to have been a necessary prelude to visual poetry, in fact it had little or no impact on the movement. Almost without exception the early poems were

this a poem? He is working line by line with visual formal features of a conventional discursive framework. Is this an essay? As the piece acquires a status as a visual object, we are able to see words working. How to proceed?

In the same year as the first issue of *The Difficulties*, Catherine Belsey wrote that all reading practices are theories of reading and "presupposes a whole theoretical discourse . . . about language and about meaning, about the relationships between meaning and the world, meaning and people, and finally about people themselves and their place in the world."[16] Accepting the link between a practice of reading as a theory of reading we approach Bernstein's visual-semantic strategy as a way of *seeing* into a reader's framework. Seeing through Belsey we can say any response to Bernstein's text is contained in a theoretical framework. The judgments which are made about this text reveal the theoretical location of the reader. Consequently, the educational value of such a text is immense. If there is educational value, we could also say that there is social value. To be given the questions Bernstein was given, and asked to respond, is one way of understanding Bernstein's innovative ability. To then be shown Bernstein's response engages the reader in a series of evaluations: How does Bernstein answer the question, and how am I responding to his text? If for example, a person simply rejects the piece as nonsense, then what, in looking back to Belsey, is his or her theoretical position?

Due to the obscurity of this text and its difficulties, no critic or anthology has embarked upon Bernstein's innovation of the grammar of spatial and visual poetics. Already, we have seen the critical issues it raises and barriers it produces. Bernstein's non-prose response to the prose question challenges reading strategies. The barrier of the challenge requires an act of charity either in the name of ethics (the desire to see alternatives change standards), or in the name of aesthetics (the pleasure of innovation). Reading Bernstein's response to the editors of *The Difficulties* challenges the very notion of a singular theoretical approach. The prose question is not given a prose answer. His text can be neither classified as prose or poetry,

---

drafted as hand written manuscripts. Not until e.e. cummings burst on the scene some nine years later did a visual poet compose on a typewriter. Only in the past thirty years has the machine come into its own as the favorite instrument of the Concretists and the Letterists." Exploring the possibilities of the typewriter on the page places Bernstein closer to Letterist or Concrete traditions.

16 Catherine Belsey, *Critical Practice* (London and New York: Methuen, 1980), 4.

but has elements of both. It can be neither classified as language or visual object, but has elements of both. It can be neither classified as a linear or a spatial text, but has elements of both. Bernstein's work, if it is to be read at all, requires a view of reading that incorporates collaboration, experimentation, and invention. Nevertheless, traditional reading models can highlight this process and, as we will see, can produce ways of viewing Bernstein's piece. Collaborating with these theories will grant us critical access but also will reveal critical limitations and the ability of the "language arts" to redraw as well as create new boundaries. Reading his response is a challenge to reading. Yet, we have theories in play a reader could use to explore this text.

Defamiliarization, a problematic concept of aesthetic perception has been employed by numerous critics for over sixty years. Shklovsky's emphasizes two interdependent structures: first, the law of perception that we carry around within us on a day to day basis; and second, the language of poetry where form and content are united to disrupt our habits and revive our sensation of life. In his theory, the reader and the text are primary, and both have a role in his understanding of defamiliarization, or "the making strange" of common habitual words and objects.[17] Bernstein in his piece, as we saw, has become "a consultant to the world outside", but this consultation is not in clear forms. Our reading is disrupted by our viewing. Our eye shifts between words as signs and signs as letters and letters as marks. Bernstein's technique of art has increased the difficulty and length of perception. The process of perception is an aesthetic end, as Shklovsky argued. The reading of Bernstein's piece goes further by vacillating between aesthetic ends and epistemological concerns. Bernstein, by increasing the process and the difficulty of perception to this level, has made the object as well as the perception interdependent. His response to the question moves between an object and a language, inside the bounds of a square, a rationality. The piece may have rational borders, but it is a rationality that contains pragmatic

---

17 Victor Shklovsky, "Art as Technique", in *Twentieth Century Literary Theory: A Reader*, ed. by K.M. Newton (New York: St. Martin's Press, 1988), 23-25. For the complete version see *Theory of Prose*, "Art as Device", trans. By Benjamin Sher (Elmwood Park: Dalkey Archive Press, 1980). The reason for starting here is that this theory widely available and can be used to work with the text. Reading Bernstein's work does not have to be a completely new endeavour. Moreover, the reading requires a creation of various models as we will see. The theories can shed light literally and metaphorically on this text.

and non-pragmatic, knowable and unknowable, linguistic realities. Because Shklovsky has a negative view of repetition, the object can be devalued. Over time the perception becomes habitual, and art "is a way of experiencing the artfulness of the object".[18] The technique of art is to extend this process as long as possible in order to keep the senses alive and habits in abeyance. Bernstein's piece has a different view toward time. No matter how long we look at its physical shape, we will not be able to know what is unknowable. In other words, Bernstein has built into perception and sensation a non-semantic physicality. He offers a valuable innovation to our conceptual understanding of the language environment. The meaning and potential meanings of the piece are not grounded in linear or dialectic epistemological categories. Bernstein's visual strategy releases meaning from familiar categories. Meaning becomes mobile, nomadic, and vacillates between and among the sign and syntax, the visual and the grammatical, the legible and the illegible. The syntagmatic residue reeks withi unrecoverable meanings. Our eye freed from the line moves about and among borders of visual knowledge. We are confronted with the/a contemporary phenomenology of the material word. Bernstein's response in other words forces us to move beyond theories of argumentation and proof to the theories of the aesthetic, formal, and constructive uses of the sign.

Is the text also a literary object? Expository and prose texts tend to offer points of verification. Bernstein's response to Beckett is like a piece of literature in that verification is problematic by traditional standards of analytic argumentation. The aspect of his response which is not verifiable is the illegible which becomes, in Iser's schematic, the literary. The illegible gains further meaning. The reader cannot verify everything, and this utopian content evades confirmation. Iser argues, "this possibility of verification that all expository texts offer is, precisely, denied by the literary text".[19] Literary texts do not refer to identical real-life situations. Truth claims in litera-

---

18 Ibid. p. 24

19 Wolfgang Iser, "Indeterminacy and the Reader's Response", in *Twentieth Century Literary Theory: A Reader*, ed. by K.M. Newton (New York: St. Martin's Press, 1988), 228. See 223–22/// where he outlines his argument of verification. All quotations are from this volume. See also, *The Fictive and the Imaginary: Charting Literary Anthropology* (Baltimore and London: Johns Hopkins University Press, 1993), 20. "The fictive, then, might be called a "transitional object," always hovering between the real and the imaginary, linking the two together. As such it exists, for it houses all the processes of interchange. Yet, in another sense, it does not exist as a discrete entity, for it consists of nothing but these transformational processes."

ture limited to a mere correspondence to real life situations, can offer little if any verification. The truth of literature or of fictional devices (metaphors, simile) must come from another point of verification. The indeterminacy created by literary texts, due to its lack of reference to any identical real-life-situation, creates the terrain of its possible verification as a projected "reality". Because the status of the text is indeterminate, its determination settles in from the reader's participation. The gaps of indeterminacy are filled by the reader's activity. The reader refers the text to the world she knows, filling in the gaps with verifiable factors. Some texts, according to Iser, lose their literary quality in the reflection. Other texts are resistant to this counterbalancing, and the world of the text begins to compete with the more familiar world of lived experience (228).

Bernstein's text presents gaps the reader will never be able to ignore or fill in. The text embedded in the material is not bound by time. What can be realized in such an environment is that the truth claims and/or ethical demands of Bernstein's text are not presented in a pure, linear fashion. Each statement, line, and word is embedded in an authorial history of the typed word. Whereas other texts are trying to record what has happened to the world, the literary text according to Iser is trying to construct a world in the reader's imagination. The literary text moves from being a three dimensional object to a four-dimensional potential. Iser would have to say that Bernstein's text is either a new form of prose, or a literary construction of a prose moment or as Sydney argued long ago, "a speaking picture". Bernstein's early comments, on how the non-standard forms of writing can be utopian content, can be read into this piece as a way of understanding its form. Since the form is neither prose (traditional or Stein-like), nor poetry (traditional or visual), we must develop further categories. If we see the piece as fictional, we lose verification. If we see it as literature, we gain a re-occurring call upon the reader's imagination. This call competes with the way things are and with the world. As Iser put it concerning a literary text: "the world of the text establishes itself as being in competition with the familiar world, a competition which must inevitably have some repercussions on the familiar one. In this case, the text may tend to function as a criticism of life" (228). Bernstein's text not only functions as a criticism of life, but as criticism of language's relationship to a discursive practice. He expands the concepts of fiction and prose through a procedure of repetition, and the use of a typewriter. Following after cummings as a poet-inventor, he liberates the word from its conventional pres-

entation, and while doing so, he creates an innovative answer to the question of reading and writing. He takes early visual strategies into new directions, creating an interactive object, dependent upon grammatical codes, yet independent from its laws.[20]
To become a consultant to the world outside is not a straightforward business. Each of the theories concerning the text, its construction, its structure, its reception, fosters heightened moments of reader-response, of the formal visual pleasure of black lettering against white, of redirected use of lettering as a form instead of a messenger, of structural investigation, and of biting political statements. Bernstein's response is not confinable to conventional discourse, but upon analysis meaning abounds. If meaning is not singular, then according to Robert Creeley collaboration is absolutely necessary: "one must recognize the absolute necessity of collaboration insofar as the information will not resolve itself as a linear and/ or "singular" pattern."[21] Collaborating among theories circulates the reading in and around the text, giving points of illumination, while not attempting to provide an explanation where it cannot be found. Easily, we can keep writing about this piece. We can argue that Bernstein sees the language environment mixed with clarity, potential workings, failures, and historical residue. If the shape of the piece is rational, we can see that the interior of the rational, or the human who uses language, is both accessible and not accessible. Here, English syntax, letter as symbol, and spatial dimensions, fill and/or describe the language environment. Bernstein's piece not only confronts the reader, but also any method of verification. The "reality" of the piece would have to be in several locations. Its reality can be found in what it does to the reader, what it does to a particular reading theory, and in those elements which correspond to the praxis

---

20 From Augusto de Campos' perspective on cummings, we can see that Bernstein is also working in the tradition of poet-inventors. As de Campos reflects upon cummings, he considers him a "poet-inventor" like Pound and Mallarmé: "Another poet-inventor, e.e. cummings, adapts the ideogram and counterpoint to the miniature. Without falling into letterisme, or the forming of sonorous groups of letters without meaning, Cummings frees the word from its grapheme, and brings its formal, visual and phonetic elements into focus in order to better release its dynamism." "Points Periphery Concrete Poetry", in *The Avant-Garde Tradition in Literature*, ed. Richard Kostelanetz (Buffalo, New York: Prometheus Books, 1982), 264-265, 259-266. Augusto de Campos' essay was originally published in *Jornal do Brasil*, Nov. 11, 1956.

21 Robert Creeley, "Some Place Enormously Moveable", *Art Forum*, Vol. 18 (Summer 1980): 39.

of the world. Its reality also comes from its visual strategy. One example among several is to think about the visual picture we are given: a square with knowable and unknowable meaning. In other words, it is a re-presentation of rationality that is limited, but still present, living with historical residue. The over-typing within the square can been seen as the historical residue that is always attached to the subject. The shape and design of the piece displays an intentionality and not a chance procedure. Because of how it was built, we can assume at some point in its construction there would have been lines, letters, and signs that were clearly visible. Over time, these moved behind the scene, still visible, but with partial access just like history and memory. How are we to enter the world of this text? We are not granted total access, but as our imagination moves over the box, we begin to see Stein's "wordness": pointing, covering, hovering. The life of this statement-poem remains outside the horizon of many theories of criticism or literature. Nevertheless, investigating Bernstein's visual strategy, informed by a willingness to attempt a theoretical practice begins a process of critical reflection. Already we gain new possibilities and come upon new demands for critical inquiry.

Bernstein's visual strategy in *The Difficulties* is unique in comparison to the rest of his early critical and creative work. With the publication of *Veil* in 1987 (the same year in which he published *The Sophist* and *Artifice of Absorption*), we are confronted with a cogent visual strategy. We can also see that his response in *The Difficulties* came from an earlier framework which he had created in 1976.[22] *Veil* begins with a quotation from the American author Nathaniel Hawthorne (1804-1864): "There is an hour to come," said he, "when all of us shall cast aside our veils. Take it not amiss, beloved friend, if I wear this piece of crape till then." [23] *Veil*, containing six pieces confronts the reader with numerous questions: Do we try and unveil this crape? How and what do we read? Does any contemporary theory of poetics provide critical guidance or acumen? We have understandable, viewable, fragments of discourse, surrounded and infused with impenetrable ink. We are called into new poetic and critical space where knowl-

22 Charles Bernstein, *Veil* (Madison, WI: Xexoxial Editions, 1976,1987). For an online version see, *Veil*, Electronic Poetry Center, State University of New York at Buffalo, 2010, http://epc.buffalo.edu/authors/bernstein/books/veil/index.html . The first edition of *Veil* is 8 ½ by 11, with a yellow cover, designed by Elizabeth Was.

23 Ibid. i. The quotation comes from the short story, "The Minister's Black Veil". Nathaniel Hawthorne, *Twice Told Tales in Two Volumes* (Boston: Ticknor and Fields, 1853), 1:57, 1:47-66.

edge is not fully realized, where the sign does not live in isolation nor is atemporal, where the reading lives on the border of semantic and iconic materiality.

In his earlier critical work ("Stray Straws, Straw Men"), Bernstein drew from Thoreau's *Walden*. In this visual work, he looks back to Hawthorne. Hawthorne's story concerns a priest who, due to his own spirituality, chooses one day to veil his face with a black veil. The veil, as we read, is a symbol of parabolic truth. Due to our actions, we are all veiled from each other. Hawthorne's parable carries a charged view of Christian piety. The piety comes from the minister's understanding of human depravity. After veiling himself in the story, the minister is seen to have a gifted ability to speak of Christian virtue and the ongoing task of turning away from sinful thoughts, words, and deeds. For Hawthorne what we are and what we've done is veiled and covered from complete sight. We are all partially hidden due to our sinful actions, and for Hawthorne's minister, the casting away of our veil will be revelatory.

In a telling interview, Bernstein transforms Hawthorne's self-awareness of the constant barrier between humans and their deity into a contemporary social description. As he discusses the project he refers to *Veil* as a " visual emblem".[24] Emblem books sought to create a dialog between image and text with the purpose of creating a third space of critical, creative and even moral reflection.[25] Bernstein inspired by Louis's Veil paintings uses the typed line as a layer of visual meaning and like Louis used these layers as stains of meaning. The stains are signs of sadness as well revelatory and re-present for Bernstein a sense of "dislocation" of "socially correct norms"(35). For him, "[n]ormalcy is the enemy of poetry—my poetry,

---

24 "Charles Bernstein", interview by Manuel Brito in *A Suite of Poetic Voices: Interviews with Contemporary American Poets* (Santa Brigida: Kadle Books, 1992), 34, 23-36. In *My Way: Speeches and Poems* (Chicago: Univesity of Chicago Press, 1999), the line "call it the everyday" is expanded: "call it (to come back to it again) the ordinary"(31).

25 The English Emblem Book Project, Penn State University Libraries' Electronic Text Center, 2004, http://emblem.libraries.psu.edu/overview.htm . This web source provides emblem texts from the University collections as well as links for further scholarly pursuit of the topic. In this context we can read Bernstein's Veil as an contemporary emblem book. As the editors suggest: "An emblem book represents a particular kind of reading. Unlike today, the eye is not intended to move rapidly from page to page. The emblem arrests the sense, leads *into* the text, both image and word, to the richness of its associations. An emblem is something like a riddle, a "hieroglyph" in the Renaissance vocabulary—what many readers considered to be a form of natural language" (Project Overview, ibid.).

"our" poetry"(35). Fusing Hawthorne's parable of unease with Louis' technique *Veil* creates yet another parable. He frames his *Veil* around Hawthorne's parable, a story built around an image with didactic implications. He also looks to Louis' work from the 1950s. The formal design implies yet another parable of language use, as "an acoustic staining"(35). Over-typing gives the piece its visual density and the density is a parabolic stain. Using language does not mean we have total transparency. "A WALL OF WORDS makes sense to everyone but you", is one found line within the *Veil*.[26] The reader is thrown into an emblem search for meaning (in this case words and phrases), and can come away with numerous understandable glimpses. "The veil acknowledges the stigma that is our common ground, our point of adjacency with one another, our 'us'ness" (35). The density, framed as a veil and as a stigma, is Bernstein's way of showing and explaining language difficulties. Bernstein believes we can't communicate without considering our own particular location in a language system, and once located we are unable to remove "our opacities and particularities, our resistances and impermeabilities—call it our mutual translucency to each other (36). *Veil*, then serves as an icon of the physical representation of communication.

His visual strategy in *Veil* is informed by Hawthorne, over-typing, Louis, and Erving Goffman's social analyses. He gives us an image of our language environment and the multiple complexities that inform writing and speech. The *Veil* becomes a material metaphor built from signs, informed by discovery and sadness, containing a multitude of possibilities. Bernstein adds, "[o]ur language is our veil, but one that too often is made invisible. Yet, hiding the veil of language, its wordness, its textures, its obstinate physicality, only makes matters worse" (36). Language itself is our veil, implying that we can never have direct contact with each other. To hide this veil only makes matters worse. Bernstein finds a form of subjectivity that goes beyond the naïve understanding that personal expression is somehow a direct one to one activity between people. He offers not just a critical theory, but also a critical and creative practice that does not hide the veil of language and allows "its wordness, its textures, its obstinate physicality". In *The Difficulties* and *Veil*, Bernstein gives an account of marks in time.

Bernstein creates a critical anxiety by confronting us with our veiled existence, just as the minister did. In Hawthorne's story, the

---

26 Bernstein, Charles, *Veil*, "Veil #3".

parishioners as well as the town spend their days trying to find the correct interpretation of why the minister is veiled. Even at the very end of the minister's life, no one has discovered the truth. Bernstein's *Veil* creates a similar, critical anxiety. The *Veil* pieces present a few problems: How do we go about reading them? Should we try to trace back all the lines to an original state? What would this give us? After we extract lines, or moments of semantic meaning, how do we interpret these extractions without forgetting their graphic, material context? As readers we are able to make out some of our shared meanings, but not all of them. In this sense Bernstein repeats Hawthorne's parabolic *Twice Told Tales*. We are able to "see" some of the meaning, but the fuller meaning awaits perusable development or change. In *Veil*, we have a veiled self placing a public object before us. Our contact is veiled and not direct. Bernstein's acoustic staining and visual strategy brings into focus the complexity of reading and writing. The architectural spaces appear as a density of signs. Moving in and out of focus we experience a graphic construction that uses letters as paint, and linguistic forms as non-linguistic modes of meaning. The linguistic moves are not abstract, spontaneous expressions, but skilled, chosen, and inserted typographical gestures that turn away from the aural toward the iconic.

In *Veil # 4* we can see that Bernstein used different size types with an oscillating density. One of the lines from this space causes even further critical involvement.

One thing I have had a hard time following is a sense of
CLEMENT GREENBERGISM

The "I" within this piece has a hard time following "a sense of Clement Greenbergism". Not only do we have a structural density innovating the borders between semantics, poetics, and the plastic arts, we now have a veiled statement concerning one of the more important critics who wrote on the avant-garde. The line's construction as well as its spatial context, follows the sense of the former critic's work. The spatial "following" beckons the reader to ponder his meaning. Greenberg's 1939 essay "Avant-Garde and Kitsch" is one of the many places a dialogue between the *Veil* and Greenberg's work could begin. Greenberg implies in his essay that the avant-garde has no need for the common or the everyday. "In turning his attention away from subject-matter or common experience, the poet or artist turns it in upon the medium of his own craft."[27] We could say Bernstein is finding common experiences through the medium of his own craft. However, common experience is not without complexities or abstractions. Instead of accepting the norms of the social contract concerning subjectivity or even common experience, Bernstein opens up Greenberg's binary opposition between experience and poetic expression. Words, intimately linked to our experience are signs requiring visual mediation and interpretation. The isolated statement within *Veil* concerning Greenberg gives us a vision not only of *Veil* as a fusion of the common experience with language as a system, but also reveals this reading's focus. Drawing from two moments in the essay simply begins the process of thinking through one response to those lines. *Veil* as a cultural emblem shows its solid connection to past American critical and poetic explorations, whether it is Hawthorne exploring daily piety, or Greenberg exploring daily life and its relationship to art. In this viewing, are we witnessing poetic experience?

Veil if looked upon demands a range of critical approaches. Quotation, a major tool in critical work, is complicated. For example, quotation as a source of isolating main or significant points, if used directly, moves critical discourse toward the visual grid.

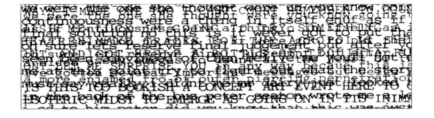

Are we unsatisfied with this quotation?[28] We can feel that something is missing. Have we drawn from the work in a way that is fair or just? On top of the other semantic and visual domains the quotation itself is brought to light as an unsettling piece removed from the whole as an elegant particular on its own. A quotation from *Veil* retains partialities of the visual strategy. The strategy moves about in this multi-dimensional textual space retaining a material enigma. Framed in psychoanalytical and religious terms, the reader experiences the

---

27 Clement Greenberg, "Avant-Garde and Kitsch", *Partisan Review* VI, No. 5 (New York: NY, 1939): 36, 34-39.

28 Ibid. 'Veil #4'.

life of the word. A text which is both a visual metaphor and linguistic metonymy of language itself. The physicality of the sign offers discourse while simultaneously offering a visual object. These pieces give us clarity and obscurity, multidimensional space and linear trajectories. Under letters, in larger letters we find:

> . . . .IS THIS TOO BOOKISH A CONCEPT ART EVENT HERE TO CHRONICLE A HIDDEN ESOTERIC MIDST TO EMERGE AS GOING ON IN ITS INIMAIABLE SEAMLESS HARMONIOUS AWFULLY NICE DIRTHITY OF SPLENDOR MAGIC ANCIENT SOUP KITCHEN AND MAGIC TERREN OF SWIRL UP SOAP SUD SEAS AGAHST WCH MAKES IT A LOT HARDER LETS FACE IT TO SAY NO NO CULT OF THE NIGHT BETWEEN ACTS OF INTERMINABLE PLAYS. . .[29]

The bookish concept of layering words on a page and binding them together is incorporated in one single page. We can take single words and offer an interpretation, or mull over combinations. Art events, to chronicle and to show a historicity of the material word, are left in such crowed linear space.

In contrast to Bernstein's *Veil*, Rosmarie Waldrop's submitted work to *Fourth Assembling* (1973) gives sharp moments of clarity (Fig. 3.4. and 3.5.).[30] Waldrop uses similar visual strategies to Bernstein.

---

29 Ibid. 'Veil #4'.

30 *Fourth Assembling*, compiled by Richard Kostelanetz, Henry Korn, Mike Metz (New York: Assembling Press, 1973), i: "For the same reason, we have persistently refused requests to print contributors' works, for one point of Assembling's concept is that, given the crisis in communication (i.e. censorship) serious writers and artists will have to learn the process of its communication from its beginnings. RK" In the introduction Kostelanetz claims that the 70s were in a state of censorship because so many could not get published. He argued that editorial styles, reviewing practices, and book store managers were censoring a large amount of contemporary writing. In response, Kostelanetz created a new publishing space. Each contributor had to print a 1000 copies and send them to the editors. Each *Assembling* volume was compiled alphabetically. Kostelanetz states the need for more counter periodicals, counter publishers, different distribution and review networks, and points out that the *Assemblings* are only a drop in the bucket. Waldrop's pieces are also in *Camp Printing* (Providence, RI: Burning Deck, 1970) but without the words "it were another matter", "it introduces waiting".

Figure 2. Rosmarie Waldrop, Fourth Assembling (1973)

The page is a space for the habitation of the material word. Her form, in strips, layers segments of previous text, whereas Bernstein layers within one frame. Waldrop's move looks backwards toward concrete poetry of the 1950s and 1960s. Bernstein's work remains veiled, but openly inviting. Waldrop inscribes the architecture of font in order to magnify choice statements. In contrast to advertising slogans, phrases like "it were a matter" can be seen but not easily followed. She has, as a backdrop, strips of letters, more or less laid on top of one another. These strips represent moments or allusions of other ongoing narratives. On top of this re-contextualized reality, going in multiple directions, Waldrop gives the reader a seemingly direct set of words that meet the eye. Bernstein's text creates layers as well, but within the same plane and without recourse to an image-statement as in Waldrop's work. Both are creating a visual and textual duality, of the seen and unseen, of the legible and illegible, and are rupturing conventional theory and discourse.

As the materiality of the sign is embraced, the difficulties of writing and communication are left in and not edited out. The textual emblem becomes, like the parable, an open invitation. Writing that is neither conventional in radical or traditional terms takes reading practices and theories outside of their established boundaries. The open, exiled, nomadic, space that this kind of innovation creates is vulnerable to hasty judgments, and yet it awaits a reading. Criticism that stops at the limits of its theory takes the vulnerability of the innovation as a threat. Reading Bernstein's visual strategy alongside a few traditional literary theories shows the limitations and the possibilities that over-spill from poetic invention. The shaped poem, the organic poem, the poem on the page, as an aesthetic, organic, or graphic object, are available grammars for contemporary visual strategies. Historical visual strategies like ancient poetic devices or emblem procedures always await further explorations. The spatial dimension of the page always has more than one kind of interpretation. Concrete, letterist, shape, or organic forms are all particular visual styles that can be investigated, invented upon, integrated. Although his work builds upon the past and the various traditions of the word, we cannot give his work one of these visual labels. The *Veil*'s backdrop of the American parable, scientific discovery, and painterly procedures give Bernstein's work a unique place in the history of poetry that does not ignore the font, the line, or the page and therefore expands the image of poesis.

The most embraced visual strategy of poetry is the line. From Latin texts onward the line break has given poetry a unique visual domain. The visual break remains the dominant strategy to poetry's page. As a naturalized schema the line has been universally taken as a given.

Yet, forms like facts are always made and can be reshaped, explored. Bernstein's visual strategy is not just limited to a "visual poetics" classically inspired from the shape work of George Herbert or the more recent page innovators such as Mallarmé, Apollinaire, or e.e. cummings. Interested in investigating commonly accepted strategies, Bernstein's "wordness" (absorbed through Stein) accepts words as objects and not just grammatical/syntactical elements. As objects all parts of the line (diction, syntax, grammar) are open to re-creation. In *Disfrutes* (1981) we find a poetry that accepts these former visual traditions but goes beyond their purity and conceptual nature. Here is a poetry of letter, suffix, prefix, of parts:

    oread
    wicket
    broach
    clap clap
    apt
    ly
    plause[31]

We surface through the parts, look up words, ponder over absences. Reading aloud, we push plause to pause, but plause alone signifies a sound without meaning. Adding sounds and parts, we make an agreement that something is aptly plausible. A divorced reader and writer have sounds without meaning. "Oread", pulled apart by the reader, brings on a command.[32] Wicket and broach are more familiar terms, waiting to be sought in a dictionary or left by themselves. The piece combines both the spatial dimensions of the word with a non-conventional grammatology. Using the dictionary as a palette, and grammatical and phonetic memory as a subtext, the lines pause, aptly rewriting words and lines altering the visual expectations of poetry.

The importance of referring to a poem from *Disfrutes* is to correct the false assumption that the work in *Veil* is "visual", whereas the poetry in *Senses of Responsibility* is not. Lines and stanzas are the forgotten visual innovations in the history of poetry. However, since the

---

31 Bernstein, *Disfrutes* (Elmwood, CT: Potes & Poets Press, Inc., 1981), 5.

32 "Oread" is also a title of a poem by H.D. *The Collected Poems of H.D.* (New York: Boni and Liveright, 1925), 81. In Greek and Latin mythology Oread is a mountain-nymph.

(re)birth of a broader visual poetics nearly a hundred years ago, the basic mechanism of poetry has, as we have seen, explored the page as a spatial dimension of poesis. Does this mean, though, that there is only one way to think about the line on the page? Can the line be reconfigured through another form of the visual? Bernstein argues he wants to create an image of poetry "that is inextricably bound up in making visible a fabricating mechanism".[33] His poetry explores where "the manufacture of the fabulous and the ordinary are indistinguishable parts of desiring production . . . " (*CD* 392). His method first calls for a visual knowledge as a sonic reality. The act(s) of composition is/are made visible where construction itself becomes the narration, where the line between categorical norms are blurred even removed. Instead of seeking a surreal image that grants access to the subterranean, or a real image that grants access to the vision of the poet, Bernstein seeks a multi-critical image of the visible. He builds into the poem "the questioning, the stoppage", and this reality "allows the *music* of the poem to be heard" (*CD* 391). He defines the music of poetic fabrication as "hearing the sound *come into* meaning rather than a play with already existing meanings by way of meter" (*CD* 391). The critical image, like all poems, creates a waiting audio-visual process.

Bernstein is concerned with mapping new grids of image construction: of seeing poetry as a larger project informed by all writing, of seeing Stein's invention put into practice where "wordness" has visible residue, of seeing the "idea of appropriating language from other written sources as [a] basic activity to writing as memory or overhearing or describing" (*CD* 393). In practice, Bernstein uses

> quotations from a vast array of sources, and just as many made-up quotations that sound like they are from a prior text. There are lines from other poems, and echoes of lines; remarks from letters (my own and others') or memos from the job; things heard and misheard. (*CD* 393–4)

Quotation, in his development of the critical image, is as basic an activity as description, memory, or overhearing. We are coming upon a poetry that works with the whole world of language construction. Description, memory, overhearing, and quotation are all forms of language used by numerous writers and poets. Bernstein's work inno-

---

33 Bernstein, "An Interview with Tom Beckett", *CD*, 392, 385-410.

vates the image of poetry by consistently taking the idea of a critical image and making visible the fabrication to the material elements of the poem: the line and the page, the letters in the word, the standard grammatical punctuations.

In the poem "The Next Available Place", we can see how making both the critical image and the fabricating mechanism of the line apparent alters visual space.

> Petratch. Foreign body sensation. Misplaced modesty.
> Like I like her. Lurker. Aimed well down. Issue,
> is you. Framed the framed. Ill (I'll)
> begets a. Unruly exstasis. Information to confound
> bike past blue notes harass (harness) looks to.
> Imbibe, imbecile. Leeds' leading legend: IN FOR.
> Nothing that I can say convinced me. With it, withheld.
> Dread, scuzzy. Perhaps Polish (polish). I
> feel rearanged, mandate a macaroon. Cuba,
> Taiwan. Indubitable dauntress fraudulent at ever
> attempting a view: binary, bisected, by the seaside,
> beside myself. Relatively few. Instantly
> benign. Bel canto. Silly trips to Everglades.[34]

Words bounce through sounds, through sectors of divergent sources and codes of culture. The construction is not static; it facilitates re-reading, not just of the text, but of meaning itself. "The poem needs less to be viewed as a fixed end, an *object d'art*, and more as a transforming agent whose exemplary features are to be used by the reader in her/his researches into the nature and products of the production of meaning" (*CD* 388). Bernstein uses a forgotten visual strategy, the period (.) to stop the reader, and he borrows from its meaning as the end of a complete thought. The words play with the sonic register: "Issue, / is you." He takes the word issue, and finds meaning in the letters, Iss—u, or the "Ill (I'll) / begets a". In a moment, the visual meaning of the apostrophe (') is reawakened. Each line has a host of meanings and Bernstein leaves large amounts of space for the reader's participation. Somehow "begets" follows the visual transformation of "Ill". The visual begets more meaning, and

---

34 Bernstein, *Controlling Interests* (New York: Roof Books, 1980), 32. Hereafter cited as *CI*.

in the English language, meaning markers of meaning beyond letters (the period, the apostrophe), beget meaning for the reader.

The poem as a transforming agent is to generate, not fixate meaning.

> Let me give an example of what "generative" might mean. I think of some of my poems as a series of remarks, either in the aphoristic sense or in the sense of observations, constructed items, etc., occurring at the level of phrases or sentences. These can be interpreted in multiple ways: they are each, perhaps to say, polyentenders (that is, any given remark can be taken as true, ironic, false, didactic, satiric, fantastical, inscrutable, sad, funny, my view someone else's view, and so on). Polyentendres suggest the continuous choices of interpretation that confronting the world involves (though that is a matter of semblance only—structural affinity to other forms of creation). Polyvalences and polyrhythms occurring overall throughout the poem create a music of the text, a music that has to do with both the rhyming/ comparing/vectoring of possible meanings, creating *chords* of the simultaneous vectors of the several interpretations of each polyentendre, and with the combination of these chords with other chords, durationally, in the sequence of the writing, and simultaneously, in the overall structure. The overall "sound" of the work is actually more important to listen for than the linear prosodic sequences, since the relation of the "chords" reinforces the sound resonances and echoes creating an intense overall vibration that adds a dynamic dimensional depth to the sound of any given linear movement. (*CD* 396-97)

Bernstein's critical image creates a further range to the sonic dimensions of linear movement. The single, specific, solitary image within one line becomes only one kind of writing instead of the manner of writing itself. In order for Bernstein to explode linear movement, to give some semblance to the "continuous choices of interpretation that confronting the world involves", he begins within the traditional line. However, once in this line new grids of multi-dimensional relations—sonic and graphic—appear one after another. The over sound of the innovated line sings polyphonically beyond the range of any one ear. Linear movement is expanded through a collage of making visible the fabricating mechanism. Its movement expands by

not carrying the whole weight of poetics. Music of words, interpretations, and critical images give an overall "sound" to the work that
"adds a dynamic dimensional depth", a spatial depth to the sound of
the line. The aural cumulative blurring builds the page of the poem.
   The poem "so really not visit a. . ." in *Controlling Interests* displays a
further development of Bernstein's visual strategy. I quote the poem
in full:

So really not visit a remember to strange
A it's always finally seems now which ago
Long that by amazed guess I thing obvious of kind
Feel can weigh a has a distance the off
That there it's then & you
While now which whatever point
Slipping constantly be to seems happening
Until fingers the like through sand
Staring there still on back look only can
Before yourself find the of window in the thoughts your at
Combing again here & times a this over gone
That for inseam or beach of section
Peering the "yet &" where exactly or when sure longer
Results tangible of terms in is it as
Thought of splint a than more no all after which is hope
Somewhere catch to looking
Or ease the that here say can what
Preclude doesn't such of difficulty
In always of necessity harsher that
Circumstance different under place
Changed to seem yet &
Are gone have that years if as
Real the if but record of matter a all
From reeling still were
Looking stop with begin to say to is which it
Puts us before to such
For necessity any rest
By if as tracings these of more
Of sort a well as
Is which place of kind one in stay to skill the with longer
Complete this view of point a than more
Annoys what here you're paper the
Unnecessary becomes flourishes

China in tea the all for again
As film the see to we are or
Else leap a such make to motivated be to need
Table this atop is solitary
Like issues discomfort of hang whatever
Mention to forgot I and you
Can't itself reform already
Like feel I want properly
The actually do to able will
Pressing more the feel to begin now
Rug the about to trips
Atumble time the by only night all window
Put that minute last the at panicking
An has delay the but expected than longer takes
On count that itself too much
Discerns imaginations a takes
I brim from handle look cluster from skyline
The same the much it find & side the over (CI 37-38)

Normal and traditional reading practices are forced to forego linear, narrative speed. Words arrive one on top of another building aural sense through linear non-sense. Words and understanding vibrate, hanging in the air.

Slipping constantly be to seems happening
Until fingers the like through sand

The traditional line disappears. Reading hums.

As film the see to we are or

Or, in the last line, the reading no longer expecting much the same, nevertheless hears those words.

The same the much it find & side the over

We "find & side the over" a rhythm not bound by syntactical logic or sense. Nevertheless, the residue of former patterns gives the reader moments of frustration or pause. What does it mean to place "slipping constantly" beside "be to seems happening"? Following the polyphonic sonic registry, the words, living in unconventional relations, still suggest possible meaning. Drawing from "normal" reading practices, we can suggest slipping constantly is a state of being that only appears to happen. The image is highly critical. We are thrown into the phenomenology of being in the world, into perceptions of actions, into questions of the human essence over daily existence, and into irresolvable, divergent images.

The sonic aspects are beautiful: "As film the see"—like film, the sea. To we, in comparison, are. Like film, the sea in comparison, like us, or . . . and, the possibilities abound. Each of the possible readings leave behind grammatical rules, yet, the sentences attain some of the same sonic depth of Bernstein's poem. The reader is given over to creating and participating. The "overall "sound" of the work" shaped in lines cannot be located in one voice. Instead, "[b]y if as tracings these of more" suggest we view the poem not as a sense of place, but as a *space* of meaning. The critical image a "making visible of fabricating mechanism" (*CD* 392) is shaped by a fusion of divergent sources: " . . . my interest in writing is to be able to incorporate material from disparate places." (*CD* 394) Not only is the source of the material topically divergent, the poem also welcomes other multiple texts.

> As writing focuses its attention less on recreating characters, place and story—presumably based on "found" situations, cities, peoples, etc.—and more on types of style and vocabulary and argument, part of the investigation, of the work, requires using other texts as material to incorporate into a poem. (*CD* 393)

Bernstein is trying to describe that the notion of "found" object has expanded to include a moment by moment existence: "You're dealing in all cases with a material, language, that is in the most fundamental was *found* . . . "(*CD* 393). He takes this to mean that the construction of a poem can include all kinds of sources, such as other texts. Poets have throughout history drawn from outside sources, so how is this practice any different? Bernstein takes the notion of inscription of the other, as a corrective to the popular notion of writing a poem. Part of the poem's work is to investigate what would happen to meaning as we build a reading of the poem such as 'so really not a visit a . . . '. When '[u]nnecessary becomes flourishes' the space of meaning moves, expands, revises.

The opening poem of *Controlling Interests*, 'Matters of Policy', provides another way to view his poetics. As the phone is off the hook, we hear:

... The telephone is off the
hook. It is written that the wisdom
of the wise will be destroyed &
the understanding of the prudent will be
brought to nothing. & so it becomes
time for a little recreation—like she can
certainly butter that popcorn.[35]

The telephone is off the hook so no one can be reached. In the break, the reader is returned to the written, where the wisdom of the wise will be destroyed. However, the break and the destruction does not lead to despair or to the desire of the *übermensch*, but rather to recreation. A reading as *recreation* as well as recreation, works within this poem. The referents of the "written" can be found in both the Hebraic and Christian scriptures.[36] In both contexts, the judgment concerns an alteration of knowledge and a release from cultural power structures. Bernstein brings this other text into his material between disconnected telephones and the making of popcorn. He quotes from different systems: phones, popcorn, power structures, not to get rid of the self, but to create another image of poetry where "the manufacture of the fabulous and the ordinary are indistinguishable parts of desire production ... " (*CD* 392). What if instead of quoting from different systems, he transposed an entire system to disrupt the power structures of the dominant icons of poetry?

A return to "so really not visit a ... ". Recalling line borders. Revisioning the image of poetry. A significant observation yet to be noted is the fact that the poem can be read from right to left. Bernstein unexpectedly brings a non-Greco-Roman logic of linear discourse into his poetics. Hebrew, Chinese, Arabic scripts read from right to left. Bernstein reshapes the Greek-Latin line English has adopted as a way of opening up the critical image. We bumped along the lines, as I have shown, moving against all normal (Greek) reading strategies without knowing it. Re-writing the text from the right to the left reveals even more procedures:

strange to remember a visit not really So

---

35 CI, 4. Also included in *All the Whisky in Heaven: Selected Poems* (New York: Farrar, Straus and Giroux, 2010) 42.

36 The "wisdom of the wise" has both a Hebrew and Christian scriptural reference. The first reference is in Isaiah 29:14 (NRSV) and the second reference can be found in 1 Corinthians 1:19 (NRSV).

ago which now seems finally always it's a
kind of obvious thing I guess amazed by that Long
off the distance has a weigh can Feel
you and then its there That
point whatever which now While
happening seems to be constantly Slipping
sand through like the fingers Until
can only look back on still there Staring
at your thoughts in window of the find yourself Before
gone over this a times & here again Combing
section of beach or inseam for That
longer sure when or exactly where "& yet " the Peering
as it is in terms of tangle results[37]

Does this translation back into Latin and Greek linear discourse make
any difference to the line? Does it make the reading any clearer? Is
this the point of reading from the left to the right? My point here
inspired by Bernstein's visual strategy is that reading can occur in
both directions. In this re-reading of Western conventional reading
patterns we are still without punctuation and each line reeks of phan-
tom ellipses. The reader must continue to find the pause and effect,
and become in the classical sense, a grammarian. This translated
poem does have moments of delight: "Combing section of beach or
inseam for that longer sure". Sure nears surety, and nears assurances.
Combing the beach every morning is still done in many parts of the
world during holiday seasons. Combing the beach also has metaphorical status, as to comb through means to look or search thoroughly.
Looking thoroughly for longer assurances: "when or exactly where '&
yet' the Peering". Perusing the visual strategy of this poem takes the
eye toward the capitalized words, toward lines without punctuation:
"happening seems to be constantly Slipping", constantly.

   The above translation has a correspondence with the poem 'As If
the Trees by Their Very Roots Had Hold of Us'. Here is the first stanza:

Strange to remember a visit, really not so
Long ago, which now seems, finally, past. Always it's a
Kind of obvious thing I guess, amazed by that
Cycle: that first you anticipate a thing & it seems

---

37   This is my translation of the poem "so really not visit a . . ." into a left to right
reading of the text.

Far off, the distance has a weight you can feel
Hanging on you, & then it's there–that
Point—whatever—which, now, while
It's happening seems to be constantly slipping away,
"Like the sand through your fingers in an old movie," until
You can only look back on it, & yet *you're* still there, staring
At your thoughts in the window of the fire you find yourself
    before.
We've gone over this a thousand times: & here again, combing
    that
same section of beach or inseam for that–I'm no
Longer sure when or exactly where–"& yet" the peering,
Unrewarding as it is, *in terms of* tangible results,
Seems so necessary.[38]

The punctuation returns, a order is fashioned, the line works as a
'line'. We read quickly, due to familiarity, but now with the knowledge that this poem is only one of several. Discovering the procedure
does not discount the strategy, nor bring closure to "so really not a
visit a. . .". In contrast to von Hallberg and Jameson, the discovery of
the procedure is only the beginning of critical reading.[39] Many critics
in the late 1970s and all through the 1980s talked about the multiple
readings of texts. Critics like Jonathan Culler, Jacques Derrida, and
even Roland Barthes read texts that were basically linear in format
and design. Others, like Stanley Fish tried to show just how many
readings one could get out of a classroom. The literature read or
seen as multi-dimensional was often graphically one-dimensional.
Consequently, the literature's *jouissance* was often simply critical and
not textual, with *S/Z* being the classic text and example.
    In regards to this text(s) we have a polyphonic register where lines
are bi-directional and sounds bump into the lack of punctuation. As

---

38   Charles Bernstein, *Senses of Responsibility* Tuumba 20 (Berkeley: Tuumba Press,
    1979), 1-2. The poem also appears in *Republics of Reality: 1975-1995*, Sun & Moon
    Classics (Los Angeles: Sun & Moon Press, 2000), 189. Also included in *All the Whisky
    in Heaven: Selected Poems* (New York: Farrar, Straus and Giroux, 2010), 25-27.

39   In the chapter "Avant-Gardes", von Hallberg accepts Jameson's reading of a
    poem by Bob Perelman in which an undisclosed procedure gave the poem its form.
    Jameson and von Hallberg were content with the discovery as an end itself (114-
    119). The discovery of new production procedures does not have to be the basis for
    or limit of the text's meaning. The difficulty with new procedures is that we can
    think that we have no need of the reception once we have unlocked the produc-
    tion.

we have gone over these poems, we have made traditional moves: analytic, grammatical, and poetic. During and after the words we are left not with a repeatable method of explaining away Bernstein's poetic, but an opening of the doors to reading itself. The translations and redrawing of lines are not mechanical reproductions; intentionality blurs repetition. Those who have not seen ancient manuscripts or who have not been in countries that do not use the Phoenician and Greek alphabets, or who have not seen Hebrew Scriptures or read Beowulf and Spencer, will have no room for this poetic of the "critical image". By-passing the rules of mass communication and the dominant mode of poetics, we are exposed to the life of collaboration, experimentation, and invention. Ancient traditions, global concerns rise up out of the local:

> the way we read today in the Western world —from left to right and from top to bottom—is by no means universal. Some scripts were read from right to left (Hebrew and Arabic), others in columns, from top to bottom (Chinese and Japanese); a few were read in pairs of vertical columns (Mayan); some had alternate lines read in opposite directions, back and forth—a method called boustrophendon, "as an ox turns to plough", in ancient Greek. Yet others meandered across the page like a game of Snakes and Ladders, the direction being signaled by lines or dots (Aztec).[40]

Like Krzystof Penderecki's *Cosmogonia* (1970), Bernstein offers a new sound grounded in the tongues and manners of the earth by transforming the local line from a global perspective.[41] Should we not know the history of punctuation, reading styles, and alphabets?

In my translation of the poem into Latin linear discourse, the location of the capitalization of the words offers a commentary on the work of the first stanza. We receive a visual mark in the capitalized letters of words that give the reader a sense of waiting and peering which seems so necessary: Slipping Until Starring Before Combing That Peering. Reading these words beside the poem brings resonance to all three poems and brings another resonance to the right side of

---

40 Alberto Manguel, *History of Reading* (New York: Harper and Collins Publishers, 1996), 48.

41 Kryzstof Penderecki's *Cosomogonia* (1972) was commissioned for the twenty-fifth anniversary of the United Nations.

the translated "so really not visit a. . .". This move does not seem to be arbitrary but adds yet another dimension to the music of the text. As if this were not enough, there is a further reference to this poem in the volume *Shade* (1978):

#23
seems, finally
it's there
& yet you're
exactly where
the peering
tangible
seems
after all
a splint
which is
looking to catch
what, I
say—here?
eases the
(really . . .
not so
new a place
we don't
by, are
it hardly
anticipates
a pack of
time's
buzzing, "maybe . . . .
or do that
of a well as[42]

All of the terms in the above text are in of "As If the Trees by Their Very Roots Had Hold of Us" and "so really not a visit a . . . ". The first eights lines correspond to the first stanza. In the above version, "seems" takes on the meaning of appearance that is placed beside a form of finality and beside a form of perception. Something is there,

---

42 Charles Bernstein, *Shade* (College Park: Sun & Moon Press, 1978), 35–36. Also in *Republics of Reality* (Los Angeles: Sun & Moon, 2000), 109–110.

and the subject is located in the tangible peering, "seems". The tangible sight is the object and the perception of the object. Bernstein brings out a form of vision and appearances along with some kind of certainty ("finally", "after all"). Each of the three versions begins with the letter "s" (strange, so, seems) and gives a sense of presence and absence of the subject's location and the object's reality. Even if we take all three of these poems and try to figure out which one was written first or even which one is the source of the other two, (if this is even the case) we do not really add anything to the reading. Each poem has potential; discovering their fraternity only adds another dimension to their liberty.

The poem in *Controlling Interests* goes further than "#23" and "As If the Trees by Their Very Roots Had Hold of Us". According to my reading and translation, the poem ends its relationship with the other two poems with the line "Of sort a well a". I have been unable to locate any other works containing the next seven lines. The end of the poem (lines 37-51) is another re-reading of the last and title poem from *Senses of Responsibility*. The poem "As If the Trees by Their Very Roots Had Hold of Us", as I have argued, calls into question perception, trace, hope, postponement and writing. The ending of the poem, "so really not visit a . . . " in *Controlling Interests* calls into question our conceptions of the visual imagination.

> On count that itself too much
> Discerns imaginations a takes
> I brim from handle look cluster from skyline
> The same the much it find & side the over

From the last and title poem of *Senses of Responsibility* we have:

> A visual imagination:
> that what it takes discerns skyline from cluster,
> handle from brim. I look over the side & find
> it much the same. "Old hat", "shoe lace", "shag
> carpet". Only you need to do some much more than
> ever could be "expected" of you.

and through my translation back into the Latin linear discourse, we have:

> takes a imaginations Discerns
> skyline from cluster look handle from brim I

over the side & find it much the same The

The poem from *Controlling Interests* does not simply mathematically change the terms, so that there is a one to one translation from a non-Latin linear discourse to a Latin based discourse. Linear qualities are not demanded. Sonic fabrication revises the line and logic of poetry and *Controlling Interests* brings the point of the visual imagination away from a solipsistic center: "Discerns imaginations a takes". Discerns is a verb (third person singular, he/she it) coming from the Latin meaning "to separate apart". The speaking subject has been removed. "A" as an article, as it is written becomes the subject: "a" the first letter of the alphabet is now a noun. So "a" takes, and "I brim from handle look cluster from skyline" and, according to the senses of the poem, the *visual* imagination is what discerns cluster from sky. In this poem, "look" takes over the control panel. Concluding with "The same the much it find" is probably the process of discerning itself as it separates cluster from skyline, handle from brim, and what it cannot integrate "& side the over". The poem "so really not so a visit . . . " not only re-works the line, it also opens new possibilities to the concept of revision, to the poem as a fixed independent unity, and to the assumption that Western linearity is the only design for the shape of an American poem. Bernstein's visual strategy, of finding another way of drawing the line, opens new rooms in the house of American poetic possibilities. Poetry, now, bypasses other forms of visual strategies: "Poetry should be at least as interesting as, and a whole lot more unexpected than, television" (*AP* 3).

Douglas Messerli who started La-bas and then Sun & Moon books, has been publishing Bernstein's work since the very beginning of his career. In his review, entitled "Making the mind whole: Charles Bernstein's *Controlling Interests*" he takes pains to show Bernstein is really John Ashbery's better self.[43] As Messerli puts it:

For, while Ashbery's vision derives from a basic juxtapositioning of antithetical positions, from an aesthetic of collage, Bernstein's poetics, with its traces of American Romanticism, functions in terms of the simultaneity of object and experience. (44)

---

43 "Both poets seek to revitalize the technological society in which they find themselves by creating a new world of language, and in pusuit [sic] of that, both interweave the technical language of the work-day world with more lyrical evocations of exotic landscapes" (43). *Paper Air* (3:1, 1982)

The difficulty of describing Bernstein's poetics this way is that Messerli does not explain what he means by "American Romanticism". He looks at the lines from "Matters of Policy" as an advancement beyond Ashbery in terms of simultaneity of object and experience.

> At last, the
> cabin cruise is over & the captain gently
> chides farewell to us with a luminous laugh.[44]

For Messerli, Bernstein "evinces his commitment to a poetry of thinking process" (40) by his ability to fuse together multiple, accessible, and simultaneous vectors of potential meaning. This poetry seeks a certain reader who is both intuitive, analytical and capable of a dash of detective work: "Like the detective, the reader must (re)construct the details; (s)he must (re)build the poem to meaning" (41). He sees Bernstein asking for a reader "in which (s)he must 'listen' for meaning as well as 'look' for it" (41). If the reader uses all of his or her faculties, he/she will be, according to Messerli, "rewarded" (41). The reward of course, is a whole mind that benefits from an "old-fashioned textual" reading, and it is a reading where he "attempts to bring his unspoken feelings about the writings in touch with the more analytical self" (44). Messerli's reading strategy is meant to counter the recent developments of theory: "Phenomenologist, Structuralist, Semiotic and other methodologies—all shifts from a reading of the poem to an exploration of what causes and determines the poetic act" (39). The whole is achieved by facing the difficulty: "it is clear that many critics of contemporary poetry find it terribly difficult to discuss a particular poem that is not *about* something, but *is* something "fixed" in perpetual process" (39).

Craig Watson reads Bernstein's volume as "concerning the socialization of the individual by means of language."[45] Reading *Controlling Interests* from within Bernstein's own definition of syntax ("Syntax is the ordering of strings of words" (*CD* 75). Watson understands that Bernstein uses a variety of devices in order "to render the compositional act visible" (158): punctuation, line breaks, prose and blank space. His conclusion about *Controlling Interests* and the poem "so not

---

44 Charles Bernstein, *Controlling Interests*, 8.

45 Craig Watson, *Sulfur* 5 (1982): 157. Watson's review shows his research, as he quotes "Thoughts Measure" in L=A=N=G=U=A=G=E 4, and *The Difficulties* #3 even before both pieces were collected in *Content's Dream*.

really visit a . . . " frames the reading as a perceptual issue, but does not explore Bernstein's visual textual strategy.

> Because the poems of *Controlling Interests* occur on the plane of immediate response in that they front thinking as the process of perception reaching for meaning, they don't attain an objective, statement level. The poet is working at an edge of consciousness which forbids another, chrono-logically-deferred process of thought, that of formal organ-ization and placement of information into an individual operating matrix. (159)

Both Messerli and Watson take pains to tie the volume to philosophi-cal concepts of perception and the process of thinking. There is no doubt their writing has applications to his work, but it does reveal critical limitations concerning innovative writing. Bernstein's poetry starts with the image as something that is built: a building which makes visible "a fabricating mechanism, so that the manufacture of the fabulous and the ordinary are indistinguishable parts of desiring production . . . " (*CD* 392). Watson sees Bernstein working on an edge or border that forbids another. He could not see the border in "so really not visit a . . . ". Instead he states: "The tonal resonance of this piece, its lack of punctuation and continuous syntactical evolution, reinforces its semantic track of individual powerlessness and search" (158). What is remarkable is that he touches upon the exiled life and nomadic meaning without even recognizing it as a formal feature of the poem.

Instead of the American errand into the wilderness, Silliman sees a war: "Poetry like war, is a pursuit of politics by other means."[46] The battle is against bourgeois universals and the goal is to show that language constructs reality. Silliman foregrounds Bernstein's training as a philosopher, as a way to understand *Controlling Interests*. He also sees Bernstein's success as a failure on philosophy's part to answer questions of Language's meaning.

> Language's ability to constitute, to generate meaning and models, to imply psychological structures, and to repre-sent, and interact with, the universe of non-linguistic expe-

---

46 Ron Silliman, "*Controlling Interests*", in *The New Sentence* (New York: Roof Books, 1995), 173.

rience, however has been the domain of another profession: philosophy. It should not be surprising, therefore,
that we should have a book of poems such as *Controlling
Interests*, composed by a poet, Charles Bernstein, trained
originally as a philosopher.[47]

Bernstein's success in *Controlling Interests* may be informed by his
philosophical training at Harvard with the Cavell and Albritton.
However, upon closer look, his innovation is rooted in a range of
modes of understanding. Bernstein's strategy in many of his works
is to re-open and innovate the domain of the line. As poetry's most
basic visual strategy, the line could remain unconsidered. Bernstein's
visual strategy does incorporate a variety of languages (quotation,
memory, the overheard), but his use of the multiple language visual
structures displays a profound grasp of the materiality of poetry.
These critics, with the exception of Watson, did not tackle one of the
more difficult poems in the collection. Their insightful readings paint
Bernstein as an innovator, but from a traditional perspective.
   Choosing to read "so really not visit a . . ." is extremely challenging. In reading this poem along with his other work, we discover a
writing practice that has moved beyond American or English based
poetics and rhetoric. Suddenly, the poem as a visual emblem attains
materiality. In hindsight, the move took years with little or no recognition. We have four poems (the reconstructed one, #23, "As If the
Trees by Their Very Roots Had Hold of Us", and "so really not visit a
. . . ") that work separately, together, and not at all. It is a programmed
and non programmed serial. Unlike the serials of an earlier generation, Williams' *Paterson*, Eliot's *Four Quartets*, Zukofsky's *A*, this serial,
this "music" has awaited the reader's participation in a way that is
unprecedented in American Poetics: no announcements were given,
no complete volume published, no critical assessment. Bernstein's
open serial re-writes the procedures of beginning, middle, and end,
re-lines Greco-Roman linear discourse, and re-designs the space of the
reader, the space of the poem, the space of a poetic practice.

Bernstein's visual strategies, as we have seen in this chapter, take
defamiliarization and multi-dimensional procedures in new directions. Directions and grids that can be only understood through a
collaboration of various graphic, linguistic, and spatial theories. The

---

47 Ibid., 174.

reader is asked new fused questions requiring perusable innovation and critical engagement. Collaboration is not only a necessity in reading his texts but is also an essential aspect of his poetics and career. He has collaborated with a musicians, painters, curators, and writers. His collaborations with Andrews as editor, with Silliman, McCaffery, DiPalma, and Andrews in *Legend* (1980) are well known. His work with Richard Tuttle, Ben Yarmolinsky, and Susan Bee are not as well known. Bernstein's ongoing collaborative work with Susan Bee has largely been ignored.[48] Examining Bernstein's visual strategies goes beyond the confines of one chapter. A picture is worth a 1000 words, a visual strategy, hung from the trees, even more.

48   See the interview, *Charles Bernstein and Susan Bee*, M/E/A/N/I/N/G Online #2, http://writing.upenn.edu/epc/meaning/02/bernstein-bee.html .Very few, if any of Bernstein's critics have explored their lengthy and voluminous collaborations which, spanning three decades, have appeared in many different forms. Bee has worked with Bernstein as designer, artist, editor, writer, and has produced over thirteen covers of his poetical works.

25

ERICA HUNT

After *Residual Rubbernecking* (a speculative non-serial anti-romance)

1.

a slide in the pronouns depends on who is speaking

to whom

dispatches from the notorious pit of self regard are addressed:

targeted people take words *personally*.

(Trust in the mirror—why not? Make a face and it's yours.) And

who could help it? A fiction that comes true everyday with parts

played by a supporting cast of the unsuspecting

equals

personality.

2.

Like shelves on the walls to hold the books

(the better to hear you) the speaker,

she hesitates being absent.

Reader take this bait—

No implication of you being she:

(the unexpurgated you being she or I or we)

we all know who they are and who the reader has become because

at various times we have been one

taking turns, not explaining ourselves

believing there is nothing to explain.

3.

A new budget would include

the cost of the labor, physical and intellectual

the expense of concealed tenses

(in past times word to word contact).

A true budget would count the beckoning

that distracts from the domestic total

subtract the subject from the household economy

and replace it with the null with its near equivalent

"was" "had been" or "formerly"

4.

Books growing between the others that the library characters don't
remember having planted. Literary volunteers.

The collection took on a new tone

now that there was to time to fill in the gaps.

Books stood upright even if they did

not always harmonize, at least they no longer

appeared as if they had been abandoned

half-way through

The collector character was apparently very pleased. She let the
breeze from the pages perfume her face.

5.

in style

private acts externalized into approximations

style jolts the ordinary into visibility

or turns into the capsizing dust

floating ever up in Brownian motion:

excited displacement. Subjectivity's almost invisible

until bruised in inter-subjective encounter.

I gloss what you gloss

You gloss what I gloss

We gloss what they gloss

(etc., a series of camouflaged surrenders).

The rest is instrumental.

6.

Fuzzy logic cooks rice

They recite the yellow pages

to say it, more or less:

the mute button is off.

"Forfeiture's plenitude" coughs up meaning

after meaning around the passing thought,

a daily traffic of drive by subjects, titles for

the multitudes, the person of the moment.

26

MICHAEL S. HENNESSEY

A Life, Spliced: On the Early Tapeworks of Charles Bernstein

I am a recording instrument
—William S. Burroughs, *Naked Lunch*[1]

Oh Charles, how could you be so cruel. Charles turn that
magadget off . . . I'm gonna get my own tape recorder and
I'm gonna tape your conversations Charles.
— Bernstein's mother, Sherry (from "#4: a portrait
of one being in family living")[2]

More than thirty-five years after the release of his first book, *Asylums*,
Charles Bernstein is justifiably recognized as one of America's most
influential living poets—a fact attested to by his recent career-span-
ning collection, *All the Whiskey in Heaven: Selected Poems* (Farrar, Strauss
and Giroux, 2010). While, as a pioneer of Language Writing, Bernstein
has made significant contributions to contemporary poetics, his work
as a scholar, editor, curator, and pedagogue are perhaps of equal,
if not greater, importance, and indeed, all of these discrete facets
work together in a complementary fashion to construct his overall aesthetic, which is equally a product of numerous extra-literary
cultural interests including music, film, drama and the visual arts.
    One major trend throughout Bernstein's life's work is a close
focus on sound and media. In a 1994 interview with Hannah Möckel-
Rieke for example, Bernstein prophesied that, "[t]he advent of audio
on the net promises to make available the sound of poetry in a way

---

1 William S. Burroughs, *Naked Lunch: the Restored Text*, (New York: Grove, 2001), 184.
2 Charles Bernstein, "#4: a portrait of one being in family living," *Early
Recorded Works*, PennSound, 2009, http://www.writing.upenn.edu/pennsound/x/
Bernstein-1975-76.html.

that has been previously stymied by the dearth of readily available audio recordings,"[3] and a decade later, he co-founded (with Al Filreis), PennSound, an online archive of recorded poetry that currently boasts more than twenty-five thousand recordings and millions of annual downloads.[4] PennSound is the culmination of several decades of tireless critical advocacy for the integral role of sound within poetics, which also includes the radio programs *Close Listening* and *LINEbreak*, the Segue Reading Series (co-founded with Ted Greenwald at the Ear Inn in 1977), and the Bernstein-edited Segue CD, *Live at the Ear* (1994), along with the groundbreaking volume *Close Listening: Poetry and the Performed Word* (Oxford University Press, 1998). Likewise, it's no stretch to see Bernstein's innovative use of technology in projects as diverse as the small press literary journal *L=A=N=G=U=A=G=E*, as well as the Electronic Poetry Center and the long-running POETICS Listserv, as being temperamentally linked to the aforementioned foci on sound, poetry, and novel modes of cultural delivery.

Because of the significance of both sound and media throughout Bernstein's long career, it's surprising that his early experiments with audio poetry—both the 1982 Widemouth Tapes cassette *Class* and the mid-1970s home recording sessions that yielded the materials for that release—have been largely neglected.[5] Arguably, one can trace all of Bernstein's sonic explorations back to this fruitful period in his early aesthetic development—when he was not only greatly inspired by contemporary music and tape manipulation, but also considered the possibility of splitting his creative focus equally between sound and poetry—and certainly these recordings are deserving of wider critical attention.

Publication History

Originally paired with Charles Stein's *theforestforthetrees* as a split release, *Class* was part of Widemouth Tapes' third series of six cassettes,

---

3 Bernstein, "An Interview with Hannah Möckel-Rieke," *My Way: Speeches and Poems*, (Chicago: University of Chicago, 1999), 72.

4 n.b. I've been a member of the PennSound project since 2007, when I joined the staff as managing editor, and was promoted to editor in 2010.

5 The entire body of Bernstein's homemade tape experiments, including *Class*, is available on PennSound (http://writing.upenn.edu/pennsound/x/Bernstein-1975-76.html), while an individual page for *Class* also exists on the site (http://writing.upenn.edu/pennsound/x/Bernstein-Class.html). All references contained herein are to these versions.

funded through a $2,400 grant from the National Endowment for the Arts. Baltimore-based poet Chris Mason, who founded Widemouth in late 1978 as part of the multifaceted Merzaum collective, had secured this funding but bowed out of the project not long before its original deadline in July 1981, handing control of the label over to tENTA-TIVELY, a cONVENIENCE, and Patty Karl, who oversaw the eventual release of these recordings and many subsequent ones.[6]

While Widemouth's original focus was documenting the underground cultural scenes of Baltimore and Washington, D.C., it soon expanded its scope to include a wide array of voices, many of whom had passed through the area to do readings, including Steve Benson and cris cheek.[7] Bernstein's *Class*—and the concurrent release of *Public Language* by L=A=N=G=U=A=G=E co-founder Bruce Andrews (on which Bernstein appears alongside Ray DiPalma, Michael Gottlieb, Peter Seaton, James Sherry, and Hannah Weiner[8])—are also emblematic of this phenomenon: Bernstein and Mason were acquainted with one another since at least the winter of 1978, when the two read together at Washington, D.C.'s Folio Books, and in Doug Lang's introduction to Bernstein's set, mention is made of his being published by both the journal, *e pod*, and his forthcoming pod books release, *Poetic Justice*, both entities also being part of the Merzaum Collective.[9]

Class was a very early addition to PennSound's archives, appearing around the time of the site's official launch in January 2005. These digitized versions, originally made by Kenneth Goldsmith for sister-site UbuWeb in 2003, made the recordings widely available for the first time in decades (technically, tapes can still be purchased from Widemouth for $50), but they had one critical flaw, as Bernstein explains: "[w]hen Kenny made the digital version for UBU it was mono, but the original was stereo. And stereo is key!"[10] This situation

6 tENTATIVELY, a cONVENIENCE, "A Brief History of Widémouth Tapes," http:// www.fyi.net/~anon/ WdmUHistory.html.

7 Ibid.

8 tENTATIVELY, a cONVENIENCE, "Widémouth Tapes Catalog," http://www.fyi. net/~anon/ WdmUCatalog.html

9 "Charles Bernstein — Readings," PennSound, http://writing.upenn.edu/ pennsound/x/Bernstein-readings.html. Interestingly, the two selections from *Poetic Justice* read at that event—"Palukaville" and "Faculty Politics"—both would appear to have roots in his recent tape experiments: the tracks "Class" (specifically, the line, "a one-way ticket to Palookaville" from *On the Waterfront*, a source-text for the track) and "Accused" (which uses a faculty senate report on a recent politically-motivated battle in CCNY's history department), respectively.

10 Bernstein, e-mail interview, February 2011.

was remedied in early 2009, when PennSound unveiled full stereo remasters of the five original tracks—along with a larger body of previously unavailable homemade tapes dating from 1975-1976, from which the *Class* tracks were chosen—engineered by Danny Snelson.

Before conducting a more thorough analysis of *Class* and exploring its historical contexts and precedents, it seems worthwhile to briefly describe and discuss each piece individually. The five final tracks were chosen by Bernstein after the project was commissioned by Mason, and since he did not yet know that Stein's *theforestforthetrees* would be accompanying his selections on the flipside, there's no conscious relationship between his work and Stein's. The "crucial" factor guiding Bernstein's choices was "the severe time limits of one side of a cassette."[11] While he strived to find those pieces that "would work best" and still fit the restrictive medium, difficult decisions were necessary: the ambitious tape-collage, "#4: a portrait of one being in family living," for example, "was too long, though in many ways it's the most complex work and I certainly liked it as much or more than 'Class.'"[12] Nonetheless, within this limited space (just shy of twenty-eight minutes), Bernstein displays a dazzling sonic heterogeneity, making use of a wide array of techniques to create five tracks that are individually distinct while simultaneously linked through a number of aesthetic traces, as we shall see when we consider each separately.

Track 1: "Piffle (Breathing)," with Susan Bee (Laufer) and Greg Ball (1976)

As the lead track on *Class*, "Piffle (Breathing)" serves as an overture of sorts, preparing listeners for many of the techniques that will be taken up throughout the cassette: a three-track stereo collage (with separate discursive elements panned hard left, hard right and center) exploring the potential of the human voice, and more specifically the textures produced when they overlap with one another. In the cassette liner notes (reproduced on PennSound's *Class* page), Bernstein characterizes "Piffle (Breathing)" as "the most formally self-reflective [track], trying to bring the process of making the piece to the fore: it's me breathing and making the commentary."[13] Moreover, though carefully constructed, it's largely a spontaneous composition—"I had

---

11 Ibid.

12 Ibid.

13 Bernstein, *Class*.

the basic architecture and concept in my head but it was unscripted,"
he notes—and this *cinéma vérité* open-endedness (inspired by French
New Wave filmmaker Jean-Luc Godard) is a key component of the
track.[14]

The piece unfolds slowly, beginning with a full thirty seconds of
Bernstein's breathing, yawning, swallowing, and snorting (which
will continue until the end of the track) in the center channel before
a track predominantly featuring Bernstein and Greg Ball ("a friend
of mine in college, boyfriend of a student, though not himself a
student"[15]) in conversation begins in the right channel. Fifteen
seconds later, a third track—featuring dialogue between Bernstein
and his partner, Susan Bee (Laufer)—starts on the left channel,
and this will continue for approximately two-and-a-half minutes,
followed by forty seconds of silence and a second exchange running
for three minutes, ending at the seven-minute mark. The right-hand
track continues without interruption until seven minutes and forty
seconds into the track, where it too cuts out, leaving just the center-
track breathing for an additional fourteen seconds. In order to more
clearly analyze the "Piffle (Breathing)," I'll address each panned
dialogue separately.

The right-hand track is largely a running meta-discussion on the
tapepoem's composition: "What we're going to do here is to record
just a conversation," Bernstein begins. "About what we're doing
here," Ball adds, and Bernstein replies, "Right, and then on the other
track we're going to have the breathing." After a brief interlude in
which they comment on Bee's new hairdo and outfit, they continue
their explanation:

> Bernstein: "So the idea is we'll then have three tracks. . ."
> Ball: "Three tracks. We could have four."
> Bernstein: "And, uh, on one track will be this conversa-
> tion."
> Ball: "And on another track will be breathing,"
> Bernstein: "Breathing, and then whatever we do over that
> final thing . . ."
> Ball: "Will be . . ."
> Bernstein: "Will be the final track."

---

14 Bernstein, e-mail interview.
15 Ibid.

With this basic plan established in the first two minutes, their conversation then shifts to other technical details, including the ideal way in which to overlay the tracks, the number of feet of tape they'll need to record to match the length of the breathing track and whether they should be recording in stereo or mono (at which point Bernstein shifts the recorder from the former to the latter, causing a noticeable difference in the sound quality). From the discussion, it's clear that this track is the last to be recorded (after the breathing itself, then the left-channel response to that tape by Bee), and aside from an attentiveness to the small details of engineering the recording, the two speakers also become somewhat self-conscious, with Bernstein making statements like, "I wonder if this kind of thing seems very self-indulgent" and "I don't know that we're being responsible toward the work." This leads into an extended soliloquy by Bernstein (with occasional interruptions by Ball) about what their intentions in the work should be:

> We should sense ourselves as if talking for posterity, and try to focus on what would be the most deep, most profound, most resonant statements or conversations or thoughts that we have, that we would want to see preserved for time immemorial. . . . Something that resonates with the particulars of time and place, that's accurate, that gives a depth and seriousness. . . . Let's just say that rather than just another contribution to throwaway culture, to conceptual, "doesn't mean anything, it's all in my mind" . . . Something that really has a permanence and beauty and a withstandingness, that pushes back, that one can come to again and again and it still has something there, as opposed to some throwaway ten minutes that we come up with to have another track to a four-track thing.

While at first we might readily interpret this as an acknowledgment of the relative permanence of the recording medium itself, Bernstein's grand monologic tone—as well as the fact that his speech dissolves into riotous laughter at several points—makes it clear that he's parodying mainstream artistic pretensions (and the interplay between this track and the sighing, yawning center track reinforces this idea nicely). Bee appears as an "interviewee," delivering the simple, damning line, "It's all piffle," which gives the piece its name, and serves as the launching point for another Bernstein monologue on ephemera, before the participants decide that they want dessert, make sure that they've recorded tape to cover the length of the other tracks, and switch the recorder off.

While the right channel addresses process, the left is concerned with the actual tape artifact itself (specifically the eight minutes of breathing) and is far more dialogic than its counterpart, with the exchanges between Bernstein and Bee taking the form of interviews. "What are your views?,," he begins provocatively, before clarifying his question: "What are your views on the breathing?" Bee can't hear him, however, due to the failure of her headphones, and answers each of his questions with a laughing "what?" before concluding, "I've lost you." After this issue is remedied, her reply is brief and direct: "I didn't like it." To Bee, the breathing is "too personal" and not "alienating enough," it's "tedious [and] boring," and she turns the tables on her interrogator by asking, "Well, did you ever listen to somebody breathing?" He acknowledges that he has, and she's quick to respond, "Well, there you have it. Bye!"

"Hang up now, it's over," she continues, shifting the medium to an approximation of a telephone conversation, however Bernstein disagrees, "it's not, you're still being recorded," and the two briefly wonder whether they should sing something instead, performing snippets of "Zip-a-Dee-Doo-Dah" and "La Marseillaise." Next, the tone shifts dramatically with Bernstein and Ball providing a summary of Bee's issues with the recording. "People don't want to hear your own private gurgling, your own internal noises," Ball concludes, to which Bee enthusiastically responds, "That's right!," bringing the first exchange to an end.

After forty seconds of the breath track alone, Bernstein and Bee begin again with him asking whether "having heard that done over again [she] likes it better with the revision." It's not clear whether he's referring to a rerecording of the breathing track or the right-channel commentary, but her response is a swift "no": "it just passed me by," she explains. Bernstein questions Bee's zombie-like voice, and in an attempt to cheer her up turns on the radio to find something worth listening to, however he quickly loses the only station that interests her, news of a thunderstorm. As he searches through the dial, adding music and voices to the track's dense palimpsest, she replies to each new program with a melodious "no" until he returns to the original channel. Bee prefers the radio to the breathing tape, "because it's more sing-song" and this leads into a particularly playful exchange between the two, riffing on the term, "sing-song," until Bernstein interrupts: "Susan, I want to leave some space at the end, so that we can just have the last dissolve come in, so I want to cut this

in a couple of feet. Do you have any final remarks to make?" "Um no
. . . sing-song," she replies, and he declares, "That's great," bringing
this track to a close.

Undoubtedly, "Piffle (Breathing)" is a challenging listening experience as one tries to engage with and sort through the two competing
dialogues simultaneously, aided and hindered by Bernstein's basso
continuo (which threads them together, encouraging elision even as
it keeps each conversation distinct), and by the poet's close miked
breathing (which seems to obscure key words and draw our attention back towards the middle). Bernstein's breathing, and its central
place within an environment of attentive listening, brings to mind
John Cage's often-told and perhaps apocryphal story of his time spent
within Harvard's anechoic chamber: "in that silent room, I heard two
sounds one high and one low," which, according to the attendant,
were the sounds of Cage's "nervous system in operation" and "blood
in circulation," respectively.[16] Similarly, in "Piffle," we begin with
a biological signifier that forces us to acknowledge our own subjective presence as active listeners. While our attention to this central
track wanes as the two hard-panned dialogues commence, it remains
a constant presence throughout—mimicked, if we're listening on
headphones, by the amplified sound of our own breathing—and
persists after the talking stops, bringing the piece to a restful close.

This meditative focus is further reinforced if we consider the track's
composition, specifically Bernstein's recording (and self-consciously
acknowledging) his own breathing for nearly eight minutes: an aural
experience reminiscent of the unwavering, panoptic camera eye
of Andy Warhol's *Screen Tests* (and both Cage and Warhol's philosophies, particularly in regards to media, were central influences on
Bernstein at this time).[17] It also fits well with the dialogues in both
channels, which touch upon issues of physicality: the left side including a critique of the breathing track itself (it's deemed too visceral,
too personally intrusive), while the right side ends with Bee's plea,
"let's have the coffee ice cream," seemingly privileging simple bodily
delights over high-minded conceptualism. Both body and breath will
figure heavily into *Class'* next track as well.

---

16 John Cage, "How to Pass, Kick, Fall, and Run," in *A Year From Monday: New Lectures and Writings* (Middletown, CT: Wesleyan, 1967), 134.

17 Bernstein, e-mail interview.

Track 2: "1-100" (1969)

"1-100" is the earliest track on *Class*, and also the earliest known recording of Bernstein, dating from 1969. A Fluxus-inspired performance piece composed during the poet's sophomore year at Harvard, "1-100" can be summed up (like all good conceptual art) relatively briefly, as Kenneth Goldsmith did when he included the track in a playlist for *The New York Times*' "Living With Music" column in 2007: "It is simply a three-minute recitation of the numbers 1 to 100 in that order. Feel the suspense as the piece slowly builds; if you last that long, things get really spicy around 75."[18]

Bernstein begins "1-100" in a normal tone of voice, rattling off the first decad with accelerating speed and force, then moves through the teens in a slightly bored fashion before delivering "twenty-one" with a burst of either anger or enthusiasm. Most of the thirties, forties and fifties are delivered in a quasi-profound tone (mocking, perhaps, an imagined stereotypical voice prevalent in contemporary poetry readings of the late-60s, from latter-day coffee house beatniks to pipe-and-tweed university bards), and this profundity gains momentum through the sixties, until the dazzling conclusion, during which the remaining numbers are screamed with animal intensity. While the first numbers of this final phase are delivered somewhat whimsically, their delivery becomes more and more blood-curdling with each passing digit, culminating in a painfully-extended, seven-second howl of "ninety-nine," followed, after a gasp for breath, by a deadpan "one hundred." This return to a mundane tone, reminiscent of Bernstein's opening "one," effectively sets up a continuum for listeners, beckoning them to begin again—to return to one, as numbers do themselves—and thus a very irregular performance ends with a recursive glance towards regularity.

It's worth noting that two different versions of "1-100" are currently available to listeners: the original 2003 digitization by Goldsmith and a 2009 (p)remaster done concurrently with Snelson's work on the other *Class* tracks, by Jim Stephens of Deep Sky Audio, who worked with Bernstein's original reel-to-reel tape from forty years earlier. While the performance in both versions is the same, the differences here are dramatic, with years of static and tape hiss (which appear to have sanded down the recording's rougher edges) stripped away.

---

18 Kenneth Goldsmith, "Living With Music: A Playlist by Kenneth Goldsmith," *The New York Times*, November 14, 2007, http://artsbeat.blogs.nytimes.com/2007/11/14/living-with-music-a-playlist-by-kenneth-goldsmith/.

Bernstein's voice becomes even more visceral and harrowing in the cleaned-up recording, taking on a buzzsaw intensity as the more whimsical tones earlier in the piece give way to distressing yelps, and a diegetic soundtrack of background music and conversation is now audible.

Aside from running longer than that original version (and also, perhaps, slightly slower), one can discern the effects of multiple-generation transfers and the limitations of the recording equipment itself on the overall fidelity here—most notably, in the metallic modulation and reverb effects on Bernstein's voice present in the master track and the clipping distortion created as he overloads the microphone, which now has an even more elemental effect upon listeners. This (p)remastering not only circumvents the minimal tone-loss caused by the 2003 digitization of the original *Class* cassette, but also any intervening redubbing between the 1969 original and the Widemouth Tapes release—done by Bernstein or the label—which seems to be somewhat considerable. Run as "a shoe-string operation," Widemouth long suffered from the inability to consistently maintain working equipment, with differences between decks often causing significant variance in the finished tapes, and this limitation was embraced by the staff.[19] In the label's online history, tENTATIVELY, a cONVENIENCE brags of their "unintentional technical amateurish-ness [and] deliberate philosophical rejection of making such concerns [first] priority at the expense of radical content," concluding that "the [end] result is often, but not always, a low-fidelity product."[20]

Nevertheless, while the new (p)remaster presents Bernstein's orig-inal performance in its purest recorded state, the previous version is perhaps the more interesting one, precisely because it wasn't a recording of a performance, but rather a recording of a recording of a performance (or more likely, a recording of a recording of a recording of a recording of a recording of a recording of a performance), serving as a reminder not only of the technological mediation inherent to any recording, but also the lovely and peculiar aesthetics inherent to that process' deterioration.

---

19 tENTATIVELY, a cONVENIENCE, "A Brief History of Widémouth Tapes."
20 Ibid.

Track 3: "My/My/My" (1976)

"My/My/My" is the sole track from *Class* with textual origins, having appeared as the untitled concluding poem in Bernstein's self-published debut collection *Asylums* (Asylum's Press, 1975) one year after its initial composition. It remained unpublished otherwise, save for a digital facsimile reissue of *Asylums* through the Eclipse archives, until appearing in *Against Expression: An Anthology of Conceptual Writing* (eds. Craig Dworkin and Kenneth Goldsmith) in late 2010. An anaphoric list-poem presented as a narrow fifteen-page column of text, "My/My/My" consists of approximately four hundred and fifty items that belong to its speaker, ranging from the physical to the visceral, the emotional to the abstract: "my game / my box / my drawer / my cup / my longing / my blotter / my distraction / my underpants / my papers / my wish / my despair / my erasure / my plantation / my candy / my thoughtfulness / my forebearance / my gracelessness / my courage / my crying."[21] In *Asylums*, "My/My/My" features an epigraph from Swami Satchidananda—"Count the number of things you call mine. This is the distance between you and enlightenment"—and though this isn't present in the recording on *Class*, Bernstein did include it in the cassette's liner notes (and subsequently on PennSound's page for the *Class* recordings).[22] Even without this introduction, however, it's still easy to see the poem as an exercise in materialism taken to absurd lengths, not only given the number of possessions, but the preposterousness of many of them as well.

Prior to its appearance on *Class*, Bernstein included "My/My/My" on two homemade cassette compilations: an eleven-minute "single track feed" on the *1975 Cassette*, consisting of a straightforward reading of the poem, followed by a five-minute "three track realization" of the poem on the *Coco-Rimbay Cassette* (1976). This version, which edits and overlays the earlier track with a newly recorded performance to create a multidimensional rendering of the poem, is the same version that would later appear on the Widemouth Tapes release.[23]

The *Coco-Rimbay/Class* version of "My/My/My" takes full advantage of the spacious stereo field, situating the three voices so that each

---

21 Bernstein, *Asylums* (New York: Asylum's Press, 1975), http://english.utah.edu/eclipse/projects/ ASYLUMS/, 33-34.

22 Ibid., 31; Bernstein, *Class*.

23 Bernstein, *Early Recorded Works*.

has plenty of room: two are panned hard right and left, respectively, the third just slightly left-of-center. Though the piece begins with the right channel, quickly bouncing to the left and then to center, it's the center voice that has the greatest prominence here, having both a higher amplitude and the greatest fidelity of the three tracks, setting up what often resembles a call-and-response exchange with the two stereo-separated tracks, a dialogue (or more truthfully, a trilogue) that's similar to the double dialogues of "Piffle (Breathing)." Though Bernstein reads at a fairly steady cadence, through variations in performance and tape recorder speeds, the three voices lapse in and out of synchronization with one another in a style reminiscent of Steve Reich's process-driven voice-phase pieces of the mid-1960s—*It's Gonna Rain* (1965) and *Come Out* (1966)—which were of great influence on Bernstein at this time.[24] William Duckworth has observed that Reich's minimalist style, "allows a relatively small amount of musical material to be cycled through all its possible permutations," and we can see Bernstein achieve a similar effect throughout *Class*, whether on a grand scale in tracks like "1-100," "My/My/My" and "Goodnight," or more discretely in certain recursive sections of "Class."[25]

As a single text realized as three overlapping tracks, the poem's already-intense litany effect is amplified exponentially, challenging listeners to parse through and follow multiple language lines, which often interrupt, contradict or distract from one another. The three voices seem to cohere momentarily on the shared long-I in "my" only to clash again as the words slip out of sync, and this push-pull effect works contrapuntally against the two-note high/low melody of Bernstein's recitations. The poem loops back upon itself as it progresses, and towards the end of the recording, the left and center tracks—which are taken from two different performances—begin to loosely mirror one another, adding yet another layer of complexity to an already dense track. The three voices continue until approximately four seconds before the end of the track, when the left channel drops out, leaving the center and right to engage in two more call-and-response exchanges before the right is abruptly cut off.

Bernstein made recordings of much of his early writing during this period, experimenting with different styles from straightforward readings to more ambitious stagings. Side two of the *1975 Cassette*

24 Bernstein, e-mail interview.
25 William Duckworth, "Steve Reich" in *Talking Music: Conversations with John Cage, Philip Glass, Laurie Anderson, and Five Generations of American Experimental Composers*, (New York: Da Capo, 1999), 292.

(where the "single track feed" of "My/My/My" is found) also contains similar solo readings by the poet of a suite of "Early Poems," *Asylums'* opening poem "Asylum," and "Lo Disfruto" (which would later also appear in *Poetic Justice*), while the *Coco-Rimbay Cassette* included two multi-voice pieces featuring Bernstein, Bee and Ball alongside the three-track version of "My/My/My": a performance of "Sentences" from *Parsing* and an "*Asylums/Parsing* medley." That out of all of these, only "My/My/My" was chosen for inclusion in *Class* is notable, particularly because it's the most altered, the most developed—the poem itself is transformed into an overlapping rondo of lines and voices, and the track's constructedness (made clear by the simultaneous voices, the tape hiss and hum, and the degradation of Bernstein's voice) is fully evident—therefore, the most closely-aligned with the *musique concrète* experiments that comprise the rest of the cassette.

Track 4: "Class" (1976)

In the penultimate track, "Class," we find Bernstein experimenting with yet another technique, creating a monophonic collage of samples from well-known films, including Marlon Brando's Oscar-winning performance in Elia Kazan's *On the Waterfront*, a brief snippet of *Casablanca*'s "As Time Goes By," and two songs from the Depression-era musical *Stand Up and Cheer* ("Baby Take a Bow" and "I'm Laughing"), which are juxtaposed with fragments of his own ambient speech. Unlike other tracks on *Class* that are carefully constructed from layers of pre-recorded tracks, the cassette's title track is the spontaneous product of intentionally crude edits.

To create the track, Bernstein used the "very low end mono cassette [recorder]" on which he'd originally recorded the track's raw materials, and "played the forward and reverse keys, like you'd play a piano" as that machine was fed into his "new fangled stereo cassette recorder."[26] The resulting sound, riddled with abrupt and unambiguously mechanical lurches, splices and repetitions that jumble syntax and jump across the frequency spectrum, blurs the lines between speech and pure sound. However, this frantic editing, while perhaps the most technically impressive facet of "Class," is only used selectively through the course of the track, which otherwise consists of lengthy, uninterrupted passages of film dialogue and song. The tension established between these macro- and micro-components

---

26 Bernstein, e-mail interview.

allows the listener a momentary respite and also effectively mimics the interplay of silence and sound (through the split-second drop-outs that accompany each edit) and the vast emotional incongruities between the source materials: the desolation of *On the Waterfront*, the wistful romance of *Casablanca* and the blithe joy of *Stand Up and Cheer!*

The piece's focal point is a stunning and stuttering deconstruc-tion of *On the Waterfront*'s famous soliloquy—"I coulda had class . . . I coulda been a contender"—as delivered by the once-promising boxer Terry Malloy (Marlon Brando), which evolves slowly over the track's length. "Class" begins (after a brief excerpt from Steve Reich's *Drumming* that also closes the track) with the speech in its entirety, running for a full ninety seconds and coming to a close at the scene's natural ending, which dissolves into the song "I'm Laughing" from *Stand Up and Cheer!* (a derisive response from the world to Malloy's troubles). When the song ends, Brando is back, repeating a smaller portion of the scene ending with the phrase, "It wasn't him, Charlie, it was you," which then loops cleanly and completely (an effect not unlike a skipping phonograph record) for forty seconds, before the intrusion of another cheerful song from the musical, "Baby, Take a Bow." The next brief interruption consists of the opening strains of *Casablanca*'s "As Time Goes By," overlaid with Bernstein's own voice, complaining to an unknown person ("you don't take any initiative and you expect me to do the whole thing")—these two tracks alter-nate once more, with the latter engaging in a brief, ragged loop, before Brando returns again, setting up the track's sonic climax.

Lasting almost four and a half minutes, this meditation on Malloy's iconic lines, "You don't understand, I coulda had class . . . I coulda been a contender . . . I coulda been somebody, instead of a bum, which is what I am, let's face it," scrambles the material into an increasingly dizzying and claustrophobic series of cuts that simul-taneously efface any meaning whatsoever (appropriately, the phrase "you don't understand" serves as a refrain throughout), while more acutely reiterating the full emotional weight of Malloy's situation, each cut accompanied by a thumping punch-in noise that hits listen-ers with as much force as the longshoremen's fists which nearly kill him at the end of the film. Bernstein's extended, virtuosic perfor-mance here yields some startling effects, both sonically and syntacti-cally, as evidenced by this transcribed approximation of one of the track's more intricate passages:

you don't understand
some money / you don't understand I

you don't understan
you don't understand
money / you don't understand, I coulda had class . . . I
coulda been a conten
I coulda been a conten
I coulda been a contender
had class
you don't understand, I coulda had class
you don't understand, I coulda had class
you don't understand, I coulda had class
saw some money / you don't understand, I coulda had class
for you, you saw some money / you don't understand, I
could had class . . .
I coulda been a contender . . . I coulda been somebody
tender . . . I coulda been somebody
contender . . . I coulda been somebody
I coulda been somebody
somebody
been somebody
I coulda been somebody
I coulda been somebody

This section is bookended by longer, uncut excerpts of the speech,
with the latter abruptly segueing into a recapitulation of "Baby, Take
a Bow" and a closing sample of *Drumming*.

"Class" is perhaps the most disembodied track on the cassette,
consisting almost exclusively of manipulated found materials, and
the source of this raw audio—largely television reruns of films from
the 30s, 40s and 50s—is notable for a number of reasons. First, one
must take into consideration the effect of television on the development of Bernstein's aesthetic imagination. Loss Pequeño Glazier,
conducting an autobiographical interview with Bernstein in 1996
recalls the poet's assertion that his work "is as influenced by *Dragnet*
as by Proust," which he interprets as "indicative of the sources of
'information' we have in a media culture like ours."[27] This hybrid
embrace of high and low culture, of literary and non-literary texts,
is a key characteristic of Bernstein's poetics. Elsewhere in the same
interview, Bernstein describes his media-saturated childhood idylls:

---

27 Bernstein with Loss Pequeño Glazier, "An Autobiographical Interview," *My Way*,
    236.

"I liked TV and hanging out at home . . . some years I missed as many as 40 days. And at home there was the chance for reverie, for sleeping late, for making tuna fish sticks sprinkled with paprika, for watching daytime TV." "I read *TV Guide* religiously in those days," he continues, "and knew all the panelists on the celebrity game shows, all the actors on the sitcoms, and all the comedy shows from the early 50s that I had missed the first time around".[28] Television also served as a vital catalyst for some of Bernstein's earliest uses of audiotape: "I got my first tape recorder when I was 12 or so," he explains, using it "to tape TV shows' themes and the like."[29]

At the same time, the specific characteristics and limitations of the television medium serve as a vital alchemical component of Bernstein's tape collage, particularly when further exploited by the process itself, similar to the inclusion of diegetic radio broadcasts in "Piffle (Breathing)." These film samples aren't purely digital, high-definition artifacts (as we would likely experience them in the present), but rather clips transformed multiply as they are broadcast terrestrially, received by a television antenna (perhaps distorted by poor tuning) and amplified through the set's tinny speaker, then recorded on one cassette tape which is, in turn, manipulated and rerecorded by another tape machine. In this chain of events, the television set plays an important role, not only significantly altering the timbre of the original sound to produce the sort of "degraded sounds" Bernstein was interested in achieving (listen, for example, to the washed out strings accompanying Brando's famous lines or the bell-like over-compressed rendition of "As Time Goes By"), but also allowing for a private viewing experience, where one is free to interact with the films in the way that he does.[30]

There are several precedents for this sort of aesthetic — both appropriative and deconstructive — within Bernstein's earliest work. "Accused," one of his very first tape experiments neatly embodies both of these characteristics. "In 1974, City College's History Department erupted into a bitter political dispute in which older faculty members . . . accused their younger colleagues of disruptive leftist agitation," Bernstein explains in the PennSound liner notes to this recording. "In this work, I perform the 1975 CUNY faculty senate

---

28   Ibid., 235. Cf. "Contradiction Turns to Rivalry," in *Islets/Irritations* (1983), which consists entirely of appropriated *TV Guide*-style show synopses.

29   Bernstein, e-mail interview.

30   Ibid.

report on the matter."³¹ Over the course of forty-five minutes, the poet makes his way through the entire text, working in a fashion similar to the recursive jump-cut style of "Class." Here, for example, is a transcription of the first twenty seconds of "Accused": "the problem / background of the problem / the problem prior / prior to / prior to the / prior to the / prior to the 1960s / prior to the 1960s the / the senior members / the senior members / the senior members / members of / of / of the / of the." The one key difference, however is that this effect is not generated by mechanical means, but rather is Bernstein's "live imitation of a tape loop or the way I would later 'play' the tape recorder."³² The resultant effect is reminiscent of both John Giorno's multi-voiced loop-influenced early appropriative poetry, or Brion Gysin's "Permutation Poems" (such as "I Am That I Am," "Kick That Habit Man" or "Junk Is No Good Baby")—which "exercise . . . a more mathematical variation of the [cut-up] concept [upon] a short phrase"³³—and Bernstein indicates that both of the aforementioned poets entered his frame of reference around the time he began his tape experiments.³⁴

"Afternoon Tape," which fills out the 1975 *Accused Cassette* also employs a milder, more conversational version of this mimicry—effectively pairing it with actual tape manipulation—and other early recordings such as "Coco-Rimbay" and "Sen-Sen" hybridize the technique, wedding repetitions (of both regular speech and Jackson Mac Low-esque gutteral phonemes) with a layering of multiple voice tracks similar to "Piffle (Breathing)." Finally, the epic tape collage, "#4: a portrait of one being in family living," is perhaps the most closely aligned to "Class," making extensive use of the rewind-button stutter loop technique on a variety of recordings, mostly self-made, whether familial field recordings, readings from a wide array of cultural artifacts or personal narratives. What's most interesting here are the myriad approaches that Bernstein takes to appropriation—while some texts are incorporated into the collage in their original forms (a recording of psychiatrist David Cooper, songs by Billie Holliday and Fats Waller, a recording of an argument between

31 Bernstein, *Early Recorded Works.*
32 Bernstein, e-mail interview.
33 Jason Weiss, *Back in No Time: The Brion Gysin Reader* (Middletown, CT: Wesleyan, 2001), 79.
34 Bernstein, e-mail interview. The poet reports meeting Gysin in Paris in the mid-1970s; he'd later appear on the 1980 Giorno Poetry Systems album *Sugar, Alcohol, & Meat.*

the poet and his parents), others are transformed from their origins as either text or sound sources, including Bernstein's recitation of dialogue from *Casablanca* and reading from the work of Poe—and the way in which these samples co-exist with the other audio fragments. It should finally be noted that this appropriative approach shaped Bernstein's early writings as well, most notably the poem "Asylum," which is constructed wholly out of excerpts from sociologist Erving Goffman's *Asylums: Essays on the Social Situation of Mental Patients and Other Inmates.*[35]

Track 5: "Goodnight," with Susan Bee (Laufer) (1976)

Class comes to a hypnotic close with "Goodnight"—a lovely, micro-cosmic meditation on the single word, "goodnight," rendered in warm and friendly tones by Susan Bee. With several tracks layered to create a gentle and near-constant delay din, and spacious stereo separation to keep each voice distinct, "Goodnight" is a lush, dense soundscape that privileges sound and syntax equally.

Moreover, like "My/My/My," this track not only bears the influence of Reich's vocal-phase technique, but further rarifies it, reducing the source material to one repeated word. The simultaneous short and long echoes create subtle variations as the multiple voicings gradually slip out of sync with one another, and the shared assonances of the drawn-out long-I sound in "night" help to create a mild phaseshifting effect, all serving to produce surprising juxtapositions and timbres here, which are augmented by a rhythmic undergirding of punch-ins and tape slurs. It's also important to note that "Goodnight" is billed as "with Susan Bee (Laufer)," not *by* her, further stressing the primacy of Bernstein's role as editor or tape operator here—certainly, the track is every bit (or even more so) a performance by him as it is her.

Finally, given the long relationship, both as partners and collabo-rators, between Bernstein and Bee—who met as teenagers in 1968, married in 1977 and remain together to this day—it's difficult for listeners not to let that knowledge inflect their interpretation of this track and "Piffle (Breathing)," making both especially charm-ing thanks to their tender and flirtatiousness interaction with one another.

---

35 Bernstein, "Acknowledgments and Notes," *All the Whiskey in Heaven: Selected Poems,* (New York: Farrar Strauss and Giroux, 2010), 299.

Contexts, Technology, and Influences

Like Bernstein's early xerographic publishing ventures—Asylum's Press and the journal, *L=A=N=G=U=A=G=E*—we see innovative alternate uses of preexisting consumer technology in both the composition and distribution of *Class*. However, *Class* is much more than a mere amplified chapbook, as we've already seen. There's a considerable gap between when the cassette's various tracks were recorded and its eventual release, and both events come at fortuitous times as Hua Hsu explains in his essay, "Thanks for the Memorex." First, "[i]n the 1970s, cassettes became a reliable, high-fidelity format for music,"[36] something they had never been before: compare, for example, the fidelity of even the (p)remastered version of "1-100," recorded on reel-to-reel, with the rest of the *Class* material (much of it recorded on cassette tape). Secondly, technological innovations resulted in increasingly smaller and more manageable machines, starting in 1962 with Philips' compact cassette recorder, and reaching its pinnacle in 1979 with the introduction of Sony's Walkman, which "immediately became a ubiquitous accessory."[37] Together with the concurrent development of the boombox and the eventual lowering of prices due to market demands, sound became portable, recordable and editable in ways previously unimagined.[38]

The audio experiments that would yield *Class*' five tracks took place alongside some of his earliest writing, and Bernstein recalls that "at the time I envisioned tape collage as being as possibly significant for me as writing and was interested in an array of electronic music, tape/music work, etc."[39] Before discussing some of these formative influences, perhaps it will be useful to briefly consider the characteristics of the tape medium itself—the creative benefits and pitfalls inherent to the recording process.

---

36 Hua Hsu, "Thanks for the Memorex," *Artforum*, February 2011, http://artforum.com/inprint/id=27399.

37 Ibid.

38 Aside from their importance to the composition of *Class*' tracks, Bernstein's various tape recorders—a stereo GE Portable Cassette deck, followed by a Walkman Pro—would faithfully record hundreds of readings in New York City, Buffalo and elsewhere, from the 1970s well into the 1990s. The vast majority of these recordings are available on PennSound, often with startlingly high fidelity given the interval between the initial recording and digitization.

39 Bernstein, e-mail interview.

In his classic essay, "The Studio as Compositional Tool," Brian Eno traces the long, symbiotic relationship between sound, composition, and recording, starting with the key idea that, "as soon as something's on tape, it becomes a substance which is malleable and mutable and cuttable and reversible."⁴⁰ This appraisal of the medium mimics Friedrich Kittler's, who posits that "tapes can execute any possible manipulation of data because they are equipped with recording, reading, and erasing heads, as well as with forward and reverse motion . . . Editing and interception control make the unmanipulable as manipulable as symbolic chains had been in the arts."⁴¹ Beyond the increased control granted by the tape recorder itself, Eno finds multi-track recording (as we find in *Class* tracks like "Piffle [Breathing]," "My/My/My," and "Goodnight") significant because it "acknowledge[s] that the performance isn't the finished item."⁴² This changes audio documentation from a mere end to a means, turning sound into raw material to be shaped at will, and therefore radically alters the creative stakes of tape-assisted composition.

Paul D. Miller (a.k.a. DJ Spooky, That Subliminal Kid) discusses the aesthetic empowerment granted by the technologically-augmented control of audio in his essay, "Algorithms: Erasures and the Art of Memory": "By using a found object—the cassette—that has the ability to hold replicated information, and in turn can be used to reproduce that very same information whenever it is activated: the cassette arrives at a point where it is the electromagnetic equivalent of the blank canvas, and 'all the world is in the mix.'"⁴³ However the full expressive promise of a given medium is neither obvious nor readily available specifically to those trained in the form. It takes a special temperament—the amateur's enthusiasm for play and subversion—to realize that potential that exists outside of prescribed use, and this re- or mis-appropriation of the audiocassette is very similar to Bernstein's use of the Xerox machine or the e-mail listserv for poetic purposes.

---

40 Brian Eno, "The Studio as Compositional Tool," in *Audio Culture: Readings in Modern Music*, Christopher Cox and Daniel Warner, eds., (London: Continuum, 2004), 128.

41 Friedrich Kittler, *Gramophone, Film, Typewriter*, Geoffrey Winthrop-Young and Michael Wutz, trans., (Stanford, CA: Stanford University, 1999), 108-109.

42 Eno, 128.

43 Paul D. Miller, "Algorithms: Erasures and the Art of Memory," in *Audio Culture: Readings in Modern Music*, 352.

Marshall McLuhan speaks to this in his manifesto, *Understanding Media: the Extensions of Man*: "It is the poets and painters who react instantly to a new medium like radio or TV."[44] Once again, he formulates Miller's leap from technology to aesthetics when he observes, "Radio and gramophone and tape recorder gave us back the poet's voice as an important dimension of the poetic experience. Words became a kind of painting with light, again."[45] For Miller, audio experiments of the sort that Bernstein is engaged in—which are "informed by a fluid dialectics of culture that places it at the center of the transition from mimetic to semiotic representation that electronic artforms are highlighting"—involve a secondary transformation, i.e. an electro-aesethetic empathy, "a migration of human cognitive structures into the abstract 'machinery' of the electronic environment."[46] Similarly, Marcus Boon stresses the primacy of physical interaction as part of this process, singing the praises of "the hand on the Pause button, coordinating with a turntable or a CD player or the radio, and the magical trace of this hand adding something personal and powerful to the recording," creating "a moment of meaning, of exchange, of contact."[47]

The link between literary and tape-mediated sonic experimentation has clear precedents in the work of William S. Burroughs, whose textual cut-up method (co-developed with Brion Gysin) soon gave way to similar experiments in both audio and film. In "The Invisible Generation," the manifesto that serves as a coda to Burroughs' novel, *The Ticket That Exploded*, the author ascribes tremendous power to the audio medium: "it's all done with tape recorders   consider this machine and what it can do   it can record and play back activating a past time set by precise association a recording can be played back any number of times you can study and analyze every pause and inflection of a recorded conversation."[48] While Burroughs' major preoccupation here is with cut-up audio as high-tech weaponry, and his "invisible generation" is a legion of undercover agents ready and waiting to effect social change through their portable recorders—he

44 Marshall McLuhan, *Understanding Media: The Extensions of Man*, (Cambridge, MA: MIT Press, 1994), 53.

45 Ibid.

46 Miller, 353.

47 Marcus Boon, *In Praise of Copying*, (Cambridge: Harvard University, 2010), 57.

48 Burroughs, "The Invisible Generation," *The Ticket That Exploded*, (New York: Grove, 1967), 205-206.

goes so far as to claim, "anyone with a tape recorder controlling the sound track can influence and create events"—the text is perhaps most useful as a detailed primer on various methods of tape manipulation.[49]

Burroughs, along with Samuel Beckett (who also featured audio-tape as a central aesthetic device in *Krapp's Last Tape*), was a major literary influence on Bernstein during his college years—when he "was consciously looking for literary equivalents for the modernist and abstract expressionist painting that [he] was so passionately taken by."[50] "I was certainly interested in the cut-up, Dada/Tzara, Burroughs/Gysin and Cage," he explains, noting in particular that it's possible that he hasn't "adequately acknowledge[d] how important [Burroughs] was to [his] thinking."[51] The work of Gertrude Stein was also a formative influence, and Bernstein recalls being "completely knocked out," by texts such as *The Making of Americans*, *Tender Buttons*, and "Composition as Explanation"—"this was what I had been looking for, what I knew must exist, and I was giddy with excitement,"[52] The jagged stop-start aesthetic of the cut-up, and Steinian recursivity are both prominent in *Class* tracks including "My/My/My," "Class," and "Goodnight.

Two other important early influences who spanned the gap between literature and performance are the talk-poet David Antin and, in particular, the multidisciplinary artist Jackson Mac Low. As Bernstein first began his tape experiments, he was a regular at New York's legendary art space, The Kitchen, where he witnessed Mac Low's "8-Voice Stereo Canon Black Tarantula Crossword Gatha" (an aleatoric piece constructed from the work of Kathy Acker and consisting of two staggered channels of four overlaid tape recordings of Mac Low's voice[53]) and reports that it "knocked [him] out."[54] While many of his more daring experiments with pure vocal sound were left off of *Class*, Mac Low's influence is felt in the prevalence of repetition in Bernstein's work, along with a spirit of openness to the aesthetic potential of chance operations (in terms of the random

---

49 Ibid., 207.

50 Bernstein, "An Autobiographical Interview," 243.

51 Bernstein, e-mail interview.

52 Bernstein, "An Autobiographical Interview," 243.

53 Jackson Mac Low, "8-Voice Stereo Canon Black Tarantula Crossword Gatha" liner notes, PennSound, http://writing.upenn.edu/pennsound/x/Mac-Low.php

54 Bernstein, e-mail interview.

interaction of overlapped sound, and especially the haphazard jump-cuts in "Class")—the latter an inheritance from Cage as well.

At the Kitchen, Bernstein also experienced the work of a wide variety of contemporary composers and musicians, including "Philip Glass, Meredith Monk, Laurie Anderson, Rhys Chatham, Michael Gordon, Terry Riley, La Monte Young, Charlemagne Palestine (who I loved), [and] Pauline Oliveros," and this first-hand exposure was simply the continuation of a long history with the genre: "I was also listening closely from college days to Karlheinz Stockhausen (especially and relevantly *Tuning*), but also Mauricio Kagel, Iannis Xenakis, [and] Morton Subotnick."[55] Bernstein has also cited a wide array of adventurous popular musicians, including the Beatles and Frank Zappa, as having shaped his approach to sound, and singles out producer Phil Spector (pioneer of the "wall of sound" aesthetic) as an influence on his explorations of overdubbing and stereo separation.[56]

"I was also interested in the history of sound poetry," he notes, and aside from the work of European *poésie sonore* artists, the combined potential of poetry and performance was revealed to Bernstein through contemporary record releases such as Tuli Kupferberg's extended exercise in appropriation, *No Deposit, No Return* (1966), *Songs of Innocence and Experience by William Blake, tuned by Allen Ginsberg* (1970) and various record releases by Giorno Poetry Systems, as well as his experience of (and participation in) poets theater, the Living Theatre and the Open Theater, which spurred his interest in creating polyvocal work through the mediation of his tape recorders: "I very much had in mind not only the collage of different voice and textures but also the overlay of the voices and different spatial locations."[57] Thus a young artist's uncompromising approach to his materials led him to embrace a hybrid form of expression, yielding—when considered as a whole—a sprawling and precocious body of work that includes the five tracks on *Class* and the broader series of sessions from which they were drawn, as well as the early books *Asylums* (1975), *Parsing* (1976), *Veil* (1976), *Shade* (1978), *Senses of Responsibility* (1979), *Poetic Justice* (1979), *Controlling Interests* (1980) and *Stigma* (1981), along with the collaborative book *LEGEND* (1980, with Bruce Andrews, Ray DiPalma, Steve McCaffery and Ron Silliman). Consider the prevalence of fragmentation, of repetition, of phonemic

---

55 Ibid.

56 Bernstein, "An Autobiographical Interview," 243; Bernstein, e-mail interview.

57 Bernstein, e-mail interview.

attention, and even typographical manipulation—most noticeable in
the Glenn Ligon-esque fields of layered text in *Veils*, or *Poetic Justice*'s
daring "Lift Off," ("a transcription from the correction tape of an IBM
Selectric typewriter,"[58] which begins, "HH/ ie,s obVrsxr:atjrn dugh
seineopcv i iibalfmgmMw"[59])—in Bernstein's early writings, and we
find temperaments and techniques very similar to those employed
in *Class*, suggesting a well-developed (if still developing) and ideologically cohesive poetics.

Conclusion: After *Class*

While Bernstein hasn't made audio compositions like those found
on *Class* since the mid-1970s—"I went on to do related things, of
course,"[60] he jokes—that doesn't mean that sonic experimentation hasn't been central to his poetics throughout the intervening years. Aside from the sound-centric editorial and curatorial
achievements listed in my introduction (*LINEbreak*, *Close Listening*
and *PennSound* being chief among them), we see traces of the enduring influence of the attitudes and habits developed during those
formative years made manifest in a number of ways. Consider, for
example, Bernstein's work in the field of opera as a librettist, first
working with Ben Yarmolinsky on the trio of imaginative pieces
collected in *Blind Witness: Three American Operas* (Factory School,
2008)—*Blind Witness* (1990), *The Subject* (1991) and *The Lenny Paschen
Show* (1992)[61]—which were followed by his collaboration with Brian
Ferneyhough, *Shadowtime* (Green Integer, 2005)[62]. This focus on song
form also carries over into his recent exploration of the gentle meter
of balladry and nursery rhyme, as best evidenced by "The Ballad of
Girly Man."

Aside from a general attention to sound and song, some of the
more technically experimental characteristics of *Class*—in particular,
appropriation, fragmentation and collage—continue to be key facets

---

58 Bernstein, "Acknowledgments and Notes," 299.
59 Bernstein, "Lift Off," *All the Whiskey in Heaven: Selected Poems*, 36.
60 Bernstein, e-mail interview.
61 Contemporary audio and video recordings of all three operas are available on
    PennSound, along with videos from the launch event for *Blind Witness*: http://writ-
    ing.upenn.edu/pennsound/x/Yarmolinsky.php
62 Aside from Green Integer's publication of the libretto, an audio CD was released
    by NCM in 2006.

of Bernstein's poetics. The same spirit guiding Bernstein's hand on the rewind and fast-forward buttons in "Class," for example, can also be seen in recent audio-visual pieces like Niels Plenge's *The Answer* (a short film in which the poet's voice is edited into a beatboxing routine)[63] or the accidental composition, "Glitch Coda," (the ending of a panel discussion between Bernstein and poet Frank Bidart turned into digital garble thanks to a portable recorder's dying batteries)[64], as well as in poems such as "Dea%r Fr~ien%d" (which employs the almost incomprehensible language of spam e-mails)[65] and "Morality" (written in a heavily-recursive style reminiscent of Bernstein's first tape experiment, "Accused").[66] The deconstructedness of these latter poems is made doubly evident when they're read aloud, the printed text becoming a challenging vocal score, though one that Bernstein handles deftly.

Indeed, the spirit of performativity has been a hallmark of Bernstein's poetics throughout his long career — his charmingly puckish demeanor shaped by childhood worship of Sid Caesar, Lenny Bruce and Spike Jones[67] — and it's worth noting, that while great poets aren't necessary charismatic readers, in Bernstein, we find both simultaneously. This underscores the importance of the recording medium, which provides not only documentation of historic events, ephemera and draft-like variant readings, but more vitally some auratic trace of the human performance, of what Barthes dubs "the grain of the voice." We're given access to this, in regards to Bernstein, for the very first time in *Class*, and the tape experiments that yielded the cassette's tracks — born of a young poet's attempts

---

63 Video available on PennSound: http://www.writing.upenn.edu/ pennsound/x/ Bernstein-Plenge.html

64 Audio available on PennSound: http://writing.upenn.edu/pennsound/x/Bernstein-talks.html#Bidart. Charles originally forwarded the audio to me for editing prior to posting on PennSound and explained the technical difficulties. When, after listening, I proposed keeping the problematic audio and making it a separate track, his response was enthusiastic: "I actually like the coda better than the main part."

65 The text of this poem is available on *Web Conjunctions* (http://www.conjunctions.com/archives/c50-cb.htm), while audio of Bernstein reading it is available on PennSound (http://writing.upenn.edu/ pennsound/x/Bernstein-Tucson.html)

66 The text of this poem is available on *onedit* (http://www.onedit.net/issue12/charlesb/charlesb.html), while several recordings of Bernstein reading it are available on PennSound: (http://writing.upenn.edu/ pennsound/x/Bernstein-readings.html)

67 Bernstein, e-mail interview.

to capture the sundry events of his everyday life and transform them into art—serve as a seed that, three decades later, would come to its fullest fruition in PennSound, where one can listen to *Class* in its entirety, along with hundreds of other recordings by Bernstein (and more than twenty-five thousand additional recordings by a panoply of poets).

Given these eventual outcomes, it's fascinating to think of the potential consequences for the world of contemporary poetry had Bernstein's priorities shifted, making his early writings a brief experimental phase concurrent with the start of his career as a tape-music composer, or if he'd opted to balance his focus on both media. While that's thankfully not the case, *Class*—an important document in his life-long aesthetic and curatorial development—has long been overlooked by poets and scholars alike. As Bernstein himself laments in his introduction to *Close Listening: Poetry and the Performed Word*, "[w]hile the performance of poetry is as old as poetry itself, critical attention to modern and contemporary poetry performance has been negligible,"[68] and though, even as early as *Class* we see Bernstein working with "sound as material, where sound is neither arbitrary nor secondary but constitutive,"[69] this sort of text is far too often treated as ancillary and unmanageable: an interesting curio, like the poet's series of commercials for *The Yellow Pages*, but nothing more. I'm hopeful, however, that an emerging generation of scholars—equally versed in poetics, sound, and media considerations, and raised to cherish the unforgetting nature of the Internet era (where ideally no data is ever lost to the tides of time)—will come to rightly see *Class* as the ur-text that it is, not just within Bernstein's poetics alone, but as a groundbreaking moment within the broader development of contemporary poetics.

---

68 Bernstein, "Introduction," *Close Listening: Poetry and the Performed Word*, (New York: Oxford University, 1998), 3.

69 Ibid., 4.

Notes on Contributors

mIEKAL aND is Professor Emeritus of the Department of Yet To Be Invented Languages at the Invisible College of the Republic of Qazingulaza. He is the author of numerous books of experimental text & visual poetry available from www.xexoxial.org. His digital poetry & hypertext works can be found at www.joglars.org. In 2011 his lifelong poem Samsara Congeries will be published by BlazeVox [books].

Caroline Bergvall. London-based writer and artist, of French-Norwegian nationality. Works across artforms, media and languages. Projects alternate between books, audio pieces, performances and language installations. Latest book: *Meddle English: New and Selected Texts* (Nightboat Books, 2011). Others include: *Fig* (2005), *Cropper* (Torque, 2008), *Alyson singes* (2008). Latest solo commission: Middling English (John Hansard Gallery). Other projects: Hammer Museum, LA (w Rodney McMillian); Oslo Poesi festival/Sonia Henie Kunstsenter (Oslo), The Poetry Marathon/Serpentine Gallery (London), MOMA (NY); Museum of Contemporary Arts (Antwerp). Director of Performance Writing, Dartington College of Arts (1995-2000), co-Chair MFA in Writing, Bard College (NY, 2004-2006), and has held visiting posts at various universities. AHRC Fellow in the Creative and Performing Arts, Southampton University (2007–2010). Writer in Residence, School of Visual Culture, University of Copenhagen (Spring 2011).

Ray Craig writes from San Bruno, California.

Michael Eng is assistant professor of philosophy at John Carroll University in Cleveland, OH, where he teaches courses in aesthetics, philosophy and literature, Marxism and Critical Theory, and philosophy and film. His areas of research include post-Heideggerian aesthetic and literary theory, philosophy of the image, philosophy and architecture, and film theory. He has published previously on Ingeborg Bachmann's *Frankfurt Lectures* and *Todesarten Projekt* and is currently at work on two manuscripts: "The Scene of the Voice: Language and the Aisthēsis of Finitude" and "The Sense of the

Image: The Metaphysical Imaginary in Cinema, Architecture, and Philosophy."

Thomas Fink. Professor of English at CUNY-LaGuardia, is the author of two books of criticism, including *A Different Sense of Power* (Fairleigh Dickinson UP, 2001), and seven books of poetry, including *Peace Conference* (Marsh Hawk Press, 2011), as well as co-editor of two anthologies. His work appears in *The Best American Poetry 2007* (Scribner's). Fink's paintings hang in various collections.

Allen Fisher is a poet, painter, publisher and art historian, lives in Hereford, UK. Emeritus Professor of Poetry & Art at Manchester Metropolitan University; over 140 single-authored publications of poetry, graphics and art documentation; exhibited in many shows from *Fluxus Britannica* Tate Britain to *Lifting from fear* King's Gallery York. Examples of his work are in the Tate Collection, the Living Museum, Iceland and various private collections in United States of America, United Arab Emirates and Britain. His last eight books were *Proposals: poem-image-commentary; Birds; Leans; Confidence in lack, essays; Singularity Stereo, Place; Entanglement; and Gravity*. His recent tour of work has been under the banner: *Complexity Manifold* which has been heard in Albany, Buffalo, Cambridge UK, London, New York and Ohio.

Kristen Gallagher is the author of *Operator* (Rubbaducky) and *We Are Here* (Truck Books). Recent poetry has been published in *West Wind Review* and *A Similar But Different Quality*, and two reviews of Tan Lin's work have appeared this academic year: an essay on Heath Plagiarism/Outsource appeared in *Criticism* in Fall 2010, and a review of Seven Controlled Vocabularies appeared in *Jacket2* in May 2011. She received her PhD from SUNY Buffalo in 2005.

Carlos Gallego is an Associate Professor of English at St. Olaf College. His research interests include 20th century American literature and cultural studies, Chicano/a studies, comparative ethnic studies, philosophy and critical theory. He has published work in the academic journals *Biography*, *Aztlán*, *Cultural Critique* and *Western Humanities Review*. His book, *Chicana/o Subjectivity and the Politics of Identity: Between Recognition and Revolution* (Palgrave Macmillan, 2011).

Madeline Gins, co-inventor of reversible destiny and procedural architecture, would seem to have existed and to be still existing. Perhaps a great deal more could be written here about her.

Michael S. Hennessey is the editor of P̲e̲n̲n̲S̲o̲u̲n̲d̲ and editor (with Julia Bloch) of *Jacket2*. His scholarly writing on sound, media and poetry has appeared in *Audiobooks, Literature, and Sound Studies* (Routledge, 2011), *Interval(le)s, English Studies in Canada,The Journal of Electronic Publishing* and *Jacket2*. Recent poetry publications include *Jacket, EOAGH, Elective Affinities, Brighton Approach: Gold Edition, Compost* and *Horse Less Review*, along with Leonard Schwartz's radio program *Cross Cultural Poetics*. He's released two chapbooks: *Last Days in the Bomb Shelter (17 Narrower Poems)* and *[static]*.

Erica Hunt is a poet, essayist and author of *Local History, Arcade,* as well as two poem chapbooks, *Piece Logic* and *Time Flies Right Before the Eyes*. Other bits published in *Boundary 2, Conjunctions, Poetics Journal, Tripwire, Recluse,* various anthologies and the St. Mark's Poetry Project newsletter. Hunt has received awards from the Foundation for Contemporary Art, the Fund for Poetry and the Djerassi Foundation.

Megan Swihart Jewell is the director of the Writing Resource Center at Case Western Reserve University in Cleveland, Ohio. She teaches courses in writing, Gender Studies, and American Literature. Her current research focuses on the intersections between innovative poetics and writing pedagogy.

Jason Lagapa is Associate Professor of English at the University of Texas—Permian Basin, where he teaches courses in twentieth-century and twenty-first century American poetry, postmodern fiction and creative writing. His articles on such poets as Leslie Scalapino, Jack Spicer, Frank O'Hara and John Yau have appeared in *Contemporary Literature, Journal of Modern Literature* and *Theory@Buffalo*. He is presently at work on a book on utopian thought and contemporary experimental American poetry.

Kimberly Lamm is assistant professor of Women's Studies at Duke University. Her research moves at the intersection of contemporary poetry, contemporary art, feminist theory, and American Studies. She is currently working on a book manuscript entitled "Inadequacies and Interruptions: Language and Feminist Reading Practices in Contemporary Art."

Steve McCaffery is the author of more than 30 books and chapbooks of criticism and poetry. A founding member of the legendary Four Horsemen sound ensemble and one of the founding theorists of Language Writing, he now resides in Buffalo where he is the David Gray Professor of Poetry and Letters ad Director of the Poetics Program.

Peter Monacell recently received his PhD from the University of Missouri. His article on James Dickey's "The Firebombing" appeared in *The James Dickey Review*, and another article, on modernist attitudes towards the suburbs, will be published in the *Journal of Modern Literature*. He lives in Columbia with his wife Michelle Diedriech.

Maggie O'Sullivan is a British-based poet, performer and visual artist. For over thirty years, her work has appeared extensively in journals and anthologies (including *Poems for the Millennium*, Volume 2) and she has performed her work, often in collaboration, internationally. She is the editor of out of everywhere: an anthology of contemporary linguistically innovative poetry by women in North America and the UK (1996). More recently is *Body of Work* (2006), *ALTO* (2009), *WATERFALLS* (2011) and *murmur* (2011). *The Salt Companion to Maggie O'Sullivan* is also available. Her website is www.maggieosullivan.co.uk

Lars Palm lives with his lovely wife, currently in Malmö (Sweden). He works in health care, writes, translates & runs a small ungovernable press. His most recent chapbooks are *what's in a* (The Red Ceilings Press, 2011) & *(s)he dead* (red ochre press, 2011).

Tim Peterson (Trace) is a poet, critic, and editor. Author of the poetry books *Since I Moved In* (Chax Press) and *Violet Speech* (2nd Avenue Poetry), Peterson has edited *EOAGH: A Journal of the Arts* since 2003 and also curates the *Tendencies: Poetics & Practice* talks series on queer poetics and the manifesto at CUNY Graduate Center. Peterson's critical writing has previously appeared in the books *Burning Interiors: David Shapiro's Poetry and Poetics*, ed Fink and Lease (Fairleigh Dickinson University Press) and *No Gender: Reflections on the Life & Work of kari edwards* (Litmus Press/Belladonna Books), as well as in journals such as *EBR, Harvard Review, ON: Contemporary Practice*, and *The Poetry Project Newsletter*. In 2006 Peterson edited a special issue of MIT Press' journal *Leonardo Electronic Almanac* on "New Media Poetry and Poetics." Peterson is currently a Ph.D. Candidate in English at CUNY Graduate Center in New York City.

Steven Salmoni received a Ph.D. in English from Stony Brook University and is currently Department Chair of English at Pima Community College in Tucson, AZ. Recent publications include poems in *Versal, Upstairs at Duroc, Sonora Review, Bombay Gin* and *Cannot Exist*, as well as articles in *The Journal of Narrative Theory, Studies in Travel Writing* and *The Critical Companion to Henry James*. He serves on the Board of Directors for "POG," a Tucson-based collective of poets and critics dedicated to the promotion of avant-garde literature and art.

James Shivers wrote the first full-length study of Charles Bernstein's work over ten years ago for his doctorate at the University of Lausanne. He was a Visiting Fellow in American Studies at Yale from 1999-2004 where he continued research in innovative poetics. While there he was an active member of the Yale Group of Contemporary Poetics. His critical and creative works have been published in England, Holland, Switzerland, and the United States. His most recent work *Planetarium* a fictional-nonfiction allo-biography is forthcoming.

Ron Silliman recently unveiled a neon sculpture at the Bury Museum of Art, Bury, Lancashire. Other recent appearances have included *Poetry, The Nation* and the Fact-Simile trading card series.

Paul Stephens' recent critical writing has appeared in *Postmodern Culture, Social Text, Paideuma, Arizona Quarterly, Journal of Modern Literature* and *Open Letter: A Canadian Journal of Writing and Theory*. He is co-editor of the journal *Convolution*, and has just completed a book manuscript titled "The Poetics of Information Overload: From Gertrude Stein to Conceptual Writing." He has taught at Bard, NYU and Emory, and currently teaches at Columbia University.

Michael Angelo Tata is the Executive Editor of the Sydney-based electronic journal of literature, art and new media **nebu[lab]**. His *Andy Warhol: Sublime Superficiality* arrived to critical acclaim from Intertheory Press in 2010. His essays appear most recently in the collections *Neurology and Modernity* (Palgrave Macmillan) and *Passage to Manhattan: Critical Essays on Meena Alexander* (Cambridge Scholars) and in the British journal *Parallax* (Routledge). Forthcoming poetry and graffiti will appear in the British journal *Rattle*.

Donald Wellman, poet, essayist, and editor, has translated the poetry of Antonio Gamoneda (Cervantes Prize 2006). Wellman's poetry includes *A North Atlantic Wall,* recently released by Dos Madres Press. In 2009, his *Prolog Pages* was published by Ahadada. Other titles include *Urika,* a chapbook from Boat Train in Gloucester, *Baroque Threads* (Mudlark) and *Fields* (Light and Dust). From 1981-1994, he edited the O.ARS series of anthologies, devoted to topics bearing on postmodern poetics, including volumes entitled *Coherence, Perception* and *Translations: Experiments in Reading.* In addition to Gamoneda, he has translated the poetry of Emilio Prados, Blaise Cendrars and Yvan Goll, among others. His translation of Gamoneda's *Gravestones* is available from the University of New Orleans Press. He teaches at Daniel Webster College in Nashua, NH.

Credits

DonaldWellman's poem was originally published in *Fields* (Kenosha: Light and Dust, 1995).

Ron Silliman's poem was published as part of *The Alphabet* (Tuscaloosa: University of Alabama Press, 2008).

mIEKAL aND's poem was originally published in *L=I=N=G=L=A=G=E* (West Lima, Wisconsin: Xexoxial Editions, 1987.

I would like to thank the writers and presses for letting us republish their works.

Acknowledgements

Many people aided in the production of this book. First, I'd like to thank Charles Bernstein himself for providing useful suggestions. Second, I'd like to thank Chris Hamilton-Emery of Salt. Without his tireless dedication to innovative poetry and, in this case, the criticism devoted to that poetry, this book would not have been produced. Third, I'd like to thank all of the contributors. They produced excellent work and were patient with the movement of this book to press. Lastly, I would like to thank my wife, Lori Ryan, who created extra time for me to work through the many details of such a collection.

"Either You're With Us and Against Us: Charles Bernstein's Girly Man, 9–11, and the Brechtian Figure of the Reader" previously appeared in *Electronic Book Review*, 2008-03-09.

Lars Palms' poem was first published in *road song for* (corrupt press, 2011).

CPSIA information can be obtained at www.ICGtesting.com
Printed in the USA
LVOW11s1747200415

435319LV00006B/1136/P